Hands-On Microsoft®
SQL Server™ 2005
Integration Services

About the Author

Ashwani Nanda develops and maintains marketing, analytical, and CRM-based database systems for medium- to large-sized enterprises. His current area of specialization is data modeling, database management, data analysis, and visualization. He started his career on the real-time mainframe systems back in the age when hard disks used to weigh a kilo per megabyte. Moving from system engineering for mainframes to networking and infrastructure support and currently to data practice, he has worked for several major hardware and software vendors. He has loved to network and integrate disparate technologies, with particular attention to productivity and security. These days he is using his integration skills with RDBMS databases and end-user tools. He can be reached at ananda@AffordingIT.co.uk.

Hands-On Microsoft® SQL Server™ 2005 Integration Services

Ashwani Nanda

New York   Chicago   San Francisco
Lisbon   London   Madrid   Mexico City   Milan
New Delhi   San Juan   Seoul   Singapore   Sydney   Toronto

The **McGraw·Hill** *Companies*

McGraw-Hill books are available at special quantity discounts to use as premiums and sales promotions, or for use in corporate training programs. For more information, please write to the Director of Special Sales, Professional Publishing, McGraw-Hill, Two Penn Plaza, New York, NY 10121-2298. Or contact your local bookstore.

Hands-On Microsoft® SQL Server™ 2005 Integration Services

34567890 CUS CUS 0198

ISBN-13: 978-0-07-226319-0

ISBN-10:   0-07-226319-9

Sponsoring Editor	Wendy Rinaldi
Editorial Supervisor	Janet Walden
Project Manager	Vasundhara Sawhney
Acquisitions Coordinator	Alexander McDonald
Technical Editor	Todd Meister
Copy Editor	Lisa Theobald
Proofreader	Jayanti Ghosh
Production Supervisor	George Anderson
Composition	International Typesetting and Composition
Illustration	International Typesetting and Composition
Art Director, Cover	Jeff Weeks
Cover Designer	Pattie Lee

To my wife, Sarita, for being an inspiration to complete this book, and to my kids, Toozy, Ritzy, and Himnish, who waited patiently for me at the dinner table.

Contents at a Glance

Contents

Acknowledgments

I would like to thank my wife Sarita for not only doing all the hard work of managing a household with three kids, especially with two young ones, but also for being supportive and understanding, and for motivating me throughout my first book writing experience. Thanks to my elder daughter Toozy, for helping her mom while also keeping her grades high. And to my younger daughter Ritzy, and son Himnish, who definitely have to sacrifice some of their gaming fun. Thanks to our parents for making us able to accomplish such a project. Thanks to my brothers for inspiration and sharing their experiences of book writing with me. Thanks so much to my friends and colleagues at work. Finally, special thanks to the team at McGraw-Hill for providing support and guidance time to time during this project.

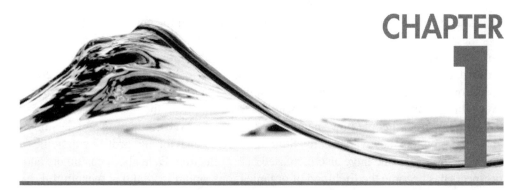

Introducing SQL Server Integration Services

In the world of database marketing, data is not only at the center of long-term decision-making by big corporations that use costly data analysis systems; these days, data is also being used by all types of organizations to drive business forward. Systems that support customer relationships—call centers and telemarketing operations, pre-sales, and post-sales, for example—have evolved at a faster rate than ever. This is primarily due to a data explosion resulting from the public's increased use of the Internet. People now spend more time on the Web comparing and deciding about the products they want to buy. Studying buyer behavior and profiling activities of visitors to a web site have also increased data collection. Data about customers and prospects has become the lifeblood of organizations, and it is vital that meaningful information hidden in the data be explored for businesses to stay healthy and grow.

However, many challenges remain to be met before an organization can compile meaningful information. In a typical corporation, data resides at geographically different locations in disparate data storage systems—such as DB2, Oracle, or SQL Server—and in different formats. It is the job of the information analyst to collect data and apply business rules to transform raw data into meaningful information to help the business make well-informed decisions. For example, you may decide to consolidate your customer data, complete with orders-placed and products-owned information, into your new SAP system, for which you may have to collect data from SQL Server–based customer relationship management (CRM) systems, product details from your legacy mainframe system, order details from an IBM DB2 database, and dealer information from an Oracle database. You will have to collect data from all these data sources, remove duplication in data, and standardize and cleanse data before loading it into your new customer database system. These tasks of *e*xtracting data from disparate data sources, *t*ransforming the extracted data, and then *l*oading the transformed data are commonly done with tools called *ETL* tools.

Another challenge resulting from the increased use of the Internet is that "the required information" must be available at all times. Customers do not want to wait. With more and more businesses expanding into global markets, collecting data from multiple locations and loading it after transformation into the diverse data stores with little or no downtime have increased work pressure on the information analyst, who needs better tools to perform the job.

The conventional ETL tools are designed around batch processes that run during off-peak hours. Usually, the data-uploading process in a data warehouse is a daily update process that runs for most of the night. This is because of the underlying design of traditional ETL tools, as they tend to stage the data during the upload process. With diverse data sources and more complex transformations and manipulations, such as text mining and fuzzy matching, the traditional ETL tools tend to stage the data even more. The more these tools stage data, the more disk operations are involved, and hence the longer the update process takes to finish. These delays in the entire process of integrating data are unacceptable to modern businesses. Emerging business needs require that the long-running, offline types of batch processes be redesigned into faster, on-demand types that fit into shorter timeframes. This requirement is beyond the traditional ETL tools regime and is exactly what Microsoft SQL Server 2005 Integration Services (SSIS) is designed to do.

SSIS was designed with the emerging needs of businesses in mind. This enterprise data transformation and data integration solution can be used to extract, transform, and consolidate data from disparate sources and move it to single or multiple destinations. SSIS provides a complete set of tools, services, and application programming interfaces (APIs) to build complex yet robust and high-performing solutions.

SSIS is built to handle all the workflow tasks and data transformations in a way that provides the best possible performance. SSIS has two different engines for managing workflow and data transformations, both optimized to perform the nature of work they must handle. The *data flow engine,* which is responsible for all data-related transformations, is built on a buffer-oriented architecture. With this architecture design, SSIS loads row sets of data in memory buffers and can perform in-memory operations on the loaded row sets for complex transformations, thus avoiding staging of data to disks. This ability enables SSIS to extend traditional ETL functionality to meet the stringent business requirements of information integration. The *run-time engine,* on the other hand, provides environmental support in executing and controlling the workflow of an SSIS package at run-time. It enables you to store SSIS packages to the file system or inside an SQL Server 2005 with facilities to migrate the package between different stores. The run-time engine also provides support for easy deployment of your packages.

The many features in Integration Services will be discussed in detail throughout this book; however, to provide a basic understanding of how SSIS provides business benefits, following is a brief discussion on the features and their uses.

Integration Services—Features and Uses

Integration Services provides a rich set of tools that are preconfigured to components and APIs that you can use to extract meaningful information from the raw data and create complex data manipulation and business applications.

Integration Services Architecture

The Integration Services architecture separates the operations-oriented workflow from the data transformation pipeline by providing two distinct engines. The Integration

Services run-time engine provides run-time services such as establishing connections to various data sources, managing variables, handling transactions, debugging, logging, and event handling. The Integration Services data flow engine uses multiple data flow sources to extract data, multiple data flow transformations to transform the extracted data in the pipeline, and multiple data flow destinations to load the transformed data into disparate data stores. The data flow engine uses buffer-oriented architecture, which enables SSIS to transform and manipulate data within the memory. Because of this, the data flow engine is optimized to avoid staging data to disk and hence can achieve very high levels of data processing in a short time span. The run-time engine provides operational support and resources to data flow at run-time, whereas the data flow engine enables you to create fast, easy-to-maintain, extensible, and reliable data transformation applications. Both engines, though separate, work together to provide high levels of performance with better control over package execution. You will study control flow components in Chapters 3 through 5 and data flow components in Chapters 9 and 10.

Integration Services Designer and Management Tools

SQL Server 2005 provides the Business Intelligence Development Studio (BIDS) as the development tool for developing Integration Services and SQL Server Management Studio for managing Integration Services packages. BIDS includes the SSIS Designer, a graphical tool built on Visual Studio's integrated development environment (IDE) that includes all the development and debugging features provided by the Visual Studio environment. This environment provides separate design surfaces for control flow, data flow, and event handlers, as well as a hierarchical view of package elements in the Package Explorer. It also provides several features that you will study later in this chapter and subsequently use throughout this book. SQL Server Management Studio allows you to connect to Integration Services to manage and view packages. You will also study SQL Server Management Studio later in this chapter.

Data Warehousing Loading

At the core, SSIS provides lots of functionality to upload data into a data warehouse. A Bulk Insert task in control flow can bulk-load data from a flat file into SQL Server tables and views. The data flow includes a SQL Server destination, which can also load data directly into a SQL Server database. If your data warehouse stores aggregated information, you can use aggregate transformation to perform functions such as SUM and Average, and use row count transformation to count the number of rows in the data flow. SSIS provides several other data flow transformations that allow you to perform all the data manipulations in the pipeline and in a single pass. These transformations help you in the following ways:

► SSIS provides three transformations—*merge, merge join,* and *union all*—to let you combine data from various sources to load into the data warehouse by running the package only once rather than multiple times for each source.

► *Aggregate transformation* can perform multiple aggregates on multiple columns.

► *Sort transformation* sorts data on the sort order key that can be specified on one or more columns.

► *Pivot transformation* can transform the relational data into a less-normalized form, which is sometimes what is saved in a data warehouse.

► *Audit transformation* lets you can add columns with lineage and other environmental information for auditing purposes.

SSIS also addresses the data warehouse need to maintain slowly changing dimension (SCD). Data flow provides a slowly changing dimension transformation that enables you to maintain SCD easily (otherwise, it is not easy to maintain). The SCD transformation includes an SCD Wizard, which configures the SCD transformation and also creates the data flow branches to load the SCD with new records, simple updates, and updates where history must be maintained.

Standardizing and Enhancing Data Quality Features

Integration Services includes the following transformations that enable you to perform various operations to standardize data:

► *Character map transformation* allows you to perform string functions to string data type columns, such as changing the case of data.

► *Data conversion transformation* allows you to convert data to a different data type.

► *Derived column transformation* allows you to create new column values based on expressions.

Integration Services can also clean and de-dupe (eliminate duplications in) data before loading it into the destination. This can be achieved either by using lookup transformation (for finding exact matches) or by using fuzzy lookup transformation (for finding fuzzy matches). You can also use both of these transformations in a package by first looking for exact matches and then looking for fuzzy matches. Fuzzy grouping transformation groups similar records together to avoid loading duplicate records into the destination. You will study data flow transformations in Chapter 10.

Converting Data into Meaningful Information

SSIS provides several components and transformations that you can use to draw meaningful information from raw data. You may need to perform one or more of the following operations to achieve the required results:

▶ Apply repeating logic to a unit of work in the workflow using For Loop or Foreach Loop containers.

▶ Convert data format or locale using data conversion transformation.

▶ Merge data from different sources using merge, merge join, or union all transformations.

▶ Distribute data by splitting it on data values using a condition.

▶ Use parameters and expressions to build decision logic.

▶ Perform text mining to identify the interesting terms in text related to business to improve customer satisfaction, products, or services.

Data Consolidation

The data in which you are interested may be stored at various locations, such as relational database systems, legacy databases, mainframes, spreadsheets, or even flat files. SSIS helps you consolidate this data by connecting to the disparate data sources, extracting and bringing the interested data into the data flow pipeline, and then merging this data together. This may sound easy, but things can get a bit tough when you are dealing with different types of data stores, different data storage technologies, and different schema settings. SSIS has a comprehensive set of data flow sources and data flow destinations that can connect to these disparate data stores and extract or load data for you.

Package Security Features

You can secure your SSIS packages with access control by encrypting the packages and by digitally signing them using a digital certificate. You can control access to packages saved into SQL Server using SQL Server roles for Integration Services. Integration Services packages can use various levels of encryption to protect sensitive information such as passwords and connection strings. You can also digitally sign your SSIS packages to establish the authenticity of the packages. You will study these security features in Chapter 7.

Service-Oriented Architecture

SSIS provides support for Service-Oriented Architecture (SOA) through a combination of the HTTP connection manager, Web Service task, and XML source. These can be used together to pull XML data from URLs into the data flow.

SSIS Package as a Data Source

SSIS provides a DataReader destination that enables an SSIS package to be used as a data source. When you use a DataReader destination in your SSIS package, you effectively convert your SSIS package into an on-demand data source that can provide integrated, transformed, and cleansed data from multiple data sources to an external application such as SQL Server Reporting Services. You can also use this feature to connect to multiple web services, extract RSS feeds, and combine and identify interesting articles to be fed back to the application on demand. This is a unique and powerful feature that places SSIS much ahead of other traditional ETL tools.

Programmability

SSIS provides a rich set of APIs in a native and managed form that enables you not only to extend the functionality provided by preconfigured components, but also develop new custom components using C++ or other languages supported by the .NET Framework (such as Visual C# and Visual Basic 2005). With the provision of this functionality, you can include your already-developed legacy applications or third-party components in SSIS processes. These custom components can be developed for both control flow and data flow environments and can be included in an SSIS toolset to be reused in enterprise-wide development projects.

Scripting

SSIS also provides scripting components in both control flow and data flow environments to allow you to add ad hoc functionality quickly within your SSIS packages using Visual Basic 2005.

Easy Management of SSIS Packages

SSIS is designed with high development productivity, easy management, and fast debugging in mind. Some of the features that contribute to achieve these goals are listed here:

► Integration Services is installed as a Microsoft Windows service, which provides storage and management functions and displays running packages for SSIS packages.

► Integration Services provides rich logging features that allow you to choose the type of information you want to log at the package level or at the component level using one of the five different log providers.

► If your package fails halfway through processing, you do not need to do all the work again. Integration Services has a restart capability that allows a failed package to be restarted from the point of failure rather than from the beginning, thus saving you time.

► Integration Services provides SSIS service and SSIS pipeline performance objects that include a set of performance counters for monitoring the running instances of packages and the performance of the data flow pipeline. Using these counters, you can fine-tune the performance of your packages.

► SSIS provides several utilities and wizards such as the dtexec utility, dtutil utility, Package Migration Wizard, and Query Builder that help you perform the work easily and quickly.

► SSIS provides the SQL Server Import and Export Wizard that lets you quickly copy data from a source to a destination. The packages saved with SQL Server Import and Export Wizard can later be opened in BIDS and extended. You will study the SQL Server Import and Export Wizard in Chapter 2.

Automating Administrative Tasks

SSIS can automate many administrative tasks, such as backing up and restoring, copying SQL Server databases and objects, and loading data.

Deployment Features

You can enable package configurations to update properties of package components dynamically with the Package Configuration Wizard and deploy packages from development to testing to production environments easily and quickly with the deployment utility. You will study deployment features and facilities in Chapter 11.

Legacy Support Features

Earlier versions of SQL Server used Data Transformation Services (DTS) to create data transformation packages. DTS has been deprecated in SQL Server 2005 and is replaced by Integration Services. (The following section provides more details.) DTS packages can still be used with Integration Services because it provides facilities for legacy support and tools to migrate your DTS packages to take advantage of new features. You will study backward-compatibility features and migration support provided in SQL Server 2005 in Chapter 12.

Where Is DTS in SQL Server 2005?

You might have worked with DTS, provided with SQL Server 2000. DTS is not an independent application in itself; rather, it is an integral component of SQL Server 2000. DTS is a nice little tool that has provided all of us with great functionality and components. Some developers have even extended DTS packages by writing custom scripts to the enterprise level. Yet DTS has some inherent shortcomings: for example, it is bound to SQL Server, is not a true ETL tool, has a limited number of preconfigured tasks and components, offers a single design interface for both workflow and data flow that is limited in extensibility, and has no built-in repeating logic. Although you could fix all these shortcomings by writing a complex script, it wouldn't be easy to maintain and would be a big challenge to develop.

With SQL Server 2005, Microsoft introduced Integration Services to replace DTS 2000. Integration Services is not a point upgrade of DTS; in fact, it is not an upgrade to DTS at all. The code for Integration Services has been written from scratch. Backward compatibility support for DTS is provided in SQL Server 2005 to allow developers and organizations to migrate existing packages to Integration Services. You will read all about the migration options in Chapter 12.

In SQL Server 2005, Integration Services is installed as a Windows service that enables you to monitor the execution of running SSIS packages and manage and view SSIS packages stored in various folders in different physical locations in a hierarchical view. DTS 2000 was not a separate Windows service; rather, it was managed under the MSSQLSERVER service instance. Also, if you migrate from SQL Server 2000 to SQL Server 2005, your existing DTS 2000 packages can still work as is with Integration Services or they can be migrated to Integration Services.

Integration Services in SQL Server 2005 Editions

Not all the editions of SQL Server 2005 include Integration Services. The following list shows how Integration Services is distributed across various editions of SQL Server 2005:

▶ **SQL Server 2005 Express Edition**   This entry-level free edition does not include Integration Services, though it does provide support for legacy DTS 2000 packages. You can run DTS 2000 packages in Express Edition, but you need to install SQL Server 2000 client tools or DTS redistributable files on the computer as Express Edition doesn't include the DTS run-time environment. Also, be aware that the Express Edition includes an Import and Export utility, which is not the same as the SQL Server Import and Export Wizard and does not use Integration Services.

▶ **SQL Server 2005 Workgroup Edition**   This edition is targeted to be used as a departmental server or as a front-end web server that is reliable, robust, and easy to manage. It includes the SQL Server Import and Export Wizard, which uses Integration Services to develop simple source to destination data movement packages without any transformation logic. The packages developed in this version of the wizard can use the Execute SQL task, OLE DB source, and destination adapters to support import and export of data with SQL Server. However, no other source or destination adapter or transformation is included. As the name suggests, SQL Server Import and Export Wizard is designed to leverage SSIS but only in relation to importing and exporting data with SQL Server. You can, however, save the packages developed with SQL Server Import and Export Wizard for later scheduling in SQL Server. This version provides legacy support to DTS 2000 packages similar to the extent in Express Edition. It also includes dtutil and dtexec—the Integration Services command line utilities.

▶ **SQL Server 2005 Standard Edition**   The Standard Edition is designed for small to medium-sized organizations that need a complete data management and analysis platform. This edition includes the full power of Integration Services, excluding some high-end components that are considered to be of importance to enterprise operations. Integration Services is installed as a Windows service, and BIDS, an Integration Services development environment, is also included. The separation of Standard Edition and Enterprise Edition is made only on the basis of high-end components and does not impose any performance or components functionalities limitations. What you get in Standard Edition works exactly as it would work in Enterprise Edition. The following components have not been included in this edition, however:

▶ Data mining query transformation

▶ Fuzzy grouping transformation

▶ Fuzzy lookup transformation

▶ Term extraction transformation

▶ Term lookup transformation

▶ Data mining model training destination adapter

▶ Dimension processing destination adapter

▶ Partition processing destination adapter

▶ **SQL Server 2005 Enterprise Edition**   The most comprehensive edition is targeted to the largest organizations and the most complex requirements. Integration Services appears with all its tools, utilities, tasks, sources, transformations, and destinations. (You will not only study all of these components but will work with most of them throughout this book.)

▶ **SQL Server 2005 Developer Edition**   This has all the features of Enterprise Edition.

32-bit Editions Versus 64-bit Editions

Technology is changing quickly, and every release of a major software platform seems to provide multiple editions and versions that can perform specific tasks. SQL Server 2005 not only introduced the Workgroup Edition, but it also brought in 64-bit flavors of Standard and Enterprise Editions. Though SQL Server 2000 was available in a 64-bit edition, it was not a fully loaded edition and ran only on Intel Itanium 64-bit CPUs (IA64). It lacked many key facilities, such as SQL Server tools on the 64-bit platform— that is, Enterprise Manager, Query Analyzer, and DTS Designer are 32-bit applications. To manage the 64-bit editions of SQL Server 2000, you must run a separate 32-bit system. Moreover, SQL Server 2000 64-bit was available in Enterprise Edition only and was a pure 64-bit edition with less facility to switch over.

On the other hand, SQL Server 2005 64-bit edition is a fully featured edition with all the SQL Server tools and services available on the 64-bit platform; that means you do not need to maintain a parallel system to manage it. SQL Server 2005 64-bit edition is available for Standard and Enterprise Editions. It can run on both IA64 and x64 platforms and is enhanced to run on Intel and AMD-based 64-bit servers. You can run SQL Server 2005 and its components in 64-bit native mode, or you can run 32-bit SQL Server and 32-bit components in WOW64 mode. SQL Server 2005 provides a complete implementation of Integration Services in the 64-bit edition. The performance benefits provided by 64-bit systems outweigh the costs and efforts involved, and it is also very simple to switch over to the 64-bit edition. If you're interested in knowing more about SQL Server 2005 Integration Services 64-bit editions, detailed information is provided in Chapter 13.

Integration Services Architecture

Now you understand the benefits Integration Services provides with its vast array of features, and you also know about various versions and feature sets associated with them. Before we move further and "get our hands dirty," let's look more closely at the architecture; this will help you appreciate how the various components perform their jobs to execute an Integration Services package successfully. Let's start with the architecture diagram provided in Microsoft SQL Server 2005 Books Online, shown in Figure 1-1.

Microsoft SQL Server 2005 Integration Services consists of the following four main components:

▶   Integration Services service

▶   Integration Services object model

▶   Integration Services run-time engine

▶   Integration Services data flow engine

You read about these components earlier in this chapter. The following discussion on each of these components and their functions will clarify how Integration Services is architected.

Integration Services Service

Shown on the top right corner of the architecture diagram (see Figure 1-1), the Integration Services service is installed as a Windows service when you specifically choose Integration Services during installation. In the next section's Hands-On exercise, you will see where you make this choice and learn that choosing Integration Services specifically during installations installs other components as well. Integration Services service allows you to execute Integration Services packages on local or remote computers, stop execution of running packages on local or remote computers, monitor

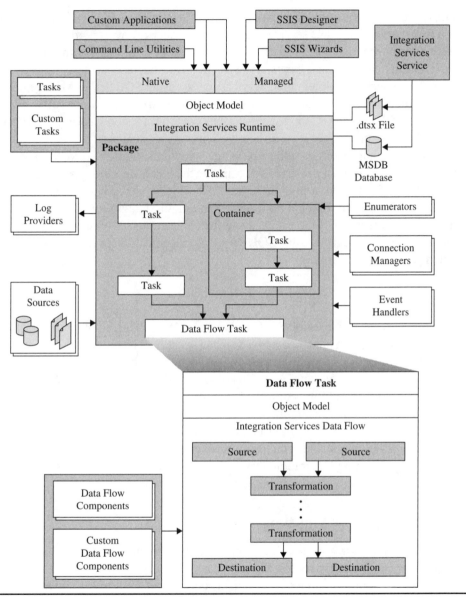

Figure 1-1   *Integration Services architecture*

running packages on local or remote computers, connect to multiple Integration Services servers to manage multiple instances, and view the Windows Event log. In Figure 1-1, the Integration Services service points to a .dtsx file and MSDB database, implying that this service can manage SSIS packages stored to a file system or in an MSDB database within SQL Server 2005. The service manages SSIS packages by importing and exporting them from one type of storage location to another. You will learn a lot more about managing packages and their storage locations in Chapter 6.

You can connect to the Integration Services service using SQL Server Management Studio, which you will do later in this chapter. Generally, with other software components, if the service is stopped, most of the components stop working. This is not true with Integration Services service, because it is a component used to monitor running packages and manage them for storage purposes—you do not need to have this service running to design and run a package. You can save the newly designed packages in BIDS on to the file system or in SQL Server 2005 MSDB database and then execute as well. However, you may find it a bit faster when running Integration Services service, as it caches the metadata of the package and the connections. Also, if you need to monitor and list the packages using SQL Server Management Studio, Integration Services service must be running.

Integration Services Object Model

As mentioned earlier, Integration Services is a new feature, with an object model that supports both native and managed APIs. You can use this object model to write custom components such as tasks and transformations using C++ or any common language runtime (CLR)–compliant language. This object model provides easy accessibility for Integration Services tools, command-line utilities, and custom applications, as shown on the top section of Figure 1-1. You can also develop custom components, build new packages, load and modify existing packages, and then execute them programmatically. This enables you to automate maintenance and execution of your packages. Programming Integration Services is a vast subject and deserves a separate book altogether. A complete discussion is beyond the scope of this book.

Integration Services Run-time

Integration Services run-time provides support for the package, containers, tasks, and event handlers during package execution. It provides run-time services such as support for logging, breakpoints, connections to data sources and data stores, and support for transactions. You read earlier that Integration Services has two separate engines— a run-time engine for workflow and another engine for data flow. Basically, Integration Services run-time consists of whatever you configure in the Control Flow tab of BIDS plus the run-time services.

Integration Services Data Flow

As mentioned, the second engine of Integration Services provides services to the data flow within a package. This data flow is also known as the *pipeline* due to the nature of data flowing through various transformations one after another. The Data Flow task is a unique task provided in the Control Flow tab of BIDS that encapsulates the data flow engine and the data flow components. Integration Services data flow consists of one or many data flow sources; none, one, or many data flow transformations; and one or more data flow destinations. The data flow engine drives the data out of data flow sources, brings it into pipeline, and lets the data flow transformations perform the aggregations and conversions, merge data streams, conditionally split data, perform lookups, derive columns, and perform several other operations before loading the data into the destination data stores using data flow destinations. You will work with data flow components in Chapters 9 and 10 in much detail.

Installing Integration Services

The next step is to install Integration Services. In real life, either you will be installing Integration Services on a *clean* Windows platform—that is, on a system where no current or previous releases of SQL Server are installed—or you will be installing it on a computer that already has DTS 2000 installed. Both these scenarios are discussed in the following sections.

Installing Integration Services on a Clean System

Most production systems are built using this method. Administrators prefer to install SQL Server on a fresh installation of Windows Server to avoid any debugging later on because of some old component on the server that doesn't work properly with SQL Server 2005 Integration Services. You can install Integration Services either using a wizard or by running the Setup program from the command prompt.

You'll install Integration Services using the SQL Server Installation Wizard in the following Hands-On exercise. You will be installing SQL Server 2005 and Integration Services together; however, note that Integration Services does not require SQL Server in order to work. You can develop packages in Integration Services that connect to mainframes, Oracle, or DB2 database servers and output in flat files without installing SQL Server. A couple of high-end transformations, such as Fuzzy Lookup transformation and Fuzzy Grouping transformation, need to create temporary tables for processing data in SQL Server 2005 and hence require connection to a SQL Server 2005 server. However, even in this case, you do not need to have SQL Server running on the same local machine where your Integration Services package is designed or executed.

Hands-On: Installing SQL Server 2005 Integration Services

In this Hands-On exercise, you will install SQL Server 2005 Integration Services using the Installation Wizard on a clean system.

Method

It is important that you follow this process step by step, as this installation will be used throughout this book to create and run Integration Services projects. If you do not have SQL Server 2005 Enterprise Edition or Development Edition software, you can download SQL Server 2005 Enterprise Evaluation Edition from Microsoft's download web site. This version is valid for 180 days and can be used for trial purposes. Details on various installation options are not covered here and are beyond the scope of this book. Refer to Microsoft SQL Server 2005 Books Online for more details on these installation options.

Exercise (Running SQL Server Installation Wizard)

Load SQL Server 2005 DVD media in your computer's DVD drive and start the installation as follows:

1. After you load the DVD, the AutoRun feature will open the Start screen, which displays various options. If AutoRun doesn't do this, browse the DVD and run splash.hta from the root folder. You can also start installation by executing the setup.exe program from the root folder. Click Server Components, Tools, Books Online, and Samples under the Install section to start the installation.

2. In the End User License Agreement screen, click the check box to accept the licensing terms and conditions; then click Next.

3. The installation program starts to install the components required for SQL Server 2005 in the Installing Prerequisites screen. Depending on what is already installed on your computer, it may install .NET Framework 2.0, Microsoft SQL Native Client, and Microsoft SQL Server 2005 Setup Support Files. When these components have been installed, click Next.

4. After the preparation phase has been completed, you will see the welcome screen of SQL Server Installation Wizard. Click Next.

5. In the System Configuration Check screen, your computer is scanned for possible issues that may cause the installation process to fail. If you receive a warning at this stage, you can view the report by clicking the hyperlink against the erroneous item in the Message column or by clicking the Report button. Once you've corrected any issues, click Next.

6. Type in your details in the Name and Company fields in the Registration Information screen. Click Next.

7. In the Components to Install screen, click check boxes to select SQL Server Database Services, Integration Services, and Workstation Components, Books Online and Development Tools, as shown in Figure 1-2.

    This is the most important step in the installation process, as you choose to install Integration Services here. However, even if you do not specifically select Integration Services, some components of Integration Services will still be installed because of their requirement in performing specific functions by other selected components. For example, SQL Server Import and Export Wizard will be installed when you install SQL Server Database Services only. Also, most of the tasks and transformations will be available to you for building packages when you install BIDS but do not choose to install Integration Services. The packages you develop without installing Integration Services may or may not work depending

Figure 1-2   *Selecting Integration Services in the Components to Install screen*

upon the tasks and transformations you've used in the package, as this won't be a complete installation of Integration Services and some components do not work, such as the Message Queue Task. When you specifically install Integration Services by selecting the check box provided in the Components to Install screen, it is installed as a Windows Service and installs backward-compatibility components to provide legacy support. Integration Services service enables you to list and monitor SSIS packages using SQL Server Management Studio. Another benefit of installing Integration Services service is that it caches metadata of package components and speeds up loading of package in BIDS. Click the Advanced button to open the Feature Selection screen.

8. First expand the Documentation, Samples, and Sample Databases node, and then expand the Sample Databases node. Select AdventureWorks Sample OLTP to install it on the local hard disk, as shown in Figure 1-3. You will be using this database in the Hands-On exercises in the chapters to come.

9. Leave the Default instance selected and click Next.

10. Select the Use a Domain User Account option on the Service Account screen and specify the Username, Password, and Domain in the provided fields. Select check boxes for SQL Server and SQL Server Agent and click Next. Use administrators account details if possible to avoid any possible issues with account rights.

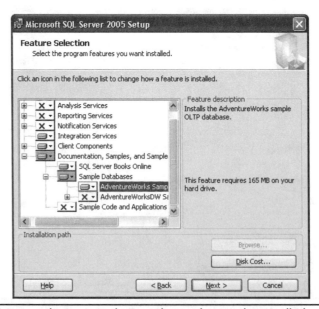

Figure 1-3 *Selecting AdventureWorks Sample Database to be installed*

11. In the Authentication Mode screen, select the Mixed Mode option and specify a password for sa (system administrator) login. Click Next.

12. In the Collation Settings screen, leave the default settings of Latin1_General and Accent Sensitive selected and click Next.

13. Click Next on the Error and Report Settings screen. You don't need to select these optional settings.

14. Review the options on the Ready to Install screen and click Install when ready.

15. You will see the installation of SQL Server 2005 components in the Setup Progress screen. This may take about 15 to 30 minutes to complete.

16. When the process completes, you will see the installation summary log in the Completing Microsoft SQL Server 2005 Setup screen. Click Finish to close the installation wizard. If prompted, restart your computer to complete the installation process.

Review

You've installed SQL Server 2005 in the default instance and SQL Server Integration Services in the Hands-On exercise. Double-click the Add or Remove Programs applet in the Control Panel and note the software components installed in this exercise. Notice that Microsoft SQL Server 2005 Backward Compatibility has also been installed. Open the Services console from the Administrative Tools and notice that SQL Server 2005 services have been installed along with SQL Server Integration Services service. Now you can play around with the software components installed by the installation wizard in the Programs group to get acquainted with various components.

Installing Integration Services from the Command Prompt

You can install Integration Services by executing setup.exe with parameters from the command prompt on a local or remote server. You can specify parameters directly in the command, or use an .ini file to pass the parameters. Installation options for Integration Services and its components are available in the command-line parameters and described next.

▶ **SQL_Engine**   This parameter installs SQL Server database engine.

▶ **SQL_Data_File**   This is the required option when you use SQL_Engine and enables you to specify the database files used.

▶ **SQL_DTS**   This option is equivalent to selecting the Integration Services check box in the preceding exercise. It installs Integration Services service and the backward-compatibility component for legacy support.

- ▶ **SQL_WarehouseDevWorkbench**   Selecting this option installs BIDS.

- ▶ **SQL_Workbench**   Selecting this option installs SQL Server Management Studio.

- ▶ **SQL_BooksOnline**   Selecting this option installs SQL Server Books Online.

For example, if you want to install SQL Server database engine, Integration Services and client tools, and online documentation, the syntax for the command will be something like this:

```
Start /wait Setup.exe /qb addlocal = "SQL_Engine, SQL_DTS,SQL_BooksOnline"
```

As mentioned earlier, you can also use an .ini file to specify the parameters. If using an .ini file, include the `/settings` switch in your command. Here's an example:

```
Start /wait setup.exe /settings c:\template.ini
```

You can see the options and the parameters in the sample template.ini file provided in the root folder of the SQL Server installation DVD. As this installation method leans more toward SQL Server 2005 installation customization options, it is not covered in full here; however, you can consult Microsoft SQL Server 2005 Books Online for more details.

Upgrading SQL Server 2000 Data Transformation Services

When you are planning to upgrade DTS to Integration Services, you have options to consider about your existing DTS 2000 packages. DTS 2000 packages can continue to run with Integration Services as is, because when you install Integration Services, it also installs backward-compatibility components. You can use the following steps to plan a smooth upgrade of Data Transformation Services to Integration Services and migration of your existing packages to the Integration Services format.

1. Microsoft provides a tool called Upgrade Advisor that can analyze the configurations of SQL Server 7.0 or SQL Server 2000 and generate a report for you to list the possible issues that may cause the upgrade process to fail. You can take corrective actions for a successful upgrade using these reports. This tool is freely downloadable from the Microsoft Download Center web site.

2. Once you have taken corrective actions to avoid possible failures of the upgrade process, you can then install SQL Server 2005 with Integration Services either using the SQL Server Installation Wizard or by running the Setup program from

the command prompt. After installation, verify that the process has installed Microsoft SQL Server 2005 backward-compatibility components from the Add or Remove Programs applet in the Control Panel. This will allow you to run DTS 2000 packages as is in the new environment using the DTS 2000 run-time.

3. Optionally, you can choose to migrate DTS 2000 packages to the Integration Services format. You must use SQL Server 2005 Standard, Enterprise, or Developer Edition if you want to migrate your existing packages to Integration Services format, as other editions do not include the Package Migration Wizard of Integration Services. Chapter 12 discusses all the migration options available for your existing DTS 2000 packages with Integration Services.

Business Intelligence Development Studio

Business Intelligence Development Studio is designed for developing business intelligence solutions including cubes, data sources, data source views, reports, and Integration Services packages. BIDS is built around Visual Studio 2005, which allows you to design, build, test, execute, deploy, and extend Integration Services packages in an integrated development environment. Because of Visual Studio 2005 integration, BIDS provides integrated development features, a debugger, integrated help, and integrated source code (Visual SourceSafe). You can use the same techniques to build and deploy Analysis Services, Reporting Services, and Integration Services projects with BIDS. You can also develop a solution using BIDS that can have multiple Integration Services, Analysis Services, and Reporting Services projects.

BIDS is based on the usual application design philosophy of solutions and projects. This provides lots of benefits, including the following:

▶ You don't need to have a SQL Server to develop Integration Services packages; rather, you can save your SSIS packages or projects in file system folders.

▶ Your development gets an organized structure so that a number of projects can be run under the context of one solution. Those projects can contain data sources, data source views, SSIS packages, and other miscellaneous files. Availability of all of the support DDL and DML files at one place makes deployment a very easy task.

▶ Direct integration with Visual SourceSafe facilitates immediate check-in whenever changes are made to projects. However, packages saved to SQL Server are not benefited with integration with SourceSafe.

▶ Being built on .NET Framework, it is easy to develop custom tasks using .NET languages such as C# or Visual Basic 2005.

The BIDS environment consists of various windows. Among the main windows are SSIS Designer, Solution Explorer, Toolbox, and Properties, in addition to other windows such as Output, Error List, and Task List. All these windows can be docked anywhere and can be tabbed on to the main Designer window, set to auto-hide, or closed. These features provide a fantastic UI configuration feature that allows developers to customize their environment (to free up working space) and boost productivity.

Let's take a closer look at BIDS. In the following Hands-On exercise, you will create a blank Integration Services project to will learn various aspects of this tool.

Hands-On: Creating a Blank Integration Services Project

The objective of this exercise is to create your first blank Integration Services project and study various aspects of BIDS while working with it. You will use this project in Chapter 2 to add packages and take it further.

Exercise (Creating a Blank Integration Services Project)

1. Choose Start | All Programs | Microsoft SQL Server 2005, and then click SQL Server Business Intelligence Development Studio.

2. When the BIDS screen appears, choose File | New, and then click Project. Alternatively, you can create a new project by clicking the Project URL next to Create in Recent Projects Section on Start Page. This will open a New Project dialog box in which the Business Intelligence Projects option is selected by default in Project Types. In the Templates pane, select Integration Services Project and then fill in the following details in the fields provided in the lower section of the dialog box (see Figure 1-4):

   Name: My First SSIS Project

   Location: C:\SSIS\Projects

   Do not select the check box for Create Directory for Solution, as we do not want a parent folder for a solution to be created in this instance. Click the OK button when you have filled in these details to create an Integration Services project.

3. A new Integration Services project window will appear, displaying you a blank designer surface and the Package.dtsx SSIS package created in the Solution Explorer window, as shown in Figure 1-5. Using Windows Explorer, go to the C:\SSIS\Projects folder and note that various files have been created in the My First SSIS Project folder. Note the extensions and types of these files, as each one of them represents a different function in your Integration Services project.

Congratulations! You have created your first Integration Services project.

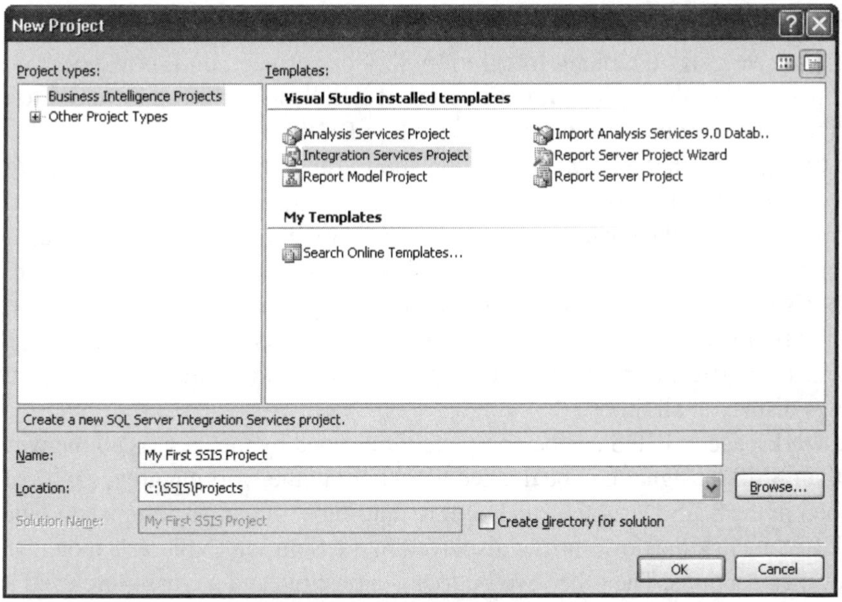

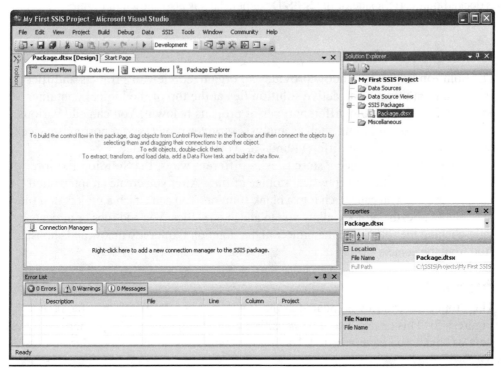

Figure 1-4   *Templates for creating new projects in BIDS*

Figure 1-5   *Your first blank Integration Services project*

Review

Though you've created a blank Integration Services project, until now you haven't been introduced to the various functionaries of BIDS. Take this opportunity to learn more about the various tabs and windows while BIDS is open.

The biggest area in the BIDS application shows four tabs—Control Flow, Data Flow, and Event Handlers to show design surfaces and one Package Explorer tab to show components used in the package in a hierarchical structure. A Connection Managers area appears in the lower section. Together this is called the SSIS Designer. The SSIS Designer's UI is particularly useful for handling large projects with many packages open at the same time. Other windows in the BIDS application are Solution Explorer, Toolbox, Properties, Error List, and Output, as shown in Figure 1-5. Not all these windows display at all times.

The workspace in BIDS can be completely managed by the user, as all the windows other than SSIS Designer can be docked anywhere in the working area, can float, can be tabbed in the SSIS Designer, can be set to auto-hide, or can be completely hidden or closed. If you click the down arrow displayed in the Solution Explorer's menu bar, you will see these options. The other two buttons—a pushpin and a cross—are used to set windows to auto-hide or hide (close), respectively. By default, the Toolbox window is in auto-hide mode, hanging on the left side of the SSIS Designer, and Solution Explorer is docked on the right side of the SSIS Designer. This is also shown in Figure 1-5.

Let's zoom in more closely to explore the various windows in BIDS.

Solution Explorer Window

The Solution Explorer window provides an organized view of projects and files associated with them. The active solution lies at the top of the logical container and contains one or more different types of projects below it. You can add various other projects to a solution, such as analysis services projects or reporting services projects, to organize your different units of work all in one place.

Because different projects store files in different ways, the Solution Explorer window does not reflect the physical storage of files. After you create an Integration Services project, you can attach it to a blank solution. You can attach a project or a file to a solution, but the projects allow you to attach only files. You add files or projects by right-clicking the solution or the project in the Solution Explorer window and choosing Add from the context menu.

Properties Window

The Properties window is located at the lower right of the BIDS interface (see Figure 1-5). This is also a context-sensitive window and shows the properties of the item or object you have selected. Having the Properties window open during design time is a great time-saver. Like other windows, you can close the window or move it around on the desktop. You can open this window again from the View menu or by pressing F4.

Toolbox

You probably noticed a tabbed window on the left side of the SSIS Designer (see Figure 1-5), called the Toolbox. The Toolbox contains all the preconfigured tasks provided by Integration Services in the Control Flow tab and Data Flow Sources, Data Flow Transformations, and Data Flow Destinations in the Data Flow tab. The tasks are organized in two sections in the Toolbox window, and it shows the tasks that are relevant to the project type you are working with. By default, the Toolbox always displays the General tab. When you are in the Control Flow tab of the Designer window and open the Toolbox, you will see Control Flow Items; if you're in the Data Flow tab of the Designer window, you will see Data Flow Sources, Data Flow Transformations, and Data Flow Destinations sections.

SSIS Designer

This is the main designer surface for developing packages for all three Business Intelligence (BI) project types. This is context sensitive—that is, each of the BI project types has its own designer surfaces. The SSIS Designer provides a graphical view of objects that makes data movement, workflow, and Integration Services development work possible with minimal or no programming. The Designer itself is made up of surfaces such as Control Flow, Data Flow, Event Handlers, Package Explorer, and Connection Managers.

Control Flow Tab

The Control Flow tab consists of the tasks arranged in the order in which they are performed—that is, precedence constraints and the workflow defined by looping structure containers For Loop, Foreach Loop, and Sequence. You can draw objects on the graphical surface of the Designer and link them with other objects by dragging and dropping an arrow that extends from one object to another. This arrow signifies a precedence constraint and can be of type OnSuccess, which appears in green; OnCompletion, which appears in blue; and OnFailure, which appears in red. By defining the tasks and the precedence constraints between them, you design the control flow of your package and thus define the workflow in your package. You can logically group tasks to simplify complex packages and annotate them with text boxes to provide an explanation of the task. You will study more about precedence constraints and other control flow components in Chapters 3 to 5.

Data Flow Tab

The Data Flow designer consists of the source adapters that extract data from heterogeneous data sources; the transformations that modify, aggregate, or extend data; and the destination adapters that load the transformed data into the final data stores. A package must include at least one Data Flow task in order to implement a data flow. You can create multiple Data Flow tasks in a package and create multiple data flows within a Data Flow task. The data is extracted from a source using source adapters and loaded to the destination using destination adapters. In between source adapters and destinations adapters you use transformations to modify, aggregate, extend column data, and apply business logic to convert data. The flow of data from source to destination with transformations along the way is linked together with green or red lines called *data flow paths*. Adding data viewers to a path enables you to see the data as it moves from source to destination. This helps you debug and locate a troublemaking component that is converting data incorrectly. Extensive error handling can be included in the Data Flow task, such as, error rows can be routed to a different destination whenever there is a row-level fault, to capture, analyze, and maybe correct and feed back to the main data flow.

Event Handlers Tab

You can extend package functionality by using event handlers, which are helpful in managing packages at run-time. Event handlers are like subpackages waiting for the events to be raised so they can come to life. They are powerful tools that can extend package functionality greatly when properly implemented. Event handlers are created for the packages, Foreach Loop container, For Loop container, Sequence container, and for the tasks in the same way as you create packages. Once created, event handlers can be explored in the Package Explorer tab by first expanding the package, then expanding the Executables, and finally expanding the Event Handlers node.

Package Explorer Tab

The Package Explorer represents the container hierarchy of the SSIS object model and lists all the package objects. This is the interface through which you can execute a package and monitor the running package. When you click the Package Explorer tab, your package appears at the top of the hierarchy. Click the package to expand and expose the variables, executables, precedence constraints, event handlers, connection managers, and log providers' objects. Event handlers are members of the event handlers collection, and all executables include this collection. When you create an event handler, SSIS adds the event handler to the event handlers collection. The Package Explorer tab in SSIS Designer lists the event handlers for an executable. Expand the Event Handlers node to view the event handlers that executable uses.

Progress Tab or Execution Result Tab

This tab doesn't show up during design time when you are still developing the package. When you run an Integration Services Package in BIDS, a Progress tab will appear within the SSIS Designer. This Progress tab converts to an Execution Result tab once the package execution is completed and you've switched back to the design mode.

Connection Managers Area

In this area, you add various connection managers depending on the requirements of your package. For example, if your package needs to connect to a flat file, you will add a flat file connection manager; if your package needs to connect to a SQL Server database, you will add an OLE DB connection manager.

BIDS provides many other windows for additional informational purposes. Some of these are described next while others will be introduced wherever used.

Code Window

You can see the code of a package or an object in the SSIS Designer. To see this, go to the Solution Explorer window, right-click Package.dtsx, and choose View Code from the context menu. An additional tab on the SSIS Designer surface appears with a listing of code in XML form.

Task List Window

In the Task List window, you can add notes for descriptive purposes or as a follow-up for later development; you can also organize and manage the building of your application. To open the task list, choose View | Task List. These tasks can be filtered and sorted based on the predefined options provided.

Output Window

The Output window displays build errors that occur during building, deployment, or run-time. Certain external tools list their output to the Output window as well. To open the Output window, choose View | Output. The Output window provides information on various panes, depending on which program is sending information to the Output window.

Error List Window

This window provides detailed description of validation errors during design time. It also shows errors, warnings, and messages for the package you are developing. To open this window, choose View | Error List.

SQL Server Management Studio

SQL Server Management Studio is the main tool used to manage SQL Server 2005 databases and run T-SQL queries against the tables and views. In this section, you will not learn how to use this tool to manage databases; instead, you will learn how to use this tool to connect to Integration Services service and manage Integration Services packages. So, instead of talking about the tool, let's start using this tool straight away with a simple Hands-On exercise.

Hands-On: Connecting to Integration Services Service

In this exercise, you will connect to Integration Services and explore where DTS 2000 packages can be managed within SQL Server Management Studio.

Exercise (Using SQL Server Management Studio)

1. Choose Start | All Programs | Microsoft SQL Server 2005. Then click SQL Server Management Studio.

2. When the SQL Server Management Studio loads, you will see the Connect to Server pop-up dialog box, where you can choose a server type to which you want to connect and provide your authentication details. Click the Server type field and select Integration Services from the drop-down list. Type **localhost** in the Server Name field to connect to the local server and then click the Connect button.

3. SQL Server Management Studio will connect to Integration Services and show you Running Packages and Stored Packages folders under Integration Services in the Object Explorer, as shown in Figure 1-6.

4. Expand these folders. You will not see any packages listed under Running Packages because no packages have yet been created. Click the Stored Packages folder and you'll see the File System and MSDB folders. This is where you will be managing the packages you've stored in the file system or the MSDB database in SQL Server. Managing these folders and the packages is covered in detail in Chapter 6.

5. Let's do a little more research to see where DTS 2000 packages go. In the Object Explorer window, click the Connect button and choose Database Engine from the drop-down list. Note that you can connect to Integration Services from here as well. Leave localhost as the Server Name and verify that Windows Authentication is selected in the Authentication field. Click the Connect button to connect to the local database server.

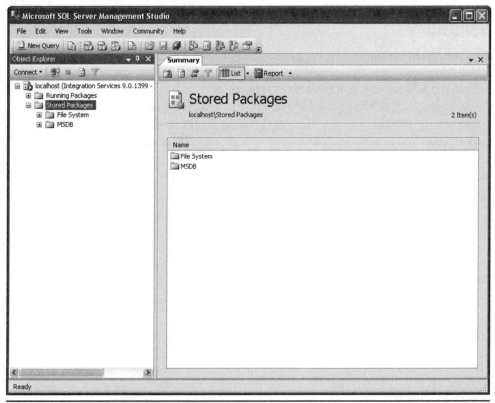

Figure 1-6   *Connecting to Integration Services service*

6. Under the database server, expand the Management node and then the Legacy node. You will see a Data Transformation Services node. This is where you will be managing DTS 2000 packages that are imported into SQL Server 2005. How you run existing DTS 2000 packages or migrate them to the Integration Services format is covered in depth in Chapter 12.

7. Close SQL Server Management Studio.

Review

Though you haven't yet built anything from the development point of view, you've seen quite a lot. If you've used DTS 2000, it may have already answered many of your questions, but if you are new to SQL Server you can appreciate how easy it is to use SQL Server Management Studio to connect to Integration Services and manage SSIS packages storage locations. Also, you know where you can see DTS 2000 packages imported into SQL Server 2005.

Summary

You have been introduced to Integration Services by following a couple of simple Hands-On exercises and reading a description of its architecture, features, and uses. You understand how various components of Integration Services work together to provide the manageability, flexibility, and scalability you need for your SSIS packages. You also appreciate the fact that all the components can be programmatically controlled and that custom tasks and transformations can be written using languages such as C++ or any CLR compatible language. You know that Integration Services has two separate engines that provide workflow and data flow functions. You are now ready to launch into the realm of bigger challenges.

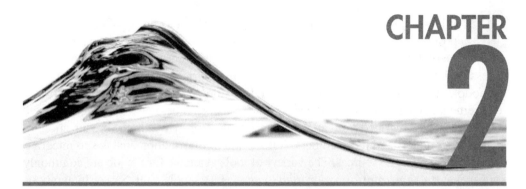

SQL Server Import and Export Wizard

IN THIS CHAPTER

Businesses of today are dealing with customers via a variety of channels—post mail, telephone, e-mail, text message, web portal, agent, dealer, direct marketing, through business partners, and the list goes on. This increased access to data means that data must be stored in a variety of places using new methodologies, and in a variety of different data storage systems. Along with storage requirement considerations, the sheer volume of data can be overwhelming.

Data must be integrated from all disparate sources rapidly within the organization to help it better understand its customers. It is the job of information analysts to integrate data stored in disparate sources. The variety of tools available for the job are commonly known as *extraction, transformation, and loading* (ETL) tools. SQL Server Integration Services (SSIS) makes the job easy by providing various components that work with most of the data sources and the data stores, and transform data to meet even the most complex requirements.

The SQL Server Import and Export Wizard (also known as SSIS Import and Export Wizard) is the easiest utility to work with. Its interactive and simple graphical user interface (GUI) allows even beginners to use the wizard for learning purposes and simple package development. Seasoned developers also use it for creating basic packages quickly, to be later extended using Business Intelligence Development Studio (BIDS) to reduce development time. The wizard is designed to perform simple tasks quickly and easily, hence it has limited transformation capabilities.

While you can use the SQL Server Import and Export Wizard to import and export data from any SQL Server database, the wizard can also move and transform data that may or may not involve SQL Server. Also, Data Transformation Services (DTS) of SQL Server 2000 could transform data stored in SQL Server only, and to transform data that resided in a different data store, you had to bring it into SQL Server first, whereas SSIS is free from this limitation and can work with data that resides in a data source other than SQL Server, bring it into its data flow, apply transformations on it, and extract it to the data store of your choice.

Starting SSIS Import and Export Wizard

SSIS Import and Export Wizard is handily available at locations where you would need it. However, unlike its predecessor, DTS Import/Export Wizard, SSIS Import and Export Wizard is not available from the Microsoft SQL Server 2005 program group in the Start menu. In SQL Server Workgroup, Standard, Enterprise, and Developer editions, the SSIS wizard uses the Integration Services engine to drive the data. Following are the locations from which you can start the wizard:

- ▶ DTSWizard.exe file
- ▶ SQL Server Management Studio
- ▶ Business Intelligence Development Studio (BIDS)

You will use different methods to start SSIS Import and Export Wizard while working in the following exercises.

Hands-On: Importing a Flat File into SQL Server 2005

In your first exercise, you will import a simple text file into SQL Server 2005 and create a new database while importing this file.

1. Choose Start | Run. In the Run dialog box's Open field, type **DTSWizard**; then click the OK button to open the SQL Server Import and Export Wizard's Welcome page, as shown in Figure 2-1. (You can also run this file from the command prompt or by double-clicking the DTSWizard.exe file in the default location of C:\Program Files\Microsoft SQL Server\90\DTS\Binn.)

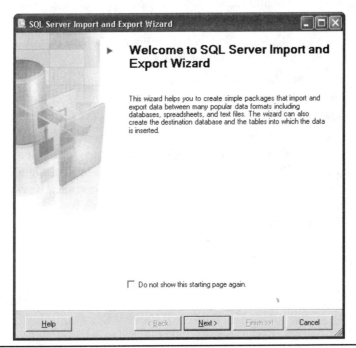

Figure 2-1   *The Import and Export Wizard's Welcome page*

2. Click the Next button to open the Choose A Data Source window. By default, the wizard is set to point to (local) server using SQL Native Client. Click the arrow next to the Data Source field to see the other available data sources to which this wizard can connect. The drop-down list shows providers for several data sources that may be installed on the local machine, including the following:

   ► Flat Files

   ► Microsoft Excel

   ► Microsoft Access

   ► .NET Framework Data Provider for SQL Server

   ► Microsoft OLE DB Provider for SQL Server and SQL Native Client

3. The Import and Export Wizard can connect to and extract data from any of these data sources. Select Flat File Source from the Data Source drop-down list. The options on screen change to match the Flat File Source requirements.

4. Click the Browse button opposite the File Name field, and in the Open dialog box navigate to the C:\SSIS\RawFiles folder. Select the CSV files (*.csv) option in the Files Of Type field to display .csv files, and then choose the RawDataTxt.csv file and click Open in the pop-up window. Most of the options will be automatically filled in for you as the wizard reads the file format.

5. Click to check the Column Names In The First Data Row option, as shown in Figure 2-2, and then click Columns in the pane on the left.

   On this page, data is listed in the bottom half of the window. Note that the Column delimiter is preselected to Comma and that the headings of columns are displayed properly and are actually picked up from the first row of the text file.

   Go to the Advanced page by clicking it in the left pane. You'll see the list of columns in the middle pane and the column properties for the selected column in the right pane. You can change column properties such as Data Type or OutputColumnWidth here. If you are working with complex data types, you can click the Suggest Types button to identify the data types and length of the columns in the flat file.

   Finally, if you click Preview, you will be able to set a value for the Data Rows to Skip property. In the Choose A Data Source window, click the Next button to move on.

6. In the Choose A Destination window, leave the default SQL Native Client selected in the Destination field. Microsoft SQL Native Client provides an OLE DB interface to Microsoft SQL Server 2005 databases, which you can use to access new features of SQL Server 2005 such as XML Data Type and Distributed queries.

Figure 2-2   *Selecting a data source in the SQL Server Import and Export Wizard*

Just to remind you once again, you don't need to have SQL Server to run the SSIS Import and Export Wizard or BIDS for developing Integration Services packages. You can actually move or transform your data from any source to any destination without involving SQL Server. So, for example, you can choose Destination as a text file and remove some of the columns from the destination file (so you generate a modified text file from a text file), one operation that isn't easy to perform on text files otherwise.

You can specify your server name in the Server Name field or select a name from the drop-down list by clicking the down arrow. Leave localhost specified for this exercise. This option can be quite useful if you want to deploy your packages on a server other than where you develop your packages. The localhost option will make the Integration Services connect to the local server wherever the package is run. For this exercise, leave the radio button for Use Windows Authentication selected.

The Database field shows <Default> specified, which indicates the default database for the login account you use. This option can also be considered for deployment purposes. You can choose a different database from the drop-down list after clicking the down arrow button. You can also opt to create a new database. The software provided for the book contains files for the Campaign database that you will use to perform various exercises. Please refer to the "How to Use the Provided Software" appendix for further details on this. If you haven't attached the provided Campaign database yet to your SQL Server database engine, you can create it here by clicking the New button. Click the New button to create a new database.

7. If your login for SQL Server is correct, a new Create Database dialog box will open, showing you the options for creating a new database. However, if you are using incorrect credentials for the server, you won't be able to connect to the server and hence can't create a new database using the New button. Type **Campaign** in the Name field. As you type, you can see the wizard has filled in the paths for Data File Name and Log File Name using the default database location (refer to Figure 2-3). Leave the options under Data File Size and Log File Size as is, and click the OK button to return to the Choose A Destination window. Note that if you're using the Campaign database provided in the software with this book, then you do not need to create the Campaign database here.

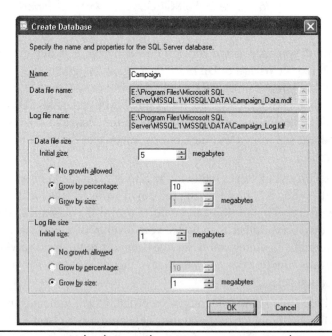

Figure 2-3 *Creating a new database in the SQL Server Import and Export Wizard*

8. Click Next to proceed. In the Select Source Tables And Views window, verify that the check box next to the file name listed under Source is selected. The Destination will automatically be filled in with a table name using the three-part notation. Click the Edit button under the Mapping column to see the Column Mappings window. Here, you have various options to configure your destination table and the way you want to insert data into it. Following is the description of each of these options:

Create Destination Table   This option will be selected in your case. Choose this option whenever you want to create a destination table. When this option is highlighted and selected, you can click the Edit SQL button to generate an SQL statement that will be used to create this new table. You can customize this SQL statement to create the table of your choice; however, if you modify the default SQL statement, you manually have to modify the column mappings shown in the Column Mappings screen.

Delete Rows In Destination Table   This option will not be available to you as the destination table is yet to be created. However, if you select an exiting table to import data into, you can then select to delete rows from the existing table.

Append Rows To The Destination Table   Alternatively, you can choose to append the rows to the existing table. However, in your case, this option will be grayed out.

Drop And Re-create Destination Table   This check box option allows loading data afresh in your table by first deleting the existing table and then re-creating and loading data into it.

Enable Identity Insert   You can use this option if you want to keep the identity in the input and want to insert into the table.

9. As in the Column Mappings window, you can change the column mappings in the Mappings section of the Column Mappings dialog box. Let's make a change to see how it works. In the Mappings section, click the drop-down box in the Destination field next to Suffix and select <Ignore>, as shown in Figure 2-4.

Now click the Edit SQL button, and note that the SQL statement for creating the destination table has picked up the change you just made. You can make changes to the SQL statement or use already existing scripts to create a table. However, once you have modified the SQL statement, any subsequent changes made from the Mappings section will not be automatically picked up by the SQL, but must be manually edited to the script. First click Cancel and then click OK to return to the Select Source Tables And Views window. Click Next to move on to the Save And Execute Package window.

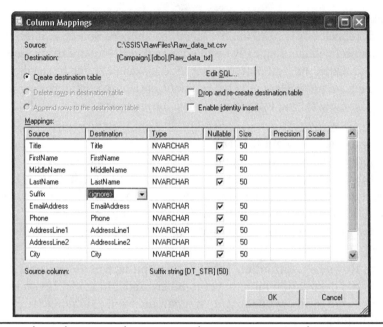

Figure 2-4   *Making changes in the mappings between Source and Destination*

10. By default, the Execute Immediately option will be selected. You will save this package in the file system. Check the Save SSIS Package option, and then select the File System radio button. Click the Next button, and the Package Protection Level dialog box will pop up. In Integration Services, you can protect your package by using various options. You will study these options in detail in Chapter 7; however, brief descriptions of these options are provided here for your quick review:

    Do Not Save Sensitive Data   Using this option, you choose not to save sensitive information such as connection strings, passwords, and so on, within the package.

    Encrypt Sensitive Data With User Key   You can save sensitive information within the package but encrypt the sensitive data using a key that is based on the user who is creating the package. With this option selected, only the user who creates the package will be able to run the package without providing the sensitive information, whereas other users who try to run the package will have to provide sensitive information manually.

    Encrypt Sensitive Data With Password   With this option, you choose to save the sensitive information in the package but encrypt it with a password. Once the package is encrypted with this option, any user will be able to execute the package by providing the password. If the user is unable to provide the password, he or she will have to provide the sensitive information manually to run the package.

Encrypt All Data With User Key Selecting this option means that you want all the information and metadata in the package to be encrypted using a key that is based on the user who is creating the package. Once the package has been encrypted using this option, only the user who created the package can run it.

Encrypt All Data With Password With this option, you can encrypt all the information and the metadata in the package by providing a password. Once the package has been encrypted with this option, it can be run only after correctly specifying the password.

11. Select the Encrypt Sensitive Data With Password option in the Package Protection Level dialog box. Type **bB987123cC** in the Password and Retype Password fields and click the OK button.

12. Type **Importing RawDataTxt** in the Name field and **Importing comma delimited RawDataTxt file** in the Description field. Type **C:\SSIS\Packages\ Importing RawDataTxt.dtsx** in the File Name field, as shown in Figure 2-5.

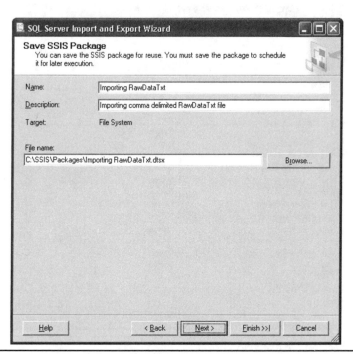

Figure 2-5 *Saving SSIS package to the file system*

13. Click the Next button to open the Complete The Wizard screen. Here you have the option of reviewing the choices you have made. Once you are happy with them, click the Finish button.

    The wizard now runs the package created, imports all the records, and shows a comprehensive report for all the intermediary steps it processed, as shown in Figure 2-6. This window not only shows any messages or errors appearing at run-time but also suggests some of the performance enhancements that can be applied to your SSIS packages.

    You can see the detailed report by clicking the Report button and selecting View Report. You can also save the report to a file, copy it to the Clipboard, and send it as an e-mail using the Report button.

14. Click the Report button and choose View Report. Scroll down to the Validating section to read that SQL Server Import and Export Wizard suggests removing the Suffix column from the source selections to improve the performance of execution, as this is not used in the Data Flow task. It is always worth taking a quick look at this report, which may offer valuable comments about the package

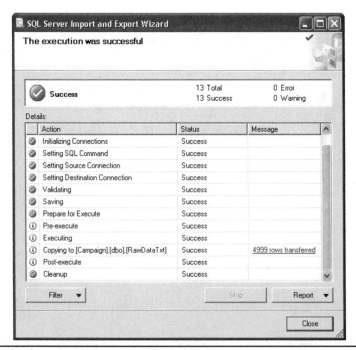

Figure 2-6 *Checking the execution results*

you have created. Close the View Report window and click the Close button to close the Import and Export Wizard.

15. Now, let's see what happened in this exercise. You have asked SSIS Import and Export Wizard to save the package and run it immediately. Start Windows Explorer and navigate to the C:\SSIS\Package folder. You will see a file called Importing RawDataTxt.dtsx saved in this folder. This is the Integration Services package saved in the XML format with an extension of *.dtsx*. Integration Services saves its packages in XML format by default. You can verify this by opening the package. Right-click this file, choose Open With, and then choose Notepad from the list of programs. You will see that the package settings listed in this file are in XML format. Close Notepad without making any changes.

16. Now let's check where the data has gone and what happened with the database you created while importing this file. Choose Start | All Programs | Microsoft SQL Server 2005, and click SQL Server Management Studio to start the program.

17. When the SQL Server Management Studio starts, you will be asked to provide authentication and connection details in the Connect To Server dialog box. In the Server Type field, select Database Engine. You can connect to various services such as Analysis Services, Reporting Services, SQL Server Mobile, and Integration Services by selecting an option from the drop-down menu. Specify the server name or simply type **localhost** to connect to the local server in the Server Name field. In the Authentication field, leave Windows Authentication selected and click the Connect button to connect to the SQL Server 2005 database engine.

18. When the SQL Server Management Studio loads, you will see Object Explorer on the left side and Summary on the right side of the window. In the Object Explorer window, expand the Databases node under the local server context. Note that in the list of databases, Campaign Database is also listed. Expand Campaign Database by clicking the plus sign next to it. Click the Tables node and you will see the RawDataTxt table in the Summary pane on the right.

19. Click the New Query button on the menu bar of Management Studio to open a query pane. Type the following in the query pane, highlight it, and press F5 to run it.

SELECT * FROM Campaign.dbo.RawDataTxt

You will see all the records imported into this table by the SSIS Import and Export Wizard displayed in the lower half of the pane.

Hands-On: Exporting an SQL Server Table to an Excel File

While we are working in SQL Server Management Studio, let's do another exercise to export the data from an SQL Server 2005 database table to an Excel file.

As mentioned earlier, you can start SSIS Import and Export Wizard from within Management Studio.

1. Right-click the Campaign database, point to Tasks, and then select Export Data from the tasks list. This will start the SQL Server Import and Export Wizard. The other option in the Tasks menu, Import Data, also starts the Import and Export Wizard. Click Next on the first window.

2. Because you've started this wizard from the Campaign database with an Export Data option, the wizard understands this and shows you the Campaign database already selected in the Database field in the Choose A Data Source window. However, it selects Windows Authentication by default and doesn't pick up your user name and password if you're connected to SQL Server using SQL Server Authentication. As you are connected using Windows Authentication, this doesn't affect you. Click the Next button to move on.

3. In the Choose A Destination window, click in the Destination field and scroll up to locate and select Microsoft Excel. In the Excel File Path field, type **C:\SSIS\ RawFiles\RawDataExcel.xls**. Leave Microsoft Excel 97-2005 selected in the Excel Version field and the First Row Has Column Names check box selected. Click the Next button to proceed.

4. Now you will see a new window, Specify Table Copy or Query, which didn't appear in the flat file import process from the preceding exercise. You can choose from the following two options:

    Copy Data From One Or More Tables Or Views   If you select this option, in the following window you will be able to select tables or views from which you want to export data. The limitation is that you won't be able to select a subset of data from the selected tables. With this option, all the data from the selected tables will be sent to an Excel file.

    Write A Query To Specify The Data To Transfer   When you select this option, the Provide A Source Query window appears, where you can type in an SQL statement or import the SQL statement from a file by clicking the Browse button. With this option, you can restrict the source data or manipulate the data, or you can get two subsets of data from two different tables using a complex query.

    Click to select Write A Query to Specify The Data To Transfer, and then click the Next button.

5. Type the following query in the SQL statement field in the Provide A Source Query window:

    SELECT * FROM [Campaign].[dbo].[RawDataTxt] WHERE CITY = 'London'

Click the Parse button to check the query. Click OK in the Confirmation dialog box and then click Next to proceed.

6. The Select Source Tables And Views window shows the [Query] as a Source selected and Query under the Destination column. This is in fact the name of the destination worksheet within the Excel file. Click in this field and rename it **London Contacts**. Click the Preview button to preview the data. Then click OK.

7. Click the Edit button to see the Column Mappings. Scroll down in the Mappings area and locate the StateProvinceID column. Click next to it under the Destination column and choose <Ignore> from the drop-down list, as shown in Figure 2-7.

    Note that all the columns are of LongText Data Type by default. Click OK and then click Next to move on to next window.

8. In the Save And Execute Package window, verify that the Execute Immediately option is already checked. Click to check the Save SSIS Package option and select File System for storage location. You will learn in detail about the storage location options in Chapter 6. Click the Next button and you will be asked to choose the package protection level in a pop-up dialog box.

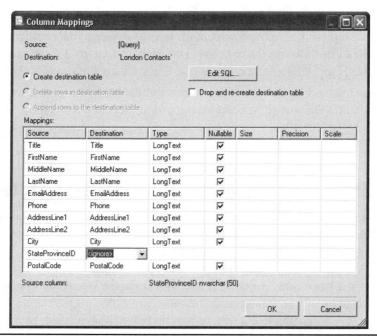

Figure 2-7   *Column mappings for London Contacts Excel worksheet*

9. Select Encrypt Sensitive Data With Password in the Package Protection Level field, as shown next. Type in **bB987123cC** in the Password and Retype Password fields and then click OK.

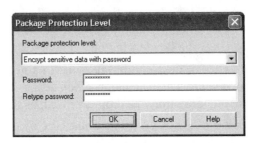

10. You will see the Save SSIS Package screen with Target selected as the File System. Specify the following in the various fields:

Name:	Exporting London Contacts
Description:	Exporting Contacts living in London from [RawDataTxt] table of [Campaign] database
File name:	C:\SSIS\Packages\Exporting London Contacts.dtsx

Click Next to complete the wizard.

11. In the Complete The Wizard screen, review the options you've selected and then click Finish to run the package. The package exports 120 records for Contacts from London to the Excel file. Click Close to close the wizard.

12. Navigate to the C:\SSIS\RawFiles folder and open the RawDataExcel.xls file to verify that the wizard has created a London_Contacts worksheet in this file, containing all the 120 exported records.

Using Business Intelligence Development Studio

One of the features of SSIS Import and Export Wizard is that the packages can be saved for later use and can be extended with BIDS. You have read about BIDS in Chapter 1 and have also created a blank Integration Services project.

In the following Hands-On exercise, you will open this blank project and then add the packages you just created using SSIS Import and Export Wizard. Don't worry if you don't understand exactly how Integration Services works; the purpose of the following exercise is to give you a preview, a feel, of how an Integration Services package looks. All the features shown are covered in detail in Chapter 3.

Hands-On: Exploring an SQL Server Import and Export Wizard Package Using BIDS

Let's open one of the packages you created in preceding exercises using BIDS. In this Hands-On exercise, you will open the various components of the Integration Services package and explore their properties and configurations. Though you will be learning about various attributes and properties of the components, the focus will be on learning how these components work together rather than understanding each component in detail.

Method

This Hands-On exercise is broken down into the following parts:

▶ You will add the package Importing RawDataTxt.dtsx that you've created earlier using the SSIS Import and Export Wizard in the Integration Services blank project created in Chapter 1.

▶ You will then explore the components in the Control Flow Designer surface and Data Flow Designer surface.

Exercise (Adding SSIS Import and Export Wizard Package in BIDS)

1. Choose Start | All Programs | Microsoft SQL Server 2005, and then click SQL Server Business Intelligent Development Studio to start the program.

2. Choose File | Open, and then click Project/Solution to open the blank project you created in Chapter 1. In the Open Project window, navigate to the C:\SSIS\ Projects\My First SSIS Project folder using the drop-down folder menu in the Look In field, select My First SSIS Project.sln, and click the Open button. You should see the blank solution you created in Chapter 1. You will now add to this blank project the package you saved while you were importing the RawDataTxt .csv text file in the preceding exercise in this chapter.

3. In Solution Explorer, right-click the SSIS Packages node and select Add Existing Package from the context menu. This will open the Add Copy Of Existing Package dialog box. Click the Package Location field to see the drop-down list and select File System, as you've saved your package in the File System. In the Package Path field, type **C:\SSIS\Packages\Importing RawDataTxt.dtsx**. Alternatively, you can use the ellipsis button (...) provided opposite the Package Path field to locate and select this package. Click OK to add this package to the SSIS Packages node of My First SSIS Project.

4. Though the package has been added to the SSIS Package node, it has not yet been loaded into the designer environment. Double-click the Importing RawDataTxt .dtsx package to load it into the designer environment. You will see the package loaded in BIDS, as shown in Figure 2-8.

5. Note that the Connection Managers tab, on the bottom half of the SSIS designer, shows two connection managers—DestinationConnectionOLEDB for choosing the Campaign database as a destination and SourceConnectionFlatFile for the source RawDataTxt.csv text file. Right-click SourceConnectionFlatFile and choose Edit from the context menu to edit this connection. You will see the Flat File Connection Manager Editor dialog box, which is similar to the window you filled in for flat file while running the SSIS Import and Export Wizard. Explore the various tabs and click the Cancel button when you're done.

6. Right-click DestinationConnectionOLEDB and click Edit. In the Connection Manager dialog box, note that the layout is different, but the settings are exactly the same as those you chose in the Choose A Destination window while running the SSIS Import and Export Wizard. Click Cancel.

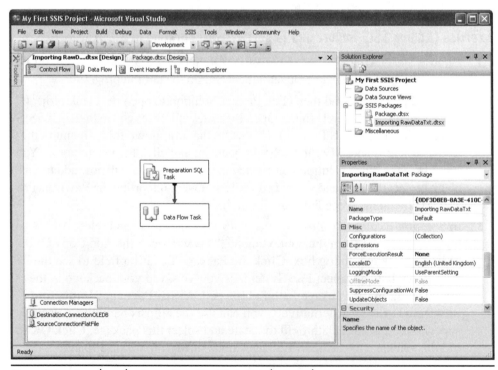

Figure 2-8   *Loading the Importing RawDataTxt.dtsx package in BIDS*

Exercise (Exploring Control Flow Components)

As you know, Integration Services has separate control flow and data flow engines to manage workflow and pipeline activities separately. The package Importing RawDataTxt.dtsx creates a table called RawDataTxt in the Campaign database while running in the control flow engine's scope. It uses Execute SQL task to perform this function. After it has created the table, it passes control over to the data flow engine to perform data-related activities.

7. In the Control Flow tab, double-click Preparation SQL Task to open the Execute SQL Task Editor dialog box, shown in Figure 2-9. You'll see various configuration options that have been set for this task.

    Note that under the SQL Statement section, the Connection field is pointing to the Campaign database using DestinationConnectionOLEDB Connection Manager. SQLSourceType is currently set to Direct Input, which gives you the option of typing an SQL statement. If you hover your mouse over SQLStatement field, you should be able to see your SQL query popup. Clicking in this field enables an ellipsis button, which you can click to open the Enter SQL Query window. In the

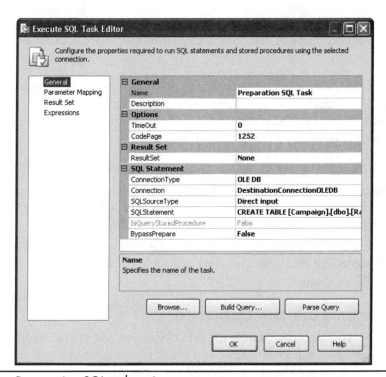

Figure 2-9 *Preparation SQL task settings*

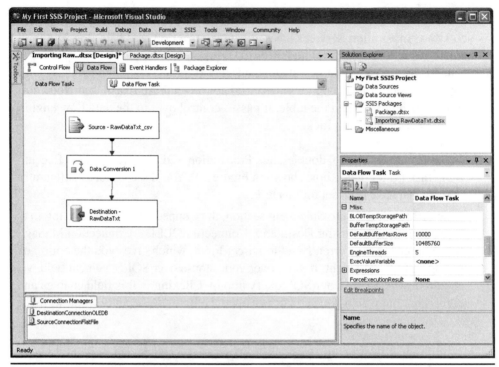

Figure 2-10 *Data Flow consists of a Source, a Transformation, and a Destination*

Enter SQL Query window, you can type in a long query or paste in an existing one. Click Cancel to close the Enter SQL Query window. You can also configure this task to read an SQL statement from a file using the Browse button, which is available only when you've selected Direct Input in the SQLSourceType field. You can also click the Build Query button to build simple queries and the Parse Query button to check the syntax of your queries. Click Cancel to undo any changes you have made and return to the SSIS Designer. The most important thing to understand at this time is that using this task, Integration Services package creates a table RawDataTxt in the Campaign database.

8. Double-click Data Flow Task to see the Data Flow tab of the BIDS. The components that constitute data flow in a package reside here. The Data Flow tab will look similar to Figure 2-10.

Exercise (Exploring Data Flow Components)

The data flow engine is responsible for data extraction, manipulation and transformation, and then loading data into the destination. In your package, these operations are performed by three different components:

- ▶ Source—RawDataTxt_csv, a Data Flow Source

- ▶ Data Conversion 1, a Data Flow Transformation

- ▶ Destination—RawDataTxt, a Data Flow Destination

The Data Flow Source, Source—RawDataTxt_csv, extracts data from the flat file RawDataTxt.csv. It then passes on the data to Data Conversion 1, Transformation, which converts the data type of incoming columns to those that match the data type of the destination columns. Finally, Destination—RawDataTxt loads the transformed data into an SQL Server table, which was created earlier by Execute SQL task in the Control Flow.

9. The first component, Source—RawDataTxt_csv in the Data Flow, is called a *Flat File Source*, which reads the data rows from the RawDataTxt.csv file row by row and forwards them to the downstream Data Conversion 1 component. If you hover your mouse on the Toolbox, which is shown as a tabbed window on the left side of the screen in Figure 2-10, it will slide out to show you all the components that can be used in the data flow. Note that Flat File Source appears in the Data Flow Sources section, Data Conversion appears in the Data Flow Transformations section, and OLE DB Destination appears in the Data Flow Destinations section. This simple package shows a typical example of a data flow that contains a Data Flow Source, a Data Flow Transformation, and a Data Flow Destination.

   The Data Conversion 1 transformation converts the data types of the data columns of data rows sent to it by the Data Flow Source. You will see later in this exercise why and how it is configured to perform this task. Finally, the Data Flow Destination, Destination—RawDataTxt, is an OLE DB destination that loads the converted records to the RawDataTxt table in the Campaign database.

10. The data flow components of an Integration Services package expose their properties in a custom user interface that is built for each component, or in the Advanced Editor that is common to all the components. Some of the components do not have a custom user interface, so they use only Advanced Editor to expose their properties and attributes. You can open the custom user interface by choosing the Edit command from the component's context menu and the Advanced Editor using the Show Advanced Editor command. Right-click the Source—RawDataTxt_csv object and choose Show Advanced Editor from the context menu.

11. You will see four tabs in this editor. The Connection Managers tab specifies SourceConnectionFlatFile connection manager that this component uses to connect to the RawDataTxt.csv flat file. If you double-click SourceConnectionFlatFile, you will see the list of two available connection managers that you have seen earlier in the Connection Managers tab on the SSIS Designer surface.

12. Move on to the Component Properties tab. Here you will see the Common Properties and Custom Properties sections that specify properties such as Name and Description.

13. Click the Column Mappings tab. In the upper half of this tab, you can see the columns mapped by the mapping lines and the lower half lists these mapped external columns with the output columns. External columns reference the data columns read from the source text file and the output columns are the columns this adapter passes on to the downstream data flow component. These output columns will become input columns for the next component in the data flow.

14. You can change these mappings if you want an External Column to be redirected to a different Output Column. Click the mapping line joining the AddressLine2 columns of Available External Columns and Available Output Columns and press the DELETE button on your keyboard. Similarly, delete the mapping line joining City columns. Now click and hold the mouse on the AddressLine2 column in the Available External Columns list and drag and drop it on the City column in the Available Output Columns list. You've created a mapping line to map AddressLine2 column to City column, which means the data in the AddressLine2 column will be sent to City column. This can also be done in the lower half of the window. Click the column that shows <Ignore>, just below City, in the Output Column. The column is converted into a drop-down list box. Click the down arrow to see the list of available columns and choose AddressLine2 from the list. As you do that, a mapping line corresponding to the affected columns will be added in the upper section. Your mappings should look as shown in Figure 2-11.

    Now right-click anywhere on the blank surface in the upper half and choose Select All Mappings to select all the mapping lines. Again right-click and choose Delete Selected Mapping. This will remove all the mappings, and the Output Column in the lower half of the window shows <Ignore> in all the columns. Again, right-click anywhere in the upper section and choose Map Items By Matching Names. This will map all the corresponding columns together.

15. Open the Input And Output Properties tab, and you can see Flat File Source Output and Flat File Source Error Output under Inputs and Outputs. Expand the Flat File Source Output node to see External Columns and Output Columns below that. As mentioned earlier, External Columns are the reference columns of the source text file and Output Columns are the columns that Flat File Source

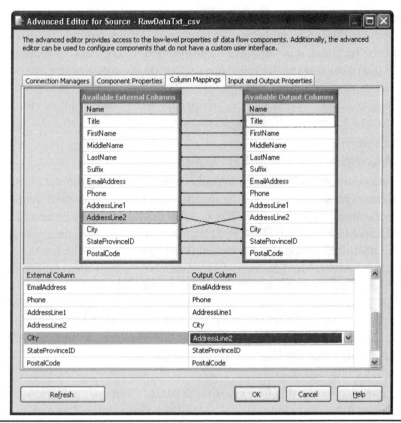

Figure 2-11 *Working with column mappings*

Adapter passes on to the downstream component in the data flow path. If you
expand External Columns and click any column, you will see column properties
such as CodePage, DataType, and Length in the right pane. If you expand
Output Columns and click any of the columns, you will see the Output Column
properties such as CodePage, DataType, Length, FastParse, SortKeyPosition,
and so on. Note that the Data Type of External Columns and Output Columns is
[DT_STR] by default. The FastParse option can be set to either True or False.
To load data between heterogeneous data sources, the source adapters parse the
data of each column to convert it to SSIS data type, and when the data is to be
loaded into a data store, the destination adapter parses the data and converts it
to the type destination requires. The two parsing techniques Fast parse (when
FastParse option is True) and Standard parse (when FastParse option is False)
are available in the Flat File source and Flat File destination adapters and the
Data Conversion and Derived Column transformations. This is because only

these data flow components convert data from a string to a binary data type, or vice versa. The FastParse option allows use of simpler (commonly used date and time formats), quicker, but locale-insensitive, fast parsing routines that SSIS provides. You can set FastParse to True on the columns that are not locale-sensitive to speed up the SSIS process. By default, FastParse is set to False, indicating Standard parse is used, which supports all the data type conversions. For more information on parsing techniques, refer to Microsoft SQL Server 2005 Books Online.

Click Cancel to return to the SSIS Designer.

16. A Data Conversion Transformation helps in converting the data type of one or more columns. While looking through the Input and Output Properties of Source—RawDataTxt_csv, you'll notice that the Data Type of External Columns and Output Columns is [DT_STR]. This is not in line with the data type you've set in the SSIS Import and Export Wizard (see Figure 2-4) in which you've set data type as NVARCHAR. The NVARCHAR data type is equivalent to [DT_WSTR] in SSIS. So, Data Conversion 1 Transformation was deployed to convert [DT_STR] to [DT_WSTR]. Double-click the Data Conversion 1 Transformation. This will open up the Data Conversion Transformation Editor, shown in Figure 2-12. Look in the lower half of the editor, where Input Columns are assigned an Output Alias and converted into the Unicode string [DT_WSTR] Data Type. Click Cancel to close the editor dialog box.

17. You can also verify this by exploring the Data Conversion 1 Transformation using the Advanced Editor. Right-click Data Conversion 1 and choose Show Advanced Editor from the context menu.

18. In the Advanced Editor for Data Conversion 1, click the Input And Output Properties tab.

19. Expand Input Columns under Data Conversion Input, and then check the Data Type of input columns by clicking the columns one by one and seeing the data type of each column. You will see that all of them are of [DT_STR] data type, as expected.

20. Now, expand Output Columns under Data Conversion Output and check the data type of all the Output Columns while moving from column to column. You will notice that the Output Columns are of Unicode string [DT_WSTR] type. This is because the transformation converts the data type from [DT_STR] to [DT_WSTR] for all of the selected columns before sending them to the output. Click Cancel.

21. An OLE DB Destination loads input records into an OLE DB–compliant data store. Now, let's explore the custom user interface of the Destination—RawDataTxt component and see how the Input Columns are mapped to the

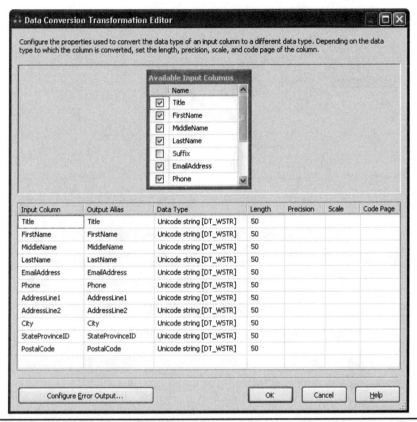

Figure 2-12 *Converting data types using the Data Conversion Transformation Editor*

Destination Columns. Double-click the Destination—RawDataTxt component to open the OLE DB Destination Editor, the custom user interface of OLE DB Destination. You will see the Connection Manager window shown in Figure 2-13.

22. Like most other destinations that need a connection manager to connect to a data store, OLE DB Destination uses an OLE DB connection manager to connect to the destination table. In this package, DestinationConnectionOLEDB is used and is specified in the OLE DB Connection Manager field.

23. Click in the Data Access Mode field, and you'll see the available five options for data access in the drop-down list:

Table or view   When you select this option, the data is loaded into a table or view in the database specified by the OLE DB connection manager, and you specify the name of the table or the view in the Name Of The Table Or The View field.

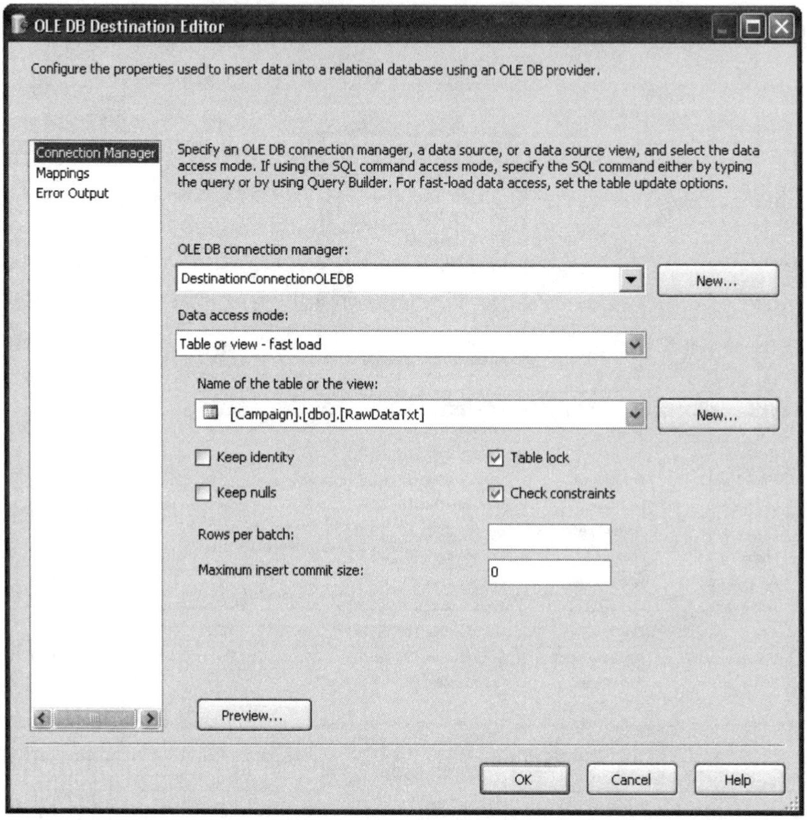

Figure 2-13 *Connection Manager window of the OLE DB Destination Editor*

Table or view—fast load   Using this data access mode, you can load data into a table or view as in the previous option, but using the fast load options such as acquiring table lock and specifying maximum insert commit size.

Table name or view name variable   Using this option, you still load data into a table or a view but instead of specifying the table or view name directly, you specify its name in a variable.

Table name or view name variable—fast load   This data access mode works like Table Or View—Fast Load access mode, except in this access mode you supply the name of the table or the view in a variable.

SQL Command   You can load the result set of an SQL statement using this option.

24. Go to the Mappings page and note that the Available Input Columns are mapped to Available Destination Columns. As the Data Conversion 1 has added the transformed columns in the data flow, you will see the Transformed column—that is, columns with Data Conversion 1 prefix are selected to map to the destination columns. You may have to scroll up and down to see the mappings properly. Click Cancel to close the editor.

Review

This Hands-On exercise presented a simple package that contains various types of components for you to see how Integration Services packages are organized. You've seen how Control Flow manages workflow in a package and makes the required objects available when they are required by Data Flow components. We haven't tried to execute this package because the package is not designed from a multiuse perspective. The Execute SQL task creates a table in a Campaign database for the first time the package is run, but what do you expect will happen if you again try to run the same package? The package will not succeed as the table that Execute SQL task tries to create in the subsequent runs already exists, and the Execute SQL task attempt will fail and hence the package will not run. If you want to run the package more than once, you could either drop the table already created before trying to create it again or use TRUNCATE TABLE command with the existing table instead of creating a new table.

You've saved another package while working with SSIS Import and Export Wizard. I would encourage you to add it to this project and explore its various components to get a feel for them. Don't worry if they don't make much sense to you now, as each of the preconfigured components that SSIS provides will be covered in detail in the chapters to come. But before you go, let's quickly perform another Hands-On exercise to build an Integration Services package directly in BIDS.

Hands-On: Importing Data from a Microsoft Access Table

This is a quick exercise in which you will build a package in BIDS. You will start SSIS Import and Export Wizard from within BIDS and build the Integration Services package straight into the designer. In the end, you will execute the package.

1. In BIDS, choose Project | SSIS Import and Export Wizard. On the Welcome window, click the Next button.

2. In the Choose A Data Source window, click in the Data Source field to expose the list of available data sources. Scroll up in this list to locate and select Microsoft Access. You will see that the field layout has changed to display the

options suitable for accessing the Microsoft Access database file. Type **C:\SSIS\ RawFiles\RawDataAccess.mdb** in the File Name field and click the Next button to proceed.

3. In the Choose A Destination window, make sure SQL Native Client is selected in the Destination field and (Local) is specified in the Server Name field. Leave the Use Windows authentication option selected in the Authentication section and select Campaign Database in the Database field from the drop-down list. Click Next to move to the next window.

4. In the Specify Table Copy Or Query window, leave the radio button selected for Copy Data From One Or More Tables Or Views. Click Next to proceed.

5. In the Select Source Tables And Views window, select the check box provided for AccessContacts In Source Column. Note that the Destination column will automatically be filled in with [Campaign].[dbo].[AccessContacts]. Click Next to move on.

6. You will notice that this wizard did not ask you to save the package, as it did when run from other locations such as command prompt or from SQL Server Management Studio. Click Finish on the Complete The Wizard window.

7. In the next window, you will see a message: "The execution was successful." Note that fewer steps were needed this time compared to when it was run from other locations. In fact, only 7 steps were executed versus 13 steps previously (see Figure 2-6). It actually did not run the package—it only validated, created, and compiled it for BIDS. Click the Close button to close the wizard and you will see that a new package was added to the project with the name Package1.dtsx.

8. Explore various components to understand how the SSIS Import and Export Wizard designed the package.

9. Press F5 to run this package. You will see that the components turn yellow and then green to show the successful execution of the package. You will see 29 rows being added to the SQL Server table in the Data Flow tab.

10. When you run the package in BIDS, you will enter debugging mode. To return to design mode after the package has completed execution, press SHIFT-F5 and the changes you made will take effect.

11. Press SHIFT-CTRL-S to save all the files and close the project from the File menu.

Review

The SSIS Import and Export Wizard can be used to build packages quickly, as you have seen in this exercise. However, you may need to customize those packages a bit to suit to your requirements. If you execute the package again, it will fail for the same reason explained in the review section of the last Hands-On exercise.

Summary

You created an Integration Services blank project in Chapter 1. In this chapter, you created packages using the SSIS Import and Export Wizard and then added those packages into your blank project. You also created a package directly in the BIDS again using the SSIS Import and Export Wizard. But, above all, you explored those packages by opening component properties and configurations and hopefully better understand the constitution of an Integration Services package. In the next chapter, you will learn about the basic components, the nuts and bolts of Integration Services packages, before jumping in to make complex packages in Chapter 4 using preconfigured components provided in BIDS.

Summary

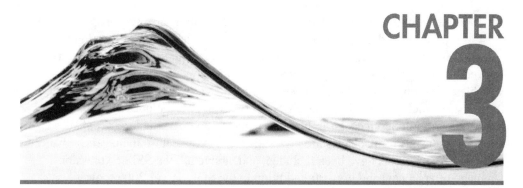

Nuts and Bolts of
the SSIS Workflow

59

S o far, you have moved data using the SSIS Import and Export Wizard and you've viewed packages by opening them in the Business Intelligence Development Studio (BIDS). In this chapter, you will learn the difference between an Integration Services project and a solution, file formats, and use of variables. If you have used Data Transformation Services (DTS 2000), you may grasp these issues quickly; don't skip this chapter, however, as it includes concepts totally new to Integration Services. Usability and management of variables are enhanced, connectivity needs for packages are now satisfied by connection managers, enhanced precedence constraints have been included, and, above all, the SSIS Expression language offers a new and powerful addition to the SQL Server 2005 toolset.

Integration Services Objects

Integration Services relies on various objects and components such as connection managers, sources, tasks and transformations, containers, event handlers, and destinations to perform its operations. All these components are threaded together to achieve the desired functionality—that is, they work hand in hand, yet they can be configured separately.

The biggest enhancement Microsoft has provided to DTS 2000 to make it SQL Server 2005 Integration Services is the separation of workflow from the data flow. SSIS provides two different designer surfaces, which are effectively different integrated development environments (IDEs) for developing packages. You can design and configure workflow in the Control Flow Designer surface and the data movement and transformations in the Data Flow Designer surface. Different components are provided based on the designer environment in which you are working—for example, the Toolbox window is unique with each environment.

The following objects are used to build an Integration Services package:

▶ **Integration Services package** The top-level object in the SSIS component hierarchy. All the work performed by SSIS tasks occurs within the context of a package.

▶ **Control flow** Helps to build the workflow in an ordered sequence using containers, tasks, and precedence constraints. Containers provide structure to the package and looping facility, tasks provide functionality, and precedence constraints build an ordered workflow by connecting containers, tasks, and other executables in an orderly fashion.

▶ **Data flow** Helps to build the data movement and transformations in a package using data adapters and transformations in ordered sequential paths.

- ▶ **Connection managers**   Handle all the connectivity needs.

- ▶ **Integration Services variables**   Help you use dynamic values at run-time.

- ▶ **Integration Services event handlers**   Help extend package functionality using events raised at run-time.

- ▶ **Integration Services log providers**   Help in capturing information when log-enabled events occur at run-time.

Throughout this book, while you are working with the SSIS components, you will be introduced to the easier and often-used objects first and will then learn about more complex configurations.

Solutions and Projects

SQL Server 2005 offers different environments for developing and managing Integration Services packages. These packages are designed and created in BIDS, while developed and deployed packages are managed for storage and execution in SQL Server Management Studio. Both environments have special features and toolsets to help you perform the jobs efficiently.

You cannot use SQL Server Management Studio to edit or design Integration Services solutions or projects. However, in both environments, you use *solutions* and *projects* to organize and manage your files and code in a logical, hierarchical manner. A *solution* is a container that allows you to bring together scattered projects so that you can organize and manage them as one unit. In general, you will use a solution to focus on one area of the business—such as one solution for accounts and a separate solution for marketing. However, complex business problems may require multiple solutions to achieve specific objectives. Figure 3-1 shows a solution that not only affects multiple projects but also includes projects of multiple types. This figure shows an analysis services project, two integration services projects, and a reporting services project all in one solution.

Within a solution, one or more projects, along with related files for databases, connections, scripts, and miscellaneous files, can be saved together. Not only can multiple projects be stored under one solution, but multiple *types* of projects can be stored under one solution. For example, while working in BIDS, you can store a data transformation project as well as a data-mining project under the same solution. Both SQL Server Management Studio and BIDS provide templates for working with different types of projects. These templates provide appropriate environments—such as designer surfaces, scripts, connections, and so on—for each project with which you are working. When you create a new project, Visual Studio tools automatically

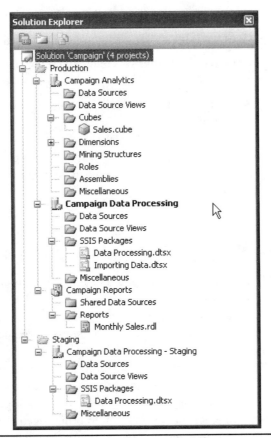

Figure 3-1   *Solution Explorer showing a solution with different types of projects*

generate a solution for you. You can then add various projects—data sources, data source views, SSIS packages, scripts, miscellaneous files—to this solution as and when required.

Grouping multiple projects in this way results in reduced development time, code reusability, interdependencies management, settings management for all the projects at a single location, and the facility to save all the projects to Visual SourceSafe. Solution Explorer lists the projects and the files contained in them in a tree view that helps you to manage the projects and the files (as shown in Figure 3-1). The logical hierarchy reflected in the tree view of a solution does not necessarily relate to the physical storage of files and folders on the hard disk drive, however. Solution Explorer provides the facility to integrate with Visual SourceSafe for version control, which is a great feature when you want to track changes or roll back code. However, although SQL Server

2005 Studio tools are based on Visual Studio, Solution Explorer doesn't actually compile the programs written in .NET languages; instead, it supports Transact-SQL (T-SQL), XML query language scripts, and XML for Analysis Services (XMLA)–related code such as XMLA methods, Multidimensional Expressions (MDX) cube calculations, and Data Mining Expressions (DMX) operations.

File Formats

Whenever an ETL tool has to integrate with legacy systems, mainframes, or any other proprietary database systems, the easiest way to transfer data between the systems is to use flat files. Integration Services can deal with flat files that are fixed width, delimited, and ragged right format types. For the benefit of users who are new to the ETL world, these formats are explained next.

Fixed Width

If you have been working with mainframes or legacy systems, you may be familiar with this format. Fixed width files use different widths for columns, but the chosen width per column stays fixed for all the rows, regardless of the contents of those columns. If you open such a file, you will likely see lots of blank spaces between the two columns. As most of the data in a column with variable data tends to be smaller than the width provided, you'll see a lot of wasted space. As a result, these types of files are more likely to be larger in size than the other formats.

Delimited

The most common format used by most of the systems to exchange data with foreign systems, delimited files separate the columns using a delimiter such as a comma or tab and typically use a character combination (for example, a combination of carriage return plus linefeed characters—{CR}{LF}) to delimit rows/records. Generally, importing data using this format is quite easy, unless the delimiter used also appears in the data. For example, if a comma is used as a column delimiter, and users are allowed to enter data in a field, some users may use commas while entering notes in the specified field. This free format data entry conflicts with the delimiter and imports data in the wrong columns. Because of potential conflicts, you need to pay particular attention to the quality of data you are dealing with while choosing a delimiter. Delimited files are usually smaller in size compared to fixed width files, as the free space is removed by the use of a delimiter.

Ragged Right

If you have a fixed width file and one of the columns (the rightmost one) is a non-uniform column, and you want to save some space, you can add a delimiter (such as {CR}{LF}) at the end of the row and make it a ragged right file. Ragged right files are similar to fixed width files except they use a delimiter to mark the *end* of a row/record—that is, in ragged right files, the last column is of variable size. This makes the file easier to work with when displayed in Notepad or imported into an application.

Connection Managers

As data grow in random places, it's the job of the information analyst to bring it all together to draw out pertinent information. The biggest problem of bringing together such data sets and merging them to a single storage location is how to handle different data sources, such as legacy mainframe systems, Oracle databases, flat files, Excel spreadsheets, Microsoft Access files, and so on. Connection managers provided in Integration Services come to the rescue. Connection managers are new features in SQL Server 2005 Integration Services.

In Chapter 2, you saw how connection managers deal with importing data. The components defined inside an Integration Services package require that physical connections be made to data stores during run-time. The source adapter reads data from the data source and then passes it on to the data flow for transformations, while the destination adapter loads the transformed data to the destination store. Not only do the extraction and loading components require connections, but these connections are also required by some of the transformations. For example, during the lookup, transformation values are read from a reference table to perform transformations based on the values in the lookup table.

A connection manager is a logical representation of a connection. You use a connection manager to describe the connection properties at design time, and these are interpreted to make a physical connection at run-time by Integration Services. For example, at design time, you can set a connection string property within a connection manager, which is then read by the Integration Services run-time engine, which makes a physical connection. A connection manager is stored in the package metadata and cannot be shared with other packages.

Connection managers enhance connection flexibility. Multiple connection managers of the same type can be created to meet the needs of Integration Services packages and enhance performance. For example, a package can use five OLE DB connection managers, all built on the same data connection.

You can add connection managers to your package using one of the following methods in BIDS:

► Choose New Connection from the SSIS menu.

► Choose the New Connection command from the context menu that opens when you right-click the blank surface in the Connection Managers area in the Control Flow Panel, Data Flow Panel, or Event Handlers Panel.

► Add a connection manager from within editor or advanced editor dialog boxes of some of the tasks, transformations, source adapters, and destination adapters that require connection to a data store.

The connection managers you add to the project at design time appear in the Connection Managers area in the BIDS designer surfaces, but they do not appear in the Connection Managers collection in Package Explorer until you run the package successfully for the first time. At run-time, Integration Services resolves the settings of all the added connections, sets the connection manager properties to each of them, and then adds them to the Connection Managers collection in Package Explorer.

You will be using many of the connection managers in Hands-On exercises while you create solutions for business problems later on. For now, open BIDS, create a new blank project, and check out the properties of all the connection managers as you read through the following descriptions.

ADO Connection Manager

This connection manager is provided for legacy applications written using an earlier version of a programming language, such as Microsoft Visual Basic 6.0, or where applications already use ADO to connect to a data source. The ADO Connection Manager is used to connect to ActiveX data objects such as a record set.

ADO.NET Connection Manager

This connection manager provides access to Microsoft SQL Server as well as data sources exposed through OLE DB and XML by using a .NET provider. You can choose from providers such as SqlClient data provider, OracleClient data provider, or ODBC data provider. The configuration options of the ADO.NET Connection Manager change depending on your choice of .NET provider.

Microsoft .NET Data Provider for mySAP Business Suite

This connection manager provides access to SAP server and enables you to execute Remote Function Call (RFC)/business API (BAPI) commands and select queries against SAP tables. This connection manager is not provided in the default installation but rather is provided as a feature pack component for SSIS. You must download it from http://msdn.microsoft.com/downloads/. This connector is built on the SAP .NET Connector 2.0 technology, which allows communication between the Microsoft .NET platform and SAP systems using Remote Function Calls (RFC) and Simple Object Access Protocol (SOAP). To use ADO.NET Data Provider for mySAP, the following prerequisites are required:

▶   Install the SAP .NET Connector 2.0 on your computer.

▶   Install two custom RFCs on your SAP server.

Once installed, the Microsoft .NET Data provider for mySAP Business Suite becomes available in the SQL Server Import and Export Wizard, the Execute SQL task, the Script task, the DataReader source, and the Script transformation.

When you go to the Microsoft site to download this feature pack component, you will download the dataproviderSAP.exe file. And when you run it, this file will unzip three files into your specified folder: the DataProviderSAP.msi file is the installable software for this data provider, the readme.htm file contains installation instructions, and the third file (SQL2005 NET Data Provider for mySAP Business Suite.doc) explains the architecture, features, and usage of this component. Sufficient information is available in these documents for you to get started; however, if you need more information on SAP .NET Connector, visit the Microsoft SAP Customer site at http://www.microsoft-sap.com/technology.aspx, expand Technologies in the left sidebar TECHNICAL SECTIONS, and then choose SAP Connector for .NET link. For further information on the syntax of queries you can run against SAP tables, refer to SQL Server Books Online.

Excel Connection Manager

This connection manager provides access to the Microsoft Excel workbook file. It is used when you add Excel source or destination objects in your package.

File Connection Manager

This connection manager enables you to reference a file or folder that already exists or is created at run-time. While executing a package, Integration Services tasks and data flow components need input for values of property attributes to perform their functions. These input values can be directly input by you within the component's properties or they can be read from external sources such as files or variables. When you configure to get this input information from a file, you use File Connection Manager. For example, the Execute SQL task executes an SQL statement, which can be directly input by you in the Execute SQL task, or this SQL statement can be read from a file.

You can use an existing file or folder, or you can create a file or a folder by using the File Connection Manager. However, you can reference only one file or folder. If you want to reference multiple files or folders, you must use a Multiple Files Connection Manager, described a bit later.

To configure this connection manager, choose from the four available options in the Usage Type field of the File Connection Manager Editor. Your choice in this field sets the FileUsageType property of the connection manager to indicate how you want to use the File Connection Manager—that is, you want to create or use an existing file or a folder. The configuration options are as follows:

Existing file   FileUsageType = 0

Create file   FileUsageType = 1

Existing folder   FileUsageType = 2

Create folder   FileUsageType = 3

Flat File Connection Manager

This connection manager provides access to data in a flat file. It is used to extract or load data from a flat file source or destination and can use delimited, fixed width, or ragged right format. This connection manager accesses only one file. If you want to reference multiple flat files, you must use a Multiple Flat Files Connection Manager.

FTP Connection Manager

Use this connection manager whenever you want to upload or download files using File Transfer Protocol (FTP). It enables you to connect to an FTP server. FTP Connection Manager can send and receive files using active or passive mode. The transfer mode is defined as active mode when the server initiates the FTP connection and passive mode when the client initiates the FTP connection.

HTTP Connection Manager

Whenever you want to upload or download files using HTTP (port 80), use this connection manager. It enables you to connect to a web server using HTTP. The Web Service task provided in Integration Services uses this connection manager.

MSMQ Connection Manager

If you want to use the Message Queue task in Integration Services, you need to add an MSMQ Connection Manager. An MSMQ Connection Manager enables a package to connect to a message queue. SSIS uses an MSMQ Connection Manager.

Analysis Services Connection Manager

This connection manager provides access to Analysis Services cube and dimension data by allowing you to connect to an Analysis Services database or an Analysis Services project in the same solution. You can connect to an Analysis Services project only at design time. The SSIS package will connect to the target server and the target database deployed by this Analysis Services project at run-time. You can use Analysis Services Connection Manager while deploying Analysis Services Processing task, Analysis Services Execute DDL task, or Data Mining Model Training destination objects in your package.

Multiple Files Connection Manager

As you can reference only one file or folder using the File Connection Manager, you will use the Multiple Files Connection Manager when you need to reference more than one file and folder that exist or that are created at run-time. When you add this connection manager, you can add multiple files or folders to be referenced. Those multiple files and folders show up as a piped delimited list in the ConnectionString property of this connection manager. To specify multiple files or folders, you can also use wildcards. Suppose, for example, that you want to use all the text files in the C:\SSIS folder. You could add the Multiple Files Connection Manager by choosing only one file in the C:\SSIS folder, going to the Properties window of the connection manager, and setting the value of the ConnectionString property to C:\SSIS*.txt.

Similar to the File Connection Manager, the Multiple Files Connection Manager has a FileUsageType property to indicate the usage type, defined as follows:

Existing file   FileUsageType = 0
Create file   FileUsageType = 1
Existing folder   FileUsageType = 2
Create folder   FileUsageType = 3

Multiple Flat Files Connection Manager

As you can reference only one flat file using Flat File Connection Manager, you use the Multiple Flat Files Connection Manager when you need to reference more than one flat file. You can access data in flat files having delimited, fixed width, or ragged right format. In the GUI of this connection manager, you can select multiple files by using the Browse button and highlighting multiple files. These files are then listed as a piped delimited list in the connection manager. You can also use wildcards to specify multiple files. Suppose, for example, that you want to use all the flat files in the C:\SSIS folder. To do this, you would add C:\SSIS*.txt in the File Names field to choose multiple files. However, note that all these files must have the same format.

ODBC Connection Manager

This connection manager enables an Integration Services package to connect to a wide range of relational database management systems (RDBMS) using Open Database Connectivity (ODBC) protocol.

OLE DB Connection Manager

This connection manager enables an Integration Services package to connect to a data source using an OLE DB provider. OLE DB is an updated ODBC standard and is designed to be faster, more efficient, and more stable than ODBC; it is an open specification for accessing all kinds of data. Many of the Integration Services tasks and data flow components use OLE DB Connection Manager. For example, the OLE DB source adapter and OLE DB destination adapter use OLE DB Connection Manager to extract and load data, and the Execute SQL task uses OLE DB Connection Manager to connect to a SQL Server database to run queries.

SMO Connection Manager

SQL Management Objects (SMO) is a collection of objects that can be programmed to manage SQL Server. SMO is an upgrade to SQL-DMO, a set of APIs you use to create and manage SQL Server database objects. SMO performs better, is more scalable, and is easy to use compared to SQL-DMO. SMO Connection Manager enables an Integration Services package to connect to an SMO server. For example, Integration Services transfer tasks use an SMO connection to transfer objects from one server to another.

SMTP Connection Manager

When you want to send mail from a package, you can use SMTP Connection Manager. SMTP Connection Manager enables an Integration Services package to connect to a Simple Mail Transfer Protocol (SMTP) server.

SQL Server Mobile Connection Manager

When you need to connect to a SQL Server mobile database, you will use SQL Server Mobile Connection Manager. SQL Server Mobile Destination adapter uses this connection to load data into a table in a SQL Server mobile database.

WMI Connection Manager

Windows Management Instrumentation (WMI) enables you to access management information in enterprise systems such as networks, computers, managed devices, and other managed components using the Web-Based Enterprise Management (WBEM) standard. Using a WMI Connection Manager, your Integration Services package can manage and automate administrative tasks in an enterprise environment.

Data Sources

You can create design-time data source objects in Integration Services, Analysis Services, and Reporting Services projects in BIDS. A *data source* is a connection to a data store—for example, a database. Once created, this data source can be used by multiple packages. Generally you will create these data source objects outside the package and use them in the package later on.

When you add a data source to a package at design time, it is resolved as an OLE DB connection at run-time. You may ask, "Why use data source, then?" This approach has several benefits. You can provide consistent approaches in your packages to make managing connections easier. You can update all the connection managers used in various packages that reference data sources by simply making changes at one place only—in the data source itself. You create data sources by using the Data Source Wizard and modify them in the Data Source Designer dialog box. Data Sources are not used when building packages programmatically.

Data Source View

A data source view, built on a data source, is a named, saved subset that defines the underlying schema of a relational data source. A data source view can include metadata that can define sources, destinations, and lookup tables for SSIS tasks, transformations, and data adapters. While a data source is a connection to a data store, you use data source views to reference more specific objects such as tables or views or their subsets. Data flow components and lookup transformations can use data source views. As you can apply filters on a data source view, you can in fact create multiple data source view objects from a data source. For example, a data source can reference a database, while different data source views can be created to reference its different tables or views. To use a data source view in a package, you must first add the data source to the package.

Using data source views can be beneficial. While you can use a data source view in multiple packages, refreshing a data source view reflects the changes in its underlying data sources. Data source views can also cache metadata of the data sources on which they are built and can extend a data source view by adding calculated columns, new relationships, and so on.

Once you add a data source view to a package, it is resolved to a SQL statement and stored in a property of the component using it. You create a data source view by using the Data Source View Wizard and then modify it in the Data Source View Designer. Data source views are not used when building packages programmatically.

SSIS Variables

Variables are used to store values. They enable SSIS objects to communicate among each other in the package as well as between parent and child packages at run-time. You can use variables in a variety of ways—for example, you can load results of an Execute SQL task to a variable, change the way a package works by dynamically updating its value at run-time using variables, control looping within a package by using a loaded variable, raise an error when a variable is altered, use them in scripts, or evaluate them as an expression.

DTS 2000 provides global variables, for which users set the values in a single area in the package and then use those values over and over. This allows users to extend the dynamic abilities of packages. As the global variables are defined at the package level, sometimes managing all the variables at a single place became quite challenging for complex packages. SSIS has developed the concept further by assigning a *scope* to variables. Scopes are discussed in greater detail a bit later in the chapter in the "User-Defined Variables" section.

Integration Services provides two types of variables—system variables and user-defined variables—that you can configure and use in your packages. System variables are made available in the package and provide environmental information or the state of the system at run-time. You don't have to create the system variable and can use these variables in your packages straightaway. However, you must *create* a user-defined variable before you can use it in your package. To see the variables available in a package in BIDS, go to the Package Explorer tab on the Designer interface and expand the Variables folder. This folder lists both user-defined variables and system variables.

System Variables

The preconfigured variables provided in Integration Services are called *system variables*. While you create user-defined variables to meet the needs of your packages, you cannot create additional system variables. They are read-only; however, you can configure them to raise an event when they change their value. System variables store informative values about the packages and their objects, which can be used in expressions to customize packages, containers, tasks, and event handlers. Different containers have different system variables available to them. For example, the Integration Services package container has about 18 different variables available. Some of the more frequently used system variables for different containers are defined in the following table.

Partial list of System Variables available in various containers		
System Variable	**Assigned to**	**Description**
CancelEvent	Package	When set to non-zero value, the task stops running
CreationDate	Package	Date when the package was created
CreatorName	Package	Name of the person who built this package
MachineName	Package	Name of the computer on which the package runs
PackageID	Package	Unique identifier of the package
PackageName	Package	Name of the package
StartTime	Package	Time that the package started to run
UserName	Package	Account of the user who started the package
VersionBuild	Package	Package version
VersionComment	Package	Comments about the package version
TaskID	Tasks	Unique identifier of a task instance
TaskName	Tasks	Name of the task instance
TaskTransactionOption	Tasks	Transaction option the task uses
ErrorCode	Event handlers	Error identifier
ErrorDescription	Event handlers	Description of the error
PercentComplete	Event handlers	Percentage of completed work
SourceDescription	Event handlers	Description of the executable in the event handler that raised the event
SourceID	Event handlers	Unique identifier of the executable in the event handler that raised the event
SourceName	Event handlers	Name of the executable in the event handler that raised the event
VariableDescription	Event handlers	Variable description
VariableID	Event handlers	Unique identifier of the variable

Using these system variables, you can actually extract interesting information from the packages on the fly. For example, at run-time using system variables, you can log who started which package at what time. This is exactly what you are going to do in the following Hands-On exercise.

Hands-On: Using System Variables to Create Custom Logs

This exercise demonstrates how you can create a custom log for an Integration Services package.

Method

You will create a simple package consisting of one task to demonstrate how you can use system variables to create custom logs, which are sometimes desirable if standard logging doesn't meet your purposes.

You will create a table in the Campaign database to host logging information and will then use the Execute SQL task to read values of system variables for logging to the earlier created table. You will also add a connection manager to connect to the Campaign database.

Exercise (Adding a Connection Manager)

1. Start SQL Server Management Studio from Microsoft SQL Server 2005 program group. Click Connect to connect to the database engine. In the Object Explorer, expand the Databases folder and click Campaign Database. You have created the Campaign database in the last chapter, but if you haven't, you can attach the Campaign database provided with the software for this book. Click the New Query button located on the Standard toolbar to open a new query pane. Type the following query in this pane to create a table CustomLog in the Campaign database.

   USE Campaign

   CREATE TABLE CustomLog (

   username varchar(50),

   machinename varchar(50),

   packagename varchar(50),

   packageID varchar(50),

   taskname varchar(50),

   starttime datetime)

Click Execute on the Toolbar to run the query and create a CustomLog table in the Campaign database. Leave SQL Server Management Studio running as you will return later to see the results.

2. Start BI Development Studio. Choose File | New | Project, or press CTRL-SHIFT-N to open the New Project window.

3. Choose Integration Services Project from the Templates pane. In the Name field, enter **Components of SSIS Workflow**. Choose the location C:\SSIS\ Projects, as shown in Figure 3-2. Verify that the Create Directory For Solution check box is not selected. Click OK to start building your new project.

4. In Solution Explorer, right-click package.dtsx under the SSIS packages folder; then choose Rename. Type **CustomLog.dtsx** and press ENTER. You'll see a message asking whether you want to rename the package object as well. Click Yes. Choose File | Save All to save the solution.

5. While you are in the BI workbench, locate the Toolbox window, which should be on the left side of the screen and may appear as a tabbed item if you have selected to auto-hide it. Hover your mouse over the Toolbox tab, and it opens. From the Toolbox window, drag and drop the Execute SQL task on to the

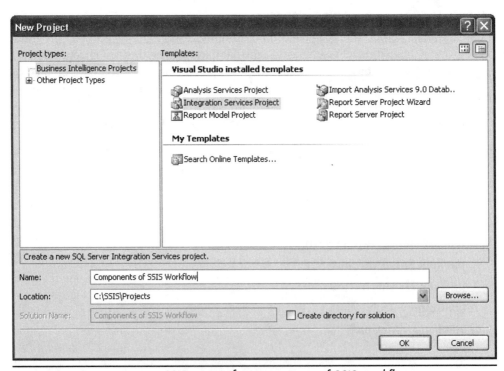

Figure 3-2 *Creating a new SSIS project for components of SSIS workflow*

Control Flow Panel. The Execute SQL task will have a crossed red circle on it. When you hover your mouse on this crossed red circle, it will show the error message, "No connection manager is specified."

6. Now create a connection manager for it. Right-click anywhere in the Connection Managers tab and choose New OLE DB Connection from the context menu. This will open the Configure OLE DB Connection Manager dialog box. As you haven't yet added any connection manager, you will see nothing under Data Connections. Click New to open a Connection Manager dialog box. You will find that the Native OLE DB\SQL Native Client has already been added in the Provider drop-down box. Click the down arrow to look at the other available OLE DB providers for this connection manager. Click Cancel to return. Type **(local)** in the Server Name selection box. Leave Use Windows Authentication in the Log On To The Server area. In the Connect To A Database area, make sure the Select Or Enter A Database Name radio button is selected. Click the down arrow and select the Campaign database from the drop-down list, as shown in Figure 3-3.

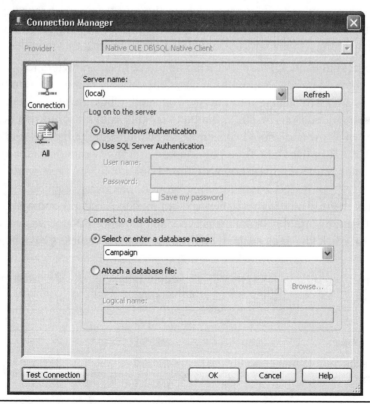

Figure 3-3   *Adding an OLE DB Connection Manager for Campaign database*

7. Click the Test Connection button to test your connection. You will see a message saying "Test connection succeeded." Click OK three times to return to the Control Flow Panel.

Exercise (Configuring Execute SQL Task)

8. Right-click the Execute SQL Task and choose Edit from the context menu to open the Execute SQL Task Editor window. In the right pane, under SQL Statement, click in the Connection box. A down arrow will appear at the far right corner of the data box. Click this down arrow to choose from the available connections. Notice that you can create a new connection from here as well. Choose (local).Campaign from the list.

9. Click in the SQLStatement data box, and an ellipsis button will appear on the far right corner of the box. Click this button to open the Enter SQL Query window. Type in the following query and then click OK.

INSERT INTO CustomLog VALUES (?,?,?,?,?,?,?)

This is a parameterised query in which the question marks represent the parameters. You need to be careful about the order of your parameters while defining them, as they will be considered in the order they are added.

10. In the left pane, click Parameter Mapping to define parameters for your query. Click the Add button. You will see a system variable being added in the dialog box. You need to change it to the one you need. Click the new variable that has just been added. As you click, the box will turn into a drop-down box. Click the down arrow and choose System::UserName from the list. Similarly, choose VARCHAR in the Data Type column and assign a value of 0 (zero) in the Parameter Name field, as shown in Figure 3-4.

Now click the Add button to add the next parameter. A second line will be added to the list. Change Variable Name, Data Type, and Parameter Name values as per the following list. Click OK to close the window once all the parameters have been defined.

Variable Name	Direction	Data Type	Parameter Name
System::UserName	Input	VARCHAR	0
System::MachineName	Input	VARCHAR	1
System::PackageName	Input	VARCHAR	2
System::PackageID	Input	VARCHAR	3
System::TaskName	Input	VARCHAR	4
System::StartTime	Input	DATE	5

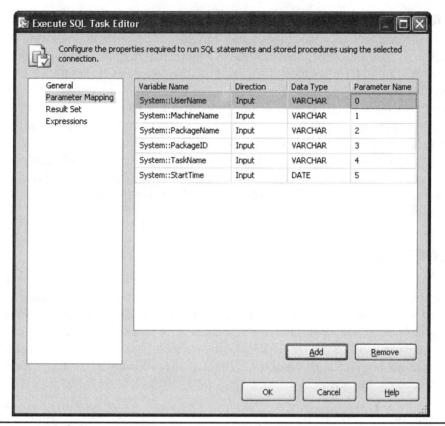

Figure 3-4 *Configuring Parameter Mapping page for Execute SQL task*

Exercise (Executing the Package to Populate CustomLog Table)

11. Choose Debug | Start Debugging to run the package in the debugging mode. The Execute SQL task will turn yellow and then green. Click the stop debugging button on the debugging toolbar and press CTRL-SHIFT-S to save all the files in the project.

12. Switch back to SQL Server Management Studio. In the query window (open a query window if this is not already open), execute the following query:

    SELECT * FROM CustomLog

You will see a record entered in the CustomLog table with all the details configured for logging.

Review

In this exercise, you read values of system variables at the point in time when the package was run and loaded those values to a table in SQL Server. SSIS provides extensive logging facilities using log providers (discussed in Chapter 8) that enable you to log in various formats—for example, log to text files or to an SQL Server table. In instances when the standard logging doesn't fit your requirements, you can use custom logging, as you've done in this Hands-On exercise. You've used Execute SQL task to run a parameterised query. If you are wondering about Execute SQL task, it will be discussed many times throughout this book and you will understand all the aspects of its usage. This is one of the main tasks provided in the Control Flow Panel of BIDS and will be covered in detail in Chapter 5 when we discuss all the preconfigured tasks provided in Control Flow.

User-defined Variables

You can configure user-defined variables for packages, Foreach Loop containers, For Loop containers, Sequence containers, tasks, and event handlers. To configure a user-defined variable you will provide a name, description, namespace, scope, and value for the variable along with choosing other properties, such as whether the variable raises an event when its value changes or whether the variable is read-only or read/write.

Before you begin creating variables, go through the following concepts to understand their creation and usage.

Namespace

SSIS keeps its variables under *namespaces*; by default, custom variables are in the User namespace, and system variables are in the System namespace. You can define custom variables in User namespace or can create an additional namespace, but you cannot modify or add the System namespace or its variables.

Scope

As mentioned earlier, Integration Services allows variables to be created in the scope of a package or within the scope of a container, task, or event handler in the package. This helps in managing variables as they are created at the location where they are used. To communicate among objects within a package and how they flow from parent package to a child package, variables follow these rules:

► *Variables defined at the container scope are available to all the tasks or containers within the parent container.* For example, all the tasks or containers within the Foreach Loop container can use the variables defined within the scope of the Foreach Loop container. Variables defined at the package scope can be used like global variables of DTS 2000, as the package is also a container and is at the top of the container hierarchy. However, for complex packages, it is recommended that you create the variables within the scope where they are needed to help manageability.

▶ *If a variable has the same name as the variable defined at its parent or grandparent, the "local" variable will supersede the one descending from the ancestor container.* Note that the variables are case-sensitive; therefore, this rule will not affect variables with the same name but with different cased letters.

▶ *Variables defined in the scope of the called package are never available to the calling package.* SSIS provides a facility to run a package as a child package inside a parent package using Execute Package task. When a package is run as a child package using Execute Package task, the variables defined within the Execute Package task scope are available to the called package. That is, the Execute Package task can pass the variables to the child packages. The process of flow of variables from parent package to child package works at run-time— that is, the child package variables get values from the parent package when run in the parent package process. If the child package is run on its own, the variable won't get updated due to the parent not being available.

Data Type and Value

While configuring a variable, you first need to choose the data type the variable is going to be. The value and the data type must be compatible with each other—for example, for an integer data type, you cannot use a string as the value. You can assign a literal or an expression to the value.

Evaluating a variable using an expression is a powerful feature that allows you to use dynamic values for variables. Each time the package tasks want to use the variable, they have to evaluate the expression to calculate the variable value. A common use of such a scenario is to load data from the update files received daily, having date as part of the file name. In this case you would need to write an expression using the GETDATE() function to evaluate the variable value. Then the expression is evaluated at run-time and the variable value is set to the expression result.

You can also change variable values using package configurations, which provide the ability for updating values of properties at run-time. Configurations are useful when deploying packages, as you can update values of variables and connection strings of connection managers. You will study more about configurations in Chapter 11.

Hands-On: Creating a Directory with User-defined Variables

Many times, while creating a workflow for SSIS packages, you need to create folders into which you'll copy files. In this exercise, you will create a folder using a user-defined variable; this will demonstrate how SSIS can use the values of variables at run-time.

Method

The File System task provided in Control Flow Panel of BIDS does many file and folder operations and can create a folder as one of its operations. You will be using this task to create a C:\SSISdirectory folder. This exercise is built in two parts: In the first part, you will use static (that is, hard-coded) values in the File System task to create the C:\SSISdirectory folder. In the second part, you will use a variable to perform the same task. While the use of variables is extensively covered in Hands-On exercises used for package developments throughout this book, here you will do a simple exercise to add a variable and see how it functions. The File System task is relatively simple to use and configure. This task is covered in detail in Chapter 5, but here the focus is on the use of variables.

Exercise (Using Hard-coded Values)

In the first part of this Hands-On exercise, you will create a folder using File System task and directly specifying the folder path and name in the task itself.

1. Start BIDS from the Microsoft SQL Server 2005 program group.
2. Choose File | New | Project to create a new project, or press CTRL-SHIFT-N. The New Project window opens.
3. In the New Project window, choose Integration Services Project from the Templates area. In the Name field type **Creating Directory** and in the Location field type **C:\SSIS\Projects**. Click the OK button, and SQL Server Integration Services will take a few seconds to create this new project.
4. After the new project is created, go to the Solution Explorer window and right-click package.dtsx under the SSIS Packages folder. Choose Rename from the context menu. Rename the package as Creating Directory.dtsx and click Yes in the confirmation box.
5. On the Control Flow Panel, locate the Toolbox window, which by default appears on the left side of the screen as a tabbed window. Hover your mouse on it, and it will open. From the Toolbox window, drag and drop the File System Task onto the Control Flow Panel. You will see a crossed red circle on the task. Hover your mouse on it and it will display a message indicating a validation error. These validation errors are a big help in debugging and creating a syntactically correct package.

6. Double-click the icon of the File System task to open File System Task Editor. With this task, you can create, move, delete, rename, and set attributes on files and directories by selecting one of these operations in the Operation field. Click in the Operation field and select Create Directory from the drop-down list. Selecting this option changes other available fields. This is one of the great features of Integration Services components—to change the available fields dynamically based on the value selected in another field. This way, you can configure only the relevant information in the component rather than getting confused with loads of options.

7. Now you need to provide the path for the folder in the SourceConnection field to create a folder. Click in the SourceConnection field and select <New connection…> from the drop-down list. This will open the File Connection Manager Editor. In the previous Hands-On for system variables, you created a connection manager by right-clicking in the Connection Managers area in the Control Flow Panel; here you are going to create a connection manager from within a task. Remember that the File Connection Manager allows you to either refer to an existing file or folder or create a new file or a folder. Don't get confused by the word *directory*, which is used in File System Task, and *folder*, which is used in File Connection Manager. They mean the same thing. It's just that different programmers used different words while developing these components.

8. In the Usage Type field, choose Create Folder from the drop-down list. In the Folder field, type **C:\SSISdirectory**. Click OK to return to the File System Task Editor. Note that *SSISdirectory* has been added in the Connection Managers area and also appears in the SourceConnection field (see Figure 3-5). Click OK to close the File System Task Editor.

9. Choose Debug | Start Debugging to execute the package you've developed. Or press F5. The File System task will quickly change to green and will show a "Package Execution Completed" message. The output window also pops up below the Connection Managers area and will show a success message. Press SHIFT-F5 to stop debugging the package and return to design mode.

10. Run Windows Explorer to see that C:\SSISdirectory has been created.

Exercise (Using a User-defined Variable to Pass the Folder Path to File System Task)

In this second part of the Hands-On, you will create a user-defined variable and assign a value to it. Then you will assign this variable to SourceConnection field in the File System task and will see that the variable value is used by the task to create the required folder.

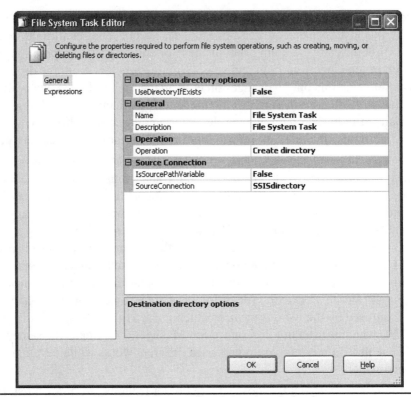

Figure 3-5 *Configuring the File System task with hard-coded values*

11. Delete the newly created folder from the C: drive and the connection manager from BIDS by simply selecting it and pressing the DELETE button. Click Yes on the pop-up dialog box to confirm deletion of the connection manager.

12. Right-click anywhere on the blank surface of the Control Flow Panel and choose Variables from the context menu. This will open the Variables window. Add a variable by clicking the Add Variable button, which is the leftmost button on the menu bar in the Variables window. In the Name column, type **directory** and change the Data Type to **String**. In the Value field, type **C:\ SSISdirectory**, as shown here:

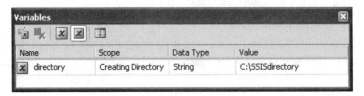

13. Double-click the File System task to open the Task Editor dialog box. In the IsSourcePathVariable field's drop-down list, select True. This converts the SourceConnection field to a SourceVariable field.

14. Click in the SourceVariable field and then click the down arrow button in the field to see the list of variables. Scroll down in the list to locate the User::directory variable and select it. The User::directory variable will be shown in the SourceVariable field. Click OK to close the File System Task Editor, as shown in Figure 3-6.

15. Press F5 to execute the package. The File System task turns green and the Output window shows the Success message.

16. Press SHIFT-F5 to stop debugging the package, or choose Debug | Stop Debugging. Switch to Windows Explorer to see that the folder has been created.

17. In BIDS, choose File | Save All and leave the project open, as you will return to this project later in the chapter.

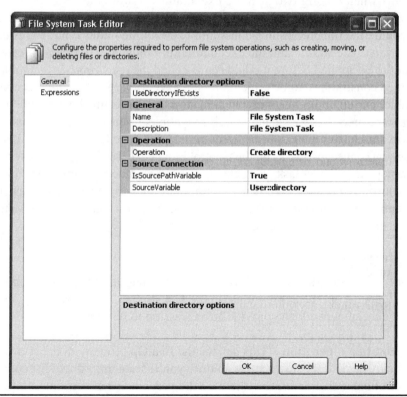

Figure 3-6   *Configuring File System Task Editor to get a value from a user-defined variable*

Review

You have created a user-defined variable and used its value to populate the SourceVariable field in the File System Task Editor. When you run this package, the File System task knows that it has to read the value of the SourceVariable field from the User::directory variable as you have specified the IsSourcePathVariable as True. Though you have defined a static value to the variable, this is a good example of how a variable can affect the task. In real-life scenarios, the variables are populated by the upstream tasks in packages at run-time and the downstream tasks or components use those variables to get dynamic values.

Precedence Constraints

While creating the workflow and linking tasks, you can decide the conditions, which can affect the running of successive tasks. To do this, you use *precedence constraints* when linking two or more executables. Within the SSIS world, an *executable* is defined as a container, a task, or an event handler. The executable for which you define the precedence constraint to be applied after it has run is called the *precedence executable* and the executable for which you define a precedence constraint to be applied before it could run is called the *constrained executable*. The precedence constraints can be affected by the execution result of the precedence executable. For example, you may wish to stop the constrained executable from running if the precedence executable fails to complete. The precedence constraints created in a package can be seen by accessing the Package Explorer tab in BIDS.

When you connect two tasks on the Control Flow Panel by dragging the green arrow from a task on to the other task, you actually use a precedence constraint. Double-click the green arrow to open the Precedence Constraint Editor, in which you can specify various options for configuring the constraints. The Editor window is divided into two parts: Constraint Options and Multiple Constraints.

Constraint Options

The precedence constraint can be based on a combination of the execution results and the evaluation of the expressions. In the Constraint Options section, you can select the execution result and provide an expression to be evaluated.

▶ **Evaluation Operation**   This defines the EvalOp property of the constraint. When you click the down arrow button, you'll see a drop-down list containing four choices that determine the way the precedence constraint combines execution results and evaluation expressions to determine whether to run the constrained executable.

▶ **Constraint**   Use only the execution result from the precedence executable to determine whether the constrained executable runs.

▶ **Expression**   Use only the Expression property to determine whether the constrained executable runs. When selected, the Expression field becomes available to enable you to define an expression, which must be a valid SSIS expression.

▶ **Expression And Constraint**   Combines the requirements of both the Constraint and the Expression.

▶ **Expression Or Constraint**   Uses either of the two options to decide the execution of the constrained executable.

▶ **Value**   This field refers to the value property of the precedence constraint and specifies the values of the execution result of the precedence executable to determine whether to run the constrained executable. When you click the down arrow button, the drop-down list shows the following three options:

▶ **Completion**   The constrained executable will run on the completion of the precedence executable with no regard to the outcome—that is, success or failure. For example, you may want to run a consistency check on your database toward the end of your nightly update operation without regard to whether the data uploading task successfully loaded data or failed to load any data.

▶ **Success**   The constrained executable will run only when the precedence executable has completed successfully.

▶ **Failure**   The constrained executable will run only when the precedence executable has failed. For example, you may want to alter the data flow when the data loading task fails.

▶ **Expression**   In this field, you can specify an expression that evaluates to Boolean true to run the constrained executable. This Expression field becomes available only when you choose the Expression And Constraint or Expression Or Constraint option in the Evaluation Operation field. The expression can include functions, operators, and system and custom variables. You can click Test to evaluate the expression or test whether the expression you have specified is syntactically correct. A simple expression is shown in Figure 3-7.

Multiple Constraints

A constrained executable can have multiple constraints—that is, more than one precedence executable may apply precedence constraints on a constrained executable. In situations for which you have multiple constraints on a constrained executable, you can specify the criteria for multiple constraints to control the execution of the constrained executable in the Multiple Constraints section of the Precedence

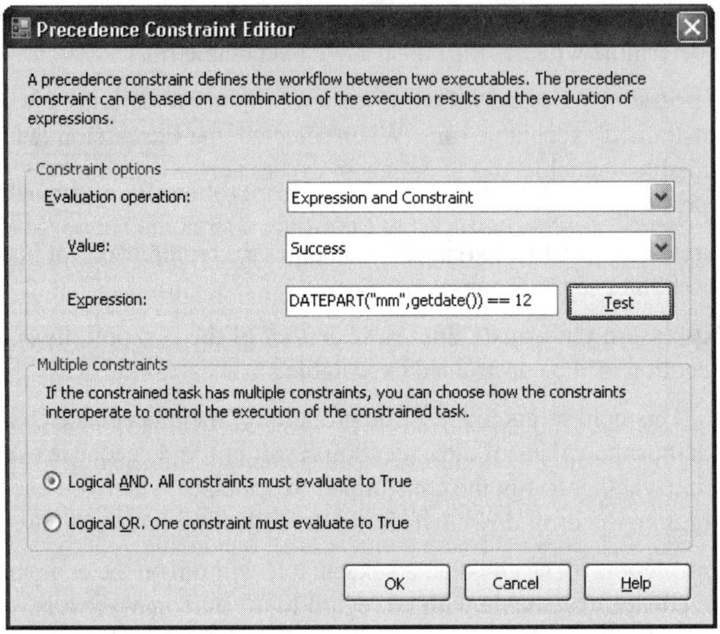

Figure 3-7   *The Precedence Constraint Editor*

Constraint Editor. You can choose one of two mutually exclusive options—Logical AND or Logical OR. Selecting Logical AND sets the LogicalAnd property of the precedence constraints to True and implies that *all* the constraints must evaluate to True before running the constrained executable. Selecting Logical OR sets the LogicalAnd property to False and implies that *one* of the constraints must evaluate to True to run the constrained executable.

You won't be doing any Hands-On exercises to see the behavior of precedence constraints in this chapter, as this requires building a package with two or more tasks—which would be a bit too much at this stage. However, the precedence constraint behaviour is covered in a Hands-On exercise in Chapter 5, where you will be able to see how the constrained executables are affected by your choice of a particular constraint.

Integration Services Expressions

Integration Services allows you to set values dynamically for fields using variables that are updated at run-time by other tasks. This facility is quite powerful and great in many respects; however, it does not solve all the real-life problems with population of configuration values. Developers must often evaluate a value for a task based on a value generated by another task. This requires that they write a custom piece of code to evaluate the required value, as the value generated by the first task can't be directly used in the second task. For example, if you want to create a folder in which the update files you receive daily are kept, and you want to add a date part in the name of the folder, you must evaluate the folder name using the two values: one for the static part and one for the dynamic date part. This is where Integration Services shows its real power. SSIS allows you to evaluate a value using expressions. SSIS tasks expose some of their properties that can be dynamically updated using expressions. Expressions can be used for the following purposes:

▶ Variables and property expressions can use expressions to update values at run-time.

▶ Integration Services has a For Loop container, which you will study in the next chapter, that uses expressions for the looping criteria.

▶ As you've seen earlier in the chapter, precedence constraints use expressions to evaluate the condition.

▶ Data flow transformations such as conditional split transformation and derived column transformation have an expression builder interface.

Integration Services expressions consist of one or more variables, columns, functions, and operators. You can use all these together to build an expression to evaluate the required value. The language of the Integration Services expressions uses syntax similar to that used in C and C#. The Expression syntax contains identifiers, literals, operators and functions. The collection of syntax, data type conversion rules, truncation rules, and string padding is called the Expression grammar.

SSIS provides GUI tools to help you build expressions. The Expression Builder is present in most of the Control Flow tasks in the Expressions page to help you apply expressions to properties of the tasks. The expressions you apply to properties are called Property Expressions. Figure 3-8 shows the example of property expression for the File System task that you used in the last Hands-On exercise. If you open the package again and open Expression Builder via the Expressions page and build the expression shown (as explained in the next paragraph), you can then click the Evaluate Expression button to evaluate this expression at design time.

In the Expression Builder, you can type information into the Expression box and drag and drop any of the items from the top two panes to the Expression box to build your expression. In the top left pane of this dialog box, you can drag and drop any of the system or user-defined variables. When you drop variables in the Expression box, the required syntax elements such as the @ prefix are automatically added to the variable names. You can also select columns from this pane if they are applicable to the task and are available there. And from the pane on the right, you can choose from

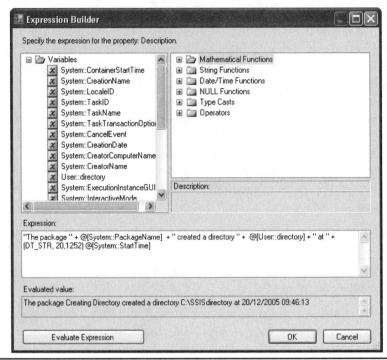

Figure 3-8 *Expression Builder user interface*

various functions and operators. Figure 3-8 also shows a sample expression, which was built using literals, concatenate operator (+) from the operators, system and user-defined variables, and a type cast to convert the date type to string.

You can also evaluate your expression by clicking the Evaluate Expression button and the result will be shown in the Evaluated Value field. This will not include any values that are not available at design time. Understand that some of the variables will be populated at run-time and they will have no value at design time; hence the evaluation may not give you the exact result that will be created at run-time. This evaluation of an expression is accomplished by the Expression Evaluator, which also determines whether expressions adhere to the rules of Expression grammar. As mentioned, property expressions can be applied to any of the exposed properties in Control Flow tasks, though the property expressions are not available in data flow components. This doesn't mean that you can't use expressions in data flow components, however; some components use expressions to a great extent. For example, the user interface for Conditional Split and Derived Column transformations is actually an Expression Builder. It's just that the data flow components don't expose their properties for you to write expressions to update them dynamically at run-time.

You can find functions and operators listed in the top right pane of the Expression Builder. Integration Services Expression language has a rich set of syntax rules and functions that cannot be covered in detail in this book. However, proper explanations for the expressions used will be provided wherever applicable. Refer to Microsoft SQL Server 2005 Books Online for more details on expressions.

Following is the brief discussion on these functions and operators.

- ▶ **Mathematical Functions**   When you expand this folder, you will see 11 functions, such as ABS, LOG, SQUARE, and SQRT. These functions perform calculations based on numeric input values provided as parameters to the functions and return numeric values.

- ▶ **String Functions**   This folder contains 14 string functions, such as LEN, LOWER, LTRIM, RIGHT, and SUBSTRING. String functions perform specified operations on string or hexadecimal input values and return a string or numeric value.

- ▶ **Date/Time Functions**   Eight Date/Time functions here, such as DATEADD, GETDATE, and MONTH, perform operations on date and time values and can return string, numeric, or date and time values.

- ▶ **NULL Functions**   Twenty functions, such as ISNULL and NULL, are available for particular data types. ISNULL returns a Boolean result based on whether an expression is null, whereas NULL returns a null value of a requested data type.

- ▶ **Type Casts**   These functions help you perform data type conversions for a variable, a column, or an expression from one data type to another, such as string to integer or date/time to string.

- ▶ **Operators**   About 22 operators, such as (+) add, (+) concatenate, (/) divide, and (>) greater than.

You will be using property expressions in various Hands-On exercises throughout this book, but just to tickle your brain, the following is a simple exercise using property expressions.

Hands-On: Using Expressions to Update Properties at Run-time

You need to create a directory to keep the update files you receive daily. But this time, you want to keep the daily update files in their own folder—you need to create a folder each night and want to include a date part in the name of the folder.

Method

You can do this in at least two ways. You can write an expression on the variable's value property to evaluate the new value and pass that value to SourceConnection field. Or you can go back to the first part of the last Hands-On exercise, in which you used a connection manager for the SourceConnection field and provided a static value of C:\SSISdirectory. As part of the second method, you can add property expression on the SSISdirectory Connection Manager to generate a connection string at run-time. As no Expression Builder is attached to the variable's properties and you have to write it manually, we will be using the second method so that you can have an introduction to Expression Builder. Follow these steps:

▶   Open the Creating Directory project and change the settings to go back to a hard-coded value for the SourceConnection field.

▶   Build a property expression on the ConnectionString property of the SSISdirectory Connection Manager.

Exercise (Configuring the File System Task with Hard-coded Values)

1.   Open the Creating Directory project with BIDS if it is not already open: choose File | Open | Project/Solution and select the Creating Directory.sln file after navigating to the project path.

2.   When the Creating Directory project is open on the designer surface, double-click the File System Task to open the editor.

3.   Click in the IsSourcePathVariable field and change the value to False.

4.   Click in the SourceConnection field and choose <New connection…> from the drop-down list. Choose Create Folder in the Usage Type field of the File Connection Manager Editor. Type **SSISdirectory** in the Folder field. You don't need to provide a path here, as that will be evaluated at run-time using the expression you are going to build. Click the OK button twice to close the File System Task Editor.

Exercise (Using Property Expressions to Evaluate ConnectionString at Run-time)

In this part, you will build an expression to evaluate the directory name, similar to C:\SSISdirectory20051220, having the date attached as a suffix to the folder name.

5.   In the Connection Manager area, right-click the SSISdirectory Connection Manager and choose Properties from the context menu.

6.   In the Properties window, click in the Expressions field and then click the ellipsis button that appears on the right of the field. This will open the Property Expressions Editor.

7. Click in the Property column and choose ConnectionString Property from the drop-down list. Click the ellipsis button to the right of this field to open the Expression Builder.

8. In the top left pane of Expression Builder, expand Variables and drag and drop the User::directory variable in the Expression area. Then do the following in sequence:

   ▶ Expand Operators and add the Concatenate (**+**) operator.

   ▶ Expand Type Casts and add (**DT_STR, <<length>>, <<code_page>>**); then change <<length>> to **4** and <<code page>> to **1252** to make it (**DT_STR, 4, 1252**).

   ▶ Expand Date/Time Functions and add **YEAR(<<date>>)**; then drop the GETDATE() function on the **<<date>>** part of the **YEAR(<<date>>)** function.

   Your expression should look like this:

   ```
   @[User::directory] + (DT_STR, 4,1252) YEAR( GETDATE() )
   ```

9. Click the Evaluate Expression button, and you will see a value of current year attached to the User::directory variable (which in my case is C:\ SSISdirectory2005 at this point in time). Complete the expression by adding the following so that the complete expression looks like one shown in Figure 3-9:

   ```
   RIGHT("0" + (DT_STR, 2, 1252)  MONTH( GETDATE()  ), 2) +
   RIGHT("0" + (DT_STR, 2, 1252)  DAY( GETDATE()  ), 2)
   ```

10. Click the OK button twice to return to the Properties window. If you expand the Expressions field you should see the expression you developed earlier.

11. Press F5 on the keyboard to execute the package. When the File System task has turned green, press SHIFT-F5 to stop debugging and go back to design mode. Choose File | Save All and then close the project.

12. Using Windows Explorer, check to see that the required folder has been created.

Review

You've learned one of the core skills that will help you create packages that can update themselves using the current values at run-time. You've used Expression Builder to write an expression. You understand that this can also be written directly without using Expression Builder's drag and drop feature to speed things up, but Expression Builder helps in providing quick syntax help.

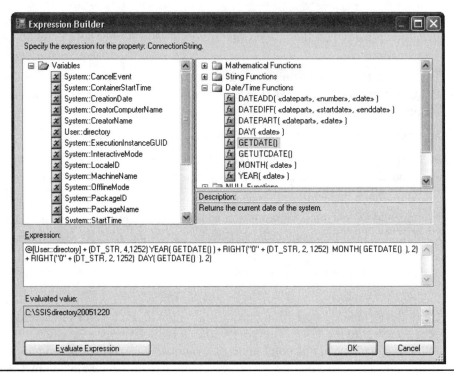

Figure 3-9   *Building property expression*

Summary

This chapter covered the basic components used for building a workflow in an SSIS package. Integration Services provides connection managers that help various tasks in the package to establish connections to the external data stores. Variables provided in SSIS are different from those in DTS 2000 as they can have scope now and are categorized as system variables that you cannot create and modify—they are read-only, and the user-defined variables that you create to meet the needs of the package. Precedence constraints are also enhanced beyond DTS 2000, as they can include expressions to consider along with execution results of the precedence executable. Finally, the most powerful feature of Integration Services is its ability to evaluate the properties dynamically at run-time. This is achieved with Property Expressions. Integration Services Expression language is rich in syntax and can be used to create complex expressions using variables, columns, functions, and operators. After having learned about connection managers, system and user-defined variables, precedence constraints, and the Expressions language, it's time for you to start building packages using these components.

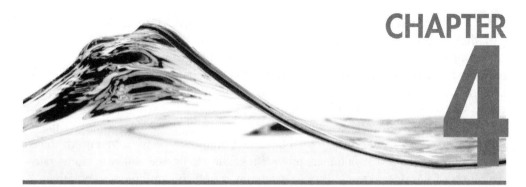

Integration Services Control Flow Containers

If you have worked with Data Transformation Services (DTS 2000), you know that the DTS packages are configured using tasks connected by precedence constraints. Integration Services (SSIS) uses a slightly different concept of building packages inside a container—that is, the container actually contains the tasks and precedence constraints. SSIS containers are the objects that represent a unit of work. A container can contain other containers and tasks. So, while you are creating an SSIS package, you will be adding and configuring tasks inside a container that will provide necessary services to your tasks to accomplish the work that needs to be done. Functionally, SSIS containers provide repeating logic, the ability to enumerate over a set of items, and the ability to group tasks and subcontainers to create an independent unit of work that can communicate with a parent container.

In this chapter, you will study the following five Integration Services containers:

▶ Integration Services package

▶ Foreach Loop container

▶ For Loop container

▶ Sequence container

▶ Task Host container

You will study another container available in SSIS, the Event Handler, in Chapter 8. Its primary function is to support a container depending on an event.

Integration Services Package

The Integration Services package is programming code that consists of executables, control flow containers, tasks, data flow transformations, connection strings, variables, event handlers, and other components that all work together. The package object is the most important object and sits at the top of the hierarchy in the Integration Services object model architecture. This means that all other containers and tasks are contained and executed within the context of a package.

You can build a package using GUI tools, such as the Import and Export Wizard or Business Intelligence Development Studio (BIDS), or you can build it programmatically. However, you may find it easier to use GUI tools, which let you build a complex package in a short time. After a package is created in BIDS, you can save it on the file system as an XML file or to SQL Server in the sysdtspackages90 table. After saving the package, you can connect to Integration Services using SQL Server Management Studio to manage your packages.

When you created your first project earlier in the book, you also created a blank package inside the solution. In the same exercise, you learned about various components and parts of a package. You can use other objects such as event handlers, variables, package configurations, breakpoints, and log providers that can greatly enhance package functionality and give you complete control over what you want to achieve and how you want to achieve it.

By now, you have learned that, broadly speaking, every package will have a control flow and most will include a data flow. One of the top selling points of SSIS is that it separates control flow and data flow in a package. This separation makes it easy for you to design, develop, debug, and maintain complex packages.

When you create a package in the BIDS, you see four tabs on the SSIS designer surface:

▶ **Control Flow tab**   Helps you create package workflow using control flow components such as tasks, connection managers, and precedence constraints.

▶ **Data Flow tab**   Helps you create a data flow using data flow components such as transformations, source adapters, and destination adapters.

▶ **Event Handlers tab**   Helps you create a control flow that runs in response to an event raised by a task or a container inside a package.

▶ **Package Explorer tab**   Shows you a hierarchical view of the elements used in the package.

Although an SSIS package sits at the top of the object model hierarchy and all the tasks and containers are executed within it, a package can be included as a child in other packages. Think of the SSIS package as a container that can contain a subcontainer—likewise, a package can contain a subpackage. SSIS includes the Execute Package task that acts as a wrapper for a package, making it a child package. You can include this task/ child package in the control flow of a parent package. This functionality makes SSIS modular in design, which means that you can create subpackages as modules, which can then be combined to form an enterprise-wide package that is even more complex. This functionality also reduces complexity in design, making it easier for you to debug and maintain smaller packages. You will learn more about the Execute Package task in the next chapter, where the Control Flow tasks are discussed.

Foreach Loop Container

While designing the workflow of an SSIS package, you may want to perform an operation on a collection. For example, you may want to read the names of the files in a folder and set the values of your variables using those names, or you may want to perform logic on each of the records in a table. The Foreach Loop container in SSIS provides this functionality by bringing the result set into the workflow; this lets you perform interesting work based on the data in the result set.

The Foreach Loop container defines an *iterative workflow*—that is, a repeating control flow in a package. This concept has been borrowed from programming languages. SSIS has made enumerating over a collection a lot easier by providing the Foreach Loop container that uses enumerators that in turn allow you to enumerate different sets of collections.

Here are some examples for which a Foreach Loop container can be used:

▶ Notifying your customers by sending out e-mails when an insurance policy is due for renewal.

▶ Processing prospects who have made enquiries during the last month.

▶ Automatically sending out welcome packs to new clients.

▶ Processing dunning letters whenever a payment is overdue by a certain number of days.

The following table lists the enumerators that SSIS provides:

Enumerator	Description
Foreach ADO	Enumerates rows in tables such as an ADO record set.
Foreach ADO.NET Schema Rowset	Enumerates the schema information about a data source. For example, enumerate all the tables in a SQL Server database.
Foreach File	Enumerates files in a folder. Can select files from the subfolders if you select Traverse Subfolders option while configuring this enumerator.
Foreach From Variable	Enumerates the contents of a variable. For example, you may have stored results of a query in a variable that you want to enumerate on.
Foreach Item	Enumerates the items in a collection, such as cells in an Excel Worksheet.
Foreach Nodelist	Enumerates the result set of an XPath expression. For example, the expression `/Products/vehicle[@Bodystyle='saloon']`.
Foreach SMO	Enumerates SQL Management Objects (SMO). For example, tables or user collections in a SQL Server database.

The Foreach Loop container repeats the control flow for each member of the collection defined by the enumerator. For example, if you want to send out an e-mail to customers on the basis of a table that has 100 rows, the Foreach loop will iterate over the Send Mail task 100 times by going to a record, sending out the e-mail for that record, and then moving on to the next record.

You can implement any business logic that requires repetition using child containers and tasks as a single unit of work within a Foreach Loop container. Once you have chosen the enumerator to implement the repetition logic, the Foreach Loop container will iterate multiple times over the business logic you want to repeat for the set of values defined by the enumerator.

Why you would want to do this? Suppose you have created a contacts table, and you want to send an e-mail to each of the contacts listed in the table. You can use Send Mail task provided in SSIS to send these e-mails; however, the challenge to fill in the e-mail addresses one by one in the Send Mail task dynamically to be able to send a mail to each of the contacts has to be overcome. This is where a Foreach loop can help: it enumerates each contact, passes the e-mail address of each using a variable to the Send Mail task, waits for the task to send the e-mail, and then moves on to the next contact until all the contacts have been sent e-mail. This functionality, which is necessary for customer relationship management (CRM) projects these days, used to mean that custom code had to be written. Now, the Foreach Loop container makes it easy.

In the following Hands-On exercise, you will configure a Foreach Loop container to send out e-mails to selected contacts.

Hands-On: Contacting Opportunities

You are tasked to send out first contact e-mail to all the persons who have made enquiries about the products your company makes in the month of May 2005.

Method

In this exercise, you will use the prospect table of the Campaign database to select persons who have made enquiries in the month of May 2005. By now, you must attach the Campaign database provided with the software for this book to your SQL Server 2005 database server; if you have not attached it, do that first so that you can complete this exercise. Attaching the Campaign database to your SQL Server 2005 was explained in the appendix "How to Use the Provided Software". You will do the following:

▶ Add an OLE DB connection manager for connecting to the Campaign database so that you can get data from the prospects table. Add another connection manager for SMTP server for sending out e-mails.

▶ Add an Execute SQL task in the control flow for selecting the prospects.

▶ Add a Foreach Loop container to include the repetition logic.

▶ Within the Foreach Loop container, add a Send Mail task for sending out e-mails. The Foreach Loop container will iterate on the selected records and execute Send Mail task for each record to send out e-mail.

Exercise (Adding the Connection Managers)

In the first part of this exercise, you will create a new project and add connection managers to connect to the Campaign database and Simple Mail Transfer Protocol (SMTP) server. These connection managers will allow your package to interface with external objects to access data and send e-mails.

1. Start Business Intelligence Development Studio. Choose File | New | Project to create a new project. In the New Project window, click OK after specifying the following:

Template	Integration Services Project
Name	Contacting Opportunities
Location	C:\SSIS\Projects

2. In the Solution Explorer window, right-click Package.dtsx and choose Rename from the context menu. Rename the package Mailing Opportunities.dtsx and click OK in the pop-up confirmation dialog box. Choose File | Save All to save the newly created package.

3. Right-click in the Connection Managers area and choose New OLE DB Connection from the context menu. In the left pane of the Configure OLE DB Connection Manager dialog box (Figure 4-1), under Data Connections, you will see a list of connections that were created earlier. Choose (local).Campaign from the list and click OK to close the window. The package gets logically linked to the Campaign database and (local).Campaign connection manager appears under the Connection Managers tab. However, if you don't find (local). Campaign connection manager listed under Data Connections, refer back to the "Using System Variables to Create Custom Logs" Hands-On exercise in Chapter 3 to learn how to create this connection manager.

4. Right-click in the Connection Managers area and choose New Connection from the context menu. In the Add SSIS Connection Manager window, click SMTP Connection Manager Type and then click Add.

Figure 4-1   *Adding OLE DB Connection Manager*

5. In the SMTP Connection Manager Editor window Name field, type **My SMTP Server**. In the Description field, type **Connection to my SMTP Server**. In the SMTP Server field, type in the name of your SMTP server, as shown here:

In the illustration, you can see that localhost is used to send e-mails. You can use your corporate SMTP server or install SMTP service component of Internet Information Services (IIS) on the local machine and forward all the messages to gateway SMTP server. You can install IIS from the Control Panel by clicking the Add or Remove Programs icon and then Add/Remove Windows Components. If you are using a Microsoft Exchange Server that is configured not to accept unauthenticated connections, select the Use Windows Authentication check box. You can also choose to encrypt communication using Secure Socket Layer (SSL) when sending e-mails from this server. Whichever way you choose to send e-mails, make sure your SMTP server is prohibited from relaying e-mails for external servers and hence prevents any potential attacks from mass mailers. For the sake of simplicity, I'm using localhost on my machine.

Click OK to return to the SSIS Designer.

Exercise (Configuring Execute SQL Task)

In the second part of this exercise, you will configure an Execute SQL Task to select prospects that have enquired in the month of May 2005. While configuring this task, you will type an SQL statement to extract the required records and will add a variable to store those extracted records.

6. In the Control Flow tab of the designer, go to the Toolbox window and drag and drop an Execute SQL Task on the control flow surface. Double-click the Execute SQL Task icon to open the Execute SQL Task Editor. Type in the following values in the General tab of the editor window:

Name	May Opportunities
Description	SQL to choose persons who inquired in the month of May 2005.

In the complex packages where you have multiple similar tasks, description lets you quickly understand what each component is doing. You don't even have to open the task—just hover your mouse on the task in the Control Flow surface and the description will be shown to you as a task hint.

7. Click in the ResultSet field and choose Full Result Set from the drop-down list.

   The choice of the option in this box depends on the result set expected from your SQL statement. In this case, the select statement is going to return more than one row, so you will choose a Full Result Set option here. These result set options are explained in detail in Chapter 5.

8. Leave the ConnectionType set to OLE DB and from the drop-down list in the Connection field choose (local).Campaign connection manager.

9. In the SQLSourceType field, leave Direct Input selected. You can see the list of available options, however, by clicking in the SQLSourceType field. You can either input your SQL statement directly in the task or input from a file or read from a variable. In this exercise, you will be entering your SQL in the task directly.

10. Click in the SQLStatement field and an ellipsis button appears in the right corner of the field. Click the ellipsis button and you will see the Enter SQL Query window. Type in the following SQL query and click OK button to return to the Execute SQL Task Editor.

```
SELECT TITLE, FIRSTNAME, LASTNAME, EMAIL, ENQUIRYDATE
FROM PROSPECTS
WHERE ENQUIRYDATE BETWEEN '2005/05/01' AND '2005/05/31'
```

11. The Execute SQL Task Editor should look as shown in Figure 4-2. Click the Parse Query button to check for any syntax errors in the script and click OK on the pop-up dialog box. You can use Query Builder plug-in provided in this task

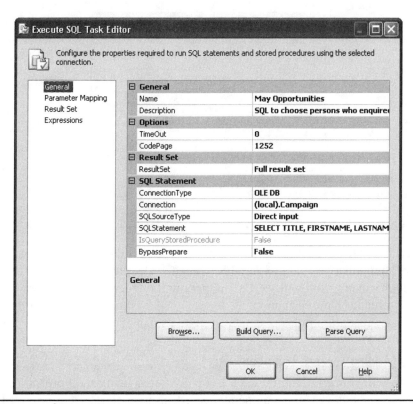

Figure 4-2 *Configuring Execute SQL Task*

by clicking the Build Query button. The Query Builder is particularly helpful when you have to select for many columns—then you don't have to type so many column names and also avoid any typos.

12. In your package, you will store the result set to a variable and then use this variable in the Foreach Loop container to let it iterate over the resultant records. To clarify further, all the records will be held in an object data type variable, which will be read by the Foreach Loop container row by row and fed into the defined tasks for further processing.

13. From the left pane of the Execute SQL Task Editor, click the Result Set page.

14. In the Result Set page, click the Add button. NewResultName will appear under the Result Name column. Delete it and type **0** (zero) in this field. Click in the field under the Variable Name column. Click the drop-down arrow to select <New variable...>. In the Add Variable window, in the Name field type **Opportunities**; leave the Namespace field set at User, and in the Value type field, select Object, as shown next:

Variables are case-sensitive, so when you type to add or to select a variable, pay attention to the case of variable. Click the OK button to return to the Task Editor window. You will see User::Opportunities added as a user variable under the Variable Name column.

15. Click OK to close Execute SQL Task Editor window.

Exercise (Adding Foreach Loop Container)

Here, you will configure the Foreach Loop container using the Foreach ADO enumerator that allows you to enumerate records from a record set as provided by opportunities variable.

16. From the Toolbox, drag and drop a Foreach Loop Container below the May Opportunities. Now click the May Opportunities and drag the green arrow appearing below it onto the Foreach Loop Container. This is the precedence control telling the Foreach Loop Container to proceed if the previous May Opportunities task has completed successfully.

17. Double-click the icon of the Foreach Loop Container to open the editor. In the General page, type in the following:

Name	Iterating May Opportunities
Description	This will iterate over the record set obtained from May Opportunities.

18. Click the Collection in the left pane to move on to the next page. Click in the Enumerator field to see the drop-down arrow, click it, and choose Foreach ADO Enumerator from the drop-down list. Note that Enumerator configuration area changes to suit the enumerator you choose.

19. In the Enumerator Configuration box, select User::Opportunities in the ADO Object Source Variable field, as shown in Figure 4-3. By specifying

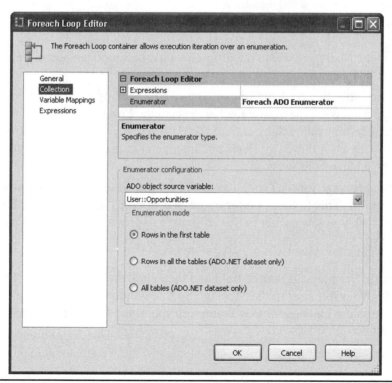

Figure 4-3   *Configuring the Foreach Loop using Foreach ADO Enumerator*

User::Opportunities here, you are telling the Foreach Loop container to get the records stored in the variable. This is a good example of tasks communicating with each other—here, the tasks are populating variables with values so that downstream components to use those values.

20. Since only one dataset will be generated in your example, make sure you select the Rows In The First Table radio button, as shown in Figure 4-3. Click OK to close Foreach Loop Editor window.

Exercise (Adding Send Mail Task and Executing the Package)

Now configure the Send Mail Task so that you can send e-mail for each of the selected records. After this, you will be executing the package to send e-mails.

21. From the Toolbox, drag and drop the Send Mail Task *inside* the Foreach Loop container.

22. Double-click the Send Mail Task icon to open the editor. In the General page, type in the following details:

Name	Mailing Opportunities
Description	It will send a mail for each of the record iterated by the Foreach Loop Container.

23. Go to the Mail page. From the drop-down list in SmtpConnection field, select My SMTP Server.

24. To keep your first package simple, you will be sending e-mails to yourself in this exercise. Type your e-mail address in the From and To fields and type **Your Enquiry** in the Subject field. You can actually read e-mail addresses from the database for these two fields using property expressions, which you will study in Chapter 8.

25. In the MessageSourceType, leave Direct Input selected, as shown in the Figure 4-4. This field is similar to the SQLSourceType field of the Execute SQL Task you saw earlier in this exercise and provides you three options: you can type your message directly in the task or get your message from a file or a variable.

26. Click in the MessageSource field and then click the ellipsis button to start typing your message in the Message Source window. I've drafted a simple message you can use for this example. Type in the following message and click OK.

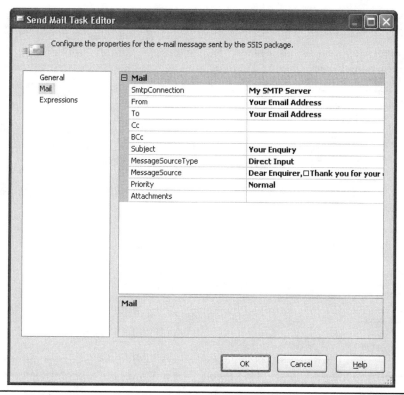

Figure 4-4   *Send Mail Task configurations*

Dear Enquirer,

Thank you for your enquiry. One of our sales representatives will be in touch with you. In the mean time, please go to our web site for more information on our products.

Thank you very much for showing interest.

Kind regards,

Sales Support Team

27. Leave Priority set to Normal, though High, Normal, or Low options are available as well. Leave the Attachments field blank. Click OK to close the dialog box.

By now, your package should look like the one shown in the Figure 4-5.

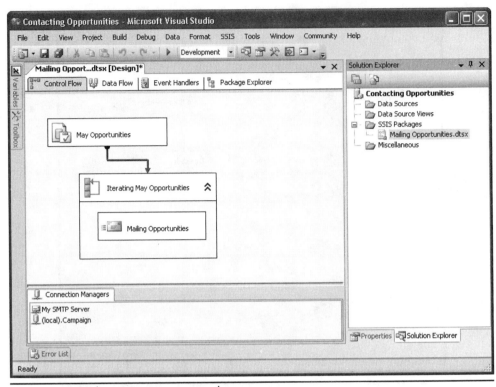

Figure 4-5   *Mailing Opportunities package*

28. Press F5 on the keyboard to start debugging. You will see the tasks changing colors. First, May Opportunities (Execute SQL Task) will turn yellow and then to green to indicate that the task has completed successfully. Then Iterating May Opportunities (Foreach Loop Container) and Mailing Opportunities (Send Mail Task) will turn from yellow to green quickly in turn for as many times as the number of records in the collection. This is a good visual experience to realise that the Foreach Loop container iterates over each item in the collection and processes the logic you design for it. Check your Inbox to see the e-mails you have sent. If your mailing system has relay restrictions, you may have to adjust them to complete the execution of the package successfully and receive e-mail in your Inbox.

29. Choose File | Save All and then choose File | Close Project to close the Contacting Opportunities project. Finally, exit from BIDS and take a coffee break after reading the review.

Review

In this exercise, you created a workflow for selecting interested parties and sent e-mails using the Execute SQL Task, Foreach Loop Container, and Send Mail Task. You have now seen most of the configuration settings for these tasks, but there are some interesting things that can still be done in this package—such as picking up e-mail addresses of the recipients from the data set; using a combination of title, first name, or last name in the addressing label; and specifying the reference by mentioning the enquiry date in the subject field. To give you a hint, all these can be done in Integration Services using property expressions. Property expressions help you dynamically update properties of a task such as the To address in the Send Mail Task. Property expressions are covered in more detail in Chapter 8, where we'll work with the advanced features of SSIS.

For Loop Container

The For Loop Container is probably the easiest container to work with. If you have worked with programming languages, you must be aware of popular For Loop statements. Generally the syntax of these statements defines a numeric variable, with a starting value, the incrementing step, and the ending value, along with statements to be executed repeatedly till the end point is reached. The For Loop Container provides a similar functionality of repeating a task or group of tasks for a defined number of times in Integration Services. The For Loop Container iterates over and over while evaluating an expression with each repeat until the expression evaluates to False.

To understand this, consider a Send Mail Task configured inside the For Loop Container. If you set to start the looping with counter value equal to zero, the increment step to one, and the maximum allowed value that can be reached to less than five, then the For Loop container will iterate the Send Mail task five times, which in turn will send out five messages. The package starts with counter value equal to zero to be increased in steps of one with each iteration. On each iteration, the current value of the counter is checked against the maximum possible value of five. If the current counter value is less than five, it is allowed to iterate the Send Mail task and increase the counter value by one until it reaches five. When the current value of the counter reaches five, it determines that the value has reached the maximum allowed and will not proceed beyond this point; it stops the execution. The evaluation expression at this point returns a value of False.

To do these iterations, the For Loop container uses the following elements:

▶ **InitExpression**   An optional initialization expression used to assign initial values to the loop counter.

▶ **EvalExpression**   A required evaluation expression used to decide whether the loop should continue or stop with each iteration.

▶ **AssignExpression**   An optional iteration expression that increments or decrements the loop counter.

You must provide an evaluation condition, but initialization and assignment expressions are optional. A For Loop Container can have only one evaluation expression and runs all the control flow tasks included in it the same number of times. You can use either literals or expressions while specifying an evaluation condition, an initialization counter value, or an assignment step value. The property expressions can include variables, which can be dynamically updated at run-time. This feature provides the For Loop Container its power to change the number of iterations each time the package is run depending upon the value of variables.

Let's compare the For Loop Container with Foreach Loop Container task, which you studied in the preceding section. The For Loop Container provides a looping functionality that conditionally iterates a control flow defined within the container, whereas the Foreach Loop Container provides a looping construct that enumerates files and objects in the control flow of a package—that is, it executes the control flow defined within the container for each item in the collection. Neither container provides any functionality; rather they provide only a structure in which you can build a repeatable control flow. To use the container functionality, you need to include at least one task in both containers. Both containers can include a control flow with multiple tasks in addition to other containers. You can in fact build nested loops and implement complex looping in your packages using these containers.

Hands-On: Removing Duplicate E-mail Addresses

You notice that the members of your portal services have been registering multiple times for different products. Corporate users have also been using a common e-mail address to log on to your site, which has created many records with the same e-mail address in your database. You want to send only one e-mail to each member, so you need to remove duplicate records with the same e-mail address from the database.

Method

In this exercise, you will delete duplicate records from the members table of Campaign database. In a similar real-life situation, developers may tend to use a cursor to achieve the results; here, you can deploy the For Loop container instead of a cursor. Integration Services provides some clever methods to remove duplicate records from a table that you will study in detail in the later chapters, here you will use the For Loop container to see its functioning and how you can use it to add iterations in your package.

This exercise uses members table in the Campaign database which is provided with the software for this book. So, before you start, make sure you have attached the Campaign database as mentioned in the "How to Use the Provided Software" appendix.

Our members table has nine distinct e-mail address records and 23 records in total. Run the following query against the members table in SQL Server Management Studio to see the nine records with distinct e-mail addresses:

```
SELECT DISTINCT emailAddress FROM members
```

If you run the following query against the members table in SQL Server Management Studio, you will see all 23 records appear, including those that have the same e-mail address. As a result of the package we develop in this Hands-On exercise, the nine records with distinct e-mail addresses will remain in the table and the duplicate records will be deleted.

```
SELECT * FROM members WHERE emailaddress IN(
SELECT emailAddress FROM members
GROUP BY emailaddress
HAVING COUNT(emailaddress) > 1)
```

Let's discuss the logic that you will use in this example. You will deal with these duplicate records in groups, and will group the records based on the emailaddress. Then you will count the records in the group and delete all the records in the group except one (that is, you'll delete all the duplicates and keep only one original). To delete all the duplicate records, you must apply the above logic to all the emailaddress groups one by one, which is cursor functionality. You will convert this cursor functionality into the looping functionality by dealing with one emailaddress group in a single iteration. In this fashion, you have to iterate on the record set for the total number of groups present. You will also need to create a temporary table to keep a record of the emailaddress groups you have covered so far during the processing. That's the core logic; make sure you understand it completely and don't mind reading this paragraph again if you have to.

Let's now break down the above logic into bite-sized chunks and give it a more practical shape.

▶ Determine the number of iterations (number of emailaddress groups).

▶ Create a temporary table to store the distinct e-mail addresses.

▶ Create a For Loop container to iterate over the emailaddress groups.

▶ Identify duplicates, delete all e-mail address records but one, and insert distinct e-mail address records into the temporary table.

▶ Delete the temporary table.

To achieve these goals, you will follow these steps:

▶ As you will be accessing SQL Server Campaign database, you will add an OLE DB connection manager for connecting to Campaign database.

▶ You will use an Execute SQL task for counting the number of emailaddress groups and store this number to a variable for use in the For Loop container.

▶ You will then add another Execute SQL task to create a temporary table to hold the e-mail addresses already iterated.

▶ You will add the For Loop Container to provide the looping functionality.

▶ Within the For Loop container, you will add an Execute SQL task for applying the SQL script to identify duplicate records, delete duplicate records but one from the emailaddress group, and insert a distinct e-mail address to the temporary table.

▶ Finally, you will add an Execute SQL task to delete the temporary table from the Campaign database.

Exercise (Adding an OLE DB Connection Manager)

1. Start BIDS. Choose File | New | Project. In the New Project window, specify the following:

Template	Integration Services Project
Name	Removing Duplicate Email Addresses
Location	C:\SSIS\Projects

Uncheck the Create Directory For Solution check box if already checked. Click OK to create a new project.

2. In the Solution Explorer window, right-click Package.dtsx and choose Rename from the context menu. Rename it Removing Duplicate Email Addresses.dtsx and click OK on the popup confirmation dialog box. Choose File | Save All to save the newly created blank package.

3. Right-click in the Connection Managers area and choose New OLE DB Connection from the context menu. A new window Configure OLE DB Connection Manager opens. Select the earlier configured (local). Campaign OLE DB connection manager listed in the Data Connections area and click OK to add this connection manager.

Exercise (Counting Distinct E-mail Addresses)

4. From the Toolbox, drag the Execute SQL task on to the designer surface of the Control Flow panel. You will see the error "No connection manager is specified" when you move your mouse on it. Double-click the icon of the task to open the Execute SQL Task Editor window. In the General page of this window, set the properties as follows:

Name	Set For Loop maxcounter
Description	This task will set the counter for the maximum number of times the For Loop Container is allowed to iterate.

5. Set the ResultSet field to Single Row by clicking the down-arrow that appears when you click in the field.

6. In the ConnectionType field, select OLE DB. Click in the Connection field and select (local).Campaign connection manager from the drop-down list.

7. In the SQLSourceType field, select Direct Input. Click in the SQLStatement field to see the ellipsis button at the far right, and then click the button to open the Enter SQL Query window. Type in the following query in the window and click OK:

```
SET NOCOUNT ON
SELECT DISTINCT emailaddress INTO #temptable FROM members
SELECT COUNT(emailaddress) AS recordcount FROM #temptable
```

As the For Loop Container has to iterate once for each e-mail address group or for each distinct e-mail address, in this query you are counting the number of distinct e-mail addresses. In the last line, you are outputting this count in the column named Recordcount, which you will bind to a user-defined variable in the following steps. The General page should appear as shown in Figure 4-6.

8. Go to Result Set page and click the Add button. You will see a line added to the Result Set page with *NewResultName* appearing under the Result Name column and nothing appearing under the Variable Name field. This is the page where you can bind the result set returned by your SQL query to a user-defined variable if the result set type is a single row, a row set, or XML. You must set the Result Name to 0 (zero) if the result set type is Full Result Set or XML, which you saw earlier in the "Contacting Opportunities" Hands-On exercise. You can bind a column of the result set to a variable by using the column name as the Result Name when the result set type is Single Row. You will be implementing this in the following step.

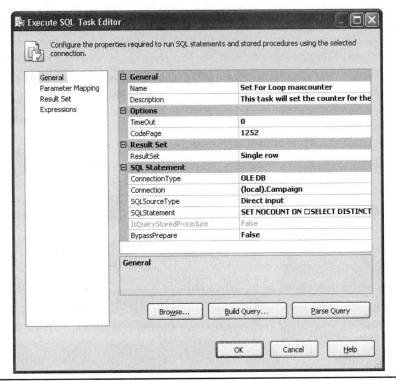

Figure 4-6 *Execute SQL Task configurations*

9. Click the NewResultName and change it to recordcount. Click in the Variable Name field and select <New variable…> from the drop-down list. Create a new variable with the following details:

Container	Removing Duplicate Email Addresses
Name	maxcounter
Namespace	User
Value type	Int32
Value	0

You will set the value equal to 0, which will be changed during run-time. Click OK to create this variable and bind it to the recordcount column of the result set. Your Result Set page should look like Figure 4-7.

10. Click OK to close the Execute SQL Task Editor window.

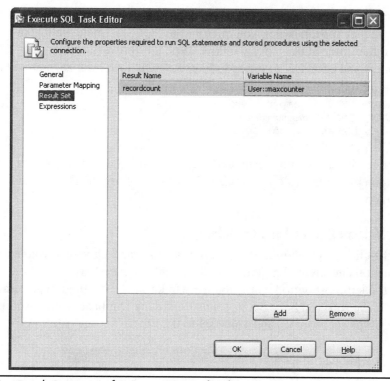

Figure 4-7   *Result Set page of Execute SQL Task Editor*

Exercise (Creating a Temporary Table)

11. From the Toolbox, drag another Execute SQL Task on to the Control Flow Designer surface just below the Set For Loop Maxcounter task.

12. Click the Set For Loop Maxcounter task and a green arrow will appear below the task. Drag the green arrow on to the new Execute SQL Task object.

13. Open the Execute SQL Task Editor window by double-clicking the icon of the task. In the General page, type the following:

Name	Creating Temporary table
Description	This task creates a temporary table for holding the email addresses that have been iterated upon.

14. As we will be creating a table only in this task and do not expect to output any data set, leave the ResultSet setting as None.

15. While OLE DB appears in the ConnectionType field, choose the previously created OLE DB connection manager from the drop-down list in Connection field.

16. Make sure Direct Input appears in the SQLSourceType field. Click the ellipsis button that appears when you click in the SQLStatement field. This should open the Enter SQL Query window. Type the following SQL query in the window and click OK to return to Execute SQL Task Editor window:

```
IF OBJECT_ID('dbo.temp_members', 'U') IS NOT NULL
DROP TABLE dbo.temp_members
CREATE TABLE temp_members
(EmailAddress varchar(100))
```

You will be inserting into this table the distinct e-mail addresses, which are to be iterated upon by the For Loop container. Click OK to close the Execute SQL Task Editor window.

Exercise (Adding the For Loop Container)

17. Right-click anywhere on the designer surface and choose Variables from context menu. In the Variables window, click the Add Variable button, which is the top left most button on the toolbar. Under the Name field, type **mincounter** and make sure you have Scope set as Removing Duplicate Email Addresses, Data Type set as Int32, and Value set to 0 (zero).

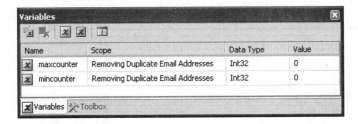

Name	Scope	Data Type	Value
maxcounter	Removing Duplicate Email Addresses	Int32	0
mincounter	Removing Duplicate Email Addresses	Int32	0

18. Drop the For Loop Container from the Toolbox on to the designer surface just below the Creating Temporary Table task. Drag the green arrow from this task on to the For Loop Container as you did earlier. (Just to remind you, this green arrow is an On Success precedence control for workflow between the two executable tasks. For more details on precedence controls, refer to Chapter 3.)

19. Right-click the For Loop Container and choose Edit from the context menu. Type the following in the For Loop page of the For Loop container:

Name	Looping for email addresses
Description	This container adds a looping structure for email addresses to be iterated upon.
InitExpression	@mincounter = 0
EvalExpression	@mincounter < @maxcounter
AssignExpression	@mincounter = @mincounter +1

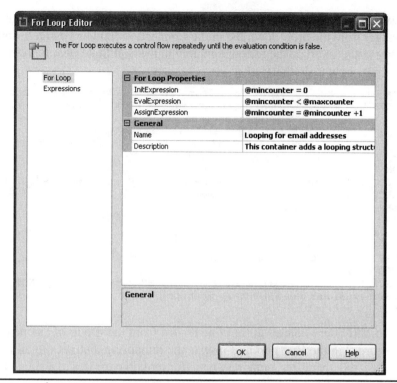

Figure 4-8   *Configuration settings of For Loop Container*

By setting these configurations, you are actually telling the For Loop container to initialize the `mincounter` with a zero value and increase it by one with each iteration. The `maxcounter` variable will be set to the number of iterations at run-time and `mincounter` will be evaluated against the run-time value of `maxcounter` on each iteration to decide whether to iterate the For Loop Container.

Click OK to close the For Loop Container. The For Loop Container configurations are shown in Figure 4-8.

Exercise (Identify and Delete Duplicate Records)

20. Drag and drop the Execute SQL task from the Toolbox inside the Looping For Email Addresses For Loop Container. Double-click the new Execute SQL task to open the Execute SQL Task Editor window. Type the following in the General page of the Execute SQL task:

Name	Identify and delete duplicate records
Description	This task deletes multiple email address records from the table.

21. Leave all the other options as they are, choose the (local). Campaign connection manager from the drop-down list in the Connection field as you have done in earlier tasks, and type the following query in the SQLStatement field (by now you know how to do that):

```
--/* Delete the multiple rows from the emailaddress group but one*/
DELETE TOP (SELECT COUNT(emailaddress)-1 FROM members
             WHERE emailaddress = (
             SELECT TOP 1 emailaddress FROM members
             WHERE emailaddress NOT IN (SELECT emailaddress FROM
temp_members)ORDER BY emailaddress))
FROM membersWHERE emailaddress = (
SELECT TOP 1 emailaddress from membersWHERE emailaddress NOT IN (
SELECT emailaddress FROM temp_members)
ORDER BY emailaddress)

--/* Insert email address to temp table once operated upon*/
INSERT INTO temp_members (emailaddress)
SELECT emailaddress FROM members
WHERE emailaddress = (
SELECT TOP 1 emailaddress FROM membersWHERE emailaddress NOT IN (
SELECT emailaddress FROM temp_members)
ORDER BY emailaddress)
```

This two-part query deletes all but one record from the group of "same e-mail address records" in the first part and inserts the remaining distinct e-mail address record to the temp_members temporary table for lookup purposes in a single iteration of the For Loop container.

Close the Execute SQL Task Editor by clicking the OK button.

Exercise (Deleting Temporary Table from the Database)

22. Drag and drop the Execute SQL task from the Toolbox on to the Control Flow Panel below the For Loop Container. Connect the green arrow from the Looping For Email addresses container to the new Execute SQL task. Type the following in the General page of Execute SQL Task Editor window:

Name	Cleanup Task
Description	This task deletes the temporary table created earlier to hold email addresses.

23. Leave all the fields at the default settings, apart from Connection field in which select (local).Campaign connection manager—and the SQLStatement field, in which type in the following command:

```
DROP TABLE temp_members
```

Click OK.

You have completed configurations for this Hands-On exercise. Your final package should look like the one shown in Figure 4-9.

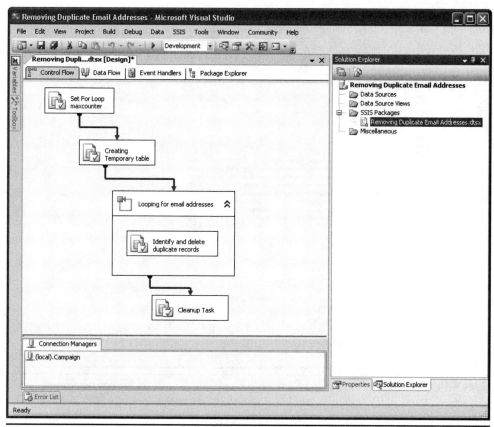

Figure 4-9 *Layout of Removing Duplicate Email Addresses package*

24. You are now ready to Start Debugging from the Debug menu or by pressing F5. You will see the tasks turn from yellow to green and particularly the Identify And Delete Duplicate Records Execute SQL task inside the For Loop Container task turning yellow and green in turn, demonstrating that this task is running many times—to be precise, it runs nine times, because only nine distinct e-mail address records exist. Once the package completes execution, stop debugging the package by pressing SHIFT-F5 and click the Execution Results tab to see how the package execution progressed (Figure 4-10).

Look in the middle of the window to watch for the Looping For Email Addresses section, which lists the For Loop Container execution results. Notice the *Start (9),* then nine lines specifying the query task 100 percent complete, and then *Stop (9).* This signifies that the "Identify and Delete Duplicate Records" task has been run nine times successfully and the tenth time, the For Loop Container evaluation expression evaluated to False, causing the process to exit from the For Loop Container iterations.

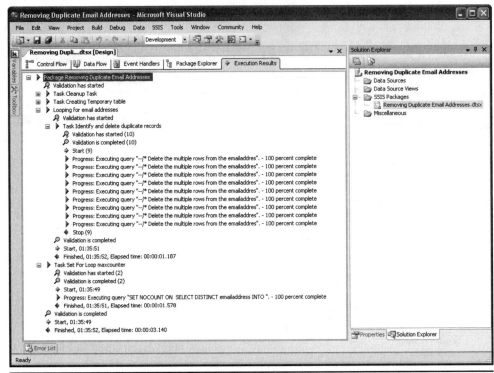

Figure 4-10 *Execution results of the Removing Duplicate Email Addresses package*

25. Press CTRL-SHIFT-S to save all the objects in the package. Close the Project and exit from BIDS. Switch to SQL Server Management Studio and run the following query to verify that now there are only 9 records with distinct e-mail addresses in the members table.

```
SELECT * FROM [Campaign].[dbo].[members]
```

Review

In this hands-on exercise, you learned how to use and configure the For Loop container. You have used the For Loop Container to replace the cursors from the data flow applications. Whichever way you use the For Loop container, the bottom line is that it allows you to add iterations to your packages whenever you need to use them.

Note that in this package, we used the For Loop container to remove duplicates. Though this is not an ideal method for removing duplicates, the above exercise has its value in terms of demonstrating how you can use For Loop containers to perform iterations on tasks. There are better methods to remove duplicates from the data that we will study in Chapter 10. If you want to run this exercise for a second time, you will have to bring members table to the original state which you can do by using members_original table that contains an initial copy of members table.

Sequence Container

The Sequence Container helps organize a complex package with several tasks by allowing the logical tasks to be grouped together. You can organize clusters of tasks with Sequence containers and hence divide the package into smaller containers, rather than dealing with one huge container (Package Container) with lots of tasks. So, a Sequence container is a subset of the package control flow containing tasks and containers within it.

While developing your Integration Services project, you can add this container from the Toolbox into Control Flow of your package. When you double-click the task, you won't see any user interface popping up where you can configure this task; rather, the context is changed to the Properties window. The Sequence Container has no custom user interface and can be configured using its Properties window; thus it behaves like a Package Container. You can build your control flow within the Sequence container by dragging and dropping the tasks and containers within it.

Following are some of the uses for which Sequence Containers can be helpful:

▶ Organizing a package by logically grouping tasks (tasks focusing on one functional area of business) makes the package easy to work with. You may choose to run one subset only from the package depending upon the need.

▶ Setting properties on a Sequence Container may apply those settings to multiple tasks within the container; this allows you to configure properties at one place instead of via individual tasks, making management easier.

▶ Such grouping of tasks makes it easy to debug the package. You can disable a Sequence Container to switch off functionality for some business area and focus on debugging the other areas.

▶ You can use the Sequence Container if you want to isolate the variables within a scope consisting of a group of tasks.

Task Host Container

You have worked with the package, the Foreach Loop Container, the For Loop Container, and the Sequence Container in BIDS by using their Editors or Properties windows. The Task Host Container is not available in BIDS so you can't configure it directly and drop tasks in it. Task Host Container empowers a task to use features of a container such as use of Event Handlers.

The benefits of having a container design in SSIS include the following:

▶ The variables can be shared among the tasks and child containers of a container.

▶ The parent container can handle the events happening within a child container.

To empower the individual tasks to use these features, Task Host containers have been created. The Task Host container encapsulates each task when the task is embedded in a workflow on the designer surface. All the tasks in a SSIS package are encapsulated within the Task Host containers. This container is configured when you configure the properties of the task it encapsulates.

Summary

The workflow in Integration Services consists of containers. Two containers, For Loop and Foreach Loop, provide the repeating logic, which was available to procedural languages previously. With the advent of SSIS, you have at your disposal the For Loop Container to perform repeating logic to the tasks contained within it, the Foreach Loop Container to perform the repeating logic for each item in a collection, and the Sequence Container to group tasks and containers, allowing you to have multiple control flows by having multiple Sequence Containers under one package.

In the beginning of the chapter, when you learned about the Package Container, you read that within the Integration Services architecture design, a package sits at the top of the container hierarchy. Yet Integration Services provides a facility to embed a package in another (parent) package by wrapping the (child) package in a wrapper task called Execute Package Task. You will study this task and do a Hands-On exercise for Execute Package task in the next chapter. Finally, you also learned that each task is treated like a container in Integration Services as a Task Host container encapsulates the task. This allows tasks to inherit the benefits of containers.

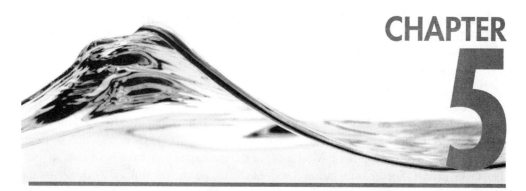

CHAPTER 5

Integration Services Control Flow Tasks

In Chapter 4, you studied control flow containers and learned how to use them in building workflow in your packages. In this chapter, you will learn more about the control flow tasks that can form a complex workflow to perform a sensible piece of work.

The chapter is divided into two main parts: the first covers tasks that play a direct role in building up workflow for your packages, and the second covers tasks that are designed to perform SQL Server maintenance, though they can also be used in the workflow. You may have already used some of these control flow tasks, such as the Execute SQL task and the Send Mail task, in the packages you have built so far. The tasks in SQL Server Integration Services (SSIS) define the unit of work necessary to create the control flow in a package. This unit of work can comprise downloading files, moving files, creating folders, running other processes and packages, sending notification mails, and the like. You will be using some of these tasks to build a couple of control flow scenarios to demonstrate how these components can be used together. SSIS provides a facility you can use to create your own custom tasks if the existing control flow tasks don't fit the bill. Integration Services supports the Microsoft .NET Framework, so you can use any .NET-compliant programming language, such as Visual Basic .NET or C#, to write custom tasks. You will also work through Hands-On exercises to work with some of the tasks.

In the later part of this chapter, you will read about Maintenance Plan tasks that can be used to perform database maintenance functions for SQL Server 2000 and SQL Server 2005 databases. Though these tasks do not directly contribute to building workflow for a package, they can be included in the control flow if required to perform maintenance of SQL Server databases or objects.

Let's wade through the Integration Services tasks first before swimming into deeper waters.

Categories of Control Flow Tasks

Though the Toolbox in BI Development Studio (BIDS) shows Control Flow Tasks in two main groups, the Control Flow tasks can be categorized on the basis of the functionality they provide. Read through the following introductions quickly to understand how these tasks are categorized and organized in the control flow. You can reread this section whenever you need a quick description of a task.

Data Flow Task

This main task performs ETL (extracting, transforming, and loading) operations using the data flow engine.

Control Flow Task	Description
Data Flow Task	Perform the ETL functions—i.e., extract data from a source, apply transformations to the extracted data, and load this data to a destination. In BIDS, this task has its own designer panel and consists mainly of source adapters, transformations, and destination adapters. This task is covered in Chapters 9 and 10.

Data Preparation Tasks

These tasks help in managing and applying operations on files and folders.

Control Flow Task	Description
File System Task	Perform operations on files and folders in the file system—i.e., you can create, move, delete, or set attributes on directories and files. You will be using this task in a Hands-On exercise later in this chapter.
FTP Task	Download and upload files and manage directories—for example, you can download data files from your customer's remote server using this task apply transformations on the data in these files using Data Flow task and then upload the transformed data file to a different folder on the customer's FTP server again using FTP Task.
Web Service Task	Read data from a Web Service method and write that data to a variable or a file—for example, you can get a list of postal codes from the local postal company using this task and use this data to cleanse or standardize your data at loading time. This task is not covered in the Hands-On exercises.
XML Task	Dynamically apply operations to XML documents using XSLT (extensible style sheet language transformation) style sheets and XPath expressions and can merge, validate, and save the updated documents to files and variables—i.e., you can get XML documents from many sources, merge these XML documents to consolidate the data, and reformat for presentation in the report form.

Workflow Tasks

Workflow tasks communicate with other processes to execute packages, run programs or batch files, send and receive messages between packages, send e-mail messages, read Windows Management Instrumentation (WMI) data, and watch for WMI events.

Control Flow Task	Description
Execute Package Task	Run child packages—i.e., develop modules of workflow and reuse them or break down the complex package into separate units of work and run them together.
Execute DTS 2000 Package Task	Run packages that were developed using the Data Transformation Services of SQL Server 2000 and include legacy packages in your Integration Services package.

Control Flow Task	Description
Execute Process Task	Run a business application or a batch file to perform specific functions that can't be done easily in SSIS, whose output can then be included in the SSIS package workflow.
Message Queue Task	Queue your messages if the destination is unavailable or busy and deliver such messages later. This task uses Microsoft Message Queuing (MSMQ) to send and receive messages.
Send Mail Task	Send messages from your packages on the basis of success or failure of the package or on the basis of an event raised during execution of the package.
WMI Data Reader Task	Run WQL (WMI Query Language) queries to get information from WMI about a computer system, enabling your package to decide what to do with the other tasks in the package.
WMI Event Watcher Task	Watch for WMI events by running WQL queries to specify the events of interest.

SQL Server Tasks

These tasks help in accessing and performing functions such as Copy, Insert, Delete, and Modify on SQL Server objects and data.

Control Flow Task	Description
Bulk Insert Task	Copy large amounts of data into SQL Server. This is the fastest method for importing data into SQL Server if you don't have to perform transformations while importing. You will use this task in a Hands-On exercise later in the chapter.
Execute SQL Task	Run SQL statements or stored procedures to perform operations such as create, alter, truncate, or drop tables; save a result set of a query or stored procedure into a variable; and so on. You have already used this task in earlier Hands-On exercises.

Scripting Tasks

These tasks help in extending the package functionality by allowing you to write your own code.

Control Flow Task	Description
ActiveX Script Task	Run existing DTS 2000 ActiveX code in SSIS packages. This task has been marked deprecated in SQL Server 2005 Integration Services; upgrade your scripts to use more advanced features provided by the Script task. This task is not covered in this book.
Script Task	Write code to perform functions that otherwise cannot be performed using built-in tasks and transformations. Uses Visual Studio for Applications Environment as its engine, for writing and running scripts with Microsoft Visual Basic 2005.

Analysis Services Tasks

These tasks allow you to work with Analysis Services objects. The Analysis Services tasks are out of scope of this book and won't be covered here. Brief functional descriptions of these tasks are provided. For more details on these tasks, refer to Microsoft SQL Server 2005 Books Online.

Control Flow Task	Description
Analysis Services Processing Task	Process Analysis Services objects such as cubes, dimensions, and mining models. This task does not work with SQL Server 2000 Analysis services and works only with analytic objects created by using the SQL Server 2005 tools.
Analysis Services Execute DDL Task	Create, alter, or drop multidimensional objects (such as cubes and dimensions) or mining models. You create data definition language (DDL) statements in Analysis Services Scripting Language (ASSL) framed in an XML for Analysis Services (XMLA) command.
Data Mining Query Task	Run prediction queries in Analysis Services using defined data mining models. The prediction query is created using Data Mining Extensions (DMX) language, which provides support for using mining models.

Transfer Tasks

SQL Server Integration Services enables you to transfer databases, error messages, SQL Server Agent jobs, transfer logins, database objects, and master stored procedures using the built-in transfer tasks.

Control Flow Task	Description
Transfer Database Task	Transfer databases from one instance to another instance of SQL Server. You can transfer database in an offline (Detach/Attach method) or online mode.
Transfer Error Messages Task	Transfer SQL Server error messages from a source SQL Server to a destination SQL Server.
Transfer Jobs Task	Copy SQL Server Agent jobs from one instance of SQL Server to the other instance.
Transfer Logins Task	Transfer logins from a source SQL Server to a destination SQL Server. You can choose to transfer all logins on the server, transfer all logins for the selected database, or transfer just the selected logins.
Transfer Objects Task	Copy database objects between databases on a source SQL Server and a destination SQL Server. You can choose to transfer indexes, primary keys, secondary keys, triggers, users, logins and roles, and so on.
Transfer Stored Procedures Task	Transfer the stored procedures saved to the master database in a source SQL Server to a destination SQL Server.

Maintenance Tasks

SSIS has built in tasks for administrative functions for databases, such as backing up and shrinking SQL Server databases, rebuilding and reorganizing indexes, and running SQL Server Agent jobs. Though these tasks are intended for maintaining SQL Server 2000 and SQL Server 2005 databases, they can also be used within SSIS packages.

Control Flow Task	Description
Back Up Database Task	You can perform different types of backups on one or more databases with this task.
Check Database Integrity Task	Check the allocation and structural integrity of all the database objects or indexes in the specified database. This task runs the DBCC CHECKDB statement.
Execute SQL Server Agent Job Task	Runs the jobs already created within the SQL Server Agent. Allows you to reuse the jobs already created in SQL Server Agent and provides a facility to perform administration from within a SSIS package.
Execute T-SQL Statement Task	Run T-SQL statements from within a SSIS package. This task is similar to the Execute SQL Task, except this task supports only Transact-SQL version of SQL.
History Cleanup Task	Deletes historical data for the specified time period from msdb tables related to backup and restore activities, SQL Server Agent jobs, and database maintenance plans.
Maintenance Cleanup Task	Deletes backup files or maintenance plan text reports based on the specified time period.
Notify Operator Task	Sends the notifications messages to SQL Server Agent operators via e-mail, pager, or Net Send communication channels.
Rebuild Index Task	Rebuilds indexes in SQL Server database tables and views.
Reorganize Index Task	Reorganize indexes in SQL Server database tables and views with this task.
Shrink Database Task	Reduce the size of SQL Server database data file and log file with Shrink Database Task. This task runs a DBCC SHRINKDATABASE command.
Update Statistics Task	Update information about the distribution of key values for one or more statistics groups in the specified table or indexed view with this task.

Custom Tasks

The object model of Integration Services provides facilities you can use to extend and program any component or complete package by writing custom code. Whether you want to extend the functionality of a component that will be used only in a package or you want to reuse the developed functionality in various packages throughout your enterprise, you will use different techniques to extend and program Integration Services. The Script task provided in the control flow, and the script component provided in the data flow environments, allow you to create and program any functionality that is not available in the preconfigured tasks and components of Integration Services. However, these components are difficult to reuse in multiple packages and support only Visual Basic .NET programming language. Alternatively, you can create your own custom tasks using any .NET-compliant programming language such as Visual Basic or C#.

After writing code for the custom task, you can create and register a user interface for the task in the SSIS Designer and reuse the developed and registered custom task or component in your packages as you would use any other built-in component. The development of custom tasks is outside the scope of this book—refer to Microsoft SQL Server 2005 Books Online for more details on how to write code for building custom tasks.

Control Flow Tasks in Detail

In the previous section, you've read brief description of each task, you'll work through Hands-On exercise or read about the options available through the task's GUI now. While working through the details of each task and Hands-On exercise, you will not follow the categorization flow. This is done intentionally to make it easier to learn and work with the tasks for business scenarios, followed by intuitive and step by step methods.

Your first project will require that you download, expand, and archive these zipped files, and then import them to a SQL Server table. This is a simple but generic scenario we all encounter in our day-to-day job functions. The solution to the scenario will be explained in all the Hands-On exercises.

So, let's start our journey with the FTP task, which will help us in downloading files from a remote FTP server.

FTP Task

Running an FTP task makes your computer an FTP client and allows you to connect to an FTP server for transferring files. When you drag and drop this task on the Control Flow Designer surface and double-click to open the FTP Task Editor, you can configure the task to perform any of the following tasks by choosing from options in the Operation field in the File Transfer page:

▶ **Send Files**   Transfers a file from the local computer to the remote FTP server.

▶ **Receive Files**   Gets a file from the remote FTP server.

▶ **Create Local Directory**   Creates a folder on the local computer.

▶ **Create Remote Directory**   Creates a folder on the FTP server.

▶ **Remove Local Directory**   Deletes the specified folder on the local computer.

▶ **Remove Remote Directory**   Deletes the specified folder on the FTP server.

▶ **Delete Local Files**   Deletes the specified file on the local computer.

▶ **Delete Remote Files**   Deletes the specified file on the FTP server.

It is easy to configure the FTP task as long as you understand how it works. During configuration of the FTP task, you may have to define the RemotePath, LocalPath, and the path variable property for both the local and the remote computers. However, the options available to you change depending upon the operation type you choose in the Operation field.

The FTP Task Editor connects to the FTP server using the FTP Connection Manager Editor. FTP Connection Manager is defined in the Connection Managers area on the Control Flow Panel in BIDS. In FTP Connection Manager Editor, you specify the server name/IP address, server port number, the credentials for accessing the FTP server, and options such as number of retries, time out, and so on. The FTP Task uses the path directly specified in the RemotePath or specified by a variable through the FTP Connection Manager and is then able to access multiple files on the FTP server. However, on the local computer, the FTP Task can access only one file if using File Connection Manager because the File Connection Manager can access only one file at a time. To access multiple files on the local computer to send or delete, you need to use a variable, by setting the IsLocalPathVariable property to True and specifying the LocalPath using a variable (see Figure 5-2). If you are using a variable, you can use wildcard characters such as * or ? for specifying multiple files. If you want to send multiple files to an FTP server or want to delete multiple files on the local computer, you must use a variable to specify the LocalPath or alternatively place the FTP Task inside the Foreach Loop Container to enumerate across multiple files.

In a real-life scenario, you will be developing packages in which the FTP task will be downloading files, and then those files will be processed by the following tasks in the same package or by a different package. At times, your FTP task will fail to download files because of their unavailability or connection problems and so on. In such scenarios, you may want not to process the subsequent tasks. For example, in scenarios for which your FTP task overwrites the exiting files with the new files downloaded daily, on the days when FTP task doesn't download files, the old files may get reprocessed, creating duplicates in data. In those scenarios when you definitely don't want to process the subsequent tasks, you can set the StopOnFailure option to True (on the General page of the task) so that the FTP task terminates when the FTP operation fails.

Let's do a Hands-On exercise with the FTP task to help you understand the various options. In this exercise, you will download files from an FTP server. But before you start, make sure you've completed the following steps to prepare yourself for the exercise.

Preparations for the Hands-On exercises in this chapter:

1. Download the software and the files from the McGraw-Hill web site and copy them to C: drive as explained in the appendix "How to Use the Provided Software."

2. By now, you should have attached the provided Campaign database to your SQL Server 2005 database server; if you have not attached it, do that now so that you can complete the exercises. Attaching the Campaign database to your SQL Server 2005 has been explained in the appendix "How to Use the Provided Software."

3. Install an FTP service on a second PC for this exercise, or have access to an FTP server. After that, create a folder called *Sales* on the FTP server root folder and copy the DealerSales01.zip and DealerSales02.zip files from the local C:\SSIS\RawFiles folder to the *Sales* folder on the FTP server.

Hands-On: Downloading Zipped Files

Dealers of Adventure Works Bikes submit their sales reports in zipped form to an FTP server, and these files need to be downloaded from the server for processing before being imported into the SQL Server database. You have been tasked with creating a project that downloads these zipped files.

Method

In this exercise, you will use the FTP task to download two files from the remote folder Sales on the FTP server. These files will be downloaded to the C:\SSIS\ downloads folder on your local computer.

Couple of points to note: Firstly, if you want to use the Downloading Zipped Files package that has been provided with this book, you will receive an error when opening the package. When you click OK on the pop-up error message, the package will load properly but without the connection string in the FTP task. This is because, by default, the sensitive information (passwords, connection strings, and so on) in the packages get encrypted using the User key, and when another user tries to open the package, an error will occur and sensitive information will be removed from the package. However, if you open the Downloading Zipped Files package after you've completed the work in this Hands-On, you will not get any such error.

Secondly, this package requires a connection to an FTP server. Many FTP sites are available from which you can download a file with this task—such as FTP sites for anti-virus updates—and build the package for this exercise in case you don't have access to a test FTP server.

Exercise (Configure FTP Task)

1. Start BI Development Studio from the Start menu.

2. In the BIDS, choose File | New | Project to open a New Project window. In this window, make sure Business Intelligence Projects is selected under Project Types, and then choose Integration Services Project from the Templates pane. Type in the following additional details and click OK to create a new project.

Name	Control Flow Tasks
Location	C:\SSIS\Projects

3. When the blank project is created, go to Solution Explorer in the BIDS and right-click the Package.dtsx package under the SSIS Packages folder; choose Rename from the context menu. Type **Downloading zipped files.dtsx** to rename the package and click the Yes button in the Visual Studio confirmation box.

4. Drag the FTP Task from the Toolbox on to the SSIS Designer. Double-click the FTP task icon to open the FTP Task Editor. On the General page, specify the following details:

Name	Download Files
Description	This task downloads sales reports files from the FTP Server.

Click in the FtpConnection field to show the down arrow button. Click the down arrow and choose <New Connection…> from the drop-down list. This will open the FTP Connection Manager Editor. In the Server Settings area, type the name of your FTP server (AIT, in my case) in the Server Name field and **21** in the Server Port field as shown in Figure 5-1. AIT is the name of the server used in the lab setup for creating the projects used in this book.

In the Credentials area, type in the user name and password to connect to the FTP server to download files. Leave other fields set to the default settings. Click the Test Connection button to test the connectivity to the FTP server. If the test reveals a successful connection, click OK twice to close the message window and the FTP Connection Manager Editor.

For more details on the FTP Connection Manager, refer to the discussion in Chapter 3.

5. In the StopOnFailure field, choose True. This will fail the package if the FTP Task can't download the files. Click on the File Transfer page from the left pane in the FTP Task Editor.

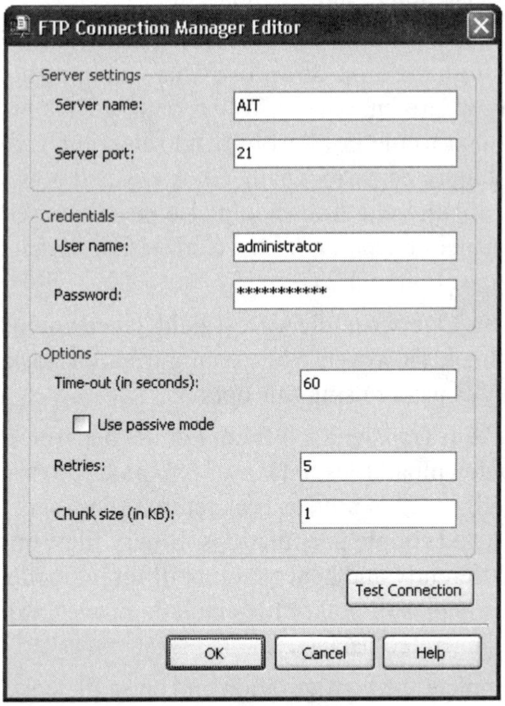

Figure 5-1 *Configuring the FTP Connection Manager*

6. Choose the operation you want to perform; this changes the available set of options. Click in the Operation field, and then click the arrow and choose Receive Files.

7. In the Remote Parameters section, leave the IsRemotePathVariable field set to False, as our remote destination is not dynamic.

8. Click in the RemotePath field and you will see an ellipsis (…) button on the far right corner of the field. Click this ellipsis button to open Browse For File window. This window shows the directory of the remote FTP server. Choose the path where you copied the files earlier while preparing for this exercise; or, if you have copied the files to the Sales folder on the Ftp server, choose the /Sales folder and then choose the DealerSales01.zip file and press the OK button. You will see /Sales/ DealerSales01.zip listed in the RemotePath field. You want to select both files listed in the folder, but you can't do that using this GUI. The FTP task does allow use of wildcard characters such as * and ? to specify file names. So change the above path in the RemotePath field by typing **/Sales/ *.zip** in the field.

9. In the Local Parameters section, leave the IsLocalPathVariable set to False, as our local path is also not variable in this exercise.

10. Click in the LocalPath field, click the down arrow, and choose <New Connection…> from the drop-down list. This will open the File Connection Manager Editor, where an existing folder path will be provided. Click the Browse button next to the Folder field and select the C:\SSIS\downloads folder by browsing to the correct path. Click OK and you will see *downloads* listed in the LocalPath field. You should also be able to see a *downloads* File Connection Manager created under the Connection Managers area on the Designer panel (see Figure 5-2).

11. Select True for the OverwriteFileAtDest field, since you will be running this package many times. However, while configuring this task for your production servers, carefully consider using this option.

12. Select True for the IsTransferAscii field. For the benefit of those who are new to using FTP to download files, FTP uses two modes to transfer files—ASCII and Binary. ASCII mode is used to transfer text files—i.e., files that contain letters, numbers, and simple punctuations. Binary files, on the other hand, are structured differently and hence require different mode of transfer—i.e., Binary mode. Examples of binary files include images, executable files, and algorithmically generated packages.

13. Click OK to complete the configuration and close the editor. Press F5 to run the package and you will see that the task turns yellow for a while; once the file

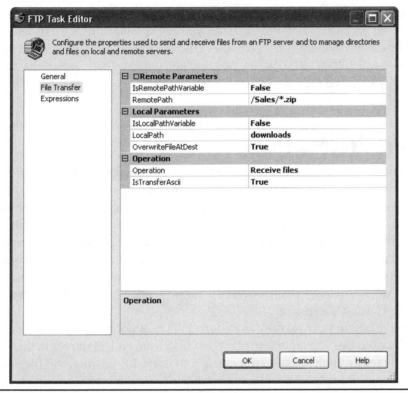

Figure 5-2   *Configuring the FTP task in the Task Editor*

downloading is completed, it will turn green. (If your network firewall or local computer firewall, such as Windows XP Firewall, is blocking the outbound connection to the FTP site, you may have to allow this connection by changing your firewall settings. See your network administrator for help on changing firewall settings.)

14. Navigate to the C:\SSIS\downloads folder and you'll notice that the two zip files have been downloaded to that folder.

15. Press CTRL-SHIFT-S to save all the files in this solution and then choose File | Close Project.

Review

In this Hands-On exercise, you learned to use the FTP task to download multiple files from a remote FTP server. You have hard-coded file paths for the RemotePath and LocalPath fields in this exercise. However, you can use variables to change these folders dynamically during run-time and download or upload files to different folders each time the package is run. For example, you can download files to the folders derived on the basis of date—i.e., the folder name includes the date as a part of the name (such as Zip20051207). When the package is run, the path variable is calculated dynamically based on the current date and loads the files to the current date folder.

Execute Process Task

Using the Execute Process task, you can run a business application or a batch file to perform specific business functions that can't be developed easily in SSIS; the good thing about this is that the output from running the business application or batch file can then be included in the SSIS package workflow. You could unzip files, call custom programs to break a huge file into smaller files that can be easily handled for transformation operations, run a custom report generation application from within SSIS, and then use a Send Mail task to distribute those reports. To keep it simple, we will use this task to unzip the files you have downloaded from the FTP server in the preceding Hands-On exercise.

You have begun your journey to understand the SSIS workflow. In the last Hands-On exercise, you downloaded zipped files from an FTP server in the C:\SSIS\ downloads folder. In the next exercise, you will unzip the downloaded files using the Execute Process task, which will run a batch file to do the trick.

Hands-On: Expanding Downloaded Files

Adventure Works Bikes dealers' reports need to be downloaded and extracted so that they can be imported into the SQL Server database. You have already downloaded these files; here you will extract flat files from the downloaded files.

Method

You have downloaded zipped files DealerSales01.zip and DealerSales02.zip in the C:\SSIS\downloads folder but can't use these files as SSIS can't read zipped files. You need to extract flat files from the zipped files to be able to import them into SQL Server using SSIS. You will run a batch file to extract the flat files from the zipped files and will deploy an Execute Process task to run this batch file at run-time. Because you want to unzip more than one file, you will enumerate the files you want to unzip; an enumeration function will be provided by a Foreach Loop container. In the last chapter, you used a Foreach Loop container with Foreach ADO enumerator to enumerate over rows; now you will be using Foreach File enumerator to enumerate over files in the following steps:

- ► Create a batch file to expand the downloaded zip file.

- ► Use a Foreach Loop container to enumerate over multiple zip files.

- ► Add an Execute Process task to call a batch file from within the SSIS package to extract flat files.

Exercise (Creating Batch File)

The downloaded files have been compressed using a Freezip freeware that has been included in the distribution software provided for this book. Go to C:\SSIS\Freeware\ Freezip to find the software files there. However, if you use some other software utility to compress files, you can use a command line interface of that utility to unzip files in the same manner as shown in this exercise.

Open a blank text file using Notepad and type the following commands:

```
DEL C:\SSIS\downloads\%1.txt
C:\SSIS\Freeware\Freezip\UNZIP %1.zip %1.txt
```

The first line deletes the previously present text file, and the second line extracts a text file from the zip file specified as an argument in the command. Save the file as C:\SSIS\RawFiles\ExtractFiles.bat. Make sure that the file has been saved with .bat extension and not with .txt extension. This file should already be available in the RawFiles folder as it has been included in the distribution software provided for this book.

Exercise (Enumerating Multiple Zipped Files)

You will add and configure a Foreach Loop container to enumerate over zip files in the downloads folder and populate the *fname* variable with the file name.

1. Start BIDS and open the Control Flow Tasks project. Go to Solution Explorer and right-click the SSIS Packages folder in the Control Flow Tasks project and choose New SSIS Package from the context menu. This will add a new package called Package1.dtsx in the project.

2. Right-click Package1.dtsx and rename it as **Expanding downloaded files.dtsx**. You will work in this package to configure the following workflow.

3. Drop a Foreach Loop container from the Toolbox onto the designer surface and open the editor by double-clicking it. Type the following in the General page:

Name	Enumerating Zip Files
Description	This task enumerates zip files in the 'C:\SSIS\downloads' folder.

4. Go to Collection page and make sure Foreach File Enumerator is selected in the Enumerator field.

5. In the Enumerator configuration area, specify C:\SSIS\downloads in the Folder field either by typing in directly or by using the Browse button to select the folder. In the Files field, type ***.zip** to specify the types of files you want the Foreach Loop container to enumerate on. Use the Files field to limit or select precisely the files you want to access in a folder containing different types of files.

6. The most interesting bit in this page is the Retrieve File Name section. This is where you will choose how the file name should be retrieved from three options. Before you jump into selecting one of the options, you must understand what these options are and how they work. The file name is treated in SSIS as consisting of three parts: the path pointing to the location where the file might be stored, the name portion of the file, and the extension of the file indicating its type.

Fully Qualified	This option will return the path, the file name, and the extension all as a single string. The path portion of the file name can be a full folder path in a universal naming convention (UNC) or absolute form. For example, the fully qualified name retrieved can be \\ComputerName\Sales\DealerSales01.zip or it can be in the form C:\SSIS\downloads\DealerSales01.zip.
Name And Extension	Choosing this option returns the name portion of the file name along with its extension—for example, DealerSales01.zip.
Name Only	Choosing this option will return only the name portion of the file name—for example, DealerSales01.

Select Name Only, as you will need only the name of the file to be passed as an argument to the batch file.

7. Go to Variable Mappings page, click in the Variable field, and select <New Variable...> to create a new variable. Name the variable **fname** in the Expanding Download Files Container with **string** type value and return to the Foreach Loop Editor. Note that the Index field has automatically been allocated a value of *0* for this variable. Make sure that you type variable name in lowercase—*fname*—as the variables are case sensitive. Click OK to complete the Foreach Loop container's configuration.

Exercise (Calling Batch File Using Execute Process Task)

Now you will add Execute Process task inside the Foreach Loop container. This task will use the *fname* variable populated by Foreach Loop container to pass as an argument to the ExtractFiles.bat file.

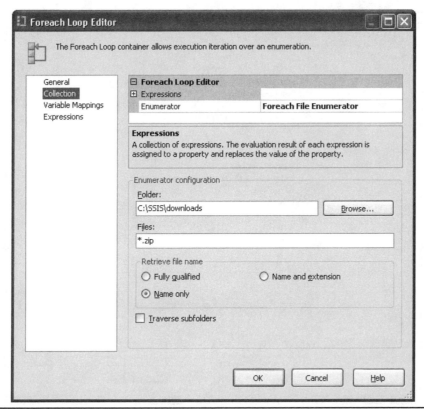

Figure 5-3   *Configuring the Foreach Loop container with Foreach file enumerator*

8. Drag and drop the Execute Process Task from the Toolbox within the Foreach Loop Container and double-click it to open the Execute Process Task Editor. Type the following in the General page of the task editor:

Name	Call ExtractFiles batch file
Description	This task extracts DealerSales flat files.

9. Go to Process page to configure options for this task. In the RequireFullFileName field, leave the default True selected. This means that the task will fail if it cannot find the batch file at specified location.

10. In the Executable field, specify C:\SSIS\RawFiles\ExtractFiles.bat to point the task to the batch file.

11. You need to specify the file name as an argument to the batch file. The file name argument has been populated in the *fname* variable in the earlier part of

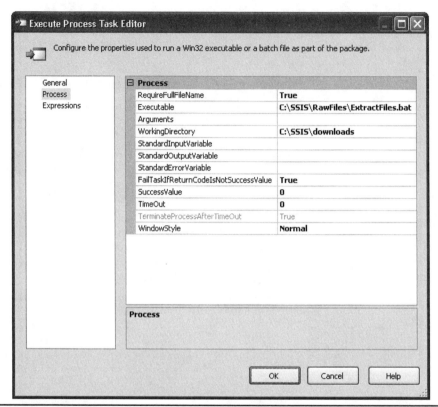

Figure 5-4   *Configurations of Execute Process task*

this exercise. However, Arguments field doesn't let you use a variable, so you will be using Property Expressions in the step 15 to attach fname variable to Arguments field. Leave Arguments field blank and in the WorkingDirectory field, specify C:\SSIS\downloads, as shown in Figure 5-4.

12. In the next three fields, you can specify variables to provide the input to the process or capture output or error output from the process. Leave them blank for this exercise.

13. Using the FailTaskIfReturnCodeIsNotSuccessValue field, you can configure the task to fail if the process exit code does not match the value you provide in the SuccessValue field.

14. Note that you can specify a time-out value in seconds and choose to terminate the task after time-out period. Finally, if it is important, you can choose the window style in which the task starts a process. Leave these fields set at their default values and move on to the Expressions page.

15. In this step, you will pass *fname* variable values to Arguments field using Property Expressions at run-time. Property Expressions are explained in detail in Chapter 8. Click the ellipsis button in the Expressions field to open Property Expressions Editor. Click in the Property field and select Arguments from the drop-down list. Click the ellipsis button in the Expression field to open Expression Builder. Expand Variables in the left pane of the window and locate the *User::fname* variable in the list. Drag this variable and drop it in the Expression box. Click the OK button three times to close the task editor.

16. Press F5 to start debugging the task. You should see the tasks turning quickly from yellow to green (see Figure 5-5).

17. Press CTRL-SHIFT-S to save all the files in this project and then choose File | Close Project.

18. Go to downloads folder and see that DealerSales01.txt and DealerSales02.txt files have been extracted.

Review

You have learned how to use Execute Process task to expand the zipped files in this Hands-On exercise. Now you know that SSIS not only provides an option to

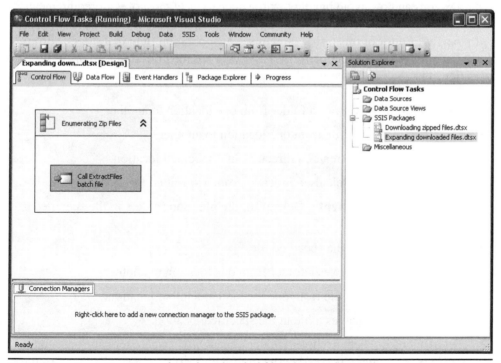

Figure 5-5 *Executing Expanding downloaded files.dtsx package*

run the custom-built applications that you need to use for day-to-day functions but also allows you to use the results of running such an application by way of StandardOutputVariable.

Execute DTS 2000 Package Task

Using this task, you can run a package that was developed using the Data Transformation Services of SQL Server 2000 and include them in your package. The task is covered in detail in Chapter 12.

File System Task

You will be using this task in your packages to perform operations on files. The File System task allows you to perform operations on the files and directories in the file system and is easy to use. If you have used DTS 2000, you might have written ActiveX code to rename, copy, or move files or folders. Though you may still have to write code to perform some of the functions using the Script Task if the requirements are complex, you can now avoid having to write code to meet most of your requirements for performing operations on files and folders by using the File System task.

In the Task Editor of this task, you will see an Operation field that offers a drop-down list of operations it can perform. Following are the brief descriptions of the operations that the File System task can perform:

► **Copy directory**   Copies a folder from one location to another.

► **Copy file**   Copies a file from one location to another.

► **Create directory**   Creates a directory in a specified location.

► **Delete directory**   Deletes a directory from a specified location.

► **Delete directory content**   Deletes all the files and folders in the specified directory.

► **Delete file**   Deletes the specified file.

► **Move directory**   Moves a folder from one location to another.

► **Move file**   Moves a file from one location to another location.

► **Rename file**   Renames a file in the specified location.

► **Set attributes**   Sets Archive, Hidden, ReadOnly, and System attributes on the files and folders. If you do not specify any attribute in your selections, the Normal attribute will be applied, which is exclusive to all the other attributes.

The File System Task has a dynamic layout in which the available fields change depending on the operation you choose. For example, the Delete Directory, Delete Directory Content, and Delete File Operations do not use a destination and hence the DestinationConnection field doesn't appear when you choose any of these operations. The SourceConnection, however, is used by all the options. The SourceConnection and the DestinationConnection can be specified by using a File Connection Manager to refer to a file or a folder or by providing a variable that contains the connection strings.

A Hands-On exercise for this task will help you understand the configuration options. Before you start, let's review what you need to do. You have downloaded and unzipped the dealer sales files and have compressed files as well as text files in the C:\SSIS\downloads folder. Your next problem is to archive the zipped files for historical purposes. In the following exercise, you will again use the Foreach Loop container to enumerate over files. Because you will be working with files, you will be using Foreach File Enumerator. As you know, the Foreach File Enumerator enumerates files specified in a folder.

Hands-On: Archiving Downloaded Files

The downloaded reports of dealers of Adventure Works Bikes are to be archived for historical purposes. You want to keep the downloaded zipped files in the Archive folder.

Method

In this exercise, you will use the Foreach Loop Container and the File System Task to copy these files one by one to the C:\SSIS\downloads\Archive folder. The step by step method is as follows:

▶ Configure the Foreach Loop Container to enumerate over files and house the File System Task in it. Your File System task will copy one file with each iteration to the Archive folder.

▶ Configure the File System task to copy files to the Archive folder one by one with each iteration of the Foreach Loop container.

Exercise (Configure Foreach Loop Container)

In first part of the exercise you will configure the Foreach Loop container to enumerate files using Foreach File enumerator and populate a variable with the file name. This variable will be used by File System task to determine the name of the file to be copied over.

1. Open the Control Flow Tasks project in BIDS. Go to Solution Explorer in BIDS and right-click the SSIS Packages folder in the Control Flow Tasks project and choose New SSIS Package from the context menu. This will add a new package Package1.dtsx in the project.

2. Right-click Package1.dtsx and rename it as **Archiving downloaded files.dtsx**. You will work in this package to configure the following workflow.

3. From the Toolbox, drag and drop the Foreach Loop Container onto the Control Flow panel.

4. Make sure that the Foreach Loop Container is selected; open the Variables window from the default position on the left side of the BIDS interface. Alternatively, click the Foreach Loop Container and choose View | Other Windows | Variables. Click the Add Variable button, the left-most button in the tool bar of the Variables window. Specify the following for this variable:

Name	fname
Scope	Foreach Loop Container
Data Type	String
Value	xyz

The value you've assigned is a placeholder that will be changed at run-time when the Foreach Loop container reads the file name and populates this variable during each iteration. This placeholder value is required for the validation phase. When you execute a package, Integration Services validates package components and variables before the start of package, and the package can fail if a variable is found to contain no value. Also, be careful with the case of the Name field, as SSIS variables are case-sensitive.

5. Right-click the Foreach Loop Container and choose Edit from the context menu to open the Foreach Loop Editor. In the General page of the container, type the following:

Name	Enumerating Files
Description	This container enumerates the files and populates the fname variable.

6. Go to the Collection page. Make sure it shows the Foreach File Enumerator in the Enumerator field and specify the options shown in Figure 5-6.

Enumerator	Foreach File Enumerator
Folder	C:\SSIS\downloads
Files	*.zip
Retrieve file name	Fully qualified

7. Move on to Variable Mappings page. You will map a variable to the file name retrieved by the Foreach Loop Container so that later on in the package you can get the file name by embedding the variable in your strings. Click in the highlighted area under the Variable column and then click the drop-down arrow that appears. From the drop-down list, select the variable *User::fname*, configured earlier in the exercise. A *0* will appear under the Index field. Index indicates the position of the string within the collection. As you will be accessing only one file name at a time, Index will be set to 0. Click OK to close the Foreach Loop Editor.

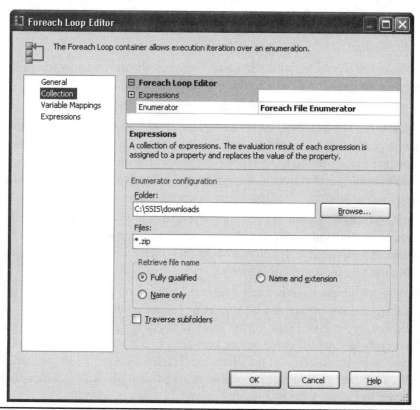

Figure 5-6   *Configuring the Foreach Loop container to enumerate fully qualified file names*

Exercise (Configure File System Task)

In this exercise, you will configure the File System task to move the downloaded zipped files from the C:\SSIS\downloads folder to the C:\SSIS\downloads\Archive folder. This task will move the files one by one with each iteration of the Foreach Loop container. It will use the variable *User::fname*, populated by Foreach Loop container, to determine the source file name.

8. Drag and drop the File System Task from the Toolbox within the Enumerating Files container.

9. Double-click the File System Task icon to open the File System Task Editor. In the Operation field in the General page of the editor, select Move File. In the General area on the right pane, fill in the following details:

Name	Archive downloaded files
Description	This task copies downloaded files from the 'downloads' folder to the 'Archive' folder.

10. In the Source Connection section, set IsSourcePathVariable to True.

11. Click in the SourceVariable field and then click the down arrow to see the drop-down list. Choose User::fname (see Figure 5-7).

12. In the Destination Connection section, set IsDestinationPathVariable to False.

13. Click in the DestinationConnection field and then click the down arrow to see the drop-down list. Choose the <New connection...> to open File Connection Manager Editor. In the Usage type field, select Existing Folder and type **C:\ SSIS\downloads\Archive** in the Folder field. The Browse button provided helps you to select an existing folder or create a new folder before selection.

14. The OverwriteDestination field allows you to overwrite the files with the same name at destination folder. Be mindful while configuring this option in the production environment. Leave it set at the default value of False. Click OK to close the File System Task Editor.

15. Now that your package is ready to be run, press F5 on the keyboard to run the package and notice how the Enumerating Files Container changes from yellow followed by Archive Downloaded Files Task changing from yellow to green. This cycle is repeated twice before both the objects stop processing and turn green to declare success of the operation. Each time Archive Downloaded Files Task changes color from yellow to green, one file has been moved. Stop debugging the package by pressing SHIFT-F5.

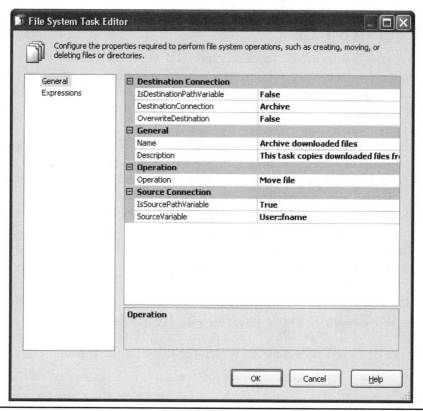

Figure 5-7   *Configuring the File System task for moving files*

16. Run Windows Explorer to check the C:\SSIS\downloads folder to see the files have disappeared, and then check the Archive subfolder in this directory to see that the files have been moved there.

17. Press CTRL-SHIFT-S to save all the files in this solution and then choose File | Close Project.

Review

You have configured the Foreach Loop container to enumerate over files in a folder and pass the file names via a variable to the File System task. The variable passed by the Foreach Loop container was used to set the source file name in the File System task, which was configured to move files from a dynamic source to the hard-coded destination Archive folder. In this exercise, you have seen the functionality provided by SSIS components to run in synchronization, where one component was reading the files one by one and passing the information to the other component that was moving those files to a different folder one by one.

Web Service Task

You can read data from a Web Service method and write that data to a variable or a file using the Web Service task. For example, you can obtain a list of postal codes from the local postal company, write it to a flat file using the Web Service task, and then do the lookup against this postal codes file to clean or standardize your data at loading time.

Similar to FTP task uses FTP Connection Manager to connect to the FTP server, Web Service task uses HTTP Connection Manager to connect to the web service. HTTP Connection Manager specifies the server URL, user credentials, optional client certificate details, time-out length, proxy settings, and so on.

Web Service Description Language (WSDL) is an XML-based language used for defining web services in a WSDL file, which lists the methods that the web service offers, the input parameters that the methods require, the responses that the methods return, and how to communicate with the web service. Thus, a web service requires a WSDL file to get details of settings to communicate with another web service. The HTTP Connection Manager can specify in the Server URL field a web site URL or a WSDL file URL. If you specify the WSDL file URL in the Server URL field, the computer can download the WSDL file automatically. However, if you are specifying the web site URL, you must copy the WSDL file to the local computer.

XML Task

Whenever you are working with XML data, you will be most likely using the XML task to perform operations on the XML documents. This task is designed to work with the XML documents from the workflow point of view, whereas if you want to bring XML data in the data flow to apply transformations, you will be using the XML Source adapter while configuring your Data Flow task. The XML Source adapter is available in the Data Flow Sources section in Toolbox when you're working with the Data Flow task on the Data Flow panel.

Using the XML task, you can perform the following operations on XML documents:

1. Retrieve XML documents and dynamically modify those documents at run-time.

2. Select a segment of the data from the XML document using XPath expressions similar to how you select data using a SQL query against database tables.

3. Transform an XML document using XSLT (extensible stylesheet language transformations) style sheets and make it compatible with your application database.

4. Merge multiple documents to make one comprehensive document at run-time and use it to create reports.

5. Validate an XML document against the specified schema definition.

6. Compare an XML document against another XML document.

The XML task can automatically retrieve a source XML document from a specified location. To perform this operation, the XML task can use a file connection manager though you can directly enter XML data in the task or specify a variable to access the XML file. If the XML task is configured to use a file connection manager, the connection string specified inside the file connection manager provides the information of the path of the XML file; however, if the XML task is configured to use a variable, the specified variable contains the path to the XML document. At run-time, other processes or tasks in the package can dynamically populate this variable. Like the retrieval process of XML documents, the XML task can save the result set after applying the defined operation to a variable or file. By now, you can guess that to write to a file, the XML task will be using a File connection manager.

The XML Task Editor has a dynamic configuration interface that changes depending upon the type of operation you choose to apply to the XML documents. Following are the descriptions of these configuration areas:

Input Section

As mentioned, the XML task can retrieve the source document that is specified under the Input section in the XML Task Editor. You can choose from three available SourceType options: Direct Input allows you to type in XML data directly in the Source field; File Connection allows you to specify a file connection manager in the Source field; and Variable allows you to specify a variable name in the Source field.

Second Operand Section

This section defines the second document required for the operation to be performed. The type of second document depends on the type of operation. For example, the second document type will be an XML document if you are merging two documents, while the second document will be an XSD document if you are trying to validate an XML document against an XSD schema. Again, like the Input section, you can choose between three types in the SecondOperandType field and specify the document in the SecondOperand field.

Output Section

In this section, you specify whether you want to save the results of the operation performed by running the XML task. You can save the results to a variable or a file by using the file connection manager to specify the destination file. You can also choose to overwrite the destination.

Operation Options Section

This section is dynamic and changes with the option selection. For example, for a Diff operation, this section will change to the Diff Options section (see Figure 5-8), and for Merge operation, this will become the Merge Options section with its specific fields relevant to the operation. The two operations XSLT and Patch do not offer this section at all.

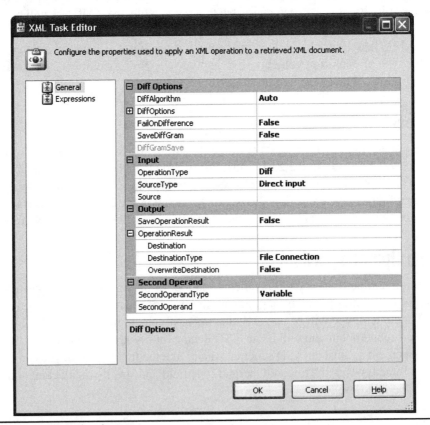

Figure 5-8 *XML Task Editor*

XML Task Operations

The XML Task has six predefined operations for you to use. The configuration layout of the options changes as soon as you select a different operation.

Validate   You can validate the XML document against a Document Type Definition (DTD) or XML Schema Definition (XSD) schema. The XML document you want to validate is specified in the Input section in the Editor and the schema document is specified in the Second Operand section. The type of schema document depends upon what you specify for ValidationType—XSD or DTD. With either type of ValidationType, you can choose to fail the operation on a validation failure in the FailOnValidationFail field.

XSLT   You can perform XSL transformations on the XML documents using XSLT style sheets. The Second Operand should contain the reference to the XSLT document, which you can type directly into the field or specify either by using the file connection manager or a variable.

XPATH   Using this operation, you can perform XPATH queries and evaluations on the XML document. The Second Operand should contain a reference to the second XML document, which you can type directly into the field or specify either by using the file connection manager or a variable. You can select the type of XPATH operation in the XPathOperation field. The XPathOperation field provides three options.

- ▶ **Evaluation**   Return the results of an XPath function such as `sum()`.
- ▶ **Node list**   Return the selected nodes as an XML fragment.
- ▶ **Values**   Return the results in a concatenated string for text values of all the selected nodes.

Merge   Using this operation, you can merge two XML documents. This operation adds the contents of the document specified in the Second Operand section into the source document. The operation can specify a merge location within the base document.

One thing to note here is that the XML task merges only the documents that have Unicode encoding. To determine whether your documents are using Unicode encoding, open the XML document with any editor or using Notepad and look at the beginning of the document to find [encoding="UTF-8"] in the declaration statement. UTF-8 indicates the 8-bit Unicode encoding.

Diff   Using this operation you can compare the source XML document to the document specified in the Second Operand section and write the differences to an XML document called a *Diffgram* document. The Diff operation provides a number of options to customize this comparison:

► **DiffAlgorithm**   Provides three choices: Auto, Fast, and Precise. You can choose between comparison algorithm to be fast or precise. The Auto option lets the Diff operation decide whether to select a fast or precise comparison based on the size of the documents being compared.

► **IgnoreProcessingInstructions**   Specifies whether the processing instructions are compared.

► **IgnoreOrderOfChildElements**   XML documents have hierarchical structure and this option specifies whether the order of child elements is compared.

► **IgnoreNamespaces**   Specifies whether the namespace URI (uniform resource identifier) of an element and its attribute names are compared.

► **IgnoreComments**   Specifies whether comment nodes are compared.

► **IgnoreXMLDeclaration**   Specifies whether the XML declarations are compared.

► **IgnorePrefixes**   Specifies whether prefixes of element and attribute names are compared.

► **IgnoreWhiteSpaces**   Specifies whether white spaces are compared.

► **IgnoreDTD**   Specifies whether the DTD is ignored.

► **FailOnDifference**   Specifies whether the task fails if the Diff operation fails.

► **SaveDiffGram**   Choose to save the comparison result in a Diffgram document.

Patch   Using this operation, you can apply the Diffgram document you saved during the Diff operation to an XML document. By doing this, you actually create a new XML document that includes the contents of the Diffgram document created earlier by the Diff operation.

Execute SQL Task

The Execute SQL task is the main workhorse task to run SQL statements or stored procedures and use the relational power of the underlying database. If you have used DTS, you may have used this task. Typically in DTS, you load data to a staging database and then apply transformations using the Execute SQL task. These transformations vary from generating salutations to Lookup transformations, deriving columns, or applying business rules using SQL Server relational engine. The design philosophy used in SQL Server 2005 Integration Services allow you to perform many of these tasks during the loading phase, thereby increasing performance by reducing repeated inefficient staging of databases. The power of the Execute SQL task is still available in SSIS in a more usable form by providing ability to use variables, to create expressions over the properties of the task, and to return a result set to the data flow that can be used to populate a variable.

Using the Execute SQL task, you can perform workflow tasks such as Create, Alter, Drop, or TRUNCATE TABLES or Views. You can run a stored procedure and store the result to a variable to be used later in the package. You can use it to run either a single SQL statement or multiple SQL statements, parameterized SQL statements, and save the rowset returned from the query in to a variable. You used this task in the "Using System Variables To Create Custom Logs" Hands-On exercise in Chapter 3, where you used a parameterized SQL statement, and in the "Contacting Opportunities" Hands-On exercise in Chapter 4, where you saved the result rowset to a variable, which then got enumerated by a Foreach Loop container.

If you scroll to the Maintenance Plan Tasks in the Control Flow Toolbox, you will see a similar task, Execute T-SQL Statement Task. The Execute T-SQL Statement task has a simple interface compared to the Execute SQL task and is focused on performing maintenance tasks on SQL Server databases using T-SQL. It doesn't give you any facility to run parameterized queries and direct the result set to the work flow, whereas the Execute SQL task has a more complex interface and is designed for use in a relatively complex workflow where you need to use variables, run parameterized queries, or direct the result set to the data flow.

Keep this task open in front of you and try various selections as we go through each option, as the task contains dynamic fields that change depending upon the choices you make in certain fields.

The Execute SQL Task Editor includes General, Parameter Mapping, Result Set, and Expressions pages.

General Page

In this page, you define a Name and Description for the task under the General section. In the Options section, you can specify a TimeOut value in seconds for the query to run before timing out. By default, the TimeOut value is 0 (zero), indicating an infinite time. The CodePage field allows you to specify the code page value.

In the Result Set section, you choose one of four options based upon the result set returned by the SQL statement you specify in this task. Based on the type of SQL statement—i.e., whether it is a SELECT statement or INSERT/UPDATE/DELETE statement—the result set may or may not be returned. Also, the result set may contain zero rows, one row, or many rows, and the following four options in the Execute SQL Task Editor ResultSet field allows you to configure them:

▶ **None**   When you use INSERT, UPDATE, or DELETE SQL statement that returns the result set containing zero rows.

▶ **Single Row**   When the SQL statement or a stored procedure returns a single row in the result set.

▶ **Full result set**   When the query returns more than one rows.

▶ **XML**   When the SQL statement returns a result set in the XML format.

In the SQL Statement section ConnectionType field, options are EXCEL, OLE DB, ODBC, ADO, ADO.NET, and SQLMOBILE connection manager types, used for connecting to a data source. Depending on the type of connection manager you've chosen, the Connection field provides a drop-down list of already configured connection managers of the same type or provides a <New connection...> option to let you add a connection manager of the appropriate type. The interface provided by the <New connection...> option changes to match your selection of the connection manager specified in the ConnectionType field.

Depending on the data source type, you can write a query using an SQL statement in the dialect the specified data source can parse. Further, you can specify the source from where the SQL statement can be read for execution in the SQLSourceType field. The selection of the source in the SQLSourceType field changes the next field dynamically (which is coupled to it) to match the SQLSourceType choice. The options available in the SQLSourceType field and how it affects the coupled field are explained here:

▶ **Direct input**   Allows you to type an SQL statement directly in the task. This changes the coupled field to SQLStatement, which provides an interface in which to type your query.

▶ **File connection**   If you have multiple SQL statements written in a file, you can choose this option to enable the Execute SQL task to get the SQL statements from the file. Selecting this option changes the coupled field to FileConnection, which allows you to specify a file connection manager to connect to an existing file containing SQL statements.

▶ **Variable**   Enables the Execute SQL Task to read the SQL statement from a variable. This option changes the coupled field to the SourceVariable field, which provides a drop-down list of all the system and user variables.

If you have chosen ADO or ADO.NET Connection Manager in the ConnectionType field earlier, the IsQueryStoredProcedure field becomes available for use and you will be able to specify that the SQL statement to be run is a stored procedure.

When you select OLE DB Connection Manager in the ConnectionType field, you can specify in the BypassPrepare field whether the task should skip preparing the query step before running it. When SQL queries are run, the SQL statement is parsed and compiled in the first step and then executed based on the execution plan prepared earlier in the compilation step. When you specify True in the BypassPrepare field, when the query is run the first time, it parses and compiles the SQL statement in the first step and keeps the execution plan in the cache of the database engine and in the next step uses this execution plan to execute the query. So when the query is run the next time, it doesn't parse and compile the statement but rather uses the existing execution plan, saving time required to parse and compile. If you're running a query multiple times, it is faster and efficient if you use a prepared execution—however, if you're running the query only once, it is not a recommended option.

Parameter Mapping Page

If you are running a parameterized SQL statement, you can map variables to the parameters in this page. The interface on this page is relatively simple and provides self-explanatory fields and options. You can click the Add button to add a parameter mapping and then click in each field to select the available values from the drop-down lists; however, in the Parameter Name field, you have to type in a value. The configuration of this page has been covered in the "Using System Variables to Create Custom Logs" Hands-On exercise in Chapter 3.

Result Set Page

If you are using a query that will return a result set and you have selected a value other than None in the ResultSet field on the General page, you can use this page to map the row set to a variable, which can be used later in the package.

Expressions Page

Using this page, you can build a property expression using SSIS expression language to update the property dynamically at run-time. In the Expression Builder, you can use

System or User variables, functions, type casts, and operators exposed by expression language to build an expression.

Bulk Insert Task

When you get large amounts of data in the flat files, say from the mainframe systems or from third parties, and you want to import this data from the flat files into an SQL Server, you can use the Bulk Insert task. This task is the quickest way to copy large amounts of data into an SQL Server table or view.

Note the following when deciding whether to use this task:

► The Bulk Insert task does not perform any transformations on the data while importing data from the source text file to the SQL Server database table or view.

► When you embed this task in an SSIS package Control Flow, only the members of the sysadmin fixed server role can run the package.

► You can use an XML or non-XML formatted file in the Bulk Insert task. A formatted file is used to store format information for each field in a data file in relationship to a specific table and provides all the format information that is required to bulk import data. This format file must be located on the server executing the SSIS package containing the Bulk Insert task.

► During the import process, some of the rows may fail to import and in turn can fail the task. You can still run this task successfully by increasing the allowed number of errors by specifying a value in the MaxErrors option. However, the rows that fail to import cannot be logged or extracted out. If you want to capture the failing rows, you need to consider alternative ways of importing data using the Data Flow task and capture the failing rows in the exception files by way of error outputs.

Message Queue Task

Microsoft Message Queuing (MSMQ) is a Windows service that allows applications or SSIS packages to send and receive messages using a queue. Message queuing is available in Windows 2000 and later released as a standard operating system component that has advantages of Active Directory Integration. This service can be extended using Message Queuing Connector to heterogeneous data sources such as CICS (IBM's Customer Information Control System) or UNIX.

In SSIS world, message queuing means one package will be sending a message to a queue while other package will be receiving that message from the queue. These packages can be on different servers and may not be running simultaneously. Using MSMQ, you can reliably exchange data between packages that may not be running on the same server and might be separated in time throughout your enterprise. Following are some of the scenarios in which you may be using Message Queue task:

▶ Send a message from an executing package to the package that is waiting for it to complete so that it can start running.

▶ If you have a small window of time to finish a large workload and you decide to distribute your workload across many servers to utilize the processing power, you can coordinate the operations on different servers using message queuing between packages.

▶ SSIS packages can communicate with the applications that utilize message queuing.

▶ Send output from a processing package to a waiting package on the other computer where the data enclosed in the message will be processed further.

You can choose from one of the different types of messages to send or receive using the Message Queue task: Data File Message, String Message, or Variable Message. When the task is configured in the receiving mode, you also get an additional String Message To Variable Message Type choice. Like other Integration Services tasks, the available fields of this are dynamic and change depending upon your choice to send or receive a message or on message type.

▶ **Data File Message**   Used to send a file that contains the message. To send a data file message, you specify Data File Message in the MessageType field and specify path of the file in the DataFileMessage field on the Send page of the Message Queue Task Editor. When receiving this type of messages, you specify Data File Message in the MessageType field, specify the name of the file in the SaveFileAs field to save message into, choose whether to overwrite the existing file, and optionally apply a filter to receive the message only from the package defined in the Identifier field on the Receive page.

▶ **Variable Message**   Used to send one or more variables. To send variables, you specify Variable Message in the MessageType field and one or more variables in the VariableMessage field on the Send page of the Message Queue Task Editor. While receiving the variables, you specify Variable Message in the MessageType field, specify the name of the variable in the Variable field to receive the message into, and optionally choose to apply a filter to receive the message only from the package defined in the Identifier field on the Receive page.

▶ **String Message**   Used to send a text string. To send text string, you specify String Message in the MessageType field and type a text string in the StringMessage field on the Send page of the Message Queue Task Editor. While receiving the text string, you specify String Message in the MessageType field and optionally specify to compare the incoming string in the Compare field with a user-defined string specified in the CompareString field on the Receive page. The string comparison options in the Compare field can be Exact Match for exact comparison, Ignore Case for case-insensitive comparison, or Containing for a substring match.

▶ **String Message To Variable**   Used to pass the source message that has been sent as a string to a destination variable and is available only when receiving messages. To configure text string message to be passed to a variable, you specify String Message To Variable in the MessageType field, specify the name of the variable in the Variable field to receive the text string into, and optionally specify to compare the incoming string in the Compare field with a user-defined string specified in the CompareString field on the Receive page. The string comparison options in the Compare field can be Exact Match for exact comparison, Ignore Case for case-insensitive comparison, or Containing for a sub string match.

To use Message Queue task to send and receive messages, you first need to install Message Queuing service using the Add or Remove Programs applet in the Control Panel followed by creating messaging queues. You can create either a public or a private queue depending upon whether you have installed the Active Directory Integration component of Message Queuing service. A public queue is created in an Active Directory environment to publish its properties and description to the Active Directory. A private queue does not publish itself to the Active Directory and works on the local computer that holds the queue.

The Message Queuing service has the following components available in Windows XP and 2003 Server for installation:

▶ **Active Directory Integration**   Provides integration with Active Directory whenever the computer belongs to a Windows domain (Windows 2000 and later). Public queues are configured and used when using this component and the queues are published in the Active Directory under MSMQ object.

▶ **Common**   Provides basic functionality required for local messaging services.

- ► **MSMQ HTTP Support**   Enables sending or receiving of messages over HTTP transport with proxy settings configured using the proxycfg.exe tool.

- ► **Triggers**   Associates the arrival of messages at a queue with triggering functionality of a COM component or a standalone application.

- ► **Downlevel Client Support**   Available in Windows 2003 Server to provide support for down-level clients.

- ► **Routing Support**   Available in Windows 2003 Server to provide routing of messages using store and forward mechanism in Active Directory transport.

For proper functioning of the Message Queue task, make sure you have installed Message Queuing service and SQL Server Integration Services service. When you install SQL Server 2005 without specifically selecting Integration Services service on the Components To Install page, you may still be able to use BIDS to design and run Integration Services packages. However, as this is a partial installation of SSIS, not all tasks will run properly and the Message Queue task is one of those tasks. For the Message Queue task to be functioning properly, you must install Integration Services fully by selecting exclusively in the Components To Install page during installation of SQL Server 2005.

You will import the expanded files into Campaign database in SQL Server using the Message Queue task and the Bulk Insert task in the following Hands-On exercises.

Hands-On: Importing Expanded Files

Dealers of Adventure Works Bikes submit the sales reports to an FTP server, and they need to be downloaded from this server and imported into the SQL Server database. You have already downloaded, expanded, and archived these report files in the previous exercises and now you have DealerSales01.txt and DealerSales02.txt files in the Downloads folder ready to be imported to the Campaign database. However, you want to run this new package independent of earlier packages and this may occur at a different time during the day.

Method

We can meet this objective in several ways: We can use the Bulk Insert task to import the data to our existing table—but we have multiple files, so we can use Foreach Loop container to read the file names one by one and pass them to the Bulk Insert task to import multiple files one at a time. However, as we want to keep the packages independent from one another and want to run the second package only when the first has completed successfully, the use of messages from the first package to pass the information to the other will be a better solution. Though in this case you will not be following the shortest and easiest solution option to achieve your goal, the solution you are going to follow is quite interesting, and I'm sure it will be relevant in real-life scenarios.

You will add the Message Queue Task at the end of the Archiving Downloaded Files package to send file names in the messages, which will be read by the Importing Expanded Files package using the Message Queue task in the receiving mode. As the package won't have to read file names from the file system, you will not be using Foreach Loop container; instead, you will use the For Loop container to read multiple messages one by one. Here's the step by step method:

▶ Install Message Queuing service and create message queues.

▶ To keep it simple and applicable to most of the users, for the sake of this exercise I've used a Windows XP machine with a private queue only. Please refer to Microsoft SQL Server 2005 Books Online for more details to create a message queuing environment suitable to your requirements.

▶ Configure the Archiving Downloaded Files package to send file names. In this step, we will add Message Queue task in the already configured Archiving Downloaded Files package.

▶ Build the Importing Expanded Files package.

▶ Execute the package and check that the two messages have been picked up from the queue and the text files have been imported into the SQL Server Campaign database.

Exercise (Install Message Queuing Service)

1. From the Control Panel, run the Add or Remove Programs applet, and then click Add/Remove Windows Components. This will open the Windows Component Wizard. Choose Message Queuing from the list of Components.

2. Click the Next button to install these components. Click Finish when the wizard completes installation.

3. Choose Run | compmgmt.msc or run the Computer Management program from Administrative Tools group of programs.

4. Expand the Services and Applications group from the left pane of the window to see Message Queuing installed there. Expand Message Queuing and then right-click the Private Queues folder. From the context menu, choose New | Private Queue. This will open the New Private Queue window. In the Queue name field, type **SSISprivQ** and then click OK.

Note that another difference between a private and public queue is that *private$* is attached to the full name of a private queue. The New Private Queue window shows that the queue will be created in *your computer name* with *private$* added in front of the name you type in. So, the full path of the queue will be *ComputerName\private$\SSISprivQ*. If this were the public queue in which we specify the queue name as *SSISpubQ*, the full path would have been *ComputerName \SSISpubQ*.

5. Expand the Private Queues folder under the Message Queuing from the left pane of the Computer Management window. Further expand the SSISPrivQ folder and you will see a Queue messages subfolder. This is where the Message Queue task will be delivering the messages and the messages will wait for a receiving Message Queue task to be picked up.

Exercise (Configure Archiving Downloaded Files Package to Send File Names)

Remember that in the Archiving Downloaded Files package, the Foreach Loop container reads the file names of zipped files lying in C:\SSIS\downloads folder and then passes those names to the File System task, which moves the zipped files to the Archive subfolder. To accomplish this, the package used a variable named *fname* to pass the zipped files names. Because you want to import text files, not the zipped files, you will derive a new variable called *txtfname* to contain the text files names from *fname* variable. This new variable will then be sent through the Message Queue task as a variable message.

6. Run BIDS and open the Control Flow Tasks project. In the Solution Explorer window, double-click the Archiving downloaded files.dtsx package to open it.

7. Open the Variables window. Click Auto Hide pushpin to dock the Variables window on the left side of the screen. On the Control Flow surface, click the Enumerating Files Foreach Loop Container and switch to the Variables window. Add a new variable named *txtfname* in the Enumerating Files Scope and set Data Type to string. Choose View | Properties, or press F4 to open the Properties window. The Properties window will open up by default on the right side of the screen, showing properties of the *txtfname* variable. (Sometimes you may not see properties for the object in which you are interested—this is because of your selection of the items on the designer. If this happens, make sure you've selected the Enumerating Files Container and then clicked the *txtfname* variable to see the properties for this variable.)

Scroll through the properties and locate the *EvaluateAsExpression* property. This property allows you to enable the variable to use the results of an expression as its value. That is, you can write an expression, which will be evaluated at run-time and the result of this evaluation will be used as the value of the variable.

Specify True for the EvaluateAsExpression property. You will see that the Expression property is now highlighted and can be edited. Type the following text in the Expression property:

```
SUBSTRING(@[User::fname] , 1, LEN(@[User::fname]) -3) + "txt"
```

This expression will evaluate *txtfname* as C:\SSIS\downloads\DealerSales01 .txt from the *fname* variable when it equals C:\SSIS\downloads\DealerSales01 .zip. If you look further down in the properties window in the Value field, you will notice (see Figure 5-9) that the full file name in fact has been resolved as C:\SSIS\downloads\.txt. You can see that nothing appears in the name portion of the file path name because the *fname* variable has not yet been populated (by the Foreach Loop container) in the design mode. However, at run-time, the Foreach Loop container provides a value for the *fname* variable and the name portion of the file name gets populated in the file path name.

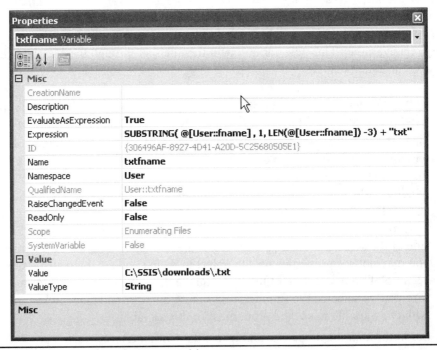

Figure 5-9 *Deriving the* txtfname *variable using property expressions*

8. Drag the Message Queue task from the Toolbox and drop it in the Enumerating Files (Foreach Loop) container below the Archive Downloaded Files (File System) task. Drag and drop the green arrow from below the Archive Downloaded Files task on to the Message Queue task. The package will look as shown in Figure 5-10 after you've configured the Message Queue task.

9. Right-click the Message Queue Task and choose Edit from the context menu. Type the following on the General Page of the task editor:

Name	Send variable message
Description	This task sends the txtfname variable to the Importing expanded files.

The task also provides a possibility to format the messages in the SQL Server 2000 Message Queue task format in the Use2000Format field. Leave the default False value set in this field.

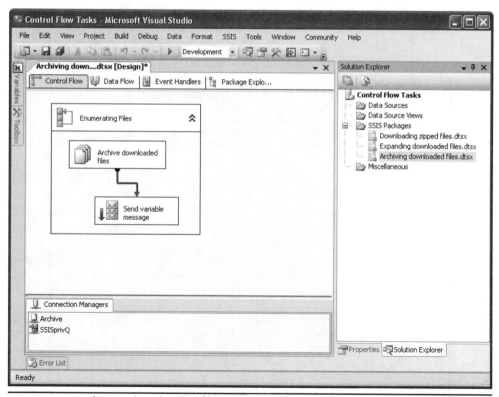

Figure 5-10 *Archiving downloaded files package after adding Message Queue task*

10. In the MSMQConnection field, select to create a new connection. In the MSMQ Connection Manager Editor, type the following:

Name	SSISprivQ
Description	Connection Manager for private Queue SSISprivQ
Path	*YourComputerName*\privateS\SSISprivQ

You can use a dot (.) instead of *YourComputerName* to indicate your local computer.

You may want to test the connection by clicking the Test button; once you get the "Test connection succeeded" message, click OK twice to return to the Message Queue Task Editor.

11. Leave the Send Message option selected in the Message field.

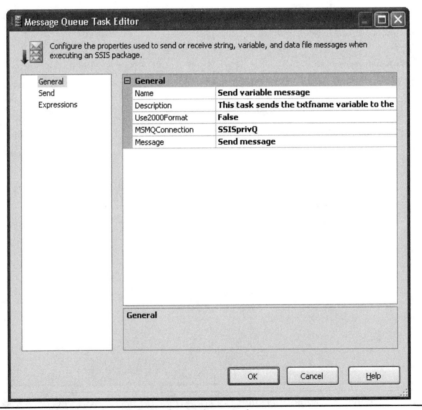

Figure 5-11 *Message Queue task configured to send messages*

12. Go to the Send page, where you can specify to encrypt your messages in the UseEncryption field, and choose an encryption algorithm (RC2 or RC4) from the EncryptionAlgorithm field. For this exercise, do not select encryption.

13. Select Variable Message in the MessageType field, as you will be sending a variable value in the message. Select User::txtfname in the VariableMessage field. Click OK to close the editor window.

14. Save the package by pressing CTRL-SHIFT-S.

15. Using Windows Explorer, move the DealerSales01.zip and DealerSales02.zip files from the C:\SSIS\downloads\Archive folder to C:\SSIS\downloads folder, which have been moved to Archive folder in earlier exercise.

16. Switch to BIDS and press F5 on the keyboard to start debugging. When the package runs, notice that the tasks change color from yellow to green twice, indicating that the package has processed two files and sent out two messages. When all the tasks turn green, stop debugging from the Debug menu or by pressing SHIFT-F5. Close the project by choosing File | Close Project.

17. Switch to the Computer Management console and notice two messages in the Queue messages folder under SSISprivQ. (You might have to refresh the folder if the window was already open.)

Exercise (Build Importing Expanded Files Package)

In this part of the exercise, you will build a new package, which will pick up variable messages sent by the Archiving Downloaded Files package earlier from the SSISprivQ messaging queue.

18. In BIDS, right-click the SSIS Packages folder in the Solution Explorer and choose New SSIS Package from the context menu. This will add a new package, Package1.dtsx, in the project. Right-click Package1.dtsx and rename it **Importing expanded files.dtsx**. You will work in this package to configure the following workflow.

19. Start building the package by dropping the For Loop Container on the Control Flow Designer surface.

20. Right-click anywhere on the Designer surface and choose Variables from the context menu. Create three variables: *filename*, *maxcounter*, and *mincounter* with the details shown in the Figure 5-12.

    Be sure to specify a value of C:\\SSIS\\RawFiles\\DealerSales_placeholder.txt to the *filename* variable and a value of 2 to the *maxcounter* variable. The *mincounter* and *maxcounter* variables will be used in the For Loop container

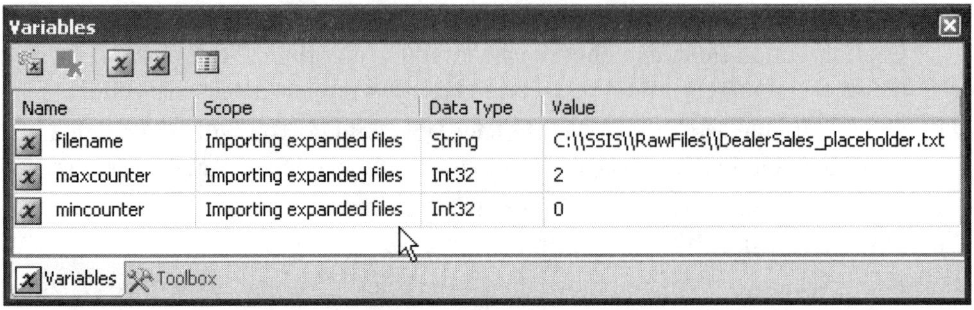

Figure 5-12 *Creating variables for the text file names and For Loop container*

while the *filename* variable will be used to receive the variable value from the messages sent by Archiving Downloaded Files package using the Message Queue task.

21. Double-click the For Loop Container icon to open the For Loop Editor. Type the following in the General page of the editor:

Name	Import Loop
Description	This For Loop Container imports DealerSales files one by one.
InitExpression	@mincounter = 0
EvalExpression	@mincounter < @maxcounter
AssignExpression	@mincounter = @mincounter + 1

As the initial value assigned to the *mincounter* variable in the InitExpression field is 0 and the maximum value specified for *maxcounter* variable while creating it is 2, the Import Loop will loop twice at run-time, after which the expression defined in EvalExpression field will become false and the loop will stop running. Click OK to close the For Loop Editor window.

22. From the Toolbox, drag and drop the Message Queue task within the Import Loop (For Loop) container. Open the Message Queue Task Editor window by double-clicking its icon and type the following on the General page:

Name	Receive variable message
Description	This task receives variable messages sent by 'Archiving downloaded files' package.

23. Leave the Use2000Format field set to default False value.

24. Create an MSMQ connection manager in the MSMQConnection field exactly as specified in step 10.

25. Select Receive Message in the Message field. Note that Send Page changes to Receive Page on the left pane of the window. Go to the Receive page.

26. On the Receive page, select True in the RemoveFromMessageQueue field. This value lets you delete the message from queue after the Message Queue task has received it. You may prefer to keep the message in the queue in situations when you have multiple subpackages to read a message.

27. You can choose to display an error message if the task fails with timeout in the ErrorIfMessageTimeout field. For now, leave it set to False. However, if you select True in this field, you will be able to specify a time-out value in seconds in the TimeoutAfter field.

28. Choose Variable Message in the MessageType field and No Filter in the Filter field. If you select From Package in the Filter field, you can specify the package in the Identifier field. This field provides a GUI to select the package by specifying the server name, storage location, and user credentials.

29. Specify User::filename in the Variable field, as shown in Figure 5-13.

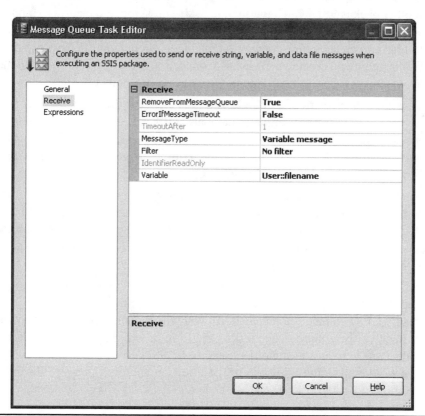

Figure 5-13 *Configuring the Message Queue task in the receive mode*

30. Click OK to close the Message Queue Task Editor.

31. Drag and drop the Bulk Insert task from the Toolbox in the Import Loop container below the Receive Variable Message task. Connect the Receive Variable Message task to the Bulk Insert task using on success (green colored line) precedence constraint.

32. Open the Bulk Insert Task Editor and type the following in the General page:

Name	Importing DealerSales
Description	This task imports DealerSales files into Campaign..DealerSales table.

33. Go to the Connection page, click in the Connection field under the Destination Connection group of options, and choose <New Connection…> to open Configure OLE DB Connection Manager window. Choose an OLE DB connection manager from the Data Connections list to connect to Campaign database, which you created in an earlier Hands-On exercises. The good thing about the OLE DB Connection Managers is that they are available for reuse in other packages, as you have seen here. If you skipped the earlier Hands-On exercises and do not see an OLE DB Connection Manager in this window, you will have to create a new connection manager by clicking the New button. For details on how to create an OLE DB Connection Manager, refer back to the "Contacting Opportunities" Hands-On exercise in Chapter 4.

34. Click in the DestinationTable field and then click the drop-down arrow to see the list of tables in the Campaign database. OLE DB Connection Manager provides this list by establishing a connection to the server and the database using the settings specified in the connection manager. Select [Campaign] .[dbo].[DealerSales] Table from the list.

35. You can choose to specify the format of the file to be imported either directly in the task or by using a file. If you choose Use File in the Format field, you have to specify the name and location of the file in the FormatFile field, which appears on selection of the Use File option. For this exercise, choose Specify in the Format field. Leave the RowDelimiter field set to {CR}{LF} and choose Vertical Bar {|} from the drop-down list in the ColumnDelimiter field.

36. Under Source Connection options group, choose <New connection…> to specify a File connection manager. As you will be using file names provided by Receive Variable Message task in the form of variables, you will specify a file name here as a placeholder. Specify C:\SSIS\RawFiles\DealerSales_ placeholder.txt in the File field of the File Connection Manager Editor (see Figure 5-14).

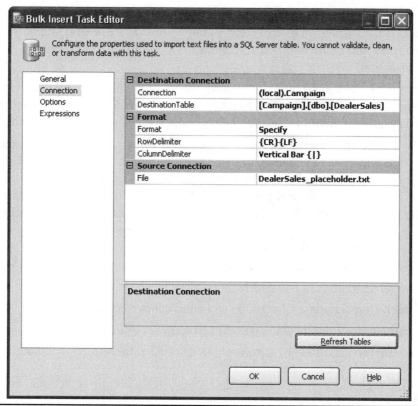

Figure 5-14 *Configuring the Bulk Insert task to import text files*

37. Go to the Options page, where you can specify code page of the text file in the CodePage field. Leave it set to the default RAW.

38. When the data is coming from various database systems, the data type may be in different formats. The Bulk Insert task provides four default data formats that can be imported. You can specify the data type of the input file using DataFileType field. The options are Character, Unicode (wide) Character, Native, and Unicode (wide) Native formats. Leave it set to Char.

39. You can specify the number of rows in a batch in the BatchSize field. The rows specified in a batch are treated together and copied to the server as one transaction. The Bulk Insert task copies files by committing all the rows in the batch as one transaction and moving over to the next batch for another transaction. In case of an error and failure of the task, all the rows in the batch will be rolled back. For example, if you set the BatchSize equal to 10,000 rows

for a table of 50,000 rows and the task fails at row number 25,001, the task will fail with 20,000 rows inserted to the table. A default value of 0 implies that all the rows will be treated as a single batch—i.e., fail or commit totally in one transaction.

40. In the LastRow field, you can specify the value of last row at which the task should stop inserting data to the table. Leave it set at the default value of 0, which means all the rows from the file will be inserted to the specified SQL table.

41. The FirstRow field is quite useful in situations where you have large amount of data to import and the quality of data results in failing the process in between. By specifying from where to start inserting the rows, you can avoid re-importing the rows that have already been imported. Using this option in conjunction with the BatchSize option helps in achieving high levels of input performance with less rework, even though the data quality may not be good. Leave the option selected to the default value of 1.

42. Moving to the Options section, you can choose any of the five options. You can also select more than one option here, listed in a comma-delimited list:

Check Constraints Checks the table and column constraints

Keep Nulls Imports blank columns from the text file as Null values

Enable Identity Insert Inserts explicit values into the identity column of the table

Table Lock Locks the table during import process

Fire Triggers Fires any existing triggers on the table while importing the data

Though none of these options will be of much help in this case, you can select Keep Nulls for this exercise.

43. You can specify the names of columns on which to sort the data in the SortedData field. This is effectively the ORDER BY clause in the bulk insert SQL statement. Leave it blank, which means do not sort on any column.

44. The rows that cannot be imported by Bulk Insert task are counted as errors. You can specify a maximum number of errors—i.e., the number of rows to fail before the task fails—in the MaxErrors field. Click OK to close the task.

You have configured all the tasks and options within the tasks apart from specifying which files to import. You can do this by mapping the connection string of the placeholder file connection manager to the value of the variable received by the Receive variable message task. Let's see how to do this.

45. Right-click the DealerSales_placeholder.txt file connection manager and choose Properties from the context menu, or press F4 on the keyboard after selecting the text file. In the Property window, click in the Expressions field and then click the ellipsis button on this field. In the Property Expressions Editor window, click in the field below the Property column and select ConnectionString from the drop-down list. Then click the ellipsis button under the Expression field to open the Expression Builder.

46. In the Expression Builder, drag User::filename from the Variables list in the Expression field, as shown in Figure 5-15. Click OK twice to finish the configurations.

47. As a last step before you run the package, make sure that you have two messages queued, which were sent by the Archiving Downloaded Files package, in the message queue folder in SSISprivQ. Also, check that the DealerSales table in the Campaign database does not have any record. Press F5 to run the package.

Notice that the Import Loop Task turns yellow followed by Receive variable message task turning yellow and then green, indicating that it has successfully

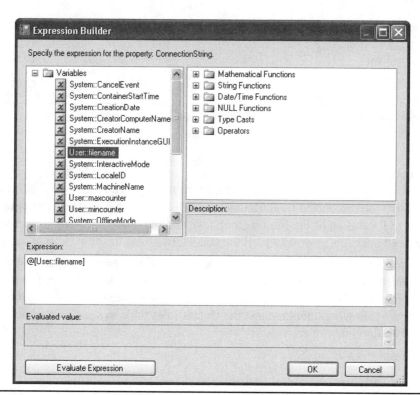

Figure 5-15 *Using Expression Builder to create a property expression for dynamically altering the connection string of the File Connection Manager*

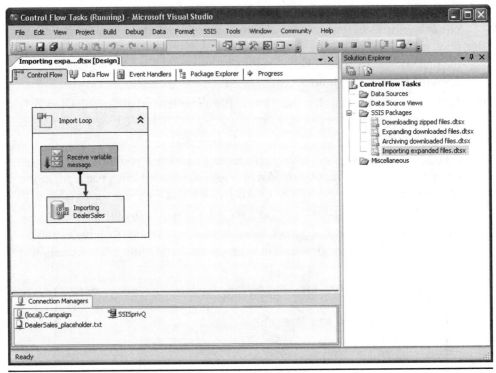

Figure 5-16 *Executing Importing expanded files package*

received the first variable message. Then Importing DealerSales turn yellow, and stays yellow for some time before turning to green indicating that it has successfully imported DealerSales01.txt file (Figure 5-16). This completes the first iteration of the Import Loop task and the process repeats itself for the second iteration, after which all the tasks turn green and stop processing.

To close the loop, check the Queue messages folder under SSISprivQ private queue by switching over to the Computer Management window and notice that the messages have been deleted. Go to SQL Server Management Studio and run the following query against the DealerSales table to see the imported data and total number of records:

```
SELECT * FROM DealerSales
```

You should see 242,634 rows displayed.

48. Press CTRL-SHIFT-S to save all the files in this solution and then choose File |
Close Project.

Review

In this exercise, you used the Message Queue task to send and receive variables from one package to another using Windows Message Queuing service. This can be quite useful for enterprise-wide implementations in which data and servers are scattered all over the network, and it makes sense to use all the processing power underutilized in those servers to help you complete the nightly processes within the allocated time. You also used the Bulk Insert task to import files to SQL Server table. This is the fastest method of importing data to an SQL Server table. In this exercise, you had encountered the For Loop Container and used it to iterate twice to receive two messages using the Message Queue task and then import two text files into the SQL Server table using Bulk Insert task. Last but not the least, and perhaps the most important thing you've learned in this exercise, you used property expressions to change ConnectionStrings of the file connection managers dynamically at run-time with the help of variables.

Execute Package Task

The Execute Package Task brings the benefits of modular design to SSIS packages. It allows an SSIS (parent) package to run other (child) packages as part of a workflow. This task can be used to run packages stored either in SQL Server msdb database or on the file system.

While developing a solution for a business problem, you tend to build smaller packages meeting specific needs. This approach is recommended as it helps your solution to be modular, which is easier to debug. This also helps you achieve quick results on some of the specific requirements. Once you have built all the modules of your complete solution, you can use the Execute Package task to fit all the smaller packages together to form an enterprise-wide solution.

Another benefit of following a modular design for SSIS packages is less work when you have to modify a child package that is used in multiple parent packages. For example, if you want to modify a child package that is used in five parent packages, you can modify your child package only once and all the same child packages will be modified in the five parent packages at the same time.

While developing your packages with the modular design concept, you can reuse packages developed as modules to perform specific functions in other packages. You may, for example, develop a send mail package that reads from a table and sends a broadcast mail to all the members in the table. This functionality can be used in any package that requires sending mails.

Using the Execute Package task, you can have better security controls in place. You can control access to sensitive data by dividing your package into packages that can have public access and other packages that can be accessed by administrator or management only. For example, you can separate out salary processing package from your main SSIS package and run that as a child package using the Execute Package task in the main SSIS package and hence avoid access to salaries data.

Probably the biggest benefit of having an Execute Package Task is that the packages are able to communicate with other packages and have an effect on the success or failure of other packages. To clarify, consider the container hierarchy in which errors and events get flagged up the hierarchy with the package being at the top of the hierarchy. When we use a child package in a parent package, the Execute Package task actually contains the child package and becomes a parent container for that child package. Any event occurring in the child package gets passed on to the Execute Package Task, which it can share with other Execute Package tasks used in the parent package. Now think of transactions that cause tasks to commit or rollback as a unit within a package. Using this task, transactions can actually span packages and can cause multiple package to commit or rollback as a unit. SSIS provides you the benefits of dealing with individual tasks and lets you use them as an independent unit, yet you are also able to integrate the packages together to work as a unit.

You can run a child package in its own process or in the process of the parent package using ExecuteOutOfProcess option. If you are following a modular design for your package and want your parent and child package to commit or fail together as a single unit, you will be using the in-process method—i.e., you will run the child package in the process of running the parent package. For this configuration, you will not be running additional processing threads and the memory required by the process will, of course, be less. In this case, the context switching will not happen and you will experience less processing overhead. However, the down side is that if a child package crashes due to some problem, that may also kill the parent package. In addition, if your system has more than 4 GB memory, SSIS won't be able to use it, as a single process in 32-bit systems can use maximum of 2 GB of virtual memory (or 3 GB if you use /3GB switch in boot.ini file). Chapter 13 discusses memory utilization of SSIS packages and pros and cons of using 32-bit versus 64-bit systems in more detail.

Alternatively, if you want to make use of full memory resource available on the system, you want to prevent parent packages from crashes in the child package due to bugs or other issues, or you want your parent package not to depend on the success or failure of a child package, then you may prefer to use the out-of-process method—i.e., the parent and the child package will run in their own process. As the package will be using multiple processes, you will see more context switching, due to the overhead of maintaining multiple processes, and the memory usage will also be more—in fact, memory utilized can grow more than 4 GB if available on the computer. The following exercise is designed to help you understand how to use the Execute Package task and the implications of connecting various tasks in a package.

Hands-On: Consolidating Workflow Packages

The packages you have developed so far to download, expand, archive, and import files are independent units of work and isolated, too. You may want to perform these functions in a sequence at one time so that you can consolidate all the packages into one package with defined sequence and understand the effect of connecting them with different constraint.

Method

In this exercise, you will use the Execute Package task to embed the given packages in the parent package and join these packages with success constraint. As a second part to this exercise, you will change the constraints and see the effects on execution results.

Exercise (Building Consolidated Package)

1. Start BIDS and open the Control Flow Tasks project. Create a new package in the Solution Explorer with the name Consolidating workflow packages.dtsx.

2. Drag and drop the Execute Package Task from the Toolbox on to the designer surface.

3. Double-click the Execute Package Task to open the Execute Package Task Editor.

4. Type the following in the General page of the editor:

Name	Downloading zipped files
Description	This task executes the named package.

5. In the Package page's Location field, select File System from the drop-down list. The other option, SQL Server, could be chosen if the package were stored in the msdb database of SQL Server. All your packages are stored in file system, so you will not be using SQL Server option.

6. Click in the Connection field and select <New connection...> to open the File Connection Manager Editor. Leave Existing file in the Usage Type field and type **C:\SSIS\Projects\Control Flow Tasks\Downloading zipped files.dtsx** in the File field to point the Execute Package task to the Downloading Zipped Files package.

7. The PackageName field is available when you select SQL Server in the Location field to allow you to choose the package from the list of packages stored in msdb store. In your case, the field is disabled as the package name has already been provided in the Connection field.

8. You can specify the password in the Password field if the package has been protected with a password. Leave it at the default setting for now.

9. As we are not using any transactions across the packages, change the ExecuteOutOfProcess field value to True. Click OK to close the Execute Package Task Editor window.

10. From the Toolbox, drop another Execute Package Task on the designer surface just below the Downloading Zipped Files task. Stretch the green arrow from the Downloading Zipped Files task and join it to the new Execute Package Task. Now, following steps 3 to 9, configure this task with the following settings:

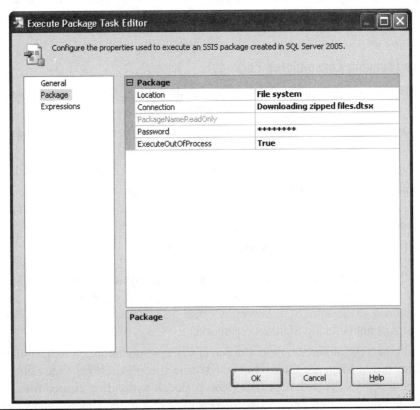

Figure 5-17 *Configuring the Execute Package task*

Name	Expanding downloaded files
Description	This task executes the named package
Location	File system
Connection	C:\SSIS\Projects\Control Flow Tasks\Expanding downloaded files.dtsx
ExecuteOutOfProcess	True

11. Similarly, add the following packages using the Execute Package task with the following details and connect them using the green arrows.

For Archiving downloaded files task:

Name	Archiving downloaded files
Description	This task executes the named package
Location	File system
Connection	C:\SSIS\Projects\Control Flow Tasks\Archiving downloaded files.dtsx
ExecuteOutOfProcess	True

For Importing expanded files task:

Name	Importing expanded files
Description	This task executes the named package
Location	File system
Connection	C:\SSIS\Projects\Control Flow Tasks\Importing expanded files.dtsx
ExecuteOutOfProcess	True

Your package should look like the one shown in Figure 5-18.

12. Before we run this package, make sure the zipped files are still available in the FTP server in the Sales folder. After checking this, delete DealerSales01 .txt and DealerSales02.txt files from the C:\SSIS\downloads folder and delete DealerSales01.zip and DealerSales02.zip from the C:\SSIS\downloads\Archive folder. Using SQL Sever Management Studio, run the following commands to delete all the rows from the DealerSales table:

```
TRUNCATE TABLE [Campaign].[dbo].[DealerSales]
```

Now that all the previous files and data have been deleted, run the package by pressing F5. You will see that the defined packages are opened and executed in sequence one after another. Once all four packages have been executed successfully, check the folders to see the files at expected places and the rows loaded into DealerSales table—242,634 in total.

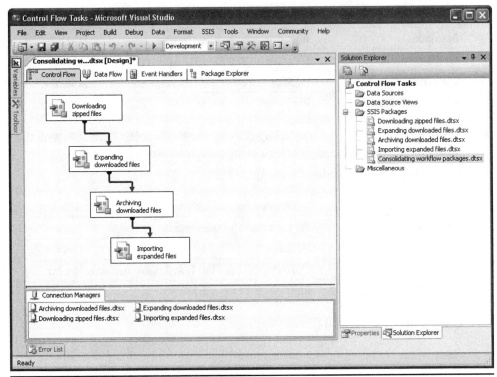

Figure 5-18 *Consolidating Workflow Packages package*

Exercise (Understanding Precedence Constraints)

In this part of the exercise, you will make changes in the ExtractFiles.bat file to fail Expanding Downloaded Files task and then study the behaviour of the package execution using success and completion constraint.

13. You have seen that the packages execute successfully. Make the following changes in the ExtractFiles.bat file to fail the Expanding Downloaded Files task:

```
REM DEL C:\SSIS\downloads\%1.txt
C:\SSIS\UNZIP %1.zip %1.txt
```

As you can now understand that when the ExtractFiles.bat file is called, it won't be able to find the UNZIP file in the C:\SSIS folder and hence will fail in operation.

Using Windows Explorer, delete DealerSales01.zip and DealerSales02.zip files from C:\SSIS\downloads\Archive folder but do not delete DealerSales01.txt and DealerSales02.txt files from the C:\SSIS\downloads folder.

14. Right-click the Consolidating Workflow Packages package in the Solution Explorer window and choose the Execute Package command from the context menu. You will see the Downloading Zipped Files package appearing on the screen and being executed successfully followed by Expanding downloaded files package being executed but failing as expected. Note that after the failure of this child package, the parent package Consolidating Workflow Packages stops immediately and doesn't execute tasks down the line. Stop debugging the package by pressing SHIFT-F5. Note that in the second to last line in the Output window, the package is declared finished with a failure. The exact message is "SSIS package "Consolidating workflow packages.dtsx" finished: Failure." (See Figure 5-19.)

If you don't see the Output window, you can open it by pressing CTRL-ALT-O.

15. Having seen the package fail when using the Success constraint, you will now change the Success constraint to a Completion constraint for the Archiving Downloaded Files task to see how the package behaves. Changing this constraint actually specifies that Archiving Downloaded Files task should run when the

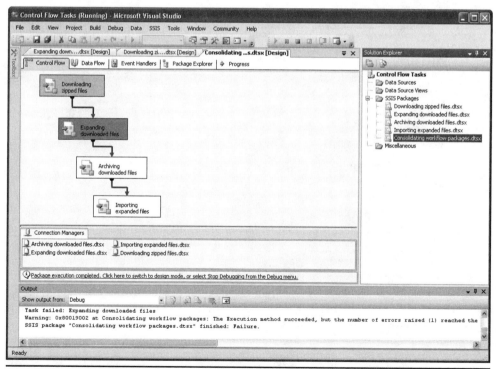

Figure 5-19 *Failing Consolidating Workflow Packages with Success constraint*

Expanding Downloaded Files task completes without regards to success or failure of Expanding Downloaded Files package.

Right-click the green arrow from the Expanding Downloaded Files task to Archiving Downloaded Files task and click Completion in the context menu. The green arrow will change to blue. This blue arrow signifies On Completion constraint for the Archiving Downloaded Files task.

Execute the Consolidating Workflow Packages package again. This time you will see the first task Downloading Zipped Files completing successfully, and then Expanding Downloaded Files task failing as expected. But your parent package doesn't stop this time; instead, it goes on to run the remaining tasks successfully and loading records in the table as the text files were available (which you didn't delete in step 13). This explains how the package behaves in case of a Completion constraint compared to a Success constraint. If you check the Output window for status, you will still see the same message you saw last time for the package being finished with a failure, but you do know for sure that this time the last two tasks ran successfully (Figure 5-20).

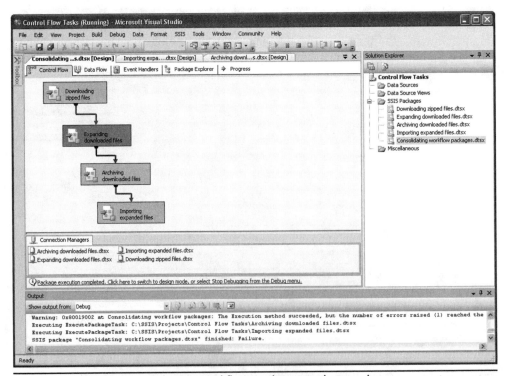

Figure 5-20 *Failing Consolidating Workflow Packages with Completion constraint*

Review

In the first part of this exercise, you used the Execute Package task to include child packages in the parent package and consolidated all the different modules into one integrated package with all the features you built separately. In the second part you learned the behavior of execution of a package with the Success constraint and later with the Completion constraint. If a task fails during run-time for any reason, the following tasks that are using the Success constraint for this package will not be executed and the package will fail immediately. On the other hand, if the failing task connects with following tasks using the Completion constraint, the remaining tasks get executed with no regard to success or failure, though the tasks that depend upon the processing of the failing task may be affected due to unavailability of data. You also learned that the final message for a package might not tell you a true story about the execution status of the package. So, you definitely need to configure logging for your packages to dig more for the failing tasks and reasons. One thing more about constraints is that expressions can also be evaluated and used along with constraints to determine the execution for the subsequent tasks in a package.

Send Mail Task

Using the Send Mail task, you can send messages from your packages on the basis of success or failure of the package or on the basis of an event raised during execution of the package. This task uses the SMTP Connection Manager to send mails using the SMTP server. You can either specify the message directly in the task, let the task read from a file, or choose a variable to be sent as a message. You can use this feature to pass messages or variables between SSIS packages running on different servers. You can also use the Send Mail task to send notification messages about success or failure of other tasks. You have already used this task in the "Contacting Opportunities" Hands-On exercise in Chapter 4, to which you can refer back for details.

WMI Data Reader Task

For the benefit of those who haven't used WMI, I will explain Windows Management Instrumentation (WMI) and its background to give you a head start. The Distributed Management Task Force (DMTF) is an industry consortium that is involved with the development, support, and maintenance of management standards for computer systems and is involved with management technologies such as Common Information Model (CIM) and Web-Based Enterprise Management (WBEM). CIM is a standard for describing management information. CIM allows different management applications to collect the required data from a variety of sources and is platform independent. WBEM uses browsers and applications to manage systems and networks throughout the enterprise. WBEM uses CIM as the database for information about computer systems and network devices. Microsoft has implemented the DMTF's CIMV2 and WBEM standards in WMI.

WMI schema is logically partitioned into namespaces for organizational and security purposes. You should use WMI Control (Computer Management | Services and Applications | WMI Control | Properties) or the Wmimgmt.msc Microsoft Management Console (MMC) snap-in to view and modify the security on WMI namespaces. Namespace actually groups a set of classes and instances that relate to a particular managed environment logically. For example, CIMV2 groups a set of classes and instances that relate to aspects of the local Windows environment. Though DMTF has defined a lot of namespaces within WBEM, Microsoft has chosen to instrument the various classes and properties that fall within the CIMV2 namespace.

The Windows Operating System provides management information through the WMI component. WMI can be used to query computer systems, networks, and applications that can be further extended to create event-monitoring applications.

Using the WMI Data Reader task you can run WQL queries to get the information from WMI such as the presence, state, or properties of hardware components, Windows event logs, and installed applications; this enables your package to decide based on the results of WQL query whether the other tasks in the package should run.

The WMI Query Language (WQL) is a subset of ANSI SQL with minor semantic changes to support WMI. You can write data, event, and schema queries using WQL. Data queries are most commonly used in WMI scripts and applications to retrieve class instances and data associations, whereas schema queries are used to retrieve class definitions and schema associations and event queries are used to raise event notifications.

The good news is that writing a WQL query is similar to writing an SQL query because they use common dialect. WQL is modified to support WMI event notification and other WMI-specific features. However, the tough bit is that WMI classes vary between versions of Windows and the WQL queries used here may not work on your system, as they have been tested only on a Windows XP machine.

Let's do a quick and short Hands-On exercise to demonstrate how to configure the WMI Data Reader task and write WQL queries.

Hands-On: Reading the Application Log

You are required to copy the application log error messages to a text file based on a criteria using the WMI Data Reader task.

Method

In this exercise, you will use the WMI Data Reader task to read an application log for error messages generated by Microsoft SQL Server after November 7, 2005.

Here's the step by step procedure:

▶ Create a WMI Connection Manager to connect to the server.

▶ Write a WQL query to read the application log.

▶ Complete configurations of the WMI Data Reader task

Exercise (Create WMI Connection Manager)

1. Run BIDS if not already running and open the Control Flow Tasks project. Add a new package to the SSIS Packages folder in the Solution Explorer window. Rename the package **Reading Application Log.dtsx**.

2. Drag the WMI Data Reader task from the Toolbox onto the SSIS Designer. Double-click the task icon to open the WMI Data Reader Task Editor. On the WMI Options page, click in the WmiConnection field and choose <New WMI connection…> from the drop-down list box. This will open the WMI Connection Manager Editor. Type the following in the Connection Manager Information area:

Name	Localhost
Description	WMI connection to localhost

Leave the following default settings in the Server And Namespace area (refer to Figure 5-21):

Server name	\\localhost
Namespace	\root\cimv2

Select the Use Windows Authentication check box and click the Test button to test the connection. When you receive the success message, click OK to close the message and click OK again to close the WMI Connection Manager Editor.

3. To specify the source where the task can access the WQL query, you can choose the Direct Input, File Connection, or Variable options. Leave the Direct Input option selected in the WqlQuerySourceType field.

4. Type in the following query in the WqlQuerySource field and click OK to return to the task editor.

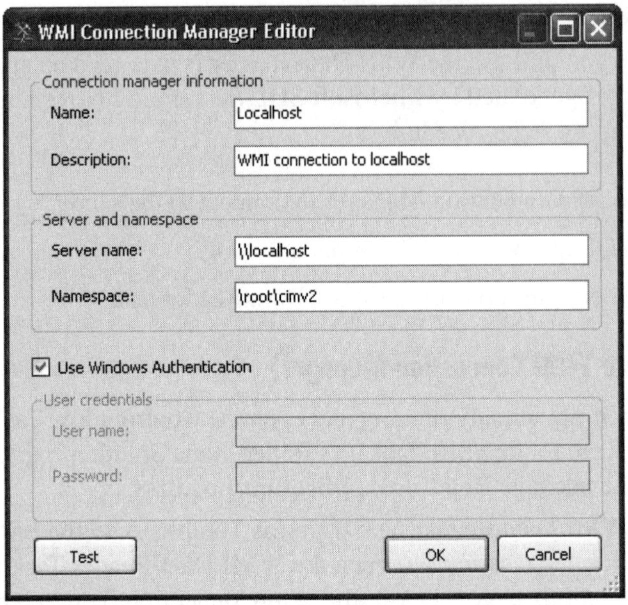

Figure 5-21   *WMI Connection Manager configured to connect to CIMV2*

```
SELECT ComputerName, EventCode, Logfile, Message, SourceName,
TimeGenerated, Type
FROM Win32_NTLogEvent
WHERE Logfile = 'Application'
AND SourceName = 'MSSQLSERVER'
AND Type = 'Error'
AND TimeGenerated > '20050731'
```

5. In the OutputType field, choose Data Table.

6. In the OverwriteDestination field, choose Overwrite Destination, as you will be running this test package many times. However, you should choose this option carefully in the production environment.

7. In the DestinationType field, you can specify to write the data to a file using the File Connection or to a variable using the Variable option. Choose File Connection in this field (see Figure 5-22).

8. In the Destination field, choose <New connection…> and select C:\SSIS\ RawFiles\ApplicationLog.txt as the existing file in the File Connection Manager Editor. This is a blank file used as a placeholder for Application Log data enclosed within the folder. If you don't find this file, create a blank text file in this folder using Notepad. Click OK twice to complete the configurations.

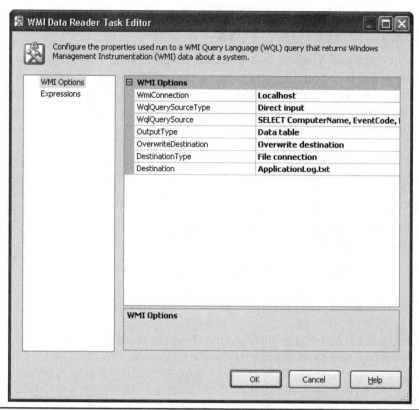

Figure 5-22 *Configuring WMI DataReader task to read application log*

9. Press F5 to start debugging the package. If you have not made any typos and the WQL configured is compatible with your system, the task will turn yellow and then green. Explore the C:\SSIS\RawFiles folder using Windows Explorer and open ApplicationLog.txt file; you will see the contents of the Windows Application log extracted in the text format.

Review

In this exercise, you learned how to configure and use the WMI Data Reader Task. You also learned about some basic concepts and terminology related to WMI. Developers use Visual Basic scripting to exploit benefits of WMI. However, while scripting for WMI, keep in mind that different versions of the Windows operating system have different sets of WMI classes in the repository. Using the WMI Data Reader task, you can harness the benefits of WMI yet avoid VB scripting using much simpler WQL language to write queries. Refer to Microsoft SQL Server 2005 Books Online to see more examples on the queries that you can use with this task.

WMI Event Watcher Task

Using the WMI Event Watcher task, you can configure your SSIS package to watch for an event, and based on the event occurrence decide whether to run the package or raise an alert using underlying WMI technology. This is a powerful feature though it requires your skills to write WQL event queries to specify the events you want to watch for. You can use this task in situations such as the following:

▶ To check for availability of enough resources (disk space, memory, and so on) on the computer system before running the package.

▶ To watch for files being added to a folder before starting the package.

▶ To wait for an e-mail (from another package) to arrive with particular subject before initiating the processing of the SSIS package.

▶ To wait for memory to be available before starting another process

Below is the step by step procedure to configure this task:

1. After you have placed this task on the Designer panel and started editing, you can specify name and description for the task on the General page.

2. On the WMI Options page, specify a WMI Connection Manager in the WmiConnection field.

3. Specify the source from where the task can read the WQL query in the WqlQuerySourceType field by choosing the Direct Input, File Connection, or Variable Option. Depending on your choice, the WqlQuerySource field changes. For example, when you choose Direct Input, you can specify the WQL query in the WqlQuerySource field.

4. In the ActionAtEvent field, you can specify the action the task should take when the event occurs. You can choose only to log the event notification and the status after the event or can choose to fire an SSIS event with the event notification and the status logged after the event (see Figure 5-23).

5. In the AfterEvent field, you can specify how the task should respond after the event. The task can be configured to return with success or failure depending on the outcome of the task, or you can configure the task to watch the event again.

6. The next two options, ActionAtTimeout and AfterTimeout, specify how the task should behave and respond when the WQL query times out.

7. In the NumberOfEvents field, you can specify the number of times the task should watch for the event.

8. Lastly, specify the time-out setting for WQL query in seconds.

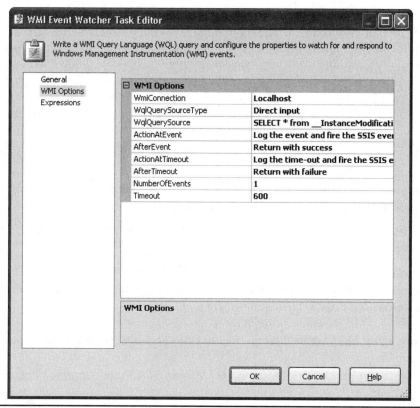

Figure 5-23 *Configurations of the WMI EventWatcher task*

ActiveX Script Task

If you have used DTS 2000, you might have used the ActiveX Script task to extend your DTS packages. This powerful task was provided in DTS 2000 and helped database developers to develop packages that otherwise wouldn't be possible. Many database developers and information analysts have exploited this task to customize data transformation; apply business logic in the DTS package; manage files and folders; dynamically set properties on tasks, connections, or global variables; and perform complex computations on the data. To help smooth migration from DTS 2000 to SSIS, Microsoft provided the ActiveX Script task in SSIS to run those custom-build scripts until such time when the scripts can be upgraded to a more advanced scripting task, simply called the Script task in SSIS.

The ActiveX Script task provided in SSIS is quite different than the one provided in DTS 2000 in look and feel. The basic purpose of the ActiveX Script task in SSIS is to allow you to run existing scripts, not develop new scripts. In fact, this task will be removed from future releases of Microsoft SQL Server. Better not to use this task to develop new scripts, and opt instead for use of the more advanced and efficient Script task for new development work.

Here are some of the benefits of using the Script task over the ActiveX Script task:

▶ The Script Task uses the Visual Studio for Applications environment, which is hosted in Visual Studio 2005 and provides an integrated development environment (IDE) rich in features such as color-coded syntax highlighting, line-by-line debugging support, and online help.

▶ Scripts developed using Visual Basic 2005 language can be precompiled in SSIS to provide excellent performance.

▶ It is easier to develop scripts in the Script Task using Visual Basic 2005 language, which is a fully featured programming language capable to refer external .NET assemblies quite easily.

To use an existing ActiveX script in your SSIS package, follow these steps:

1. Drop the ActiveX Script task on the Designer surface and double-click it to configure it.

2. Specify a Name and Description for the task in the General page.

3. In the Script page Language field drop-down list, choose a scripting language that was used to write the ActiveX script. The default choices are VB Script Language, Jscript Language, SignedJavaScript Class, and SignedVBScript Class; the ActiveX Script task can support other scripting languages based on the scripting engines installed on the local computer.

4. The Script field provides an interface where you can type in your ActiveX script. However, if you want to access your existing ActiveX script file, you can click Browse and select the file, and your script will be read in by the task and shown in the Script field. Click Save to save the contents of the Script field to a file and click Parse to parse the script.

5. The EntryMethod specifies the name of the method that is called from the ActiveX Script task at run-time.

Script Task

The Script Task lets you write your own code to extend the package functionality and get the job done. The ability to use your own code is provided by the Script task in Control Flow and by the Script component in Data Flow. To provide an IDE, the Script task and the Script component uses Visual Studio for Applications (VSA).

Using VSA, you can write scripts with Visual Basic 2005. This is the only supported language in the current release of SSIS, which means you cannot use other .NET languages such as C# or J#. Not to worry, though, as Visual Basic 2005 is a fully featured object-oriented language and is easy to program. If your business rules are already coded in .NET languages such as C# or J#, you can compile it into a .NET assembly and use it within the Script task using Visual Basic 2005 as it can call the external .NET assemblies. The Visual Basic 2005 code written in VSA is completely integrated with Integration Services—for example, the breakpoints in VSA work seamlessly with breakpoints in Integration Services. You do need to make sure that the VSA engine is installed on the computer before you run a package containing a Script Task and a Visual Basic 2005 script in it.

So, whether you want to achieve extra functionality or use existing code, the Script task provides enough facilities to allow you to accomplish your goals. You can use the Script task for any of the following:

▶ To extend your packages to use external .NET assemblies and leverage powerful .NET libraries.

▶ To connect to data stores for which preconfigured connection managers are not available.

▶ To work or skip certain rows from data specified by business rules to prevent uploading unwanted data.

When you open the Script Task Editor to configure this task, you will see three pages to configure. The following steps are necessary to configure this task:

1. In the General page, you specify a name and description for the Script task.
2. In the Script page, note that ScriptLanguage field shows Microsoft Visual Basic .NET selected. Though this is a drop-down list field, this is the only option available. Perhaps more languages will be made available here in the future.
3. Specify whether the script is precompiled into binary code before the task is run in the PrecompileScriptIntoBinaryCode field. This feature enhances the performance of your package and makes it run faster because it won't need

to be compiled at run-time. If you choose False for this option, your scripts won't be compiled when the package is saved and will be compiled when the package is run. To compile, the VSA engine must load and convert the script into binary code. This process takes time and slows down the package execution. Precompiling your scripts is highly recommended though the compiled files may consume more space.

4. Specify the entry point for your script in the EntryPoint field.

5. In the next two fields, you can specify the variables you want to work with in the script. It is worth mentioning the variables in the ReadOnlyVariables field if you do not want to update their value, as it protects the variables from accidentally being overwritten. The variables whose values will be updated in the script can be mentioned in the ReadWriteVariables field.

6. When you click the Design Script button, the VSA environment opens with a default script embedded in it, as shown in Figure 5-24. The first three lines that are commented out with a single quote describe the script. The next four lines

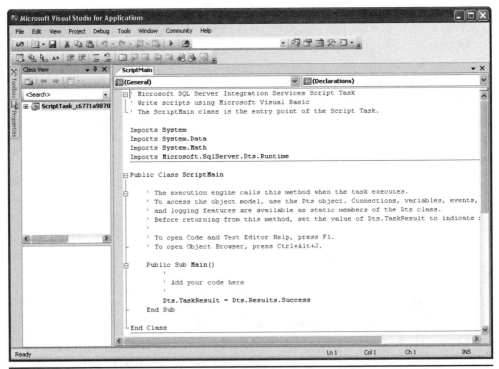

Figure 5-24 *VSA environment for writing scripts*

that start with `Imports` are the Imports statements for the script. By using Imports statements, the Script task includes some .NET Framework system libraries to make it easier for you to call functions and also includes the SSIS run-time engine. At run-time, the script gets executed by calling a class, which is ScriptMain by default. This ScriptMain class is declared in the next line that states `Public Class ScriptMain`. The ScriptMain class declares the Main sunroutine in the line `Public Sub Main()`. Below this you can add your own code. After writing your script, you can close VSA environment, which automatically saves the script for you when you close it.

7. After configuring your script, you can either close the task to go back to Control Flow or use Expressions page to configure some of the properties for the task using property expressions.

We haven't included any exercise for this task; however, if you know how to write script in Visual Basic, using this task into your package after reading above description shouldn't be difficult. Lots of examples of Visual Basic codes are available on the Web and in Microsoft SQL Server 2005 Books Online. This task is quite powerful and, in fact, scripting this task alone can create a fully functional package. However, if you are a hard-core programmer and prefer to use high-end .NET languages such as C# or J#, you can consider programming your code to create custom tasks to include in SSIS. This will also satisfy the requirement in case you need to use the same piece of code multiple times in various packages.

Transfer Database Task

The Transfer Database task transfers a database from the source SQL Server to the destination SQL Server; you can copy or move your database. This task can use DatabaseOnline or DatabaseOffline method of transfer. When you choose online transfer of the database, the source database stays online even during transfer and can respond to user queries; in the offline method, the source database is detached and the database files are copied over to the destination server. You can specify to reattach the source database or leave it offline.

You configure the Transfer Database task in the following ways:

▶ Once you open the task editor, you will see three pages: General, Databases, and Expressions. You specify name and description in the General page.

▶ Specify a SourceConnection and DestinationConnection to the source and destination servers using SMO Connection Manager in the Connections section.

▶ On the Databases page, you specify the Action from the drop-down list to copy or move the database and specify the DatabaseOnline or DatabaseOffline transfer method in the Method field. Then choose the database you want to transfer from the drop-down list provided in the SourceDatabaseName field and select the files for the database in the SourceDatabaseFiles field. You can select to ReattachSourceDatabase by selecting a value of True in this field (see Figure 5-25).

▶ In the Destination Database section, you can specify the appropriate values in the DestinationDatabaseName and the DestinationDatabaseFiles fields. Finally, you can choose to overwrite the files if they exist at destination.

▶ Use the Expressions page to modify any property at run-time using property expressions.

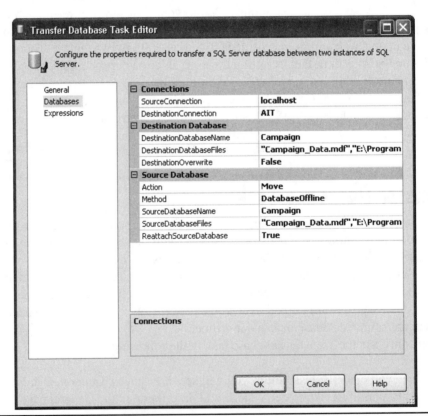

Figure 5-25 *Configurations for the Transfer Databases task*

Transfer Error Messages Task

The Transfer Error Messages task copies one or more SQL Server user-defined error messages from one SQL Server to another. Once you define error messages on one SQL Server for your application, you might like to make those error messages available at all the servers wherever you install your application. This task helps avoid the rework in creating these error messages. You create the error messages on the first server by using the sp_addmessage stored procedure and use this task to copy the defined error messages to the remaining servers. These messages can be viewed using the sys.messages catalog view.

You can configure the task as follows:

1. This task editor has three pages. Specify name and description for this task in the General page.

2. In the Messages page, you specify most of the options for this task. Specify a SourceConnection and DestinationConnection to the source and destination servers using SMO Connection Manager in the Connections section.

3. You can choose FailTask, Overwrite, or Skip if the error message already exists at the destination server in the IfObjectExists field (see Figure 5-26).

4. Then you can choose to transfer all error messages by selecting True in the TransferAllErrorMessages field. However, if you select False in the field, ErrorMessagesList and ErrorMessageLanguagesList fields become available and you can specify the error messages you want to transfer by selecting from the collection in the ErrorMessagesList field.

5. You can also select the languages for which you want to transfer user-defined error messages in the ErrorMessageLanguagesList field.

6. Use the Expressions page to modify any property at run-time using property expressions.

Transfer Jobs Task

The Transfer Jobs task copies SQL Server Agent jobs from the source SQL Server instance to the destination SQL Server instance. This task uses the SMO Connection Manager to connect to the source and destination SQL Server instances. The task is quite straightforward to configure.

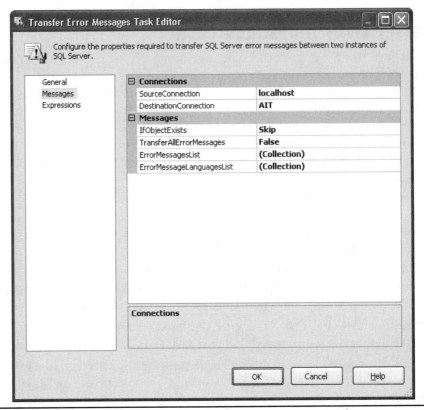

Figure 5-26   *Configuration options for the Transfer Error Messages task*

Following are the steps you will be performing to configure this task:

1. Open the editor window for the task and specify the name and description in the General page.

2. You will specify most settings in the Jobs page. Specify a SourceConnection and DestinationConnection to connect to source and destination servers using the SMO Connection Manager in the Connections section.

3. In the Jobs area, you can specify to copy all the jobs to the destination SQL Server or select from the list provided in the JobsList field. The selected jobs will be displayed as a collection in the field (see Figure 5-27).

4. After selecting the jobs you want to transfer, you can fail the task, overwrite, or skip the jobs if jobs of the same name already exist on the destination SQL Server. You can also choose to enable the jobs at the destination SQL Server.

5. Like the previous task, you can use the Expressions page to modify any property at run-time using a property expressions.

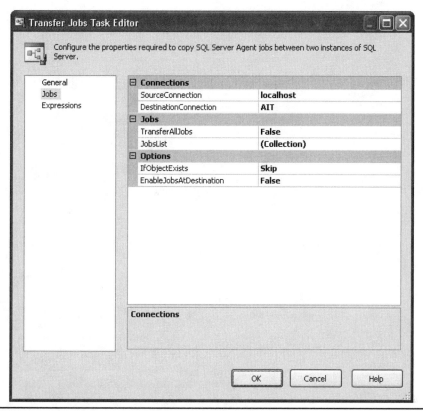

Figure 5-27 *Configuration options for the Transfer Jobs task*

Transfer Logins Task

The Transfer Logins task allows you to copy logins from the source SQL Server instance to the destination SQL Server instance. You can choose to transfer all the logins on the server or the selected servers or all the logins for the selected databases. The following steps let you configure this task on the Designer panel:

1. Open the editor window for the task to configure. Then specify a name and description in the General page.

2. You can specify most of your settings in the Logins page. Specify a SourceConnection and DestinationConnection to connect to source and destination servers using the SMO Connection Manager in the Connections section.

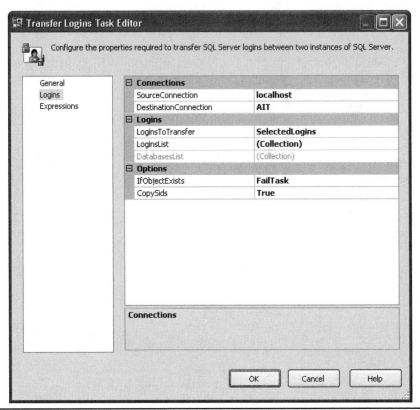

Figure 5-28 *Configuration options for Transfer Logins task*

3. In the Logins section, choose from the three options to specify the logging you want to transfer in the LoginsToTransfer field:

AllLogins	Choose to transfer all logins from the source SQL Server instance to the destination SQL Server instance. When you select this option, the subsequent two fields LoginsList and DatabasesList become unavailable.
SelectedLogins	Choose to transfer only the selected logins from the source SQL Server instance to the destination SQL Server instance. When you select this option, the LoginsList field becomes available and you can select the logins to transfer from the list provided in this field (see Figure 5-28).
AllLoginsFromSelectedDatabases	Choose this option to transfer all the logins from the selected databases. When you select this option, the DatabasesList field becomes available and you can select the databases from the list provided in this field for which you want to transfer the logins.

4. Finally, in the Options area, you can choose to fail the task, overwrite the logins, or skip the logins if they already exist in the destination server. You can also choose to copy the SIDs associated with the logins to the destination SQL Server instance using CopySids field. Each login is assigned a unique security identifier in SQL Server. The database users are then linked to SQL Server logins using these SIDs. When you transfer a database to a different server, the database users get transferred with the database, but their associated logins are not transferred as logins do not reside in the database context and creating new logins even with the same name on the destination server would not help as the newly created logins will be getting their own SIDs. To map logins on the destination server with database users, you will need their SIDs. So, when you transfer a database using Transfer Database task, you must set CopySids property to True so that the transferred database users can be mapped to the transferred logins. If you do not set CopySids value to True, the destination server will assign new SIDs to the transferred logins and the database will not be able to map users to these logins.

5. You can use the Expressions page to modify any property at run-time using property expressions.

Transfer SQL Server Objects Task

The Transfer SQL Server Objects task transfers SQL Server objects such as Schema, Tables, Primary Keys, and so on, along with other types of objects from the source SQL Server instance to the destination SQL Server instance. Following are the steps you perform to configure the options for this task:

1. Specify the name and the description for the task in the General page of the editor window.

2. In the Objects page, configure source connection and the destination connection using the SMO Connection Manager. Choose the source database and the destination database from the list provided in the database fields of the relevant connections.

3. All the remaining options are binary options for which you either select True to indicate the acceptance for the option or False. For options that you don't want to be applied to all the objects and hence you select False as a choice, you choose the objects from the list provided in the immediately following field. The default is False in all the options.

4. In the Destination Copy Options section, indicate whether you want the task to copy all objects or specific objects. If you select False, the ObjectsToCopy field becomes available for you to choose the objects you want to copy. When you expand this field, you will see a list of objects categorized based on the type of object. For each of the object types in the category list, you can choose either to copy all the objects of that type or select from the list provided in the List field. The object types you can choose here are Tables, Views, Stored Procedures, User Defined Functions, Defaults, User Defined Data Types, and Schema (see Figure 5-29).

5. In the Destination section, you can choose to drop objects at the destination server before the transfer, determine whether the extended properties are to be transferred, choose to copy schema or to include collation in the transfer, and choose whether to include the dependant objects in the transfer. You can also choose to copy data, and if selected, you can also specify whether to replace the existing data or append the data to the existing data.

6. In the Security section, you can select whether to transfer the database users, database roles, SQL Server logins, and Object level permissions.

7. In the Table options section, you can select to include Indexes, Full-Text Indexes, Triggers, Primary Keys, and Foreign Keys in the transfer. You can also specify whether the script generated by this task to transfer the object is in Unicode format.

8. Finally, you can use the Expressions page to modify any property at run-time using property expressions.

Transfer Master Stored Procedures Task

The Transfer Master Stored Procedures task copies user-defined stored procedures that are stored in the master database of the source SQL Server instance to the master database of the destination SQL Server instance. Following are the steps you would take to configure this task:

1. Specify the name and the description for the task in the General page of the editor window.

2. Specify the source and destination connections using the SMO Connection Manager.

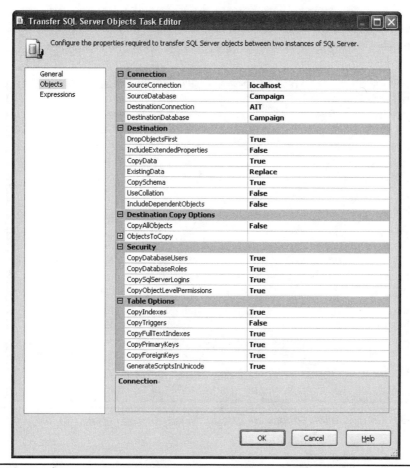

Figure 5-29 *Configuration options for Transfer SQL Server Objects task*

3. Choose to copy all or specific stored procedures defined in the master database in the TransferAllStoredProcedures field. You can select the stored procedures from the list provided in the StoredProceduresList field if you choose to transfer only the specific stored procedures (see Figure 5-30).

4. Finally, you can choose to fail the task or overwrite the stored procedures or skip over the stored procedures that already exist at the destination.

5. You can use the Expressions page to modify any property at run-time using property expressions.

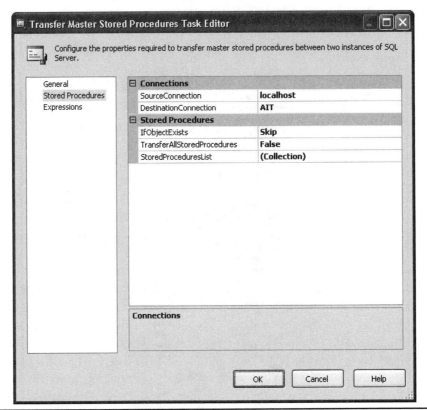

Figure 5-30 *Configuration options for Transfer Master Stored Procedures task*

Back Up Database Task

The Back Up Database task uses the BACKUP DATABASE statement to perform different types of SQL Server database backups. Using the Back Up Database task, a package can back up a single database or multiple databases. Following is the step by step method to configure this task:

1. Specify a connection to the SQL Server using the ADO.Net Connection Manager in the Connection field.

   Choose the databases you want to back up in the Databases field from the available options: All databases, All system databases (master, msdb, model), All user databases (excluding master, msdb, model and tempdb) or selected databases from the provided list.

2. Specify the Backup type by selecting from the available options of Full, Differential, or Transaction Log Only.

3. If you've selected a single database for backup, you can choose the backup component by choosing for Database or its files and filegroups.

4. Specify the destination where you want to back up the database. The available options are Disk and Tape.

5. Choose to back up single or multiple databases across one or more files or choose to back up each database to a separate file (see Figure 5-31). Spend some time to understand the available options in either method.

6. Select to verify the integrity of the backup files.

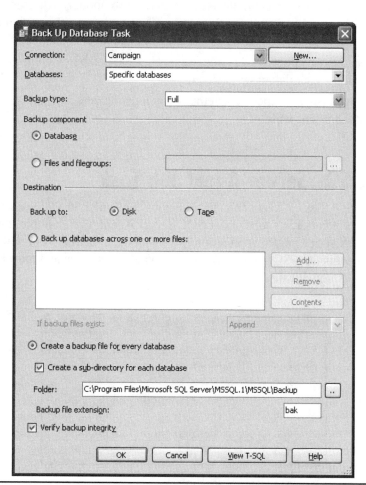

Figure 5-31 *Configuration settings for the Backup Database task*

Check Database Integrity Task

The Check Database Integrity task uses DBCC CHECKDB statement to check the allocation and structural integrity of all the objects in the specified databases.

The task is simple to configure:

1. Drag and drop this task on the Designer panel and start editing, and then specify a connection to the SQL Server using the ADO.Net Connection Manager.

   Choose the databases from Databases field. When you click the down arrow in the field, following list of options appear:

   All databases, All system databases (master, msdb, model), All user databases (excluding master, msdb, model and tempdb) or select databases from the provided list.

2. You can choose either single database or multiple databases—Figure 5-32 shows all the user databases selected.

3. Finally, you can also specify whether to include the database indexes in the Integrity check as well.

Execute SQL Server Agent Job Task

The Execute SQL Server Agent Job task runs jobs configured in SQL Server Agent. You can create a variety of jobs under SQL Server Agent. For example, the jobs can be ActiveX script jobs or replication jobs, which can be run from within SSIS package using this task. SQL Server Agent is a Windows service and must be running for jobs to run automatically.

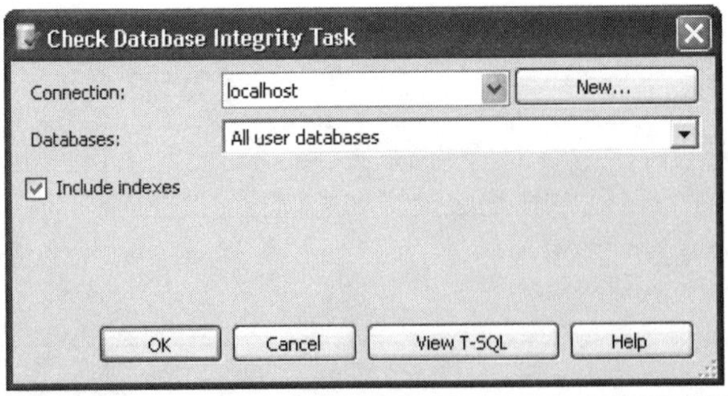

Figure 5-32 *Check Database Integrity Task interface*

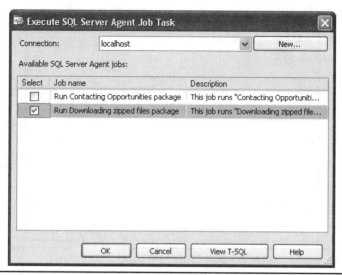

Figure 5-33 *Interface for Execute SQL Server Agent Job task*

The task interface is intuitive and easy to configure as you can make out from Figure 5-33. You specify a connection to the SQL Server. The task reads the SQL Server Agent jobs from the specified SQL Server and lists them under the Available SQL Server Agent Jobs area. You then select the job you want to run from the list provided.

Execute T-SQL Statement Task

Using the Execute T-SQL Statement task, you can run Transact-SQL (T-SQL) statements against specified database. This task supports only the T-SQL version of the SQL language and cannot be used to run statements on the servers that use other dialects of the SQL language. The Execute T-SQL Statement task cannot run parameterized queries and cannot save result sets to variables. This task is mainly designed to run T-SQL commands that can be used to maintain SQL Server. SSIS provides many other maintenance tasks for SQL Server; however, in certain situations you may find this task quite handy and easy to configure to achieve the desired results quickly and efficiently.

This task is quite simple to configure as you can see from Figure 5-34. You specify a connection to the SQL Server in the Connection field and type your T-SQL command in the space provided. Optionally, you can specify an execution time out value to the task.

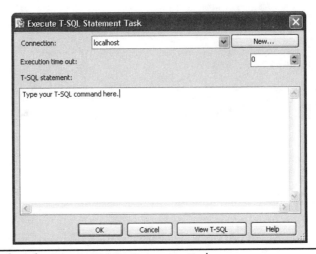

Figure 5-34 *Interface for Execute T-SQL Statement Task*

History Cleanup Task

When SQL Server Agent runs jobs for a considerable period of time, the job history, which is kept in msdb database tables, can fill up the database with lot of unwanted data. The History Cleanup task enables a package to delete the historical data stored in tables of msdb database for backup and restore activities, SQL Server Agent jobs, and database maintenance plans. The tables of the msdb database that get affected are backupfile, backupfilegroup, backupmediafamily, backupmediaset, backupset, restorefile, restorefilegroup, and restorehistory. Here's the step by step configuration method for this task:

1. Connect to the SQL Server while trying to configure this task. This task uses the ADO.Net (SqlClient Data Provider) Connection Manager to create an SQL Server connection.

2. Choose the historical data that you want to delete from the three available options: Backup and Restore History, SQL Server Agent Job History, and Maintenance Plan History (Figure 5-35).

3. Specify the time period for the oldest date of the data that you want to be retained in the database. You can specify the time period by number of days, weeks, months, or years from the date the task is run.

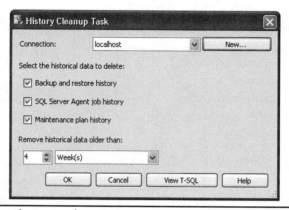

Figure 5-35 *History Cleanup task options*

Maintenance Cleanup Task

While the History Cleanup task clears the stale data such as backup and restore activities or job histories from the tables in the msdb database, the Maintenance Cleanup task deletes database backup files or Maintenance Plan text reports files based on the time period specified.

Here are the steps you take to configure this task:

1. In the user interface, specify a connection to the server. You can create a new connection by clicking the New button and specifying a name to the connection, and then specifying the database server to which you want to connect using Windows or SQL Server user authentication. This task uses the ADO.Net (SqlClient Data Provider) Connection Manager to connect to the SQL Server.

2. Choose the type of files you want to delete from the available backup files or Maintenance Plan text reports options (Figure 5-36).

3. Specify a folder to look for the type of files already chosen, or point the task to the specific file.

4. Specify a value for the time period for which you want to delete files older than the specified value. You can specify this value by providing a number, and unit of time in day, week, month, or year.

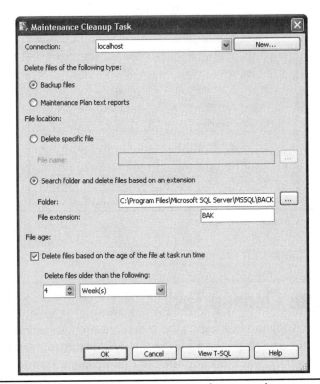

Figure 5-36 *Configuration options for Maintenance Cleanup task*

Notify Operator Task

The Notify Operator task sends notification messages to SQL Server Agent operators. For this task to work properly, you need to have SQL Server Agent service working; for the task to show you the list of operators, you need to have operators defined in SQL Server Agent and assign them an e-mail address. This task lists only users that have an e-mail address associated with them.

Following is the step by step method to configure this task:

1. Drag and drop this task on the Control Flow panel of your package, and then connect to the SQL Server. This task uses the ADO.Net (SqlClient Data Provider) Connection Manager to create a server connection.

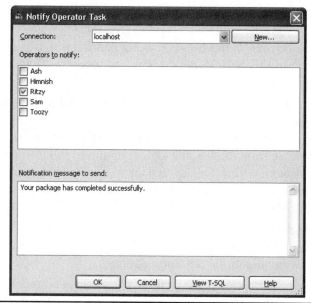

Figure 5-37   *User Interface for Notify Operator task*

2. Select the operators you want to notify from the list, as shown in Figure 5-37 under the Operators To Notify area. If you do not have any operator configured with an e-mail address to which you are trying to connect, you will receive the error message "There are no operators with e-mail addresses defined on this server." You can configure operators using SQL Server Management Studio.

3. Type in the message you want to send and click OK to complete the configuration.

Rebuild Index Task

When you insert, update, or delete records from tables, the indexes become fragmented and the performance suffers. To keep the performance at the optimum level, you may decide to rebuild indexes as part of your SSIS package. The Rebuild Index task drops the index and creates a new one using the specified fill factor for SQL Server database tables and views. By rebuilding the index, this task removes fragmentation of pages, compacts the tables, reclaims disk space, and orders the rows in the contiguous pages, thus improving performance. This task effectively runs the ALTER INDEX REBUILD T-SQL command.

Here is the step by step method to configure this task:

1. Drag the task on the Control Flow Designer panel and start configuring this task. First connect to the SQL Server. This task uses the ADO.Net Connection Manager to create a server connection.

2. Choose the databases from the following options: All databases, All system databases (master, msdb, model), All user databases (excluding master, msdb, model and tempdb) or select databases from the provided list. If you choose a single database from the list, the Object option highlights, enabling you to choose tables or views for which you want to update statistics. However, if you choose multiple databases, you can't select the tables or views and the Object option is dimmed.

3. If you have selected single database in the Databases option, you can select Table, View, or Tables and Views in the Object option (Figure 5-38). Selecting Table or View highlights the Selection option.

4. When the Selection option is available, you can select either all objects or select objects from the list.

5. Choose how much free space you want to leave in a page. This free space is governed by FILLFACTOR represented in percentage. You can either use the original FILLFACTOR by selecting Reorganize Pages With The Default

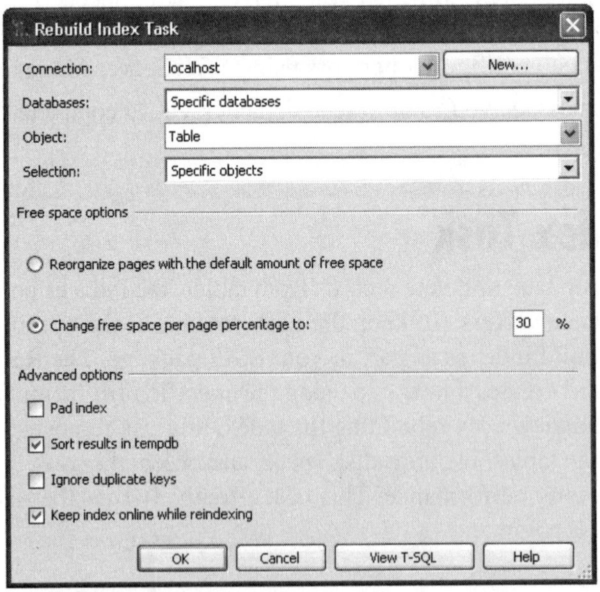

Figure 5-38 *Configuration options for Rebuild Index task*

Amount Of Free Space or you can type in the value for FILLFACTOR in percentage when you select Change free Space Per Page Percentage To option. Fill factor values 0 and 100 are treated in the similar respect and the pages are filled to the capacity.

6. Select the Pad Index Advanced Option to allocate percentage of free space specified by FILLFACTOR to the intermediate-level pages of the index.

7. When you build the index, the intermediate sort results are generally stored in the same database. However, you can also store these sort results in the tempdb. By doing this, you can reduce the time required to build an index, when the tempdb is on a separate set of disks than the database in question. Note that this may put extra requirements of space on the tempdb. So, when you want to use tempdb to sort results to reduce time, you can select the Sort Results In Tempdb Advanced Option to store the intermediate sort result used to rebuild the index in tempdb.

8. Selecting the Ignore Duplicate Keys Advanced Option allows only the rows that violate the unique index to fail in a multiple-row insert operation. All other rows that do not violate the unique constraints are inserted.

9. Choose the Keep Index Online While Reindexing Advanced Option to let the queries or updates happen to the underlying table during re-indexing.

Reorganize Index Task

When you insert, update, or delete records from tables, the indexes become fragmented and the performance suffers. To fix this, you can use this task in your SSIS packages along with other tasks such as bulk insert. The Reorganize Index task reorganizes indexes in SQL Server database tables and views and does the defragmenting of indexes by re-ordering leaf level pages and compaction. This task effectively runs the `ALTER INDEX T-SQL` command and uses the `REORGANIZE WITH (LOB_COMPACTION = ON)` clause in the command.

Here is the step by step method to configure this task:

1. Drag the task on the Control Flow Designer panel and start configuring this task. First connect to the SQL Server. You use the ADO.Net Connection Manager to create a server connection.

   Choose the databases from the option list (refer to Figure 5-39): All databases, All system databases (master, msdb, model), All user databases (excluding master, msdb, model and tempdb) or select databases from the provided list.

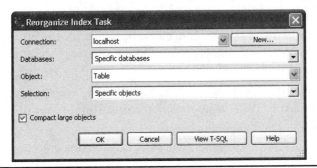

Figure 5-39 *Interface for Reorganize Index task*

If you choose a single database from the list, the Object option highlights, enabling you to choose tables or views for which you want to update statistics. However, if you choose multiple databases in this option, you can't select the tables or views and the Object option is dimmed.

2. If you have selected a single database in the Databases option, you can select Table, View, or Tables and Views in the Object option. Selecting Table or View highlights the Selection option.

3. When the Selection option is available, you can select either all objects or select objects from the list.

4. You can choose to compact the large objects. The data with the image, text, ntext, varchar(max), nvarchar(max), varbinary(max), or xml data type is considered as the Large object data. You can optionally choose to view the T-SQL code.

Shrink Database Task

This task runs the DBCC SHRINKDATABASE T-SQL command to shrink the specified database. The step by step configuration process goes like this:

1. Drag the task on the Designer panel and start configuring this task. First connect to the SQL Server. This task uses the ADO.Net Connection Manager to create connection to the server.

   Choose the databases from the option list: All databases, All system databases (master, msdb, model), All user databases (excluding master, msdb, model and tempdb) or select databases from the provided list.

2. After selecting the database, specify when you want this task to execute by typing in the size in megabytes in the Shrink database when it grows beyond option.

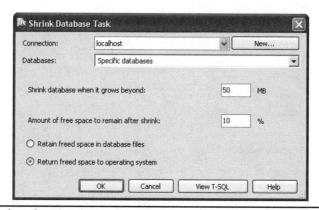

Figure 5-40 *Interface for Shrink Database task*

3. Specify how much free space you want to leave in the database by typing in a value in percentage (from 0 through 100) in the Amount Of Free Space To Remain After Shrink option (see Figure 5-40). This percentage value is calculated on the space occupied by the data in the database and not the total size of the database. For example, when you have a database of 100 MB with 40 MB of data and 60 MB of free space, specifying 50 percent value in the Amount of Free Space To Remain After Shrink option will shrink the database to 60 MB, having 40 MB of data and 20 MB of free space.

4. Choose between the two options Retain Freed Space in Database Files or Return Freed Space to Operating System after shrinking. At this time, you can view the T-SQL code if you have an interest or simply click OK to close the task dialog box.

Update Statistics Task

This task runs UPDATE STATISTICS T-SQL command to update information about the distribution of key values for one or more statistics groups (collections) in the specified databases. Following is the step by step procedure for configuring this task:

1. Drag and drop this task on the Control Flow Designer surface and start configuring this task. First create a server connection for this task by clicking the New button. This task uses the ADO.Net (SqlClient Data Provider) Connection Manager to connect to the server.

   Choose one or more databases from the option list: All databases, All system databases (master, msdb, model), All user databases (excluding master, msdb, model and tempdb) or select databases from the provided list.

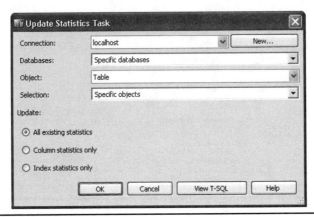

Figure 5-41 *Update Statistics task interface*

2. If you choose a single database from the list, the Object option highlights, enabling you to choose tables or views for which you want to update statistics (see Figure 5-41). However, if you choose multiple databases in this option, you can't select the tables or views and the Object option is dimmed.

3. If you have selected Single Database in the Databases option, you can select Table, View, or Tables And Views in the Object option. Selecting Table or View highlights the Selection option.

4. When the Selection option is available, you can select all objects or select objects from the list.

5. Choose between the three options to update All Existing Statistics or Column Statistics Only or Index Statistics Only. If you view the T-SQL code, you will see that the Column Statistics Only option adds the `WITH COLUMN` clause and Index statistics adds only the `WITH INDEX` clause to the SQL code.

Summary

We have covered a lot of ground in this chapter—all the Control Flow tasks, and we've used some of them in Hands-On exercises. We have also used variables and property expressions, along with a little exercise on precedence constraints. By now you must be getting ready to create packages involving complex features and data manipulation. Before we get into advanced features of event handling and logging (Chapter 8) and Data Flow (Chapters 9 and 10), we will cover administration of SSIS packages in next two chapters so that you have time to settle in with the knowledge you've gained from in this chapter.

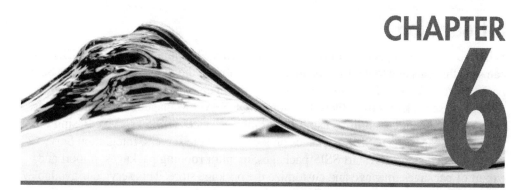

Administrating Integration Services

Introduction

When you develop a package in Business Intelligence Development Studio (BIDS), you can save this package to the file system, inside a table in the SQL Server, or in the SSIS package store. You will then use SQL Server Management Studio to run, monitor, or manage these packages from these locations. SQL Server Management Studio provides these management capabilities using Integration Services (SSIS) service. Using this service you can manage SSIS packages on local or remote servers. Integration Services service lets you stop and start SSIS packages, monitor running packages, import and export of packages, manage and customize the package store. This service is available only in SQL Server Management Studio, which means that you must install SQL Server Management Studio to manage stored and running SSIS packages.

During installation, when you choose Integration Services in the Components to Install section, SSIS service is installed. After Installation is completed, this service is not started by default and must be started before you can connect it or use it. If you don't install or start the SSIS service, you cannot save your packages to SQL Server unless you start SSIS service; however, you can save your packages to the file system without having SSIS service started. Also, you cannot run your SSIS packages using Integration Services in SQL Server Management Studio unless SSIS service has been started. However, you can run your SSIS packages using the SQL Server Import and Export Wizard, the Package Execution utility, and DTExec command prompt utility without running SSIS service. Another benefit of having SSIS service started is that it caches the Integration Services components metadata when the package is loaded the first time and speeds up subsequent loading of the package.

Let's do a quick Hands-On exercise to enable Integration Services Service.

Hands-On: Enabling the SSIS Service

In this exercise, we will enable the SSIS service.

Method

Though you can use other methods such as Services MMC (Microsoft Management Console) or the command prompt to enable SSIS, as this is a standard Windows-based service, we will take this opportunity to use the SQL Server Surface Area Configuration tool, a new security tool provided in SQL Server 2005, to enable SSIS service.

Exercise (Use the SQL Server Surface Area Configuration Tool)

1. Run SQL Server Management Studio from the Start menu (Start | All Programs | Microsoft SQL Server 2005 program group). When the program loads, choose Integration Services in the Server Type field of the Connect To Server dialog box and type in the name of your server in the Server Name field. Then click the

Connect button. If you have not already enabled Integration Services, you will get an error message stating the SSIS service failed to start because it is disabled. Click OK to close the error message. In the following steps we will enable the SSIS service. Leave the Connect to Server dialog box open in SQL Server Management Studio. We will return to this UI to connect to Integration Services.

2. Choose Start | All Programs | Microsoft SQL Server 2005, and go to the Configuration Tools group and click SQL Server Surface Area Configuration.

   SQL Server 2005's new security architecture is secure by default—i.e., many features are disabled by default in the new installations. This has been done to reduce the attackable surface area of the system. The SQL Server Surface Area Configuration tool allows you to enable and disable key services and features selectively.

   Spend a few minutes reading the description shown for this tool (see Figure 6-1). From here, you can launch the following tools:

   ▶ **Surface Area Configuration for Services and Connections**   Used to enable or disable Windows services and network protocols.

   ▶ **Surface Area Configuration for Features**   Used to enable and disable features of the database engine, Analysis Services, and Reporting Services.

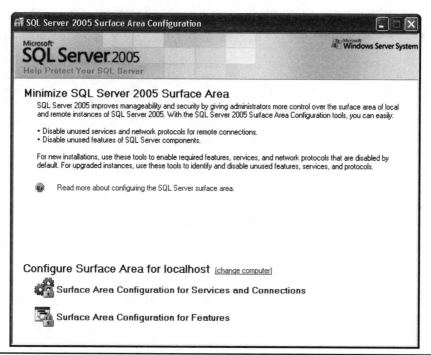

Figure 6-1 *SQL Server 2005 Surface Area Configuration tool*

You can use the SQL Server Surface Area Configuration tool to enable or disable remote SQL Server Services. We will use Surface Area Configuration for Services and Connections tool to enable SSIS service on our local server. For more information on SQL Server Surface Area Configuration tool, refer to Microsoft SQL Server 2005 Books Online.

3. Click the Surface Area Configuration for Services and Connections tool, and in the dialog box that appears, you can begin to configure services and connections for SQL Server 2005 components. In the left pane, click Integration Services, and you will see the service name showing *MsDtsServer* and a description telling you that this service provides management support for SSIS package storage and execution.

4. Change the Startup Type to Automatic by selecting it from the drop-down box. Click Apply.

5. Once the settings have been applied to the service to start it automatically on server restart, click Start (see Figure 6-2) to start the service. The Surface Area Configuration tool will try to start the service. When the service has been started, click OK to close the Surface Area Configuration for Services and Connections window. Close the SQL Server 2005 Surface Area Configuration window also.

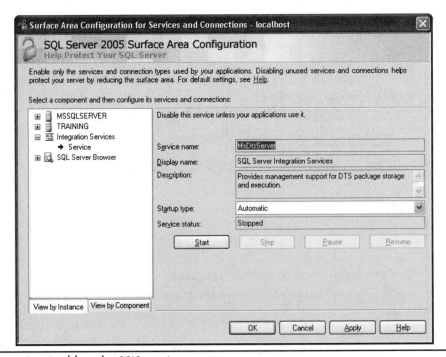

Figure 6-2   *Enabling the SSIS service*

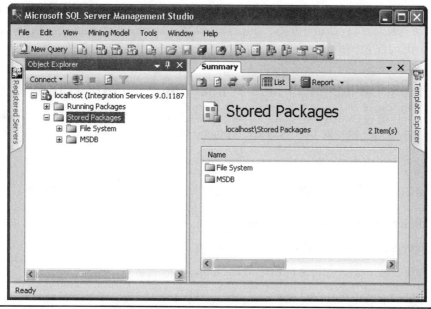

Figure 6-3   *Integration Services folders in Object Explorer*

6. Congratulations! You've enabled and started SSIS service, and you can now connect to Integration Services in SQL Server Management Studio to manage and run SSIS packages. Switch back to the Connect to Server window in SQL Server Management Studio. Click Connect. This time you will be connected to Integration Services and will be seeing the top-level folders (see Figure 6-3) of SSIS. Leave the SQL Server Management Studio for a minute and read on; we will return to Management Studio a bit later to explore further.

Review

In this exercise, you enabled and started SSIS service and could connect to it using SQL Server Management Studio. You have also seen the top-level folders of SSIS service, which are discussed next.

Working with Integration Services Folders and Packages

As you have seen, Integration Services provides two top-level folders—Running Packages and Stored Packages. The Running Packages folder lists the currently running packages. You will be monitoring long running packages from this place.

Stored Packages lists the packages saved to the file system or to the SQL Server msdb database. This area is configurable and extensible. You will be working with this area a lot to manage the storage of your folders.

Hands-On: Managing Storage of Integration Services Package

In this exercise, you will learn about the storage areas where you can save packages and how you can change their storage type and location.

Method

The following will be completed:

▶ Understand the folders and their locations

▶ Save a package to SSIS Package Store

▶ Add a root level folder to Stored Packages

▶ Import and export packages

Exercise (Understand the Folders and Their Locations)

1. Switch back to SQL Server Management Studio, where you should see the top-level folders Running Packages and Stored Packages. Expand both the folders to see the folder hierarchy.

2. On expanding the Running Packages folder, you will realize that it doesn't have any subfolder and you will not be able to create a subfolder under it. This is because the Running Packages folder is not extensible.

3. Expand the Stored Packages folder and the folders you see within it—the File System and MSDB folders are called *root level folders*. The File System folder lists the packages stored in the file system. The default location of this folder is %Program Files%\Microsoft SQL Server\90\DTS\Packages. Right-click the File System folder and choose New Folder from the context menu. Type **Campaigns** in the Create New Folder window and click OK to close the dialog box. Right-click the File System folder and choose Refresh. You will see Campaigns subfolder under the File System folder. Now explore to the %Program Files%\ Microsoft SQL Server\90\DTS\Packages folder and you will see Campaigns folder there.

   You can also create subfolders in MSDB folder. Packages saved to the SQL Server msdb database appear under the MSDB folder in Integration Services.

To sum up, you can create subfolders under the File System folder and MSDB folder to manage your packages in a hierarchical order. You can then delete or rename these subfolders; however, you cannot delete or rename the root folders.

Exercise (Save a Package to an SSIS Package Store)

4. Start BIDS and open the Contacting Opportunities solution. When the solution loads, go to the Solution Explorer window and double-click the Mailing Opportunities.dtsx package under the SSIS Packages node to open the package in the Designer. When the package appears on screen, choose File | Save Copy of Mailing Opportunities.dtsx As. This will open the Save Copy of Package dialog box, which gives you choices of where you want to save your package.

   Click the down arrow in the Package Location field to see the locations where you can save your packages. You have three options:

   ► SQL Server

   ► File System

   ► SSIS Package Store

   Choosing SQL Server lets you save your packages to the sysdtspackages90 table of the msdb database in SQL Server. The File System option allows you to save your package anywhere on the file system. You can specify a path in the Package Path field for saving the package. Selecting SSIS Package Store allows you to save your package to the defined storage area on the file system. It's worth noting the difference between the File System option and SSIS Package Store. The File System option allows you to save your package anywhere on the file system and these packages will not be visible in SQL Server Management Studio, while selecting the SSIS Package Store option lets you save your package only under the Stored Packages root folder defined in Integration Services, which will be available in SQL Server Management Studio.

   Note that a naming issue exists with the File System folder. In SQL Server Management Console, the File System folder means SSIS Package Store, which points to the location as defined in the configuration file of Integration Services, but in the Save Copy of Package dialog box, the File System option means you can save your package anywhere on the file system. The packages saved on the file system other than the SSIS Package Store will not be available for management under SQL Server Management Studio.

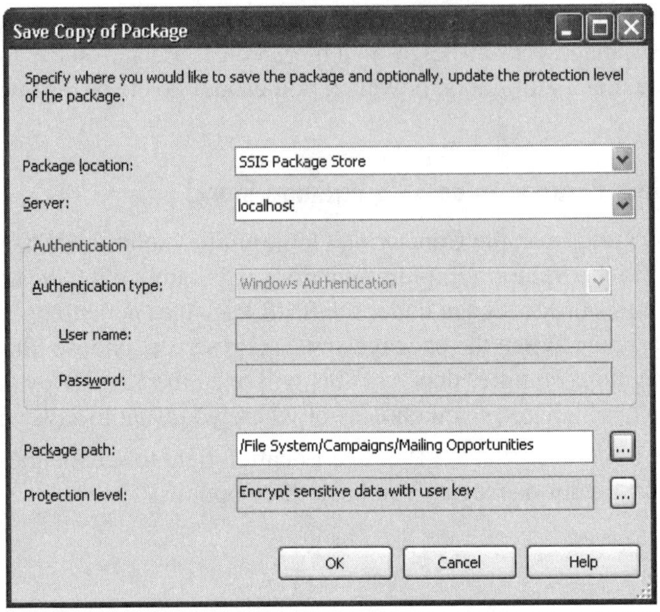

Figure 6-4   *Saving your package to the SSIS Package Store*

5. Select SSIS Package Store in the Package Location field. Type in your server name or localhost if you're saving locally. Click the ellipsis (...) button opposite to Package Path field to open the SSIS Package window with the same folder structure available in SQL Server Management Studio. Expand the File System folder then select Campaigns, and then type **Mailing Opportunities** in the Name Of The Package field. Click OK to return to Save Copy of Package dialog box (see Figure 6-4). Click OK again to save the package.

6. Switch to SQL Server Management Studio, right-click the File System folder, and choose Refresh. Expand the File System and then Campaigns folders to see the Mailing Opportunities package.

    Also, if you explore to Campaigns folder under the %Program Files%\Microsoft SQL Server\90\DTS\ packages folder, you will see the Mailing Opportunities.dtsx file saved there as well. This is the default location specified in the Integration Services configuration file which is discussed in the next part.

Exercise (Add a Root Level Folder to Stored Packages)

You have seen by now that the root folders can contain subfolders. But what if you want to store your packages at a different place than where the root folders point to by default? You can achieve this objective with the help of a configuration file provided to configure Integration Services.

7. Explore to the folder C:\Program Files\Microsoft SQL Server\90\DTS\Binn and look for file MsDtsSrvr.ini.xml. This is the default location of the Integration Services configuration file. Right-click the file and choose Open With | Notepad. You will see the following XML configuration code in the file:

```
<?xml version="1.0" encoding="utf-8"?>
<DtsServiceConfiguration xmlns:xsd="http://www.w3.org/2001/
XMLSchema" xmlns:xsi="http://www.w3.org/2001/XMLSchema-instance">
   <StopExecutingPackagesOnShutdown>true
    </StopExecutingPackagesOnShutdown>
   <TopLevelFolders>
     <Folder xsi:type="SqlServerFolder">
       <Name>MSDB</Name>
       <ServerName>.</ServerName>
     </Folder>
     <Folder xsi:type="FileSystemFolder">
       <Name>File System</Name>
       <StorePath>..\Packages</StorePath>
     </Folder>
   </TopLevelFolders>
</DtsServiceConfiguration>
```

Locate the XML element <StopExecutingPackagesOnShutdown> and note that you can control how Integration Services treats the running packages when the service is stopped. By default, it is set to True, which means that the running packages will be stopped when the SSIS service is stopped. By changing True to False in this line, you can configure Integration Services to continue running packages even if the SSIS service has been stopped.

8. We will now add a root file system folder so that we can save our packages to a different area. Move to the XML element <Folder xsi: type="FileSystemFolder"> in the configuration file. Note that the storage path ..\Packages actually points to %Program Files%\Microsoft SQL Server\90\DTS\Packages. Copy the <Folder> element—i.e., copy four lines starting from <Folder xsi:type="FileSystemFolder"> to </Folder>. Now add these lines between the </Folder> and the </TopLevelFolders> elements. In the new lines, change the values of <Name> element to SSIS Package Store and <StorePath> element to C:\SSIS\Packages. Your new lines should look like this:

```
<Folder xsi:type="FileSystemFolder">
  <Name>SSIS Packages Store</Name>
  <StorePath>C:\SSIS\Packages</StorePath>
</Folder>
```

Save the configuration file. To see the changes, restart the Integration Service.

Open the Services MMC (Microsoft Management Console) from the Administrative Tools. Locate the SQL Server SSIS service from the list. Right-click SQL Server Integration Services and choose Restart. Once the service stops and starts again, switch to SQL Server Management Studio and refresh Stored Packages to see the newly added folder SSIS Packages Store. This folder actually points to C:\SSIS\Packages folder on the file system.

Exercise (Import and Export Packages)

You can change the storage format and location of packages by using the import and export features of the Integration Services. This can also be done from the command prompt using the dtutil utility. In this exercise, you will import the Mailing Opportunities package to the MSDB folder and then export this package to SSIS Packages Store you created previously.

9. Switch to SQL Server Management Studio, right-click the MSDB folder and choose Import Package. An Import Package window will open. This window is similar to the Save Copy of Package dialog box, except it has an extra field for specifying the package name to be imported. In the Package Location field drop-down list, choose SSIS Package Store and type **localhost** in the Server field. Click the ellipsis (...) button opposite to the Package Path field. In the SSIS Package dialog box, expand the File System folder, then the Campaigns folder, and then select the Mailing Opportunities package (see Figure 6-5). Click OK to return.

Figure 6-5 *Selecting a package to import*

10. Click in the Package Name field and the Mailing Opportunities will be automatically filled in for you. Click OK to start importing the package. Refresh the MSDB folder to see the Mailing Opportunities package imported there.

11. In the Object Explorer window of SQL Server Management Studio, click the Connect button and connect to the database engine. Open a query pane by clicking the New Query button and run the following Query against the msdb database:

    ```
    SELECT * FROM msdb.dbo.sysdtspackages90
    ```

    The result set will contain all the information about the Mailing Opportunities package.

12. Let's export our package to an area on the file system, which is not defined in the SSIS Package Store. Go to Integration Services in the Object Explorer of SQL Server Management Studio, right-click the package Mailing Opportunities stored under MSDB folder, and choose Export Package from the list of options.

13. An Export Package–\MSDB\Mailing Opportunities dialog box opens. In the Package location field, choose SSIS Package Store and type **localhost** in the Server field. These settings enable Integration Services to read storage locations from the MsDtsSrvr.ini.xml file on the local server. Note that the SSIS Package Store is an Integration Services option, whereas you've created the SSIS Packages Store (with an *s* in *Packages*) as a folder in Integration Services, which points to the C:\SSIS\Packages folder in the file system.

14. Click the ellipsis button next to the Package Path field to open the SSIS Package dialog box. Here you can see the SSIS Packages Store folder you created earlier in Integration Services. Select the SSIS Packages Store folder and note that the Package Name already has *Mailing Opportunities* filled in. Click the OK button to close this dialog box. You will see the */SSIS Packages Store/Mailing Opportunities* value specified in the Package Path field. This is a user-friendly option that allows you to create a storage location pointer in Integration Services; all users can save packages without bothering about the actual storage location of the package. This is also quite helpful in case you want to keep your packages on a central server for archiving on your network storage. You also get an opportunity to define a new name to your package here, which is helpful in case you are saving with version numbers attached in the end of the package name. Click OK button to export the package. Explore to the C:\SSIS\Packages folder to verify that the package has been saved there. Leave the SQL Server Management Studio running (if you're not ready for a break yet!) as we will return to it in the next exercise.

Review

In this exercise, you worked with root folders of SSIS service and managed to create a subfolder to the root folder, save a package to it, and saw the options available for saving a copy of the package. You also learned about where you can monitor the running packages and where you can save them. After that, you used the configuration file for Integration Services to create an additional root folder in the SSIS Package Store area. You also saw how to use import and export features to change the storage type and location of the packages.

While we are discussing the configuration file options, you might find a couple of other options useful. If you want to use a named instance for storing your Integration Services packages, you can do so by specifying the instance name in the <ServerName> element of configuration file. You can specify the named instance in the format *InstanceName\ServerName*. Save the file, restart the SSIS service, and you are ready to store your packages in a named instance of SQL Server.

The second option is to use an alternative configuration file. Integration Services does allow you to set up and use an alternative configuration file. By default, Integration Services refers to the MsDtsSrvr.ini.xml configuration file located at C:\Program Files\ Microsoft SQL Server\90\DTS\Binn\ MsDtsSrvr.ini.xml. This location is mentioned in the Windows registry. You can change the location of the default configuration file by modifying the value of the registry key HKEY_LOCAL_MACHINE\SOFTWARE\ Microsoft\MSDTS\ServiceConfigFile. After making this change, all you need to do is restart SSIS service and Integration Services will read the new file from the location you specified in the registry.

Dtutil Utility

You have worked with Integration Services from within SQL Server Management Studio and have imported and exported your SSIS packages with the help of GUI tools. Having used these tools, you have realized how easy it is to manage your Integration Services packages from the tools' GUI. However, sometimes you need a command-line tool to write scripts to do the work in batches, you may want to automate tasks, or perhaps you want to schedule jobs. In this section you will learn how to manage Integration Services packages using Dtutil, a command prompt utility provided with SQL Server 2005.

Dtutil can be used for the following:

▶   Verifying the existence of a SSIS package

▶   Copying SSIS packages

▶   Moving SSIS packages

▶ Deleting SSIS packages

▶ Signing SSIS packages

All these usages involve the three defined storage locations—i.e., msdb database in SQL Server, anywhere on the file system, and the SSIS Package Store.

Here is the base syntax:

```
dtutil /option [value] [/option [value]]…
```

The parameters can be in any order and are not case-sensitive. Also, they are defined in terms of *option and value pairs*. The options must begin with a slash (/) or a minus sign (-). You will notice a pipe (|)at some places in the syntax, which is used as an OR operator to show the possible values of the arguments.

It is easy to learn the commands by practicing them than trying to memorize the syntax. So we will learn the utility with Hands-On exercises.

Hands-On: Using dtutil

In this Hands-On exercise, we will use dtutil against various scenarios.

Method

We will work through some exercises to study the utility to understand how it works and learn the syntax along the way. Start SQL Server Management Studio and connect to Integration Services. Also, open Windows Explorer and the command prompt and be ready to switch windows to see the results.

Exercise (Verify the Existence of an SSIS Package)

You can check the existence of a package using EXISTS option of dtutil:

```
dtutil /EXISTS [/option [value]]…
```

1. Verify whether the Mailing Opportunities package exists in the msdb database of the local server instance:

    ```
    dtutil /EXISTS /SQL "Mailing Opportunities"
    ```

    You will see the "The specified package exists" message. However, if the package doesn't exist in the local instance, you will see "The specified package does not exist". The SQL option checks for packages stored in the msdb database of SQL Server. Note that the SQL option cannot be specified with the DTS or FILE option as they are mutually exclusive to each other. However, you can use user, Password, or Server options to extend the SQL option usage.

2. Verify that the Mailing Opportunities package exists in the C:\SSIS\Packages folder of the local server:

```
dtutil /EXISTS /FILE "C:\SSIS\Packages\Mailing Opportunities.dtsx"
```

The `FILE` option checks the specified file system folder for the existence of the package. Note that `FILE` option cannot be specified with the `DTS`, `SQL`, `User`, `Password`, or `Server` options.

3. Verify that the Mailing Opportunities package exists in the shared folder called Data, of the remote server named AIT:

```
dtutil /EXISTS /FILE "\\AIT\Data\Mailing Opportunities.dtsx"
```

In this example, we used a UNC path to specify the location of the package. *AIT* is the name of the second server I'm using to test Integration Services packages designed for this book.

4. Verify that the Mailing Opportunities package exists in the SSIS Package Store:

```
dtutil /EXISTS /DTS "\SSIS Packages Store\Mailing Opportunities"
```

The `DTS` option specifies that the verification for existence of the package should be done on the SSIS Package Store. Please note that the `DTS` option cannot be specified with the `FILE`, `SQL`, `Server`, `User`, or `Password` options.

Exercise (Copy SSIS Packages)

If you have used the `COPY` command of the good old DOS (this is still available at the command prompt but hardly anyone uses it now), you will find copying packages similar. Using the DOS `COPY` command, you provide the source path and name of the file to be copied and destination path and name of the file to be copied to. With dtutil, you provide similar parameters but in a slightly more complex manner because of multiple storage locations (SQL, DTS, and FILE) are involved here. The syntax for the `COPY` command is shown here:

```
dtutil /{SourceLocation} [SourcePathandPackageName] /COPY
{DestinationLocation};[DestinationPathandPackageName] ...
```

Please note that you do not use a backslash (/) when you provide the destination location after the `COPY` command.

5. You have saved your package in the file system while designing the package using BIDS. Now you want to copy your package from the file system to the msdb database of the SQL Server called SARTH.

```
dtutil /FILE "C:\SSIS\Packages\Mailing Opportunities.dtsx" /COPY
SQL;"Mailing Opportunities" /DestS SARTH
```

If you still have the Mailing Opportunities package saved to the msdb database of your server, you will see a confirmation prompt, "Package "Mailing Opportunities" already exists. Are you sure you want to overwrite it?" Typing **Y** will overwrite the package and typing **N** will cancel the command. To stop such confirmation prompts, you can use /Quiet option in the command while trying to copy, move, or sign the package. The option DestS specifies the destination SQL Server. If this option is missing in the dtutil command, the local SQL Server will be used.

Try the same command by changing the destination package name to *Mailing Opportunities01*. When you see the message "The operation completed successfully" switch to SQL Server Management Studio; refresh the MSDB folder under Stored Packages in Integration Services to see this new package there.

6. You have a package in the msdb database and want to copy it to the file system on a different server:

```
dtutil /SQL "Mailing Opportunities" /SourceS SARTH /COPY
FILE;"\\AIT\Data\Mailing Opportunities.dtsx"
```

By now, you must have noted that I'm using double quotation marks on the package path and name. This is because the package has a white space in its name; you don't need to use double quotes if your package doesn't have white space in its path or name. The SourceS option specifies the source SQL Server name. Again to clarify, *SARTH* and *AIT* are the names of servers I use in my little test lab. You should replace the names with your computer names to perform this test. Once the command has been run successfully, check the destination location to see the package copied there.

Exercise (Move SSIS Packages)

The MOVE option moves an SSIS package from one storage location to another storage location. The syntax for this option is quite similar to the syntax of the COPY option.

```
dtutil /{SourceLocation} [SourcePathandPackageName] /MOVE
{DestinationLocation};[DestinationPathandPackageName] …
```

7. You have a package in your SSIS Package Store, which you want to archive— i.e., you want to remove it from the SSIS Package Store and copy it to the central archival location.

```
dtutil /DTS "\SSIS Packages Store\Mailing Opportunities" /MOVE
FILE;"\\AIT\Data\Mailing Opportunities.dtsx"
```

You will see a prompt to confirm that you want to write the existing package. Type **Y** to overwrite. Once the package is moved successfully, switch over to

SQL Server Management Studio and refresh the SSIS Packages Store folder to see that the package has been removed from there. Check the destination folder to find the package copied there.

8. Another instance of SQL Server is running on your server and you want to move a package from the default instance to the named instance:

```
dtutil /SQL "Mailing Opportunities" /MOVE SQL;"Mailing Opportunities"
/DestU admin /DestP Tra1n1n9 /DestS SARTH\TRAINING
```

Exercise (Delete SSIS Packages)

You can delete a package using the delete (DEL) option. The generic syntax for using the option is shown here:

```
dtutil /DEL /{SQL | DTS} [DestinationPathandPackageName]...
```

9. You want to delete an existing package from a shared folder on the network:

```
dtutil /DEL /FILE "\\AIT\Data\Mailing Opportunities.dtsx"
```

When you see the message "The operation completed successfully" switch over to Windows Explorer and check that the package has been deleted from the specified folder.

10. You want to delete a package from the msdb database in SQL Server:

```
dtutil /DEL /SQL "Mailing Opportunities01"
```

On successful deletion, switch over to SQL Server Management Studio and go to the MSDB folder; then refresh it to find that the package is no longer there. This option uses Windows Authentication, which is more secure. It is recommended that you use Windows Authentication whenever possible; however, you can use SQL logins to operate dtutil by specifying a SQL user name and password for the SQL Server. Dtutil uses different options for passing user credential details of source and destination server. For source server details, dtutil uses these options:

SourceS for source server

SourceU for user name at source server

SourceP for password of the above-mentioned user

And dtutil uses the following options for destination server details:

DestS for destination server

DestU for user name at destination server

DestP for password of the above-mentioned user

Exercise (Sign SSIS Packages)

When you are working on developing a complex SSIS project consisting of several packages, you may want to deploy the packages when they have achieved a certain level of functionality, even while the development team continues further development. In such scenarios, if you are concerned that your packages can be changed and run accidentally by others working with you on the same project, you can use the SIGN option to sign the packages and prevent these changed packages from being loading and running.

```
dtutil /Si[gn] {SQL | FILE | DTS};Path;Hash
```

The SIGN option uses three arguments separated by semicolons. A SQL destination can include the DESTU, DESTP, and DESTS options. The Path argument specifies the location of the package on which to take action and the Hash argument specifies a certificate identifier expressed as a hexadecimal string of varying length.

11. For protecting your package saved in the file system, use the following command:

```
dtutil /FILE "C:\SSIS\Packages\mailing Opportunities.dtsx" /SIGN
FILE;C:\SSIS\Packages\SignedPackage.dtsx;
7B18F301A198B83778B5E546729B0539A0D4E758
```

The hash value actually corresponds to the digital certificate I've installed on my computer, which you should change accordingly when you use this command.

Exercise (Encrypt SSIS Packages)

Properties containing information such as a password or connection string can be treated as a sensitive data. Properties containing sensitive data can be protected using encryption. Integration Services packages have a property called *ProtectionLevel* that you can use to set the level of protection for your packages. If you are creating a custom task, you can specify that the properties be treated as sensitive. Following are the ProtectionLevel options available:

▶ Level 0 strips the sensitive information.

▶ Level 1 encrypts sensitive data using the local user credentials.

▶ Level 2 encrypts sensitive data using the required password.

▶ Level 3 encrypts the package using the required password.

▶ Level 4 encrypts the package using the local user credentials.

▶ Level 5 encrypts the package using SQL Server storage encryption.

The generic syntax for encryption option is shown here:

```
dtutil /En[crypt] {SQL | FILE};Path;ProtectionLevel;Password
```

12. You want to encrypt a package stored in the file system by using a password, use this command:

```
dtutil /FILE "C:\SSIS\packages\mailing opportunities.dtsx" /ENCRYPT File;
"C:\ssis\packages\Encrypted mailing opportunities.dtsx";3;abcd
```

Now, if you open this newly created package Encrypted mailing opportunities .dtsx after adding it to a project in BIDS, you will have to specify the encryption password *abcd* while adding and opening the package. You may be wondering by now how one can decrypt the encrypted packages. Yes, you are right, dtutil has a `Decrypt` option. Using this option lets you set the decryption password when loading a package with password encryption.

Exercise (List Contents of Folders)

You may want to check the contents of folders and subfolders in SSIS Packages Store area and SQL Server (msdb database) storage area. `FDi` is a short form of asking dtutil to show folder directory:

```
dtutil /FDi {SQL | DTS}; FolderPath [; S]
```

13. Here's how you check the contents in SSIS Packages Store area:

```
dtutil /FDi DTS
```

When you use this command, the contents of the root folder will be returned, showing you the three folders File System, MSDB, and SSIS Packages Store.

14. To see the contents of SSIS Packages Store, type this:

```
dtutil /FDi DTS;"SSIS Packages Store"
```

You can also use the `S` argument with this command if you want to see the contents of subfolders.

Exercise (Create a Folder)

You can also create subfolders in SSIS Packages Store area or msdb database for storing packages in a hierarchical manner using dtutil with the syntax shown next. *ParentFolderPath* is the location for the new folder. *NewFolderName* is the name of the new folder.

```
dtutil /FC[reate] {SQL | DTS};ParentFolderPath;NewFolderName
```

15. Create a folder in the msdb database:

```
dtutil /FC SQL;\;MyPackages
```

When you see "The operation completed successfully" message, run the following command:

```
dtutil /FDi SQL
```

You will see the MyPackages folder created in msdb database. You can also verify the existence of a folder as we did for packages. To verify the MyPackages folder, type this:

```
dtutil /FE SQL;MyPackages
```

The FE command option stands for Folder Exists.

Exercise (Rename a Folder)

The folders created in SSIS Packages Store area and msdb database can be renamed using the FR option in dtutil. *ParentFolderPath* is the location of the folder to rename. *OldFolderName* is the current name of the folder. *NewFolderName* is the new name.

```
dtutil /FR[ename] {SQL | DTS};ParentFolderPath;OldFolderName;NewFolderName
```

16. Rename the MyPackages folder.

```
dtutil /FR SQL;\;MyPackages;Archives
```

Exercise (Delete a Folder)

You can delete a folder using the FDe command option existing on SSIS Packages Store area or msdb database of SQL Server. *ParentFolderPath* is the location of the folder to delete. *FolderName* is the name of the folder to delete.

```
dtutil /FDe[lete] {SQL | DTS};ParentFolderPath;FolderName
```

17. Delete the Archives folder from the MSDB database:

```
dtutil /FDe SQL;\;Archives
```

Once the operation is completed, switch over to SQL Server Management Studio to verify the deletion of the folder from the MSDB folder under the Stored Packages folder.

Review

In this exercise, you learned how to use the dtutil utility to manage your packages and the storage areas. You used it to copy, move, delete, sign, and encrypt packages stored in various storage areas. You also used the dtutil utility to see the contents of folders; to create, rename, and delete a folder from various storage areas; and to verify the existence of a folder or a package in a particular storage area.

Running Packages

You can use various options to run an Integration Services package. Your choice of tool or utility can be guided by various factors.

BIDS

You can run your packages from within BIDS while you are developing, debugging, and testing your packages. You can run your package by pressing F5 or by right-clicking the package in Solution Explorer and choosing Execute Package option from the context menu. You have already used these options while developing packages in the last chapter. Remember that when you run a package in BIDS, a Progress tab appears to show how the package is doing while the package is running, which finally converts into an Execution Results tab when you switch to design mode or stop debugging on package completion. The packages run in this fashion in SSIS Designer run immediately and cannot be scheduled. If your solution contains multiple projects and packages, you have to mark your package as a start-up package in the project to execute the correct package.

SQL Server Import and Export Wizard

The SQL Server Import and Export Wizard is the easiest utility to work with. Its interactive GUI provides a simple interface to build and run Integration Services packages. You have already used this tool a lot in variety of scenarios to create and run packages. For more details on SQL Server Import and Export Wizard refer to Chapter 2.

Package Execution Utility

The Package Execution Utility (DTExecUI) is a GUI-based version of the DTExec command prompt utility covered in the following section. To run a package using DTExecUI, connect to Integration Services in SQL Server Management Studio, right-click the package, and select the Run Package option from the context menu. You can run packages stored in the File System, MSDB, and SSIS Package Store root folder of the Integration Services storage area.

Hands-On: Running an SSIS Package Using the Package Execution Utility

In this exercise, you will learn how to use the Package Execution utility to run SSIS packages.

Method

You can start this utility from inside SQL Server Management Studio or from the command prompt by typing **DTExecUI**. We will use SQL Server Management Studio to start this utility and run the Mailing Opportunities package.

Exercise (Work with the Package Execution Utility)

1. Switch to SQL Server Management Studio if you haven't closed it; otherwise, start it from the Start menu and connect to Integration Services.

2. Under the Stored Packages area, expand the MSDB folder, right-click the Mailing Opportunities package, and choose Run Package. After a few seconds, an Execute Package Utility dialog box shown in Figure 6-6 will appear.

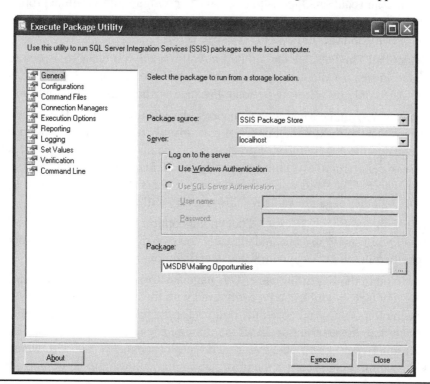

Figure 6-6   *Running the Execute Package utility*

You can run your package by clicking the Execute button without any additional run-time options. However, you may want to go through some of the useful configurations while deciding how to run your package.

3. Click Configurations on the left pane to see the configuration files options. The Package Execution utility can read the configuration files to modify the properties of your package at run-time. You can specify the order in which these files are to be loaded. This is important, as the configurations load in order starting from the top of the list, and if multiple configurations modify the same property, the configuration that loads last prevails.

4. Similar to configuration files, the Package Execution utility can read the command files to include execution command lines to your package at run-time. Click Command Files to see the interface. You can specify the order of your command files using the arrow buttons provided on the right side of this window.

5. Go to the Connection Managers page. You can edit the connection string of the connection manager that the package uses by selecting the check box provided in front of the connection manager.

6. Open the Execution Options page. You can configure the run-time properties such as validation behavior and maximum number of concurrent executables, and specify checkpoints for the package here.

   Select Fail The Package On Validation Warnings if you want your package to fail in case a validation warning occurs, and specify that the package be validated only by selecting Validate Package Without Executing Option.

   Notice the *-1* in the Maximum Concurrent Executables option. The value of *-1* means that the maximum number of concurrently running executables allowed is equal to the total number of processors on the machine executing the package, plus two. Alternatively, you can specify the maximum number of concurrent executables. The valid values are positive numbers starting from *1*. Specifying a 0 or any other negative value for this property will fail the package.

   Checking the Enable Package Checkpoints option lets you specify a checkpoint file if you want to use one and also lets you override restart options already specified in the package with those specified here.

7. Move on to the Reporting page. This page has Console Events and Console Logging boxes, which can be configured with the options provided. You can use the Reporting page to set the options for the package by selecting the events and the information about the running package to report to the console. Console Events specify the events and types of messages to report, whereas Console Logging specifies the information that you want to be written to the log when the selected event occurs.

8. In the Logging page, you can tell the Package Execution utility which log providers to use at run-time by specifying the log providers and the connection string for connecting to log. The options for log providers are as follows:

    ▶ SSIS Log Provider For Text Files

    ▶ SSIS log provider for SQL profiler

    ▶ SSIS Log Provider For SQL Server

    ▶ SSIS Log Provider For Windows Event Log

    ▶ SSIS Log Provider For XML Files

    Click in the field under the Log Provider column to choose from one of the available log providers. Then you can specify the connection string in the Connection String field.

9. The Set Values page is probably the one you will be using most often when you want to update property values of packages, executables, connections, variables, and log providers at run-time. This useful feature makes deploying packages easier. You can modify the property values by typing in the modified value and the path to the property. The path can be specified using a backslash (\) before the container, the period (.) before the property, and including a collection member within the brackets. Refer to Chapter 11 on deployment of Integration Services packages if you are getting curious to know why would you want to set property values.

10. In the Verification page, you can set the attributes that must be met before allowing a package to run. For example, you can set the attributes to run only signed packages. Other options are to verify the package for the build number, package ID number, or version ID number.

11. Finally, the Command Line page allows you to review and optionally edit the command (see Figure 6-7) that has been generated by the options you selected in the various pages.

    Select the Edit The Command Line Manually radio button to make changes in the command line. If you accidentally make mistakes here and want to undo your changes, you can do so by selecting the Restore The Original Options radio button. Please note that when you select options in the other pages of the Package Execution utility, the command line gets updated; however, this is not the case if you make changes to the command line—i.e., these changes don't get reflected in the options of relevant pages. Also, these changes are not validated for the same reason.

12. Now click the Execute button to run the package, and you will see the progress of the running package in Package Execution Progress window.

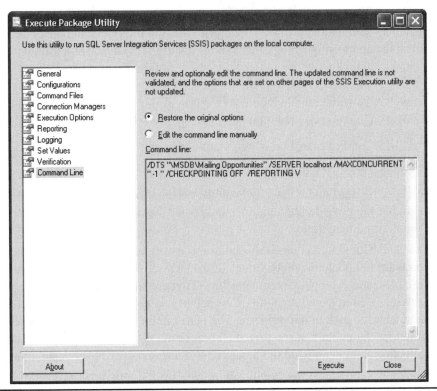

Figure 6-7   *Command generated by the Package Execution utility*

Review

In this exercise, you learned about the Package Execution utility that you can run from within the SQL Server Management Studio or from the command prompt. You also learned various options and how to set values for the properties at run-time. You saw that this utility generates a command line that can be copied to a file and used with the CommandFile option in DTExec, or pasted directly to the Command Prompt window when running a package using DTExec. The DTExecUI user interface provides the facility to select several options that you find difficult to write syntactically correct and create command lines that can be passed on to the DTExec command prompt tool. The main difference in DTExecUI and DTExec is that DTExecUI is a GUI-based tool that helps you create command lines easily but lacks the ability to extend the functionality of automatically the running of packages. DTExec is a handy and powerful command prompt tool that is a bit difficult to program, especially if you are not deploying packages day and night, but once the command line is created, it can automate running of packages with the help of SQL Server Agent service. So you will use DTExecUI when you want to run a package one off or manually each time and also when you want to write a complex command line for running a package automatically using

DTExec and SQL Server Agent. You will study both DTExec and SQL Server Agent service in the following sections.

DTExec Utility

SSIS provides the command prompt utility DTExec to configure and execute SSIS packages; it replaces the DTSRun utility provided in Data Transformation Services of SQL Server 2000. By default, the DTExec utility is located in %Program Files%\ Microsoft SQL Server\90\DTS\Binn folder. DTExec is a powerful utility that lets you access packages saved to SQL Server anywhere on the file system or in the SSIS Package Store. It allows you to configure connections, checkpoints, variables, logging, and reporting for the package you want to run. However, you have to use SQL Server Agent to schedule your package, which is discussed in the next section. As mentioned earlier, you can use DTExecUI utility to create a command line with all the options you require and use it directly with DTExec.

The basic syntax for the command is shown next; the parameters are specified as the option-value pairs. The options are specified beginning either with a (-) minus sign or a slash (/)and are not case-sensitive barring passwords.

```
DTExec /option [value] [/option [value]]...
```

When the DTExec utility is executed, it passes through different phases depending upon the parameters specified in the command line and in the end can return an exit code as well. Let's study these phases and the parameters that decide the behavior of DTExec.

Command Sourcing Phase

This is the initialization phase in which the DTExec utility reads the parameters— i.e., the list of options and arguments specified. If you want to see only the help on the commands using a /? or /H option, for example, DTExec will run for this phase only and all the subsequent phases will be skipped. If you specify an argument along with help options, DTExec will display help for that argument. Refer to the following code example and Figure 6-8.

```
DTExec /H DTS
```

/Rem is another option that is parsed in this phase. Using /Rem, you can include remarks on the command prompt or more appropriately in command files. These remarks are discarded during command sourcing phase.

In the command sourcing phase, if the /CommandFile (/com) option is used, DTExec opens up the file specified with the /CommandFile option and reads all the options from the file till EOF is reached. You can either use the complete option

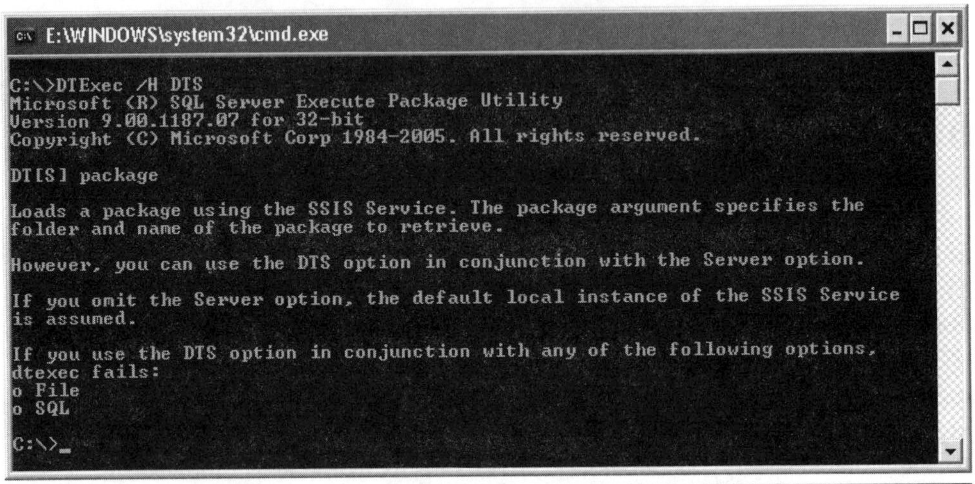

Figure 6-8 *Asking for help from DTExec utility*

name or can use the short form of the option shown in parenthesis with each option. The file specified with /CommandFile option is a text file that contains additional DTExec command options.

Here's an example: Open a blank text file in Notepad and type **/DTS "\msdb\ mailing opportunities"** at the beginning of the file. Save this as C:\dtscmds.txt. Then go to command prompt and type this command:

```
DTExec /com "C:\dtscmds.txt"
```

You will see that the Mailing Opportunities package has executed successfully. DTExec doesn't put any restriction on how you write command options—i.e., on the same line or on the different lines in the command file.

Package Load Phase

After passing through the first phase, DTExec goes on to load the package from the storage specified by the /SQL, /FILE, or /DTS option.

To load a package stored in msdb database of SQL Server, type the following command using the /SQL (/SQ) option:

```
DTExec /SQL "Mailing Opportunities"
```

The /File (/F) option loads a package saved in the file system. The file path can be specified in either Universal Naming Convention (UNC) format or as a local path.

```
DTExec /F "C:\SSIS\Packages\Mailing Opportunities.dtsx"
```

Don't forget to include the file extension when using the /File option.

Finally, to load a package saved in the SSIS Package Store, you will use the /DTS (/DT) option.

```
DTExec /DTS "\MSDB\Mailing Opportunities"
```

You can use only one of these three options, as they are mutually exclusive. Using these options together will cause the package to fail. You can also use the following supportive options:

► /User This can be used with the /SQL option when the package is protected by SQL Server Authentication. If you omit the /User option, Windows Authentication is used. It is recommended that you use Windows Authentication whenever possible.

► /Password (/P) This option is used with the /User option. If you omit the /Password option, a blank password will be used.

► /Decrypt (/De) If the package to be loaded is encrypted with password encryption, this option is used to set the decryption password.

► /Server (/Ser) You use this option to specify the server from which to retrieve the package when the /SQL or /DTS option is specified. If you omit the /Server option when using /SQL or /DTS, the local server instance will be used to retrieve the package.

The following command will run the package stored at remoteserver:

```
DTExec /SQL "\MSDB\Mailing Opportunities" /Ser remoteserver
```

Configuration Phase

After the package is loaded, DTExec goes on to process rest of the options that set flags, variables, or properties; verify the package versioning; and specify the logging and reporting. These options are as follows:

► /CheckPointing (/CheckP) This option is used when you want to include checkpoints during the package execution. The valid values are *on* or *off*. The default is *on* when the option is specified without a value. The checkpoints enable a failed package to rerun from the point of failure. For example, if you want to import 1 million records but your package fails after importing 600,000 records, then using checkpoints will enable this failed package to rerun from the 600,000th position and save the processing for already imported records. To achieve this, the DTExec utility records the current position in a file called CheckFile.

► /CheckFile (/CheckF) The file used by DTExec when the failed package restarts can be specified using /CheckFile option. The file name specified with the /CheckFile option is used to update the value of CheckPointFileName property of the package.

▶ /ConfigFile (/Conf)   You use this option at run-time when you want to set different configuration values than what were specified at design time. The run-time values can be stored in an XML file and loaded before executing the package using the /ConfigFile option.

▶ /Connection (/Conn)   You can change connection managers at run-time using this option. You have to specify the connection manager name or ID used in the package along with the connection string to which you want to change.

▶ /ConsoleLog (/Cons)   You can use this option to display the specified log entries to the console (see Figure 6-9). You can specify the columns you want to see by using the *displayoptions* parameter for which the values include *N* for Name, *C* for Computer, *O* for Operator, *S* for Source Name, *G* for Source GUID, *X* for Execution GUID, *M* for Message, and *T* for time. If you do not specify the option parameters, no column is displayed, and if you specify the option parameters, all the values for the selected columns will be displayed that you may want to limit. For limiting the display of log entries on the console, you use extended options that are called *list_options*. The list_options allow you to

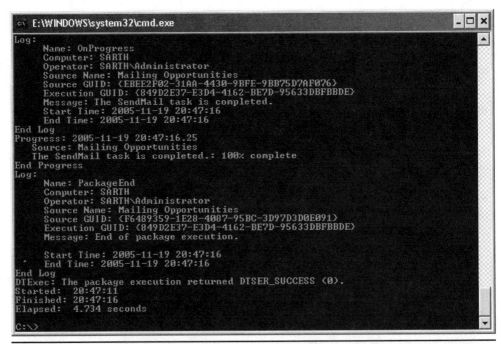

Figure 6-9   *Use of the /ConsoleLog option displays the execution log on the screen*

log only the sources that are specified with parameter (I) for inclusion or only the sources that are not explicitly excluded with parameter (E) using a list.

▶ /Logger (/L): Using the /Logger option, you can choose one or more log providers to be used at run-time by specifying an ID and a connection string to establish a connection to the destination store for log entries. The options of the log providers are as follows:

SSIS log provider for Text files

SSIS log provider for SQL Profiler

SSIS log provider for SQL Server

SSIS log provider for Windows Event Log

SSIS log provider for XML files

▶ /Reporting (/Rep) By default, DTExec will report errors, warnings, and progress of the events when the package is executed. However, you can specify the types of messages to report using /Reporting option. You can choose from the options listed in the following table:

Option Symbol and Name	Description
N – No Reporting	A mutually exclusive option with all other options and should be specified alone.
E – Errors	Errors are reported.
W – Warnings	Warnings are reported.
I – Information	Informational messages are reported.
C – Custom Events	Custom events are reported.
D – Data Flow Task Events	Events related to Data Flow task are reported.
P – Progress	Progress of the execution of package is reported.
V – Verbose Reporting	A mutually exclusive option with all other options and should be specified alone.

▶ /Restart (/Res) This option specifies a new value for the CheckpointUsage property on the package. The possible parameters are shown next:

Deny	Sets CheckpointUsage property to DTSCU_NEVER.
Force	(Default) Sets CheckpointUsage property to DTSCU_ALWAYS.
ifPossible	Sets CheckpointUsage property to DTSCU_IFEXISTS.

▶ /Set You can modify the configuration values of variables, properties, containers, log providers, Foreach enumerator, or connections at run-time. Both property path and the value are to be specified according to specific syntax rules. The syntax uses backslash (\) as a container separator, period (.) to delimit properties, square brackets ([]) to specify collection members, and semicolon (;) to separate the property path and its value.

▶ /MaxConcurrent (/M) You can limit the number of executables running in parallel on your machine using this option. You can specify a positive non-zero integer value or –1. A value of –1 means the maximum concurrently running executables (total number of processors on the computer plus two) are allowed.

▶ /Sum (/Su) This is an optional switch that shows the number of rows that will be passed on to the next component.

▶ /VerifyBuild (/VerifyB) During the development stage when you will be making lots of changes to your package, you may want to make sure that the package is executed with a stable version of the build while you can carry on the development work without jeopardizing the normal running of the tasks. You can specify the build numbers you want to run and verify your package against those numbers. In case of a mismatch, the package will fail to run. The /VerifyBuild option has three arguments, major, minor, and build, which can be specified in three forms: *major*; *major, minor*; *major, minor, build*.

▶ /VerifyPackageID (/VerifyP) Similar to the /VerifyBuild option, you can specify the package ID with this option to let it verify against the package GUID.

▶ /VerifySigned (/VerifyS) This is a security option to check that the package is signed. If the package is not signed the execution of the package will fail.

▶ /VerifyVersionID (VerifyV) You can verify the version ID of a package to be executed against the version ID you specify with this option.

Validation and Execution Phase

In this phase, the package is validated and then finally run. However, you can also choose only to validate the package without running it.

▶ /Validate (/Va) Use this option to validate only without running the package.

▶ /WarnAsError (/W) You can go one step further in validation by specifying this option along with the /Validate option, so that the package will treat the warnings as errors and will fail if a warning occurs during validation phase.

Finally, DTExec utility can return exit code depending upon the state of the package loading and execution. The exit codes are values from 0 through 6 that can be interpreted as follows:

Exit Code	Description
0	The package was executed successfully.
1	The package failed to execute.
3	The user cancelled execution of the package.
4	The package could not be found at the specified location.
5	The package could not be loaded.
6	The command line could not be interpreted due to syntax or semantic errors.

SQL Server Agent Service

Running SSIS packages can be automated using the SQL Server Agent service of SQL Server 2005. SQL Server Agent jobs can have one or more steps, each providing a different package and a bit of work that the agent can do for you. The jobs can also be scheduled to run at specific times. SQL Server Agent needs to be started before you can use it to run packages on the local server or send jobs to the target server.

Hands-On: Automating Running an SSIS Package with SQL Server Agent Service

In this exercise, you will learn how to use the SQL Server Agent service to create and automate jobs for running SSIS packages.

Method

We will use SQL Server Agent in SQL Server Management Studio to

- ► Create a new job
- ► Add a package (step) to the job
- ► Create a schedule to execute the package
- ► View the job history after running

For this exercise, we will again use the Mailing Opportunities package as a test package.

Exercise (Create a New Job)

1. Start SQL Server Management Studio and connect to the database engine.

2. Before moving on, verify that SQL Server Agent service is started. If it is not, start SQL Server Agent service by right-clicking SQL Server Agent in the Object Explorer pane and choosing the Start option. Then expand SQL Server Agent and right-click Jobs; then choose New Job from the context menu to open the New Job dialog box.

3. Type **Running Mailing Opportunities** in the Name field.

4. Leave the Owner field setting with your logon details. Also, note that Enabled should be checked before moving on to the Steps page.

   Note that several security enhancements have been made in SQL Server 2005 that affect the ways jobs run in SQL Server Agent. In previous versions of SQL Server, the SQL Server Agent service account had to be a member of the local Administrators group when executing the xp_cmdshell extended stored procedure, ActiveX scripting, or CmdExec jobs owned by users who were not members of the SysAdmin fixed server roles. This is not required in SQL Server 2005 as it has hierarchy of fixed database roles (msdb database) to control access to SQL Server Agent. For example, users who are members of SQLAgentUserRole (SQL Server Agent fixed database role) can create or execute jobs locally. Also, the Sysadmin fixed server role can create multiple proxy accounts and assign each account to a separate step of a SQL Server Agent job. For more details on SQL Server Agent fixed database roles, refer to Microsoft SQL Server 2005 Books Online.

Exercise (Add a Package to the Job Using the Steps Page)

5. Go to the Steps page and click New to create a new step for this job. In the Step Name field of the New Job Step window, type **Executing Mailing Opportunities Step**.

6. In the Type field, click the down arrow to display the list of job types and choose SQL Server Integration Services Package. As you choose this option, the window changes to include the options for running an Integration Services package.

7. In the Run as field, leave SQL Agent Service Account selected.

8. In the General tab, set the Package Source field to SSIS Package Store, type **localhost** in the Server field, and leave Use Windows Authentication selected in the Log On To The Server area. Click the ellipsis button next to the Package field to choose an SSIS package—the Mailing Opportunities package under the MSDB storage folder. Click OK. Note the package path shown in Figure 6-10.

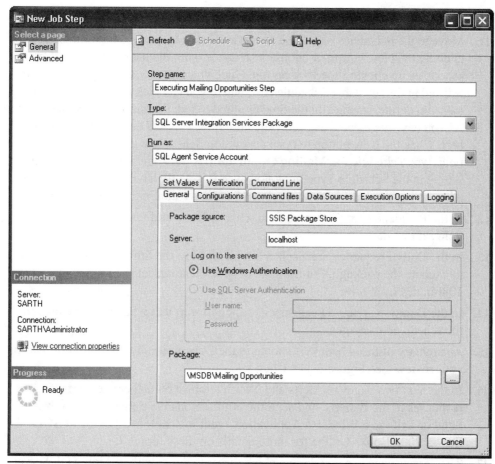

Figure 6-10 *Configuring a step for SQL Server Agent job*

9. Look through various tabs in the Steps page to see the options available. You will soon realize that these options are similar to those provided in the Package Execution utility (DTExecUI) pages except for a few differences.

10. Click the Advanced page in the New Job Step window to see the available options. You can specify what should happen on the success or failure of a step. The default for success of a step is to go to the next step, and the default for the failure of a step is to quit the job and report failure. You can also specify the number of retry attempts and the time to wait between retries here. Click OK to close this window and return to the New Job window. You should see the package listed in the Job step list area. Notice the arrow buttons on the lower left side of this page; you can use these to move your job steps up and down and hence change the order in which they are executed.

Exercise (Create a Schedule to Execute the Package)

11. Move to the Schedules page. You can now create a new schedule for this job by clicking the New button or choose a schedule from the list of already defined schedules by clicking the Pick button. Once you create a schedule for a job, it is listed in the Available Schedules list, where you can pick a schedule for other jobs you define, saving you the time required to redefine similar schedules again. As you have not created any schedule until now, you will create a new schedule here. Click the New button to open a New Job Schedule window. In the Name field, type **Schedule for Mailing Opportunities package**. Leave the Recurring setting in the Schedule Type field; however, it is worth having a quick look at the other option available in the drop-down list. Leave the Enabled option checked.

12. In the Frequency area's Occurs field, choose Daily and leave Recurs Every field set to 1 day.

13. In the Daily Frequency area, select a time equal to the time when you want to execute the package. For the sake of quick testing, set the time about 10 minutes from now.

14. In the Duration area, you can specify when to start and when to stop executing the scheduled packages.

15. A summary of the schedule is shown in the Description box in plain English for your review (see Figure 6-11). Click OK.

16. In the next two pages of Alerts and Notifications, you can create alerts, define responses to those alerts, and send the notifications via e-mail, page, or Net Send or write to a Windows Application event log. Refer to Microsoft SQL Server 2005 Books Online for more details on these topics.

17. The Targets page lets you define which server to target with this job. SQL Server 2005 includes a new feature called *multiserver administration* to manage two or more servers by designating them a master server and target servers. The master server distributes jobs to the target servers and receives events from them to keep the status information. Target servers periodically connect to master servers to get the new schedules for the jobs allocated, download new jobs, or update the master server with the latest status about the jobs being run. You can create a master server or target server from multiserver administration by right-clicking SQL Server Agent in the SQL Server Management Studio. If no target servers are listed, the only option is to run the job from the local server. For more details on multiserver administration and how to make a master server or target server, refer to Microsoft SQL Server 2005 Books Online.

18. Click OK to create the job. You will see this job listed in the Jobs node under SQL Server Agent. Have a cup of coffee, and by the time you return to your computer you will see the test mails in your mailbox.

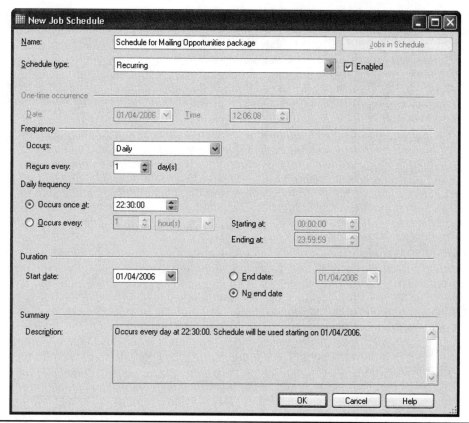

Figure 6-11 *Creating a schedule for a job*

Exercise (View the Job History)

Let's now study how you can obtain the status of a jobs:

► You can configure a notification to be sent to you via e-mail while configuring the job in the Notifications tab.

► You can choose to write to Windows Application event log in the Notifications tab while configuring the job.

► You can select to see the Job History from the Report drop-down list box in the Summary sheet of Jobs in SQL Server Management Studio.

► To see the detailed job history, you can right-click the job and choose View History. When you choose the View History option, you will see the history as shown in the Log File Viewer window (see Figure 6-12).

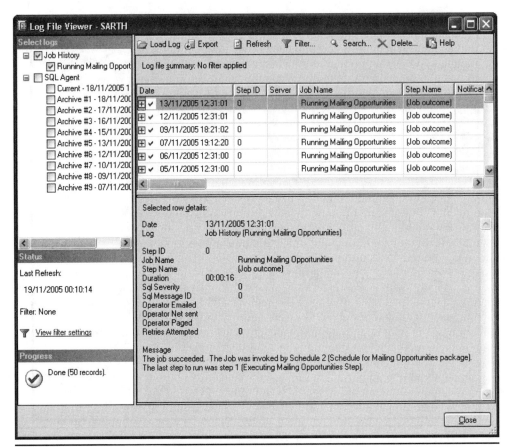

Figure 6-12 *Job History in Log File Viewer window*

Review

In this exercise, you learned how to automate execution of an SSIS package using SQL Server Agent. You learned how to create a new job, add steps to the job, and specify a schedule for the job. You have also seen some of the new features introduced in this version of SQL Server:

▶ The user account under which the job executes doesn't need to be sysadmin anymore; you can use a proxy account to run the packages.

▶ The steps of a job have a new type—SQL Server Integration Services Package—defined for them that allows you to configure all the options required to run a SSIS package in this category.

▶ You can choose a schedule from the already defined schedules and don't need to define one each time you add a job.

▶ Multiserver administration has been introduced in SQL Server 2005 that lets you manage two or more servers by creating a hierarchy of master and target servers.

▶ You have seen an enhanced version of job history.

Summary

SQL Server 2005 provides several tools that enable you to manage Integration Services and Integration Services packages effectively and easily. You started this chapter by enabling the SSIS service and then learned how to manage storage locations for storing Integration Services packages. You've used SQL Server Management Studio and dtutil to manage storage and Integration Services packages. You also learned how to import and export an Integration Services package from one storage location to the other. In the process, you created a new storage location on the file system for these packages. You learned about various tools to run an Integration Services package that include the use of the Package Execution Utility and the DTExec command line utility. You automated running of a package by creating a job and its schedule using SQL Server Agent. In the next chapter we will discuss securing Integration Services packages in detail.

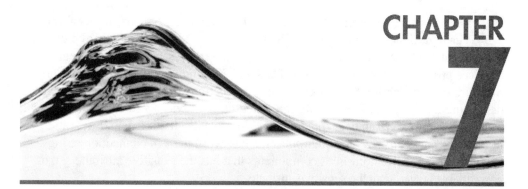

Securing Integration Services Packages

ecurity in SQL Server 2005 and that of Integration Services has been enhanced a great deal more compared to DTS 2000. DTS uses package password protection, SQL Server Security, and SQL Server Agent service security, while Integration Services provides the features used by DTS and a lot more to enhance data security. SSIS provides the ability to secure data and connections from various perspectives depending upon the situation. By design, Integration Services will communicate with SQL Server only over an encrypted channel to protect sensitive data. Integration Services defines *sensitive information* as the password used in connection strings, any property of the custom-built components that has the sensitive attribute set, or any variable tagged with the sensitive attribute.

Integration Services secures your packages and data by providing the facilities to do the following:

- ▶ Digitally sign the package
- ▶ Exclude sensitive information from the package
- ▶ Encrypt sensitive information in the package
- ▶ Encrypt all the contents of the package
- ▶ Control access to the package by using database-level roles
- ▶ Secure storage areas

Let's take a detailed look at these options and what they offer in terms of securing a package.

Digitally Signing the Package

Development of a complex Integration Services solution involves several developers who create many smaller packages to join as modules and form a complex solution for the business problem. During development phase, a package that has been tested successfully to perform a part of the function can be deployed while it is still under development for additional functionality. In such a scenario, you need to avoid the deployment of modified packages while they are still under testing. For example, you may be working to solve a complex scenario for which you have proposed a solution that can be developed and deployed in multiple stages. While development is still underway and many developers have access to SSIS packages, the last thing you would want to do is to run an untested package in the production environment.

To avoid such situations and guarantee the integrity of packages, you can digitally sign a package with a certificate so that each time the package is loaded, it is verified for digital signatures and hence altered packages wouldn't be loaded. You need to have a digital certificate installed on the server to digitally sign your packages. Once you have that in place, all you need to do is follow these instructions:

► Using Business Intelligence Development Studio (BIDS), open the package you want to digitally sign.

► On the menu bar, click the SSIS menu and choose Digital Signing. This will open the Digital Signing window.

► You will see a message in the window saying "This package is not signed." Click the Sign button to select a certificate to sign the package.

► After signing the package, right-click anywhere on the blank surface of the designer and choose Properties from the context menu. Locate the CheckSignatureOnLoad property and set it to True. This will require that the digital signature on the package be checked every time the package is loaded.

Excluding Sensitive Information from the Package

Integration Services identifies the properties containing sensitive data (i.e., passwords or connection strings) in a package and sets the sensitive attribute of these properties. Integration Services identifies the sensitive properties automatically and doesn't let you change any sensitive attributes of these properties. However, you can specify the properties you want to be treated as sensitive for your custom-built SSIS components.

You can opt not to save sensitive data in the package. The list of options is available in the ProtectionLevel property of the package, shown in Figure 7-1. When you choose the DontSaveSensitive option, the sensitive information is removed from the package when saved and is unavailable for future executions of the package. So each time you want to execute the package, you have to provide the required information in order for the package to run successfully. If you change this option to any other option later on, the sensitive information is populated with blank data and you will have to provide the correct sensitive information (i.e., passwords and so on) in the relevant area of the package to make this information available for encryption or other options.

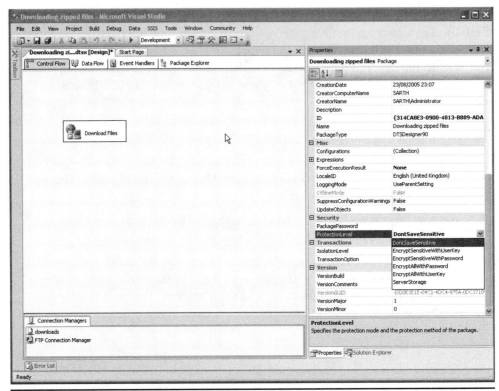

Figure 7-1   *ProtectionLevel property in properties of a package*

Encrypting Sensitive Information in the Package

When you want to save sensitive information in the package and want to protect this information, Integration Services provides two options in the ProtectionLevel package property to encrypt this information: EncryptSensitiveWithUserKey and EncryptSensitiveWithPassword. These options are used to encrypt the package using a user key or using a password. Microsoft Data Protection API (DPAPI), which is a cryptography component, is used to fulfill all the encryption needs of ProtectionLevel security options.

EncryptSensitiveWithUserKey is the default encryption level for a package. So sensitive information in the package is, by default, encrypted using the current user key, which has been created based on the user profile. Only the current user using the same profile can load this package. If another user tries to load the package, the sensitive information fields are populated with the blank data and the package will fail to execute, unless the user trying to run the package provides the sensitive information.

EncryptSensitiveWithPassword package protection level allows you to save the sensitive information in the package and encrypt it using a password, supplied in the PackagePassword property. By using a password as an encryption key for the sensitive information, you can let other developers open the package by supplying a password and hence make the package accessible to all members of the development team. Each time the package is loaded or the ProtectionLevel option is changed, the user must provide the package password. If the package password is not provided, the package is opened without the sensitive information. So to sum up, you will use the EncryptSensitiveWithUserKey option to encrypt the packages that you probably will not share with anybody else and the EncryptSensitiveWithPassword option when you will share the package.

Encrypting All the Information in the Package

Two options are available for encrypting the whole package: EncryptAllWithUserKey and EncryptAllWithPassword. These use a user key or a package password, respectively, to encrypt all the information in a package.

Using the EncryptAllWithUserKey option, you encrypt all the information in the package using a user key. As the user key is generated based on the user profile, only the user who created or exported the package using the same profile can open the package.

Using the EncryptAllWithPassword option, you encrypt all the information in the package using a password specified in the PackagePassword property. You can use this option to secure the contents of the package yet allow the development team to work on it; a custom-developed package for your application that includes an intellectual property is a good example for this. A package encrypted in such a way can be opened only by providing the password. You cannot load the package if you fail to provide the password.

Hands-On: Understanding Package Protection Levels

This Hands-On exercise is designed to enhance the understanding of package protection levels.

Method

In this exercise, we will use each package protection level in turn to see how it works and the effects it has on the security of the package. We will use the Downloading zipped files package, as it requires a password to connect to an FTP server, to see the effects of using it with various protection levels.

Note that if you want to use the Downloading zipped files package that has been provided with this book, you will receive an error when opening the package. When you click OK on the pop-up error message, the package will load properly but without the connection string in the FTP task. This is because, by default, the sensitive information (passwords, connection strings, and so on) in the packages get encrypted using the user key, and when another user tries to open the package, an error will occur and sensitive information will be removed from the package. However, if you open the Downloading zipped files package that you developed yourself in Chapter 5, you will not get any such error.

In addition, this package requires a connection to an FTP server. If you've skipped building this package Chapter 5, you should find an FTP server and build the package to complete this Hands-On exercise. The provided package may not be of much help as it is pointing to a computer used in the lab setup for this book, which is obviously not accessible to you. Better to use the package that you created earlier.

Exercise (Excluding Sensitive Information from the Package)

After this exercise, you will be able to exclude sensitive information from the package using the DontSaveSensitive option in the ProtectionLevel property.

1. Open BIDS and create a new Integration Services project with the name Downloading zipped files in the location C:\SSIS\Projects. In the Solution Explorer window, expand SSIS Packages | right click on Package.dtsx and choose Delete from the context menu. Click OK to confirm deletion. Right click on SSIS Packages node and choose Add Existing Package from the context menu. In the Add Copy of Existing Package window, choose File System in the Package location field and type C:\SSIS\Projects\Control Flow Tasks\Downloading zipped files.dtsx in the Package path field. Click OK to add this package in your project. Expand SSIS Packages node and double click on the Downloading zipped files.dtsx package to load it on the Designer.

2. Right-click anywhere on the blank surface of the Designer and choose Properties from the context menu. In the Properties window, you can view the properties in two ways—Categorized view or Alphabetical view. These views can be set using the two buttons provided in the command bar on the top of the window. In the Categorized view, the properties are grouped together on the category basis while Alphabetical view simply lists the properties using alphabetical sort order. Use Categorized view.

3. Scroll down in the Properties window and locate the Security section. Note that the ProtectionLevel field shows EncryptSensitiveWithUserKey selected.

4. Press CTRL-ALT-L to open Solution Explorer. Right-click the Downloading zipped files.dtsx package under SSIS packages folder and choose View Code from the context menu. The package code in XML will be shown in a new tab in BIDS.

5. Press CTRL-F and find *Password* in the XML document. The `ServerPassword` property in the XML document is immediately after `ServerUserName` property and you will be taken to the following XML node:

```
<DTS:Property DTS:Name="ServerUserName">administrator </DTS:Property>

<DTS:Property DTS:Name="ServerPassword" Sensitive="1" Encrypted="1">AQAAANC
Mnd8BFdERjHoAwE/Cl+sBAAAAgp969y9CpkO6k07L3IdJGwAAAAAIAAAARABUAFMAAADZgAAqA
AAABAAAABhZumzf3dqV1SXY5667BryAAAAAASAAACgAAAAEAAAAMW+xn039fmW+00yN32EHG4YA
AAAAE5rsrl9TvzImKtVSb+UWoZbYuJXBwtLFAAAAMTOWe+5xETOTECqeJbMTSIq/c9e

</DTS:Property>
```

In this node, note that the `ServerPassword` property is attributed as sensitive data and is set for encryption. Also note that data in this node is all encrypted. This encryption is due to the default EncryptSensitiveWithUserKey setting.

6. Switch to the Designer tab of the package and press F4 to highlight the Properties window. In the Security section, click in the ProtectionLevel field and choose DontSaveSensitive from the drop-down list.

7. Switch to Code view and search for *Password*. This time you will see the same XML node with no encryption attribute and no data in it:

```
<DTS:Property DTS:Name="ServerPassword" Sensitive="1"> </DTS:Property>
```

This is because the password has been removed from the package.

8. Press F5 to run the package. The package will fail. Stop debugging and click the Execution Results tab. You will see the following error declaring that the password was not allowed:

```
[Connection manager "FTP Connection Manager"] Error: An error
occurred in the requested FTP operation. Detailed error description:
The password was not allowed.
```

9. Double-click the FTP Connection Manager in the Connection Managers area in the Designer and provide a password to connect to the FTP server in the Credentials section of the FTP Connection Manager Editor window. Click OK to close it.

10. Press F5 to run the package; this time the package will succeed. You can run a package that has been saved excluding the sensitive information by supplying the sensitive (password) information.

Exercise (Encrypting Sensitive Information in the Package Using a User Key)

When you use a user key to encrypt the package, the package encryption gets associated with the user profile. We will create a test user account ISUser01 to log on and open a package that has already been encrypted using a user key by another user and will establish that the sensitive information is replaced when a different user tries to load the package. This package can be successfully executed only by providing the sensitive information in the package.

11. Open or highlight the Properties window by pressing F4. Change the ProtectionLevel property value to EncryptSensitiveWithUserKey. Switch to XML code of the package and search for *Password* to see that it has been encrypted, like the one shown in the preceding exercise.

12. Choose Start | right click My Computer and choose Manage from the context menu. In the Computer Management window, expand the Local Users and Groups folder, right-click the Users folder, and choose New User from the context menu. This will open a New User window where you can create a user. Fill in the following details to create a user account:

User name	ISUser01
Password	ISUp@ss01

    Clear the User Must Change Password At Next Logon option check box before clicking the Create button.

    Create another user with the following details that you will be using in a later exercise in this chapter:

User name	ISUser02
Password	ISUp@ss02

13. Close all the applications and log off and log back on as ISUser01 with the assigned password.

14. Choose Start | All Programs | Microsoft SQL Server 2005 | SQL Server Business Intelligence Development Studio.

15. In BIDS, choose File | Open | Project/Solution; or you can press CTRL-SHIFT-O to open the Open Project dialog box. Select Downloading zipped files.sln in the File Name field by going to the C:\SSIS\projects\downloading zipped files folder and clicking the Open button.

16. If you see the solution loaded in the Solution Explorer but nothing appearing on the Designer surface, it means the package is not configured as a startup package. To open the package, double-click the Downloading zipped files.dtsx package under SSIS Packages folder. When BIDS tries to load the package, you will see an error on the screen informing you that the package might be corrupted and prompts you to see the Error List for details.

17. When you click OK to close the error, you will see that the package is loaded. If you don't have the Error List window open in BIDS, press CTRL-\ followed by CTRL-E to open the Error List window. Alternatively, you can open Error List window from the View menu. In the Error List window, you will see the detailed error message explaining that the encryption key is not valid:

```
"Error loading Downloading zipped files.dtsx: Failed to decrypt
protected XML node "DTS:Property" with error 0x8009000B "Key not
valid for use in specified state.". You may not be authorized
to access this information. This error occurs when there is a
cryptographic error. Verify that the correct key is available."
```

18. Press F5 to run the package. The package will fail. Press SHIFT-F5 to stop debugging. Go to the Execution Results page and read the error message, which states that the FTP password was not allowed. This certifies that the FTP password was replaced when we tried to load the package as a different user.

19. Double-click the FTP Connection Manager in the Connection Managers area in the Designer and provide the password to connect to the FTP server in the Credentials section of the FTP Connection Manager Editor window. Click OK.

20. Press F5 to run the package; this time the package will succeed. This certifies that when the package is encrypted with the user key you can still load the package and use it if you know the sensitive information and can supply the correct password.

Exercise (Encrypting Sensitive Information in the Package Using the Package Password)

When you opt to encrypt a package using EncryptSensitiveWithPassword ProtectionLevel property, you then provide an encryption password using the PackagePassword property in the Security section of the Properties window. Here you will learn that if you encrypt the sensitive information in a package using a password, other users can access the sensitive information by specifying the PackagePassword. However, if other users try to load the package without specifying the PackagePassword, the sensitive information is replaced with blanks. You will be performing these steps while still logged on as ISUser01. In the following steps, you will use a package password to encrypt the sensitive information in the package.

21. Click anywhere on the blank surface of the Designer and press F4 to open the properties for the package. Change the ProtectionLevel property to EncryptSensitiveWithPassword and specify a password *bB12345cC* in the PackagePassword field.

22. Open the XML code view for the project from the Solution Explorer, as explained in step 4. In XML code view, if you try to find the word *Password* in the document, you will not get any result, since this word doesn't exist in the document. Instead, find the ServerUserName property, as you are interested in the property that appears after it. You will see something like this in the XML code view:

```
<DTS:Property DTS:Name="ServerUserName">administrator </DTS:Property>

<EncryptedData Type="http://www.w3.org/2001/04/xmlenc#Element" Salt="oOBw/
g9GpA==" IV="5YsCDRU2aMM=" xmlns="http://www.w3.org/2001/04/xmlenc#"><Enc
ryptionMethod Algorithm="http://www.w3.org/2001/04/xmlenc#tripledes-cbc"/
><CipherData><CipherValue>5YsCDRU2aMM9jrGvOlsQSXNFzBG13LDuBBBI/tK07k/Z1BX
BYNSQEOWFYD3WgRhEDQ56TKlATw2Tvi7UU7OAJfDXDSnnoYPAwtmgTj3d/Qk72HJwlzNjqJ/
FiGjC+2sfN4VNzpLSVGQCkV27tDchXriytPz/2pTI1EY58wui1LPAkulpSbunbg==</
CipherValue></CipherData>

</EncryptedData>
```

The data encrypted in the package has been encrypted using TripleDES with CBC algorithm.

23. Press CTRL-SHIFT-S to save all the items in the package. Close all the applications and log off. Log back on using the administrator user account.

24. Run BIDS and load the Downloading zipped files solution. You may have to double-click the Downloading zipped files.dtsx package under SSIS Packages folder in the Solution Explorer to load the package on the Designer. When BIDS loads the package, you will see the Package Password prompt to provide the password (Figure 7-2).

25. If you provide the correct package password, the package will load and you can run the package successfully. However, we will observe the behavior in case someone tries to load the package without the password. Click Cancel to load the package without the password.

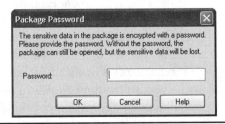

Figure 7-2 *A password is required to open packages saved with the EncryptSensitiveWithPassword option*

26. You will see an error message saying that there were errors while loading the package, which prompts you to see the Error List for more details. Click OK to proceed further.

27. The package will be loaded. Open the Error List window, and you will see an error explaining that the package will be loaded without the encrypted information:

```
Error loading Downloading zipped files.dtsx: Failed to decrypt
an encrypted XML node because the password was not specified or
not correct. Package load will attempt to continue without the
encrypted information.
```

Press F5 to run the package, which will fail, specifying that the password was not allowed in the Execution Results pane.

28. In the Connection Managers area, double-click the FTP Connection Manager and specify the password in the credentials area. Click OK to close this window. Press F5 to run the package. The package won't run; instead it returns an error similar to the one shown in Figure 7-3.

You get this error because you are still using the EncryptSensitiveWithPassword protection level and haven't provided a package password to decrypt the encrypted information. Until you supply the package password or populate the encrypted information with blank data, you won't be able to run or save the package. So how do we populate the encrypted information with blank data? Well, one way is to change the PrtoectionLevel property to EncryptSensitiveWithUserKey and provide the FTP password in the FTP Connection Manager. Click OK twice to close the error windows.

29. Press F4 to highlight the Properties for the package. Scroll to the Security category and change the ProtectionLevel property to EncryptSensitiveWithUserKey.

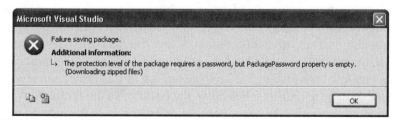

Figure 7-3   *Error returned on running a package without specifying a package password*

30. Double-click the FTP Connection Manager in the Connection Managers area and specify the FTP password in the Credentials section. Close the Connection Manager window and press F5 to run the package. The package executes successfully this time.

Exercise (Encrypting All Information in the Package Using a User Key)

Using the EncryptAllWithUserKey option in the ProtectionLevel property encrypts all the metadata of a package and renders it useless of other users.

31. Switch to the package Properties window and change the ProtectionLevel property to EncryptAllWithUserKey.

32. If the XML View Code tab is not already open, go to Solution Explorer, right-click Downloading zipped files.dtsx, and choose View Code from the context menu to open the package code in a new tab. See the package code to note that all the code of the package has been encrypted.

33. Save the package, close all the applications, and log off.

34. Log back on with ISUser01 account and open the Downloading zipped files solution using BIDS.

35. The package won't load by itself. Go to Solution Explorer and double-click the Downloading zipped files.dtsx package under SSIS Packages folder to load the package.

36. The package still doesn't load. Instead, it returns an error saying that the package could not be loaded and the package might be corrupted. This is because BIDS could not remove the package encryption. Click OK, and then go on to read the detailed error message from the Error List window (Figure 7-4).

    As you can see, the Error List window displays the much-detailed error messages. This is unlike the EncryptSensitiveWithUserKey option, in which the sensitive information is replaced with blank information when other users try to load the package and then these other users can use the package by providing the sensitive information. Using the EncryptAllWithUserKey option, the other users can't load the package at all. This is the most restricted protection level possible in SSIS. However, use of this protection level should be done with great care as it ties down the package to the creator's profile; if the creator loses access to his or her profile, the package is rendered useless. The most eligible uses of this protection level may be ad-hoc or short-term deployment of highly security sensitive packages.

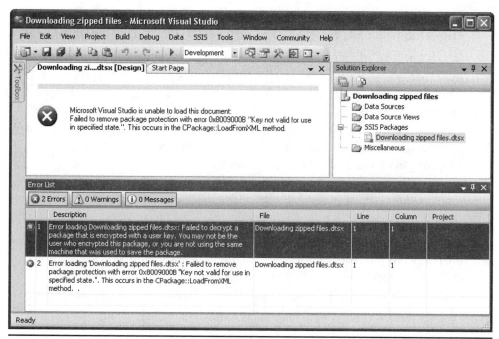

Figure 7-4 *Error loading package with EncryptAllWithUserKey protection level*

Exercise (Encrypting All Information in the Package Using a Package Password)

In this exercise, you will learn that the EncryptAllWithPassword option of the ProtectionLevel property is the most secure option that allows sharing your package with other users.

37. If you already have our test package open and are following up from the preceding exercise, close all the applications and log off, as we cannot use this package with the previously encrypted method. Log on using the administrator account and open the Downloading zipped files solution using BIDS.

38. Open package properties by first clicking anywhere on the blank area on the Designer surface and then pressing F4. Scroll down to the Security category and change the ProtectionLevel property to EncryptAllWithPassword.

39. Click in the PackagePassword property and then click the ellipsis button, which appears when you click in the field. Provide the password *bB12345cC* in the Property Editor window, confirm it, and click OK.

40. View the package code and notice that this time the encryption method used is TripleDES with CBC algorithm. Press CTRL-SHIFT-S to save all the files. Close all the applications and log off.

41. Log on as ISUser01 user and open the Downloading zipped files solution in BIDS.

42. The package may not load by itself; double-click the package in the Solution Explorer to load it. You will be asked to provide a password because the package is encrypted. If you provide the password, the package will load and you can successfully execute the package. But, for the sake of testing what happens otherwise, click the Cancel button here.

43. An error message will tell you that the package could not be loaded, as it might be corrupted, and asks you to see Error List for details. Click OK.

44. The package will not load and you will receive an error message on the Designer saying that Microsoft Visual Studio is unable to load the document, as the password was not specified or not correct. Almost similar errors appeared in the Error List:

```
Error loading 'Downloading zipped files.dtsx' : Failed to remove
package protection with error 0xC0014037 "The package is encrypted
with a password. The password was not specified, or is not
correct.". This occurs in the CPackage::LoadFromXML method.
```

This exercise shows that using the EncryptAllWithPassword protection level option doesn't let other users use the package until they specify the correct package password. If the other users use wrong password or do not specify a password, the package is simply not loaded and hence not available. This is quite useful feature as it allows you to share the package within a team yet keep it encrypted to avoid any unauthorized access.

Review

You have used five out of six available ProtectionLevel property options in this exercise. You first learned that you could choose to exclude the sensitive information from a package using the DontSaveSensitive option. Then you learned that two options use a user profile to encrypt sensitive information in a package or to encrypt a complete package: EncryptSensitiveWithUserKey for encrypting sensitive information and EncryptAllWithUserKey for encrypting the complete package. You studied two more options to encrypt sensitive data or the complete package using an encryption password to be specified in the PackagePassword property: EncryptSensitiveWithPassword for encrypting sensitive information and EncryptAllWithPassword for encrypting the complete package. These options let you share packages with other users while keeping them secure from unauthorized access. The ServerStorage option that you have not used in this exercise is covered next.

Note that when you create and save a package, your package may use other miscellaneous files that may reside outside the package. Using the above protection options may lead to a false impression that all the data is secured. So you should carefully consider all the files you refer to in a package and where these files are saved. These files may include checkpoint files, configuration files, or log files. You need to apply access control to these files using access control list permissions depending upon where they are stored.

Using Integration Services Fixed Database Level Roles

Integration Services enables you to control access to SSIS packages by providing three fixed database-level roles: db_dtsadmin, db_dtsltduser, and db_dtsoperator. These are available in msdb database and can be applied to only the packages that are saved to the msdb database in SQL Server. The packages stored in MSDB storage area in Integration Services are saved in sysdtspackages90 table of the msdb database. The sysdtspackages90 table defines the access permissions for the packages in the readrole, writerole, and ownersid columns of the table.

Fixed Database Level Roles and Their Permissions

When you use the ServerStorage option for the ProtectionLevel property, the access to the packages saved to msdb is controlled by fixed database-level roles. These roles have been assigned read or write privileges in three levels, as described next:

▶ **db_dtsoperator role**   This is the weakest role among the three available roles. You generally assign this role to users who need to execute the packages. This role cannot perform any write operation—i.e., it cannot import or create packages and has only read permissions. It can list, view, execute, and export all the packages stored within a storage area. It can also schedule package execution using SQL Server Agent service.

▶ **db_dtsltduser role**   This role is designed to give user access to developers who need to create and manage their own packages. As the name suggests, this role can perform functions limited to owned packages and can import any package, delete only owned packages, and manage owned package roles. And for the read functions, this role can list owned or all packages and can view, execute, or export only the owned packages.

▶ **db_dtsadmin role**   This role is designed for administrators to manage packages and package roles. They have all the read and write permissions to perform any operation on the SSIS packages. The role can list, view, execute, and export owned or other users' packages. This role can perform the write operations for importing, deleting, and managing package roles for owned or other users' packages.

Let's save the Downloading zipped files package to MSDB and see how these roles affect the access to this package.

Hands-On: Control Access to a Package Using Database-level Roles

A database-level role is another access control method provided in SQL Server 2005 Integration Services. SSIS provides three fixed database level roles that can be used to apply access control to Integration Services packages. In this exercise, we will study how these roles can be enabled and configured to control access.

Method

This is a two-step method. To use database level roles to protect SSIS packages, you first have to enable this by telling Integration Services to use the ServerStorage ProtectionLevel and then configure the database level roles that you want to use. The steps involved are:

▶ Configure ServerStorage ProtectionLevel

▶ Configure permissions for database level roles

Exercise (Applying ServerStorage ProtectionLevel to the Downloading Zipped Files Package)

1. Make sure you are logged on as administrator. Open the Downloading zipped files.sln solution using BIDS, and provide the package password when asked.

2. Choose File | Save Copy of Downloading zipped files.dtsx As. This will open the Save Copy of Package dialog box. Provide the following details in the dialog box, as we will be storing our package to SQL Server:

Package Location	SQL Server
Server	Provide your SQL Server Name
Authentication Type	Windows Authentication
Package Path:	/Downloading zipped files

Click the ellipsis button in the Protection Level field and choose Rely On Server Storage And Roles For Access Control for the Package Protection Level, as shown in Figure 7-5. Then click OK. Click OK again to close the Save Copy of Package dialog box.

3. Choose File | Close Project and exit from BIDS.

4. Open SQL Server Management Studio and connect to Integration Services.

5. In the Object Explorer, expand the Stored Packages folder and then expand the MSDB folder. You will see a list of packages stored in the MSDB storage area. Right-click the Downloading zipped files package and choose Package Roles from the context menu.

6. This will open Package Roles window, showing the package name and the default settings for Reader Role and Writer Role (see Figure 7-6).

Note that by default, Reader Role permission is assigned to db_dtsadmin, db_dtsltduser, and db_dtsoperator fixed database-level roles and Writer Role permission is assigned to db_dtsadmin, Owner (creator) of the package. Reader Role permission allows a role or a user to enumerate (list) the packages, view the package contents, and export the package, whereas Writer Role permission allows a role or a user to delete, rename, edit, and save a package. Members of a sysadmin server role are given the permissions of db_dtsadmin role.

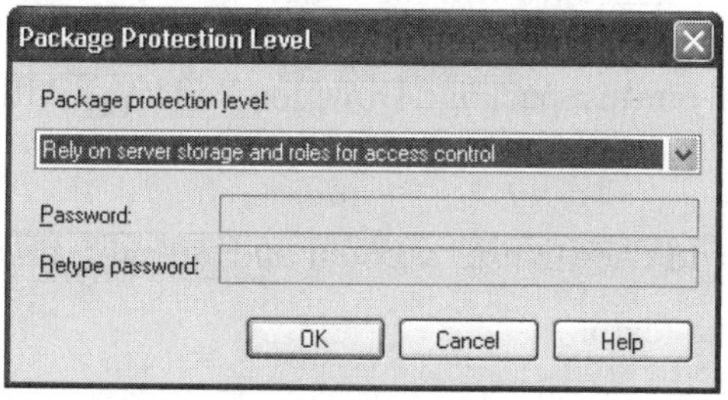

Figure 7-5   *Selecting the ServerStorage option while saving a package*

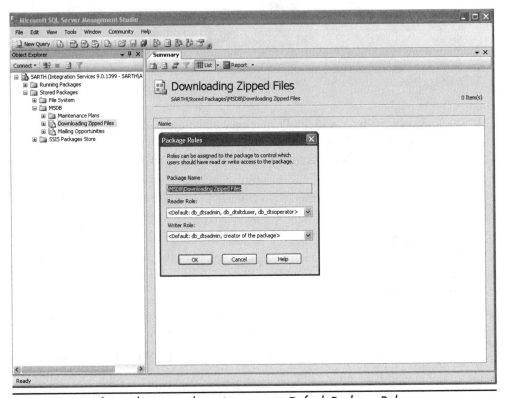

Figure 7-6   *Reader and Writer role assignments to Default Package Roles*

Exercise (Assigning Permission to Execute the Downloading Zipped Files Package)

The detailed permissions for the fixed database-level roles tell us that db_dtsoperator is able to execute any package. We will focus only on assigning the db_dtsoperator role to our user. In this exercise, we will assign execute package permission to a group (team) and will execute our test package Downloading zipped files. The steps of the process are as follows:

▶ Create a login for ISUser02 user account and a user-defined role team.

▶ Add the user to the team.

▶ Assign the team group to db_dtsoperator.

To assign permissions to a group of users, you will create a user-defined role, make users members of this role, and assign permissions to this role to access the package and the database objects the package needs to access to execute successfully. Finally, you will add the user-defined role to the pertinent fixed database-level roles.

7. In SQL Server Management Studio, connect to the database engine, open a new query tab, and type the following query:

```
USE msdb
CREATE ROLE Team
CREATE LOGIN [SARTH\ISUser02] FROM WINDOWS
CREATE USER ISUser02 FOR LOGIN [SARTH\ISUser02]
EXEC sp_addrolemember 'Team' , 'ISUser02'
```

This creates a user-defined role Team. Next create a login and user account for ISUser02 in the msdb database and then add ISUser02 as a member to the role Team. (Note that SARTH is the computer name used in the setup environment used for writing this book. You need to replace this name with the name of your computer.)

8. Choose Start | All Programs | Accessories. Right-click the command prompt and choose Run as from the context menu. In the Run As window, specify the following:

User name	ISUser02
Password	ISUp@ss02

Click OK to open Command Prompt window with ISUser02 credentials.

9. Type the following at the command prompt and press ENTER:

```
DTEXEC /SQL "Downloading zipped files"
```

The package fails with the following error:

```
Could not load package "downloading zipped files" because of
error 0xC0014062. Description: The LoadFromSQLServer method has
encountered OLE DB error code 0x80040E09 (EXECUTE permission
denied on object 'sp_dts_getpackage', database 'msdb', schema
'dbo'.). The SQL statement that was issued has failed.
```

This is OK, as the ISUser02 user account doesn't have rights to execute the package yet.

10. You can assign execute permissions (i.e., Reader Role) in several ways to the ISUser02 user account or user-defined role Team. One way is to assign Reader Role to Team and then add the Team role to database-level db_dtsoperator role. However, we will add the Team role to a fixed database-level role db_dtsoperator, and this should be sufficient, as the db_dtsoperator role by

default has Reader Role privileges. Switch to SQL Server Management Studio and run the following T-SQL in the query pane:

```
EXEC sp_addrolemember 'db_dtsoperator' , 'Team'
```

This will add Team as a member to the fixed database-level db_dtsoperator role.

11. Switch to the command prompt opened earlier for user ISUser02. Try to execute the Downloading zipped files package. You will get a success message this time:

```
DTExec: The package execution returned DTSER_SUCCESS (0).
```

Review

In this Hands-On exercise, you learned how to assign a group a reader role. You first created a user-defined role, then added the required database user to the role, and then linked that role to the fixed database-level role db_dtsoperator. Similarly, you can assign a writer role to user accounts or groups. What we did not do is to assign Reader Role directly to the user-defined group and then link that role to a fixed database-level role. Alternatively, you could have added users directly to the fixed database-level role. Whichever way you choose to go, make sure you assign a reader or writer role to the user or user-defined group and link them to the fixed database-level roles. Just for the better clarity on this point, perform a few simple steps here:

1. Check the sysdtspackages90 table in msdb database for reader role and writer role by running the following T-SQL command:

```
USE msdb
SELECT name, readrolesid, writerolesid from sysdtspackages90
WHERE name = 'Downloading zipped files'
```

You will get NULL for both the readrolesid and writerolesid fields.

If the Reader Role and Writer Role have default fixed database-level roles assigned, you will see Nulls in the above-mentioned fields.

2. In the Integration Services Connection, go to the Package Roles of Downloading zipped files package as we did earlier. Here you can add *Team* in the Reader Role comma-separated list or have it listed on its own, as shown in Figure 7-7.

3. Now, if you run the same T-SQL again to see the roles in sysdtspackages90 table, you will see the SID for role Team added in the readrolesid field.

Now all you have to do is add the user-defined role—i.e., Team—in the relevant default role to have access permissions.

Figure 7-7   *Assigning a Reader Role to the Team role*

Another point worth mentioning here is that any metadata or configuration files and the like that are saved outside the package cannot be protected solely by the database-level roles. Carefully consider where you want to store your configuration files or other miscellaneous files so that they are properly protected. Examples of such files that can be saved outside the package are configuration files, checkpoint files, or log files. If you are saving these files to SQL Server (but outside the package) or on to the files system, you need to secure them using appropriate security measures. For more details on this, refer to the next section.

Last but not least, you also need to assign permissions to user-defined roles on the objects (such as tables, views, and so on) being accessed by your package; otherwise the package will run but will fail for not being able to access the objects.

Protecting Packages and Metadata at the Storage Level

You need to protect the Integration Services packages and the package metadata from unauthorized access or hardware failures. Integration Services packages may have associated configuration files that have been saved outside the package. These configuration files are used to update values of properties at run-time, making it easier to deploy packages from a development environment to a production environment. While both the package and the package configurations can be saved in SQL Server or file system, they need to be protected irrespective to where they have been saved.

Considerations for Saving to SQL Server

When you save SSIS packages to SQL Server, you actually save them to the sysdtspackages90 table in the msdb database. If you are using a legacy package—i.e., DTS 2000 package in SQL Server 2005—Integration Services saves it to the sysdtspackages table in the msdb database. This means when you save your packages in the msdb database, they are protected by server, database, and table-level permissions. Packages developed from the ground up using BIDS (and not using DTS 2000 package)—i.e., the packages saved in the sysdtspackages90 table—are also protected by fixed database-level roles as you have studied earlier.

Like SSIS packages, package configurations can also be saved to any SQL Server 2005 database table, not necessarily the msdb database. When saved in a SQL Server database table, package configurations are protected with server, database, and table-level permissions.

To protect your packages from hardware failures or miscellaneous types of data losses, you need to develop a backup plan that includes backup of the msdb database, as this will back up sysdtspackages90 and sysdtspackages tables stored in the msdb database. For package configurations, you need to make sure that the table containing package configurations is also included in the backup plans to provide complete protection from hardware failures.

Considerations for Saving to the File System

When saved to the file system, an Integration Services package is stored in an XML file (.dtsx), and package configurations can also be saved to XML file types. If you decide to save your packages and package configurations to the file system, you need to secure them using file system permissions. It's better to create a folder hierarchy for a solution to keep all the projects, their packages, configuration files, and other miscellaneous files if possible and protect this folder hierarchy using file system permissions. This also helps in making it easy to back up all the code and the files for related projects in the same backup job.

Summary

Security is the most often discussed topic these days in the IT industry. As a DBA or information analyst, you need to make sure that the contents of SSIS packages are secure. You have seen that the Integration Services provides a facility to sign a package to check for its integrity and provides six package protection levels out of which four are for encrypting packages, one is for excluding sensitive information, and one is for using database level roles. You have learned how to exclude sensitive information in your packages and encrypt sensitive information in packages using a user key or password. You have also used database level roles to protect the package with read or write access controls. You should understand the various considerations necessary to store packages. Remember to consider carefully where to store each file used in a SSIS solution and make sure these files are also protected.

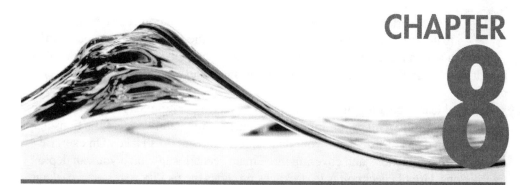

Advanced Features of Integration Services

IN THIS CHAPTER

Y ou've worked with various tasks of control flow and have used various features and properties of the tasks to configure your package to perform a job. In this chapter you will learn about some of the advanced functionalities inbuilt into Integration Services that you can leverage to extend functionality of your packages.

You will learn about logging and log providers in Integration Services, which help you to monitor the events at run-time and provide auditing abilities. Transactions help you maintain data consistency in your data stores. You will do a Hands-On exercise dealing with transactions and covering three main scenarios in which you can deploy transactions. Use of checkpoints in packages provides the facility to restart a package from the point of failure and reduce the work to be done to complete the regular data processing jobs. Checkpoints and their usability are covered in detail in this chapter. Though you've already been introduced to variables and property expressions and have also used them to basic level, you will be using them extensively in this chapter. Finally, you will learn how you can make your packages respond to the events occurring during run-time and take appropriate actions.

Let's start with the easiest and the most basic requirement of logging events and activities at run-time.

Logging and Log Providers in SSIS

You can use logging in Integration Services to log information about events happening at run-time for auditing and troubleshooting purposes. SSIS containers expose their properties as log entries to enable you to log information from them. Integration Services provides detailed levels of logging within packages. An Integration Services package is a container, and an Integration Services task is enclosed inside a task host container, so you can enable logging at the package level, at the container level, or even at the task level. You do not need to enable logging at the package level to log information for a container or at the container level to enable logging for the task within the container. Logging can be configured independently from the container hierarchy point of view. However, the logs can be created only at the package level.

You need to add the logs to which you want to log information in a package. Integration Services provides five different types of preconfigured log providers; plus, you can create custom log providers. The log providers specify the format and the storage type of the log. Depending on the log provider, you may also choose a connection manager. To add a log to a package, first select the log provider and then specify a connection manager to specify the location of the log. Let's explore the types of log providers available in Integration Services:

SSIS log provider for text files   This log provider adds the simplest and most used type of logs in the form of text files that can be transferred anywhere and can be read by other applications. This log provider writes the logging information into a CSV (comma-separated value) formatted text file that you specify using a file connection manager.

SSIS log provider for SQL Profiler   One of the big improvements in SQL Server 2005 is the ability to link Windows performance logs with the Profiler traces so that you can match the events happening inside SQL Server against the overall performance behavior of the server. For such scenarios, when you want to analyze the execution of the package step by step against the performance logs, you will select this log provider to log information in a format that can be read by SQL Server Profiler. The log file name extension must be *.trc* for it to be used with the SQL Server Profiler. This provider uses a file connection manager to write log entries to a file with .trc extension.

SSIS log provider for SQL Server   When you want to write the logging information into an SQL Server database so that you can query for certain events, you will select this log provider. It writes the log entries into the sysdtslog90 table that it creates when the package is run the first time with this log provider selected and configured. You use an OLE DB Connection Manager to specify the database to which you want it to create a sysdtslog90 table.

SSIS log provider for Windows Event Log   When you use this log provider, your package will log entries into Windows Application Event Log on the local computer. This is the simplest form of log provider to work with, as you do not need to configure any connection manager.

SSIS log provider for XML files   When you want to write the logging information in XML format, you will use this log provider. You will then use a file connection manager to specify a file with an .xml extension into which it writes log entries.

A few words about log providers in general: You can add more than one log of each type of log providers in your package. For example, you can add the SSIS log provider for Text files twice in your package to contain different set of information in the different files. Once you've added the logs and have specified their connection managers, you can then enable logging for the tasks and containers in your package and select the events to log to one or more types of logs that you've added into your package.

By this time, you can well imagine that with the ability to write events happening within the container to multiple logs, you can write different events in different logs. Also, with different levels of containers and tasks within the package, you can select relevant events to be logged based on the role or level of the container within the package. For example, you may want to log package start time and end time at the package level but may want to log much more information at the task level. By default,

Integration Services provides several types of information for logging against each event or log entry. This information, called *Integration Services log schema*, consists of the following elements:

▶ **Event** Name of the event or log entry.

▶ **Computer** Name of the computer where the event occurred.

▶ **Operator** Name of the user under whose context the package is being executed.

▶ **SourceName** Name of the container or task where the event occurred.

▶ **SourceID** Each task or container in the Integration Services package is assigned a unique ID, which is displayed in the ID field in the Properties window. This field refers that unique ID of the task or container where the event occurred.

▶ **ExecutionID** Each time a package is executed, it is assigned a globally unique execution ID that is recorded in the logs by this element.

▶ **MessageText** Some events or log entries generate a message such as "Beginning of package execution" during run-time that is logged by this element.

▶ **DataBytes** Specifies a byte array (BLOB) that is specific to the log entry.

You will find some additional elements available in the logs depending on the type of log such as ID, StartTime, EndTime, and DataCode. Other features are associated with logging functionality, such as inheritance of logging options and facility to apply templates of logging configurations to keep consistency across the organisation. These features are best understood visually while working with them, so let's do a Hands-On exercise to configure logging in a package.

Hands-On: Configure Logging in a Package

The objective of this Hands-On exercise is to enable and configure logging in a package and see the log results after executing the package.

Method

To implement logging, we will be using the Contacting Opportunities package that you created in Chapter 4. However, to avoid version conflict and confusion of these two packages, we will create a new Integration Services project and add the Mailing Opportunities.dtsx package to this. The main steps involved are as follows:

- ▶ Create a new Integration Services project.
- ▶ Add the Mailing Opportunities.dtsx package in newly created project.
- ▶ Enable logging and configure log entries at various levels in the package.
- ▶ Execute the package and observe the logs.

Exercise (Create a New Integration Services Project)

1. Open BIDS and press CTRL-SHIFT-N to create a new project.
2. In the New Project dialog box, select the Integration Services Project template and fill the following details in fields:

Name	Contacting Opportunities with Logging
Project	C:\SSIS\Projects

Uncheck the Create Directory For Solution check box and click OK to create a new project.

3. After the project has been created, go to Solution Explorer window, right-click the SSIS Packages node, and select Add Existing Package. In the Add Copy of Existing Package dialog box, choose SQL Server in the Package Location field if it is not already selected. In the Server field, type **localhost** and leave Windows Authentication selected in the Authentication type field. Click the ellipsis button next to the Package Path field to open the SSIS Package window, which should display the Mailing Opportunities package under SSIS Packages folder, which you imported to MSDB in Chapter 6. However, if you skipped Chapter 6 and this package is not there, add this package from file system instead. Select Mailing Opportunities from the list and click the OK button. Close the Add Copy of Existing Package dialog box by clicking OK. You will see the Mailing Opportunities.dtsx package added under SSIS Packages node in Solution Explorer.
4. Select the Package.dtsx package and press the DELETE key on the keyboard. Click OK to confirm deletion of this package. Press CTRL-SHIFT-S to save this project. Double-click the Mailing Opportunities.dtsx package in Solution Explorer to load it in the Designer.

Exercise (Enable and Configure Logging)

5. Right-click anywhere on the blank surface in the Control Flow tab and select Logging from the context menu. This will open the Configure SSIS Logs dialog box, which shows an alert prompting you to enable logging. Click the

check box to the left of Mailing Opportunities to enable logging at the package level in the Containers pane and get rid of the alert message.

6. On the right pane of the Providers and Logs tab, click in the Provider Type field to see the list of log providers, and select SSIS log provider for SQL Server from the list. Click the Add button to add a log of this type and you will see a log added in the logs area. Similarly, add another log of SSIS Log Provider for Text Files at the package level. You have added two different types of log providers to your package as you will be logging the package level information to SQL Server and the Send Mail task level logging information to the text file.

7. Click in the Name field of the SSIS Log Provider for SQL Server log and rename it *Package Level log to SQL Server.* Similarly rename the SSIS Log Provider for Text Files log name as *SMTP Task level log to Text file.*

8. Click under the Configuration field of Package Level Log To SQL Server and the field will convert to a drop-down list box. Click the down arrow and select (local).Campaign.

9. Click under the Configuration field of SMTP Task Level Log To Text File and the field converts to a drop-down list box. Click the down arrow and select <New connection...>. This will open a File Connection Manager Editor.

10. Click in the Usage Type field and select Create File from the drop-down list. Type **C:\SSIS\Projects\Contacting Opportunities with Logging\ SMTPTaskLevel.log** in the File field and click OK. At this stage, your Configure SSIS Logs dialog box should look like the one shown in Figure 8-1.

11. Now that you have enabled logging for your package, you can select the log entries against which you want to log information. As you will be logging package level information to SQL Server table, select the Package Level Log To SQL Server Log check box.

12. Go to the Details tab and select the check box provided to the left of Events column to select all the events listed below it, as shown in Figure 8-2.

    You can select the desired events from the list of various types of events provided for the container or the task. Spend some time here reading the description provided for each event.

13. After enabling logging and the log entries at package level, you can move on to configure subcontainers and tasks. Click Iterating May Opportunities, the Details tab will gray out and an alert will ask you to enable logging if you want to implement unique logging options for this container. Also note that the check in the check box on the left of this container is grayed out. This means that the logging options will be inherited from the immediate parent container—i.e., you

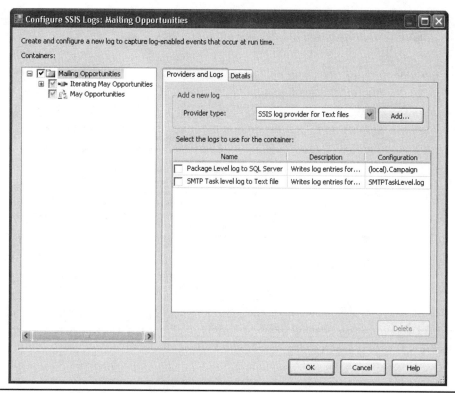

Figure 8-1   *Enabling logging in an Integration Services package*

do not need to define logging options specifically for child containers or tasks. This makes logging easy and quick to implement. However, if you want to control the logging level for each container or task, this option is available. Each container or task in the package can have three levels of logging modes that are defined by a property called LoggingMode of the container or task: UseParentSetting, Enabled, or Disabled. You can set the logging mode on a container either from the Properties window of the selected object or by using the check boxes provided for each container or task in the Configure SSIS Logs dialog box. If you click the Iterating May Opportunities Container check box to clear the checkmark, this disables the LoggingMode, and if you click again to apply a checkmark in the check box, it will enable the LoggingMode property, which means that you can define unique logging options for this container. As we do not want to set separate logging options for this container, disable the check box to imply that the parent logging options will be used.

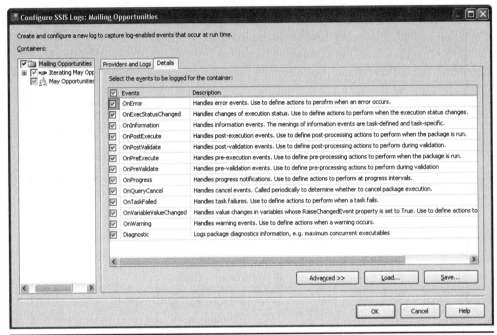

Figure 8-2 *Enabling events to log entries into logs*

14. Expand the Iterating May Opportunities container and select the Mailing Opportunities task. Note that the events on the Details tab remain the same as the logging options have been inherited from the parent, Iterating May Opportunities. Double-click on the check box to the left of Mailing Opportunities in the left pane to place a highlighted tick in the check box and change the LoggingMode to Enabled for this task. As you do that, you will notice that three new events—SendMailTaskBegin, SendMailTaskEnd, and SendMailTaskInfo—have been added to the list in the Details pane. This is because not all the tasks and containers provide the same types of events or log entries; many of the Integration Services components of course provide additional log entries for logging specific information related to their functionality only.

15. Click the Advanced button and you will see the information fields that will be logged when the selected events occur. These log schema fields have been described earlier in this chapter. Select OnProgress, SendMailTaskBegin, SendMailTaskEnd, and SendMailTaskInfo events only, as shown in Figure 8-3. Note that all the fields of log schema are selected by default.

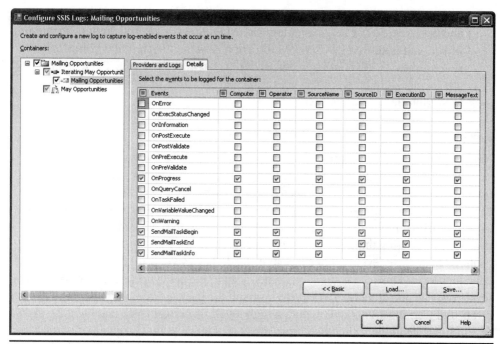

Figure 8-3   *Configuring unique log entries for the Mailing Opportunities task*

16. Click the Providers and Logs tab. Select the check box for SMTP Task Level Log To Text File Log, as you want to log events to a text file for Mailing Opportunities Task. Click OK to close the Configure SSIS Logs dialog box. You've successfully configured logging for this package.

Exercise (Analyze Integration Services Logs)

17. Press the F5 key to execute the package. You will see the components changing color from yellow to green. When the package execution completes, press SHIFT-F5 to return to design mode.

18. Run SQL Server Management Studio and connect to the database engine. Run the following query in the Query pane:

```
Select * from [Campaign].[dbo].[sysdtslog90]
```

Look through the results and particularly note the OnPreExecute event and OnPostExecute event of Iterating May Opportunities. Note the start time and end time of these events.

19. Explore to the C:\SSIS\Projects\Contacting Opportunities with Logging folder and open the SMTPTaskLevel.log file using Notepad. Scroll right to the end of file and note that the Send Mail task has been initiated and completed seven times, corresponding to the seven messages it sent out. These events also occurred in between the start time and end time of the Iterating May Opportunities container.

Review

You've enabled and configured logging options in this exercise with unique logging options on the Mailing Opportunities task. You've seen how the inherited logging options work and that you do not need to set any configurations. However, if you need to save disk space and tighten up logging only for the required events, you can do so by configuring unique log entries as you have done with the Mailing Opportunities task. One interesting thing to note is that events such as OnError and OnWarning not captured at the task level do not get lost; instead, they travel up and can be captured at container level. This means that you do not need to log everything at every component level. You can actually choose discrete levels in the package where you want to capture errors and warnings. This will maintain high levels of performance and keep the disks free of unwanted logs. Otherwise, from the best practice point of view, you should be logging heavily during development and debugging phases while reducing the logging to the minimum required level at normal production runs.

Transactions in Integration Services Packages

Transactions enable you to implement data integrity and consistency within your packages. In DBMS world, a transaction is considered an atomic piece of work that must be completed entirely or rolled back altogether. Sometimes it becomes imperative to use transactions when working with database systems. For example, in banking systems, when somebody transfers money from his account to someone else's account, the money has to be debited and credited in a single transaction—either both operations of debiting and crediting will happen or both will be rolled back if the system is unable to complete the transaction at any stage while processing this transaction. In this way, you can be sure that the data integrity will be maintained. Transactions are required to possess the ACID properties (Atomicity, Consistency, Isolation, and Durability), without which the integrity of the transacted data cannot be guaranteed. Integration Services also allows you to use transactions within a package or among one or more packages.

Containers within an Integration Services package can be configured to use transactions by setting the TransactionOption property to Required or Supported in the Transactions section of the container's Properties window. As the tasks are enclosed within the task host containers, the tasks can also be configured to use transactions using the TransactionOption property. This property can have one of three possible values:

▶ **Required**   The container must participate in a transaction when the TransactionOption is set to Required. That is, if the parent of this container has already started a transaction, this container will join that transaction; if no transaction exists, this container will start a new transaction.

▶ **Supported**   The container will participate in a transaction if it already exists when the TransactionOption is set to Supported. However, if a transaction doesn't exist, it will not start a new transaction.

▶ **NotSupported**   The container will not participate in a transaction even if a transaction exists. That is, the containers having TransactionOption set as NotSupported will neither start a transaction nor join an existing transaction.

You can use transactions with various types of possibilities and scenarios. Because Integration Services tasks support programming SQL Server, you can effectively use native transactions supported by SQL Server. But for most of the work, you will be using Microsoft Distributed Transaction Coordinator (MSDTC) to support transactions in Integration Services. MSDTC is a Windows service that provides transaction infrastructure across multiple computer systems or distributed computing environments.

You can configure transactions involving tasks in a container, you can involve multiple containers in a transaction, or you can have a transaction spanning over multiple packages. These packages can be running on different machines, effectively resulting in a transaction running in a distributed environment. Multiple transactions can be included in a package and multiple packages can be run under one transaction.

How package transactions are run depend on you how you configure transactions on the containers and subcontainers and how you configure transactions when the package is run as a child package under the context of an Execute Package task. When a package is run under the context of an Execute Package task, it can inherit the transaction started by the parent package if the Execute Package task and the package are configured to join this transaction. In addition, while configuring multiple transactions within a package, you may have transactions running within a transaction. These *nested transactions* go hand in hand with the container hierarchy within a package. However, issues arise when you use nested transactions that are not related—i.e., do not fall particularly within single parent transaction which can cause tasks not to roll back completely as desired. While configuring transactions within your package, try to keep child transactions within the scope of a single parent transaction and, as a best practice, test thoroughly before deploying to production.

Hands-On: Maintaining Data Integrity with Transactions

You are tasked with making sure that the data is always kept in consistent state, irrespective of the data sources from where the data is coming. You are trying to identify how the data could become inconsistent; you determined that one of the reasons could be the data import process, when part of a record could not be imported. Various packages and processes are importing data, and you want to determine exactly how transactions can protect your data.

Method

In this exercise, you will be simulating various scenarios of data import and will work with transaction options to maintain data integrity. You can configure transactions within a package in various ways, but to help you understand how they work, you will deal with three main cases in which transactions can be used. The main steps involved in this exercise are as follows:

▶ Create a package and understand how data consistency can be affected with loading operations.

▶ Case I covers use of transaction involving multiple tasks but in a single container.

▶ Case II covers transactions spanning multiple containers

▶ Case III covers transactions spanning multiple packages.

Exercise (Create a Simulation Package for Data Consistency Issues)

1. Open SQL Server Management Studio, connect to the database engine, and run the following queries to create three tables after opening a new query pane:

```
USE [Campaign]
GO
CREATE TABLE [dbo].[NewCustomer](
    [CustomerID] [varchar](10) NOT NULL,
    [FirstName] [varchar](50) NULL,
    [SurName] [varchar](50) NULL
) ON [PRIMARY]
Go
CREATE TABLE [dbo].[EmailAddress](
    [CustomerID] [varchar](10) NOT NULL,
    [Email] [varchar](100) NOT NULL,
    [Type] [varchar](50) NULL
) ON [PRIMARY]
```

```
Go
CREATE TABLE [dbo].[Vehicle](
   [CustomerID] [varchar](10) NULL,
   [VIN] [varchar](20) NOT NULL,
   [Series] [varchar](50) NULL,
   [Model] [varchar](50) NULL
) ON [PRIMARY]
GO
```

2. Open BIDS and create a new Integration Services project with the following
    details in the New Project dialog box:

Name	Maintaining data Integrity with Transactions
Location	C:\SSIS\Projects

    Verify that Create A Directory For Solution Option is unchecked and click OK.

3. When the Integration Services designer loads up the new project, right-click in
    the Connection Managers area and choose New OLE DB Connection. In the
    Configure OLE DB Connection Manager dialog box, choose (local).Campaign
    and click OK. You've added a connection manager to connect to the Campaign
    database.

4. Drop an Execute SQL Task from the Toolbox onto the Control Flow surface.
    Rename this task Loading NewCustomer.

5. Open the Execute SQL Task Editor by double-clicking its icon. In the
    Connection field's drop-down list, choose (local).Campaign.

6. With SQLSourceType set to Direct Input, click in the SQLStatement field, and
    then click the ellipsis button that appears in the right corner of the field to open the
    Enter SQL Query dialog box. Type the following SQL statement in this dialog box
    and click OK.

    ```
    INSERT INTO NewCustomer (CustomerID, FirstName, SurName)
    VALUES ('N501', 'Will', 'Harrison')
    ```

    Click the Parse Query button to parse the SQL statement and click OK to close
    the pop-up message box. After the query has parsed correctly, click OK.

7. Repeat steps 4 to 6 to add a second Execute SQL task to your package. Rename
    this task Loading EmailAddress and edit it to add (local).Campaign connection
    manager. Close the task after assigning the following SQL statement to it:

    ```
    INSERT INTO EmailAddress (CustomerID, Email, Type) VALUES
    ('N501', 'wharrison@AffordingIT.co.uk', 'Work')
    ```

    Join the Loading NewCustomer task with this task using an on-success
    precedence constraint.

8. Repeat steps from 4 to 6 to add a third Execute SQL task to your package. Rename this task Loading Vehicle and edit it to add the (local).Campaign connection manager. Close the task after assigning the following SQL statement to it:

```
INSERT INTO Vehicle (CustomerID, VIN, Series, Model) VALUES
('N501', 'UV123WX456YZ789', 'X11 Series', 'Saloon')
```

Join the Loading EmailAddress task with this third task using an on-success precedence constraint. Your package should look like the one shown in Figure 8-4.

9. Execute this package by pressing the F5 key. When all the tasks have changed to green and the package has completed execution, press SHIFT-F5 to return to design mode.

10. Switch to SQL Server Management Studio and run the following query:

```
SELECT n.[CustomerID], [FirstName], [SurName], [Email],
[Type], [VIN], [Series], [Model]
```

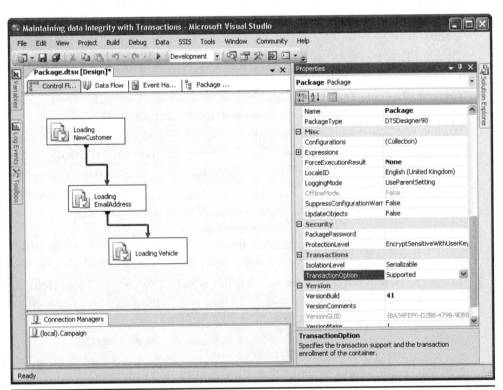

Figure 8-4 *Creating a simulation package for data consistency checks*

```
FROM [Campaign].[dbo].[NewCustomer] n LEFT OUTER JOIN
[Campaign].[dbo].[EmailAddress] e
ON n.CustomerID = e.CustomerID
LEFT OUTER JOIN [Campaign].[dbo].[Vehicle] v
ON n.CustomerID = v.CustomerID
```

You will see the result contains customer details, the customer's e-mail address, and the vehicle details, all as you wanted (see Figure 8-5), irrespective to the fact that the data is stored in different tables.

11. Note the TransactionOption property of the package in Figure 8-4, which is set at the default value of Supported. This property has a Supported value for all the three tasks as well. Only the containers with TransactionOption set as Required can start a transaction, so no container started a transaction while this package was executed. So far so good. Now, let's see what happens if a task fails and doesn't import a particular row.

Data uploading can fail for a particular record for various reasons. The most common is a data type mismatch or a constraint on the column. If you go to the Campaign database, expand the Vehicle table, and then look in the Columns node in the Object Explorer in SQL Server Management Studio, you will see the column properties of the Vehicle table. Note that the VIN field is a mandatory (not null) field and must have a known value. If no data is received for this field during the import process, that row will not be inserted.

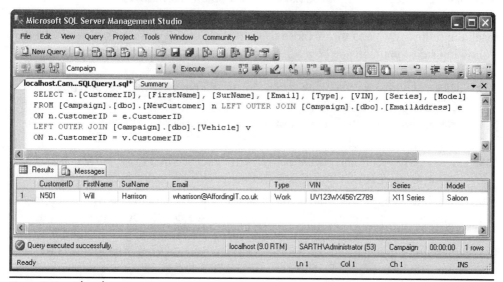

Figure 8-5   *The data consistency you want to see in your database*

12. Before you proceed, let's clean up our tables. Run the following queries in the Query pane to delete all the data from the existing tables:

```
DELETE [Campaign].[dbo].[NewCustomer]
DELETE [Campaign].[dbo].[EmailAddress]
DELETE [Campaign].[dbo].[Vehicle]
```

13. Switch to BIDS and modify the SQL statement in the Loading Vehicle task by removing the VIN information from the SQL statement; your statement should look as follows:

```
INSERT INTO Vehicle (CustomerID, Series, Model) VALUES
('N501', 'X11 Series', 'Saloon')
```

14. After you've made the change, press F5 to execute the package again. Keep in mind that you've still not implemented transaction in the package. This time, you will see that the first two tasks execute successfully while the Loading Vehicle task fails and turns red.

15. Switch to SQL Server Management Studio and execute the query written in step 10 to see the results this time. You will see that the three fields—VIN, Series, and Model—have NULL values. You have discovered how your data can become inconsistent during the loading process.

16. Run the delete SQL statements written in step 12 to cleanse this data from all the tables.

Exercise (Case I: Avoiding Inconsistency in a Single Container)

In real life, you either commit all the data from all the tasks in the tables or roll back the failing rows and throw those rows out and deal with them separately. In the following steps, you will see how you can roll back the data by using transactions.

17. Click anywhere on the blank surface of the Control Flow panel and press F4 to open the Properties window. Scroll down the Properties window and locate the Transactions section. Change the TransactionOption value from Supported to Required.

18. Press F5 to execute the package. You will again see that the first two tasks complete successfully whereas the Loading Vehicle task fails as expected.

19. Switch to SQL Server Management Studio and execute the query written in step 10 to see the results. This time, you will see no data at all in the output query. Setting the TransactionOption to Required resulted in the use of a transaction under which all the three tasks were executed. As the third task failed, the data loaded by first two tasks was rolled back.

Exercise (Case II: Transaction Spanning over Multiple Containers)

The preceding exercise demonstrated how you can use a transaction to avoid inconsistency in data during loading operation. This was quite simple, involving only one container in the package. What if a data-loading package uses multiple containers? Let's see how that can be handled.

20. Drop the Sequence Container twice on the Control Flow surface from the Toolbox. Delete the precedence constraint connecting Loading EmailAddress with Loading Vehicle.

21. Select Loading NewCustomer and Loading EmailAddress by pressing and holding the CONTROL key on the keyboard and clicking these tasks one by one. With these tasks selected, drag and drop them inside the first Sequence container.

22. Drag and drop Loading Vehicle inside Sequence Container 1. Drag the green arrow from the Sequence Container and drop it on Sequence Container 1 to join these containers so that the tables are loaded in sequence. (Note that this step is not required for running of the package though). Your package will look like the one shown in Figure 8-6.

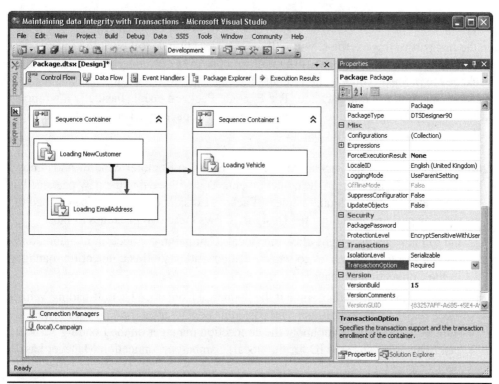

Figure 8-6   *Package consisting of multiple containers*

23. Your package is now using two sequence containers to load the data. Verify that the two new containers have their TransactionOption set to default value of Supported and the Package container's TransactionOption property still has the Required value set previously.

24. Press F5 to run the package. You will see that the first container with the two tasks in it successfully executes and turns green. However, the second sequence container with the Loading Vehicle task in it fails and turns red. Press SHIFT-F5 to switch back to design mode.

25. Switch to SQL Server Management Studio and run the SQL statement you wrote in step 10 to see what's been loaded in the database. You will see that no data for the NewCustomer and EmailAddress tables has been added, even though the loading tasks were successful. This is because both the containers were running under one transaction, and when one of the tasks in a container fails, the transaction rolls back all the work done by previous tasks. One lesson to learn from this exercise is that the parent container, which is the package in this case, must have its TransactionOption property set to Required to start a transaction, and the child containers need to have at least the Supported attribute for this property.

Exercise (Case III: Transaction Spanning over Multiple Packages)

In the last part of this exercise, you will use a transaction to roll back the inconsistent data when your loading process uses multiple packages. When you have multiple packages to process, you use the Execute Package task to embed them inside a single package and then run this package. The Execute Package task is basically a wrapper task that enables a package to be used inside another package. The Execute Package task is explained in detail in Chapter 5.

26. Right-click the SSIS Packages node in the Solution Explorer window and choose New SSIS Package from the context menu. You will see that the new package has been added with the default name of Package1.dtsx and the screen is switched to the new package. Note that the Designer shows these two packages as tabs.

27. Go to Package.dtsx, right-click the (local).Campaign connection manager, and choose Copy. Switch back to Package1.dtsx and paste this connection manager in the Connection Managers area.

28. Again go to Package.dtsx and cut the Sequence Container 1 with Loading Vehicle Task, return to Package1.dtsx, and paste this container on the Control Flow. You will see a validation error about the connection manager on the Loading Vehicle task. This is because the ID for the (local).Campaign Connection Manager has been changed.

29. Double-click the Loading Vehicle task icon to open the editor. In the Connection field, choose (local).Campaign Connection Manager from the drop-down list and click OK. You've divided the first package into two separate packages. To run these two packages as a single job, you need to create a new package and call these two packages using the Package Execute task.

30. Right-click the SSIS Packages node in the Solution Explorer window and choose New SSIS Package from the context menu. When the new blank package is loaded, drop two Execute Package tasks on the Control Flow surface.

31. Rename the first Execute Package task *Package* and the second task *Package1*. Join Package to Package1 using an on-success precedence constraint.

32. Double-click the Package icon to open the editor. Go to the Package page and change the Location field value to File System.

33. Click in the Connection field and then click the drop-down arrow and choose <New connection…>. In the File Connection Manager Editor's File field, type **C:\SSIS\Projects\Maintaining data Integrity with Transactions\Package .dtsx** and click OK. You will see *Package.dtsx* displayed in the Connection field. Click OK to close the Execute Package Task Editor.

34. As in the last two steps, open the editor for the Package1 task, change the Location to File System, and add a file connection manager in the Connection field point as **C:\SSIS\Projects\Maintaining data Integrity with Transactions\ Package1.dtsx** existing file. Close the Execute Package Task Editor after making these changes.

35. Click anywhere on the blank surface of the Control Flow panel and press F4 to open the Properties window for the package. Scroll down and locate the Transactions section and set the TransactionOption property to Required. This will run both the tasks and hence the package in the context of a single transaction. However, before proceeding any further, verify that the TransactionOption is set to the default value on Package and Package1 tasks and on the Package1.dtsx package. The Package.dtsx will have this property set to Required, which is OK, as this will also enable it to join the transaction started by Package2.dtsx. At this time, your package will look like the one shown in Figure 8-7.

36. Go to the Solution Explorer window, right-click Package2.dtsx, and then select Execute Package from the context menu. You will see that the Package.dtsx will execute successfully and then Package1.dtsx will execute, but it fails, and the components will turn red.

37. Switch to SQL Server Management Studio and run the command you created in step 10 to see the results. You will see that still no record has been added to

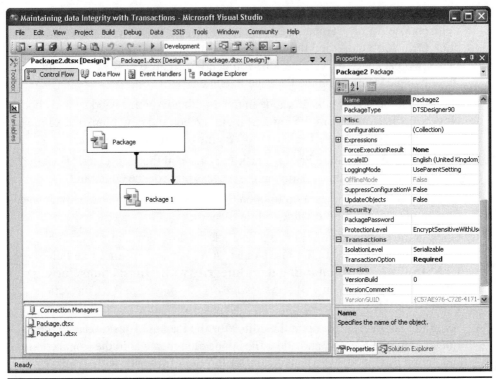

Figure 8-7 *Calling multiple packages using the Execute Package tasks.*

the tables, despite the fact that Package1.dtsx executed successfully. This is because both the packages were running under one transaction, and when the Loading Vehicle task failed in the Package1.dtsx package, the transaction rolled back not only all the tasks in this package but also the tasks in the other package, Package.dtsx.

Review

You've seen how you can use a transaction to combine various tasks and containers and even the packages to behave as a single unit and create atomicity among them that will commit or roll back as a unit. You've worked with the Sequence container to combine set of tasks as a logical unit and have learned a new trick of copying and pasting tasks among packages to increase productivity.

Restarting Packages with Checkpoints

If you're like most other information analysts and you update your data warehouse every night, this feature will be of much interest to you. After having set up logging for your packages, every morning you'd be checking the logs for the last night's update process to see how the update went. You usually expect that the update process has been successful, but what if the update process has failed? You will have to rerun your package during the daytime—and I know you wouldn't be happy about this, because doing this work during business hours involves some serious implications. Your users will not get the latest updates and will experience poor performance of the database server while you rerun the update process. If you've worked with DTS 2000 packages, you know that DTS 2000 doesn't support restating a package from the point of failure. You have to rerun the package from the start or manually run the tasks individually, which is quite involving and sometimes impossible to do. This is where Integration Services comes to the rescue by providing improved functionality of restarting a package.

By using checkpoints with Integration Services packages, you can restart your failed packages from the point of failure and can save the work that has completed successfully. Integration Services writes all the information that is required to restart a failed package in a *checkpoint* file. This file is created whenever you run a package the first time after a successful completion, and it is deleted when the package successfully completes. However, if an Integration Services package fails and is configured to use checkpoints, the checkpoint file is not deleted; instead, it is updated with information that is required to rerun the package from that point. When you rerun your package, Integration Services checks two things before executing the package: whether the package is configured to use checkpoints and whether the package was successfully executed last time. If it finds that the package configured to use checkpoints has actually failed the last time it was run, it then reads the checkpoint file associated with the package, gets the required information from the file, and restarts the package from the point of failure.

The checkpoint file contains all the necessary information for a package to restart at the point of failure. You decide the key positions in your package that would be good candidates for the point of restart and can be written as checkpoints in the file. For example, you would definitely designate a checkpoint immediately after the task that loads a large data set or downloads multiple large files from an FTP site. In case of failure of the package after successfully downloading files or completing loading the data set, the package will be restarted after these tasks, as the checkpoint defines the starting place. The checkpoint file also contains the package configuration information—i.e., the information about the environment into which the package was running. This avoids loading of package configurations, as this is read from the checkpoint file and hence maintains the original environment into which the package was running at the time of failure.

To enable your package to record checkpoints information, you set the following properties at the package level:

- ▶ **CheckpointUsage**   You can access this property in the Checkpoints section of the package Properties window. This property can have one of three values: Never, Always, or IfExists. The default value is Never, which means the checkpoints are not enabled and no checkpoint file will be created; hence the package will always start processing from the beginning whenever it is executed. The second value is Always, which, if selected, will make the package use a checkpoint file always. If the package has failed in the previous execution and you've somehow deleted or lost the checkpoint file, the package will fail to execute. The third possible value is IfExists, which, when selected, makes the package use a checkpoint file if it exists and start the package from the point of failure in the previous execution. However, if the checkpoint file doesn't exist, the package will always start from the beginning.

- ▶ **SaveCheckpoints**   After enabling your package to use checkpoints, you can set this property to True to indicate that checkpoints should be saved.

- ▶ **CheckpointFileName**   Using this property, you can specify the path and the file into which you would like to save checkpoints.

Along with these properties, you also need to set the FailPackageOnFailure property, available in the Execution section in Properties window on the package and the containers, to True to specify that the package will fail when a failure occurs. This property helps in setting the checkpoints on the tasks that you want to make as points of restart. If you do not set this property on any task or container in the package, the checkpoint file will not include any information for the containers on failure and will restart the package from the beginning. It is interesting to note the following points concerning the smallest unit that can be restarted:

- ▶ The smallest unit that can be restarted is a task.

- ▶ The Data Flow Task, which is a special task in Integration Services enclosing the data flow engine, can consist of several data flow transformations. This task is considered similar to any other Control Flow Task as far as checkpoints are concerned and cannot be started from halfway where it failed. If you have massive data flow operations in your package and you're concerned about rerunning packages, it is better that you divide up the data transformations work between multiple Data Flow tasks.

▶ The Foreach Loop Container is also considered an atomic unit of work that will either commit or restart completely to iterate over all the values provided by the enumerator used.

The use of an atomic unit of work actually calls for a discussion on transactions and checkpoints, as transactions convert the components involved into an atomic unit of work. Before we get deeper into that, let's understand the checkpoints and their operation within the scope of a transaction in the following Hands-On exercise.

Hands-On: Restarting a Failed Package Using Checkpoints

In this exercise, you will simulate a package failure and configure your package with checkpoints to restart it from the point of failure.

Method

You will use the package you developed earlier in the last exercise and apply checkpoint configurations to it. In the second step, you will use transactions over the package to see its behavior.

Exercise (Apply Checkpoint Configurations to Your Package)

1. Open BIDS and create a new Integration Services Project with the following details:

Name	Restarting failed package
Location	C:\SSIS\Projects

   Verify that Create A Directory For Solution option is unchecked and click the OK button.

2. When a blank project is created, go to the Solution Explorer window and select the Package.dtsx package in the SSIS Packages node. Then press the DELETE key on your keyboard. Click OK to confirm the deletion. Right-click the SSIS Packages node and choose Add Existing Package from the context menu.

3. In the Add Copy of Existing Package dialog box, select Package Location as the File System. In the Package path field, type **C:\SSIS\Projects\Maintaining data Integrity with Transactions\Package.dtsx** and click the OK button to add this package. Once the package has been added, expand the SSIS Packages folder and double-click the Package.dtsx package to open it in the Designer.

4. Drop an Execute SQL task from the Toolbox on to the Designer surface outside the Sequence container and rename this task Loading Vehicle. Double-click the task icon to open the editor. In the General page's Connection field, choose Add (local).Campaign connection manager and type the following SQL statement in the SQLStatement field:

```
INSERT INTO Vehicle (CustomerID, Series, Model) VALUES
('N501', 'X11 Series', 'Saloon')
```

You already know that this SQL statement is without the mandatory VIN field; hence it will fail the Loading Vehicle task. Join the Sequence Container with the Loading Vehicle task using an on-success precedence constraint.

5. Click anywhere on the blank surface of the Designer and press F4 to open the Properties of the package. First, make sure that the package is not configured to use transactions. Scroll down and locate the TransactionOption property, and change its value to Supported.

6. Scroll up in the Properties window and locate the Checkpoints section. Specify the following settings in this section:

SaveCheckpoints	True
CheckpointUsage	IfExists
CheckPointFileName	C:\SSIS\Projects\Restarting failed package\checkpoints.chk

7. Because we want to include the restart information of the Loading Vehicle task in the checkpoints file, click the Loading Vehicle task on the Designer surface. You will see that the context of Properties window changes to show the properties of the Loading Vehicle task. Locate the FailPackageOnFailure property in the Execution section and change its value to True.

8. Press F5 to execute the package. You probably already know the result of the execution. The Sequence Container and the two Execute SQL tasks in it successfully execute and turn green, but the Loading Vehicle task fails and shows up in red. Press SHIFT-F5 to switch back to designer mode.

9. Let's see what has happened in the background while the package was executing. Open SQL Server Management Studio and run the following query to see the records imported into the database:

```
SELECT n.[CustomerID], [FirstName], [SurName], [Email],
[Type], [VIN], [Series], [Model]
FROM [Campaign].[dbo].[NewCustomer] n LEFT OUTER JOIN
[Campaign].[dbo].[EmailAddress] e
ON n.CustomerID = e.CustomerID
LEFT OUTER JOIN [Campaign].[dbo].[Vehicle] v
ON n.CustomerID = v.CustomerID
```

You will see that the customer and its e-mail information has been loaded while the vehicle information fields have null values.

Using Windows Explorer, navigate to the C:\SSIS\Projects\Restarting failed package folder and note that the checkpoints.chk file has been created and contains some information indicated by its size > 0 KB.

10. Change the SQL statement of the Loading Vehicle task to include the VIN information with the following query:

```
INSERT INTO Vehicle (CustomerID, VIN, Series, Model) VALUES
('N501', 'UV123WX456YZ789', 'X11 Series', 'Saloon')
```

11. Again execute the package. This time you will see that only the Loading Vehicle task is executed and the earlier two tasks and the Sequence container did not run at all (see Figure 8-8). This is because the package reads the checkpoint file before executing and finds the information about where to start executing. Press SHIFT-F5 to switch back to design mode.

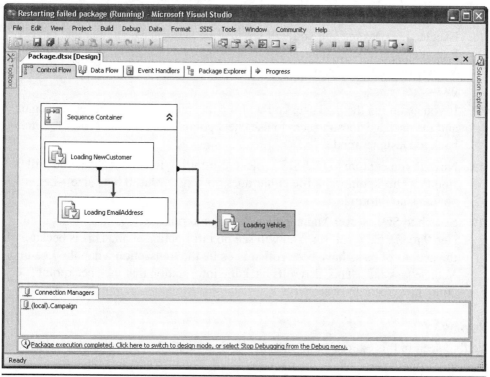

Figure 8-8   *Restarting package with checkpoints*

12. Explore to the C:\SSIS\Projects\Restarting failed package folder and note that the checkpoints.chk file does not exist.

13. Switch to SQL Server Management Studio and run the script specified in step 9 to see the result set. You will see one record containing customer, e-mail, and vehicle information. Run the following queries to clear the tables:

```
DELETE [Campaign].[dbo].[NewCustomer]
DELETE [Campaign].[dbo].[EmailAddress]
DELETE [Campaign].[dbo].[Vehicle]
```

Exercise (Effect of transaction on checkpoints)

14. Open the editor for Loading Vehicle task and remove the VIN information to fail the task. The SQLStatement should be configured this time with the query used in step 4. Click OK to close the task.

15. Click anywhere on the blank surface of the Control Flow Panel and press F4 to open Properties window. Scroll down and locate the TransactionOption property in the Transactions section. Set it to the Required value so that it starts a transaction.

16. Execute the package and you will see that the Sequence container and the two Execute SQL tasks in it successfully execute and turn green, but the Loading Vehicle task fails and shows up in red. Press SHIFT-F5 to switch back to Designer mode.

17. If you again run the package, you will see that all the tasks get executed again and the package doesn't seem to use checkpoints file. Press SHIFT-F5 to switch back to Designer mode.

18. Now, if you explore to C:\SSIS\Projects\Restarting failed package, you will find that checkpoints.chk file either does not exist or has 0 byte size—i.e., it contains no information.

19. Switch to SQL Server Management Studio and run the SQL statements used in step 9 to see the result set. You will see no information at all. This is because all the actions of tasks have been rolled back by the transaction when the Loading Vehicle task fails. This also rolls back the information that the checkpoint file could have recorded otherwise.

Review

You've seen in this exercise that the checkpoints can help you restart a package precisely from the task where the package failed. You also saw that the transactions roll back the information of the checkpoint file and cause that package to execute all over again. This is actually applicable to containers also. If you are using a transaction on a container, any failure in the container will roll back actions of all the tasks in the container that have already executed and no information will be recorded in the checkpoint file. This will cause the container to execute all over again. There is a catch here, though. Read the following points:

If your package consists of a complex container hierarchy and a subcontainer commits before the parent container fails, the subcontainers do not get rolled back and also do not get recorded in the checkpoint file. This causes those subcontainers to be executed again when the parent container is restarted. Similarly, the Foreach Loop container does not record any information in the checkpoint file about the iterations it may have already done before failing and gets executed all over again when restarted.

Expressions and Variables

You learned about variables and property expressions in Chapter 3 and have used them in various Hands-On exercises in subsequent chapters. With DTS 2000, use of variables was considered an advanced feature that allowed you to add some dynamic behavior to your packages. However, use of variables in Integration Services is made easier and has been tied into SSIS package design so much that the packages developed without using variables are reduced to ad hoc data operations, most of which can be done using the SQL Server Import and Export Wizard. On the other hand, use of property expressions is a new feature in Integration Services that provides an ability to set values for component properties dynamically using variables that are updated at run-time by other tasks. Property Expressions allow you to evaluate values generated at run-time by other tasks and use the evaluated values to update properties exposed by the concerned task at run-time. This is quite a powerful feature, as it allows you to read and evaluate the values that exist only at run-time and modify the property or behavior of other tasks in the package.

Though you've used variables and expressions in the Hands-On exercises earlier, here you will do another exercise that uses variables and particularly property expressions extensively to update properties of the send mail task to generate personalized mails.

Hands-On: Extending the Contacting Opportunities Package with Property Expressions

In Chapter 4, you created an Integration Services project called Contacting Opportunities that sends mail to persons who raised a query in May 2005. However, during the package development, you used static values in the To field, Subject field, and Message field.

You are now to extend the package so that these values are read from the table and evaluated for each person to create personalized messages.

Method

You will add the Mailing Opportunities package from the Contacting Opportunities package to the new package to keep the package separate from a learning point of view. The Mailing Opportunities package sends mails to seven persons who made enquiries in May 2005 using static values. To make the package dynamic, you will update the e-mail addresses in the Prospects table with your e-mail address so that you can see the messages that are being generated and sent out by this package. Then you will create variables that will capture values from the Prospects table to pass on to property expressions at run-time. Finally, you will create property expressions and will also learn about the DelayValidation property towards the end of this exercise.

Exercise (Build Property Expressions for Mailing Opportunities package)

1. Open SQL Server Management Studio, choose Databases | Campaign | Tables, and then select the Prospects table in the Object Explorer. Click the New Query button from the menu bar to open a new query pane. Type the following SQL statement in this new pane:

```
UPDATE [Campaign].[dbo].[Prospects]
SET email = 'youremailaddress'
WHERE ENQUIRYDATE BETWEEN '2005/05/01' AND '2005/05/31'
```

   Replace *youremailaddress* in the above query with your e-mail address and then execute this query to update the seven records.

2. Open BIDS and create a new Integration Services project with the following details:

Name	Contacting Opportunities with Property Expressions
Location	C:\SSIS\Projects

   Verify that the Create A Directory For Solution option is unchecked and click the OK button.

3. When the blank project is created, go to the Solution Explorer window and select the Package.dtsx package in the SSIS Packages node; then press the DELETE key on the keyboard. Click the OK button to confirm the deletion. Right-click the SSIS Packages node and choose Add Existing Package from the context menu.

4. In the Add Copy of Existing Package dialog box, select Package Location as the File System from the drop-down list. Type **C:\SSIS\Projects\Contacting Opportunities\Mailing Opportunities.dtsx** in the Package Path field and

click the OK button to add this package. Once the package has been added, double-click the Mailing Opportunities.dtsx package in the SSIS Packages folder to open it on the Designer.

5. Double-click the Iterating May Opportunities Foreach Loop container to open the editor. This package enumerates over the User::Opportunities variable. Earlier, no value was been picked up and used in the package, so let's fill the gap now. Go to the Variable Mappings page and click in the Variable column and then click the down arrow and choose <New Variable...> from the drop-down list.

6. Leave Mailing Opportunities selected in the Container field in the Add Variable pop-up dialog box. Type **Title** in the Name field and leave the Namespace as User and Value type set to String. Variables are case-sensitive so type the name all in lowercase to avoid any issues later on. Click the OK button to add this variable. You will see that User::title has been added in the Variable column and assigned an Index value of 0.

7. Similar to step 6, create four more variables and assign them Index values as per the following table:

Variable	Index	Value Type
fname	1	String
lname	2	String
email	3	String
enquiry_date	4	DateTime

For the variable enquiry_date, you will need to assign a value in the format *06/06/2006*, as this type of variable cannot be defined without a value. The Variable Mappings settings should look similar to Figure 8-9. Click the OK button to close the editor.

8. Now that you've mapped the values from the table to the variables, it is time to make use of them in the package. Double-click the Mailing Opportunities Send Mail task icon to open the editor. Go to the Mail page where you will be using Property Expressions to derive and modify values assigned to various fields at run-time. To be absolutely sure that the e-mail address in the To address of the e-mails is being read from table and not from the value you've typed directly in the field, type **test@test.com** in the To field.

9. Go to the Expressions page and click in the Expressions field. Then click the ellipsis button to open the Property Expressions Editor.

10. Click in the Property column and then click the drop-down arrow and select the ToLine property. Now you can either type an expression directly in the

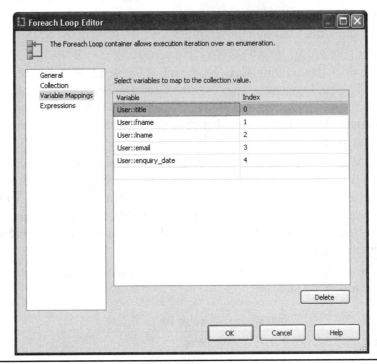

Figure 8-9   *Adding variables to the package*

Expression field to evaluate a property or use an Expression Builder to build an expression by clicking the ellipsis button next to the Expression field. For now, click the ellipsis button to open the Expression Builder. In the top-left pane, expand Variables, locate the User::email variable, and drag and drop it into the Expression box. Click the OK button to return to the Property Expression Editor.

11. Similarly, add the Subject property in the next row in the Property column and then click the ellipsis button. First type **"Your enquiry dated "** + in the Expression box and then expand the Type Casts node in the top-right pane. Locate the (DT_WSTR, <<*length*>>) type cast and add it after the plus sign in the expression. Replace <<*length*>> with **20** and then drag the User:: enquiry_date variable from the top-left Variables node into the expression. Click the Evaluate Expression button to check whether the expression has been built properly. Refer to Figure 8-10 to see how it should look. Click the OK button.

12. Again, click in the next row in the Property column, then click the drop-down arrow, and this time select the MessageSource property. Click the ellipsis button to open the Expression Builder. Build the following expression in the Expression box:

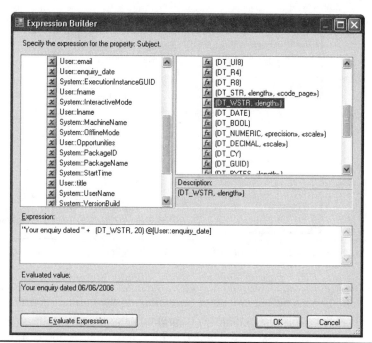

Figure 8-10 *Building an expression for the Subject property*

```
"Dear " + @[User::title] + @[User::lname] + "," + "

Thank you for your enquiry. One of our sales representatives will
be in touch with you. In the meantime, please go to our web site
for more information on our products. Thank you very much for
showing interest.

Kind regards,
Sales Support Team"
```

When you're done, click OK to close the Expression Builder. Your Property Expression Editor should now look as shown in Figure 8-11. Click the OK button twice to close the editor and the Mailing Opportunities Task Editor.

13. Press the F5 key to execute the package—but the package fails to execute and a package validation error appears, as shown in Figure 8-12.

14. The error message "No recipient is specified" indicates that during the validation process of execution, Integration Services found that no value was assigned to the To property. If you open the Mailing Opportunities Task Editor, you will find that the earlier assigned direct value of test@test.com no longer exists in the To field and the To field is blank. This is because when the package execution starts,

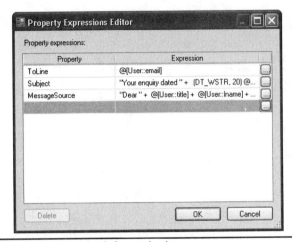

Figure 8-11 *Property expressions built for multiple properties*

validation happens before any other operation. At the validation time, Integration Services knows that the To property has to be populated from the ToLine property expression and hence ignores any direct value assigned in the field; it failed to find a value because the property expression further needed a value from User::email variable, which was not available because the package had not been executed yet. This type of error is quite normal when using Property Expressions that use variables at run-time that are not yet available. To overcome this situation, Integration Services provides a facility to delay validation for such components of the package until the actual run-time for the component. Click the Mailing Opportunities task and press F4 to open the Properties window. Locate the DelayValidation property in the Execution section and change its value to True.

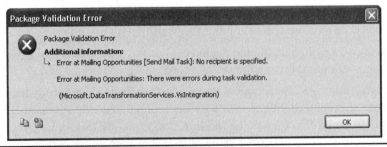

Figure 8-12 *Validation error due to ToLine property having blank value*

15. Press F5 to execute the package, and this time the package will run and complete successfully. If you check your mailbox after some time, you will see the seven personalized messages.

Review

You've used property expressions in this exercise to evaluate properties from static values and also variables that in turn get their value only at run-time. This proves how you can dynamically modify a package at run-time based on the values of other attributes in the package. You also understood the use of the DelayValidation property, which is handy to use when you are developing a package that uses lots of property expressions.

Handling Events at Package Run-time

When the packages are executed, variables change values, and data flows from files to tables and gets transformed along the way by various tasks. These tasks and processes come across changing data and environments at run-time, which sometimes results in alerts or events being raised. In such situations, you may wish to be present at run-time so that you can sort out events raised by the tasks. Integration Services comes to the rescue by providing event handlers that can act as your agents and be present at the run-time configured to respond to events and add intelligence to the packages by properly handling the events raised.

As containers have subcontainers, so do packages have event handlers. Event handlers are like subpackages waiting for the events to be raised so they can come to action. These powerful tools can extend package functionality greatly when properly implemented. Some of the tasks that can be done with custom event handlers include precharging a cache, sending you an e-mail or raising a warning when a task fails, dropping the temporary tables created during the package run, processing log files post execution, or perhaps following an alternative workflow on an event. Event handlers can be created for the packages, Foreach Loop containers, For Loop containers, Sequence containers, and Control Flow tasks as well.

Creating event handlers is like creating a control flow for a package. The Event Handlers tab is used in the SSIS Designer to create event handlers in your package; once created, the event handlers can be explored in the Package Explorer under the Event Handlers node. You can also define connection managers in the Event Handlers tab in case event handlers need to connect to any data source.

When the tasks and packages raise events during run-time, event handlers come into play. The raised event is captured by Integration Services and passed to an event handler for further action. If an event has no event handler defined on the container, it is passed on to the parent container. The parent container runs the event handler in response to this event; however, if the parent container doesn't have an event handler defined, it is flagged up the hierarchy, and so on. This passing on of events up the container hierarchy applies not only at the package level but can travel up the parent package if the package itself is run as a child package using the Execute Package task.

However, before you get carried away using this functionality, you need to know that every bit of functionality comes at a cost. If you try to handle all the events at the package level, your package will have too much to manage. In addition, it can be detrimental to performance to let events travel up the ladder when they could easily be handled at the task or container level. You can strategically use event handlers with different types of events handled at different levels. To avoid the extra load, which can degrade performance, you can strike a balance by handling events at various levels and at the same time filter out unwanted events from traveling up the ladder. When you design your event handling strategy for a package, you don't need to worry about identifying where the event has been raised irrespective of where it is captured in the hierarchy, because the source of the event is retained. This makes it easier to identify where the event has been raised.

Let's do a simple Hands-On exercise to create event handlers for one of the packages created earlier in this chapter.

Hands-On: Creating Event Handlers in a SSIS Package

As the title suggests, you will be creating event handlers in an Integration Services package to understand their configurations and behavior.

Method

In this exercise, you will add the Package1.dtsx package you created earlier in the Maintaining Data Integrity with Transactions project and then will create event handlers to respond on OnTaskFailed and OnPostExecute events.

Exercise (Work with Event Handlers)

1. Open BIDS and create a new Integration Services project with the following details:

Name	Working with Event Handlers
Location	C:\SSIS\Projects

Verify that the Create A Directory For Solution option is unchecked and click the OK button.

2. When the blank project is created, go to the Solution Explorer window and select Package.dtsx in the SSIS Packages node and press the DELETE key on the keyboard. Click the OK button to confirm the deletion. Right-click the SSIS Packages node and select Add Existing Package from the context menu.

3. In the Add Copy of Existing Package dialog box, select Package Location as File System from the drop-down list. Type **C:\SSIS\Projects\Maintaining data Integrity with Transactions\Package1.dtsx** in the Package Path field and click the OK button to add this package. Once the package has been added, expand the SSIS Packages folder and double-click the Package1.dtsx package to open it in the Designer.

4. On the Designer surface, go to the Event Handlers tab and click the down arrow in the Executable field, which will open a Package Explorer window. Expand Package1 | Executables | Sequence Container 1 | Executables | Loading Vehicle (see Figure 8-13). Note that you can select a package object, container,

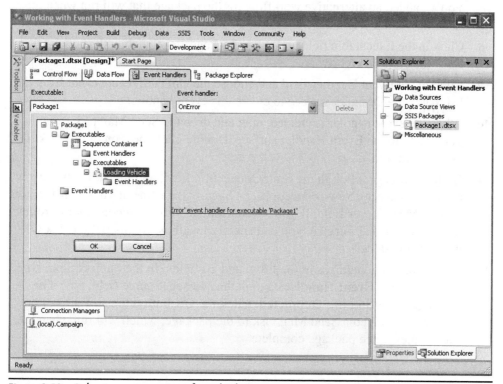

Figure 8-13 *Selecting a container for which to create event handlers*

or a task from here. Once you've selected the object for which you want to build event handlers, click the OK button to close this window.

5. For the selected Loading Vehicle executable, you can specify the type of event handler you want to create. Click the down arrow in the Event Handler field and select OnTaskFailed; this indicates that when the Loading Vehicle task fails, this event handler will be executed. Take a moment to go through the other events available. For more details on each of these event types, refer to Microsoft SQL Server 2005 Books Online.

6. Click the Designer surface to create an OnTaskFailed event handler for the Loading Vehicle task. When the Designer surface becomes available, drag and drop the Execute SQL task from the Toolbox onto the Event Handlers surface. Double-click the Execute SQL Task icon to open the editor.

7. In the General page, select (local).Campaign Connection Manager in the Connection field. Type the following SQL statement in the SQLStatement field and click the OK button to close this editor:

```
INSERT INTO Vehicle (CustomerID, VIN, Series, Model) VALUES
('N501', 'UV123WX456YZ789' ,'X11—Series', 'Saloon')
```

You've added an alternative workflow for the package that will run when the Loading Vehicle task fails.

8. Click in the Executable field and select Package 1 executable; then click OK to close the drop-down box.

9. Click in the Event Handler field and choose the OnPostExecute event from the list. Click the Designer surface to create this event handler.

10. When the event handler is created, drag and drop the Send Mail task from the Toolbox onto the Event Handler surface. Double-click the icon of this task to open the editor.

11. Go to Mail page, click in the SmtpConnection field, and then click the arrow button and select <New connection…>. Specify the name of your SMTP server in the SMTP Server field. If you've configured your local computer to route mails using SMTP service, you can specify localhost in this field. Click OK when you're done.

12. Type your e-mail address in the From and To fields. In the Subject field, type **Working with Event Handlers** and in the MessageSource field, type **The package execution has completed.** Click the OK button to close the editor. Now you've added a Send Mail task to the package, which will run when the executables in the package complete.

13. Press the F5 key to execute the package. You will see that the Control Flow components in the package fail while the event handlers successfully execute. You can select the executable from the Executables field to see its event handlers' status. Press SHIFT-F5 to switch back to design mode.

14. Run SQL Server Management Studio, connect to Database Engine, and run the following query in the New Query pane:

```
select * from [Campaign].[dbo].[Vehicle]
```

You will see one record in the result set that has been added in the Vehicle table by the event handler created on the Loading Vehicle task.

Check your e-mail and you will see that you've received four mails instead of one. This is because of the multiple executables raising the OnPostExecute event to kick off this Send Mail task. This is why you need to be careful to design and configure a strategy for handling events at various levels.

Review

Event Handlers are like subpackages that can respond to events occurring at run-time, and if properly designed and developed, they can let you get a good night's sleep most nights. In this exercise, you created simple event handlers for OnTaskFailed and OnPostExecute events and have seen how these event handlers wake up on the occurrence of these events and perform the work they are configured to perform. You can create quite a complex event handler to perform alternative actions if a particular event happens. However, you also need to be careful while using these event handlers, as the events are flagged up to the parent container at the cost of CPU cycles, unless you filter out the events not to be sent to parent container.

Summary

This was an absorbing chapter, as you've worked through various advanced features provided in Integration Services to enhance the service quality of your packages. You've worked with logging and log providers and have enabled logging for a package in the Hands-On exercise. Then you worked with transactions and configured your package to use transaction to handle three different kinds of scenarios for processing transactional data. You also used checkpoints to restart your package from the point of failure and learned about the effect of using transactions on checkpoints. Later in the chapter you extended the Contacting Opportunities package to create personalized e-mails using variables and property expressions. In the last Hands-On exercise, you created event handlers in your package and saw how they become active when a specified event happens.

With this chapter, you've concluded the workflow configurations of Integration Services projects and their administration. In the next two chapters, you will learn all about the data flow engine and how to transform data using Integration Services Data Flow transformations. Till now, your packages did not include any data flow or Data Flow tasks; however, from now on, we will focus mainly on data flow components and their configurations and will not do much in Control flow. Note that you cannot exclude control flow from your packages as it is a must be part of an Integration Services package.

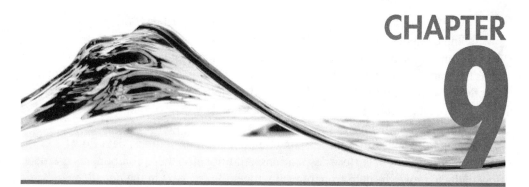

CHAPTER 9

Data Flow Components

SQL Server 2005 Integration Services provides several data-oriented services and components. The data flow within a package extracts the data from a data source; performs the transformations, computations, and derivations; and then loads the transformed data to the data destination. The assembly used to represent a data flow is called a *data flow pipeline*. The data flow engine of Integration Services is a data-driven execution engine that provides a steady flow of data streams onto which atomic computations or processes are applied through the pipeline.

The data flow constitutes three main components: data sources, data flow transformations, and data flow destinations. Additionally, these components use data flow paths to move the data from one component to the next in the data flow.

This chapter discusses the separation of data flow from the control flow and the benefits thus achieved. It then discusses the data flow components consisting of data flow sources, data flow transformations, data flow destinations, and data flow paths, plus the inputs, outputs, error outputs, and the external columns to explain their functions. At the end of the chapter, you will work through a Hands-On exercise to use these components.

Separating Data Flow from Control Flow

An Integration Services package relies on control flow and data flow as integral parts, though other parts such as event handlers and log providers also support the package. The data flow consists of three major components—data flow sources, data flow transformations, and data flow destinations—which are connected via data flow paths.

One of the key enhancements in SQL Server 2005 Integration Services is the separation of control flow and data flow engines. SSIS predecessor—i.e., SQL Server 2000 Data Transformation Services—had all the control and data flow features available in one engine and hence was difficult to use for creating complex packages to meet stringent data requirements of big enterprises. SQL Server 2005 Integration Services introduces two engines, called the integration services run-time engine and integration services data flow engine, which separate data flow from control flow.

Inherently, the requirements of control flow and data flow are different for operational and performance reasons. The requirements that drive the creation of an ETL package are to extract data, perform some transformations, and load; when you get to design board, you realize that the package needs to populate variables along the way, wait for data to be available that might be populated by other part of the package, perform operations in a particular order, move data from buffer to buffer, and so on. This order of tasks, availability of data, and ability to move data as fast as possible from a buffer to another buffer after applying transformations drive the designers in two opposing directions—applying control to the package work flow and applying transformations as fast as possible to the data flow. Although DTS 2000 fits the bill for tackling these operations, it lacks the ability to strike a perfect balance between control and data flow requirements for the packages you design for various purposes.

The provision of a separate run-time engine and data flow engine provides better control over packages and enhances the way the packages are designed with separate data flow. The run-time engine controls the order of the package workflow and provides associated services, such as ability to define an alternative workflow on the occurrence of an event, to apply breakpoints on the tasks, to manage connections to the data sources, to log data, and to manage transactions and variables. The Data Flow Engine provides high-performance data movement functionality, transformations optimized for speed, and great extensibility by allowing you to create custom transformations on top of prebuilt data sources, transformations, and destinations to load data capable of meeting most of your requirements. You can include multiple data flow tasks in a package, with each data flow task able to support multiple data sources, transformations, and destinations.

When you drop the Data Flow Task on the Control Flow Designer surface, you invoke the data flow engine. The Data Flow Task is a special task provided in Integration Services that allows you to create data movements and transformations for data in a package. The Data Flow Task replaces the DTS 2000 tasks, such as the Data Transformation Task and the Data Driven Query Task, that used to provide data movement and manipulation functionalities. Unlike other tasks, double-clicking the Data Flow Task doesn't invoke the Properties or Editor dialog box; instead, it opens another designer surface represented by the Data Flow Tab in BI Development Studio (BIDS). The Data Flow Task i.e. Data Flow tab provides many additional components such as data sources, transformations, and destinations to build your data movement and transformation part of the package. The following section covers the components available in the Integration Services Data Flow tab.

Data Flow Component Interfaces

The Data Flow Task consists of source and destination adapters that extract and load data between heterogeneous data stores; transformations that modify, summarize, cleanse, and extend data; and the paths that link these components together by connecting output of one component to the input of the other component, thus providing a sequence to the data flow. As mentioned, the Data Flow task can have multiple data sources, transformations, and destinations. These components are designed for high performance with a focus on data movement and manipulation efficiency.

All these components are available in the Toolbox window of the Data Flow tab, and you can drag and drop them onto the Data Flow Designer surface. These components are categorized in three ways: data flow sources, data flow transformations, and data flow destinations. Data flow sources are used to extract data, data flow transformations help in modifying the extracted data, and this modified data is finally loaded into the data silos using data flow destinations. While these components perform their functions, they use data flow paths to move data from a source component to the destination component. These data flow paths are similar to pipes in a pipeline. A data flow path is interesting from the debugging and visualisation of data point of view. You can see the data and metadata of the data flowing through data flow path using data viewers. Data flow paths are covered in detail later in the chapter.

Each of the data flow components can have one or more inputs, outputs, or error outputs associated with it. These outputs consist of data columns that expose their properties to the SSIS object model, the custom editor for the component, or in the Input and Output Properties tab of the Advanced Editor.

Inputs and Outputs

The data flow source reads the data from the data source, such as a flat file or a table of a relational database, using its external interface. It then makes this data available to the downstream components. A data flow source uses outputs to send the data in one or more columns via the data flow path to the inputs of the transformations or destinations.

External Columns

This interface writes or reads data to and from external data stores (these are not SSIS components—for example, an Excel worksheet) and keeps a copy of their metadata. During design time, when you create a data flow and add sources to your package, the metadata of the data from the sources is copied to the external columns on data flow sources. Similarly, a data flow destination keeps a copy of the destination metadata in its external columns as a snapshot of the destination data store and compares the data schema with this snapshot before writing to the data store. These external columns keep a snapshot of the schema and help in the process of package validation. So if a data store is to be created at run-time that doesn't exist at design time, or you make changes to a data store without updating the package, you will get validation errors or warnings displayed by SSIS components.

Inputs

Inputs receive data from the data flow path in the input columns. This data can be validated against schema available in external columns depending upon the data flow component configured for this. In the Advanced Editor, you configure inputs for a component. This component-specific editor lets you specify whether to fail the component, ignore errors, or redirect the error rows in case the inputs receive errors in the input columns. In Integration Services data flow, destinations and transformations components have inputs. You might think that as the data flow sources bring in data to the data flow, they have inputs, but this is not the case. Inputs and outputs (discussed in the next sections) are used only when the data flows from one data flow component to another data flow component. Whenever external data sources or storages are involved, the data flows directly through the data flow sources or data flow destinations.

Outputs

The data is sent out from the outputs of the sources and transformations through the data flow path to the inputs of the downstream component. The output columns' data can be validated against the external column schema depending on the data flow components configured for this. The output columns are exposed in the Input and Output Properties tab of the Advanced Editor, where you can configure them.

Error Outputs

When the data flows through the processing logic of the component, errors and mismatches can occur. These errors could be related to the data type mismatch between the input data coming in a particular column and the corresponding metadata of an external column, or the data coming in may be longer than the length defined in the corresponding external column. These kinds of mismatches may cause data rows to raise errors or truncations. You can configure the error handling in the component to either fail the component on an error, ignore the error, or redirect the failing rows to an error output. You can specify the error handling behavior for each column using one of three options. Whenever the failing rows are redirected to error output, two additional columns, ErrorColumn and ErrorCode, are also added to indicate the failing column and the code of failure.

Considerations when Bringing Data into Data Flow

Integration Services uses the data flow engine to extract data from a data source, transform and modify the data once it is in the data flow, and then load it to an external data store. The data flow engine uses data flow sources for extracting data from a data store. Figure 9-1 shows how the data is being extracted and parsed by a data source; it also shows how an erroneous record will be handled.

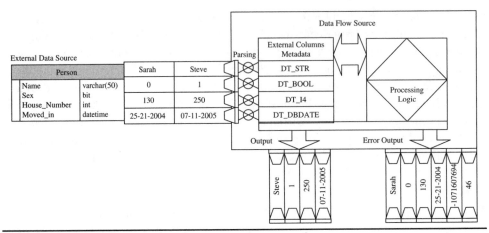

Figure 9-1 *A data flow source extracting and parsing data*

In Figure 9-1, two records demonstrate how data flows through a data flow source. As the data flow source reads the data from the external source, it translates the source data in to the Integration Services data type. During design time, when you drop the data flow source on to Data Flow Designer surface and configure it to connect to an external data source from which data will be read, the data flow source copies the metadata—i.e., schema of the data—to its external columns metadata. At run-time, when the data is being pulled in, the incoming data columns are parsed into the Integration Services data types using external columns metadata. In the example, the names Steve and Sarah are parsed into DT_STR data type, sex, which is indicated using 1 and 0, and have been assigned DT_BOOL; House_ Number has been assigned DT_I4; and the Moved_in data has been assigned DT_ DBTIMESTAMP data type. Integration Services provides 26 different data types to cover for various types of data, such as character data, numerical data, Boolean, dates, text, and image fields. Integration Services provides a wide range of data types and is particular about how they are used; hence, if data has a data type that does not match with the data types available in Integration Services, an error occurs. We will explore many data types along the way as we progress with our Hands-On exercises; however, to know more about each data type, refer to Microsoft SQL Server 2005 Books Online.

The process that converts the source data into Integration Services data types is called *data parsing*. Data flow components can be configured to use either *fast parsing* or *standard parsing*. Fast parsing supports the most commonly used data types with a simple set of routines and can be configured at the column level. Because it uses simple routines and does not check for many other data types, it can achieve high levels of performance. However, it is not available for most of the data flow components and can parse only a narrow range of data types. For example, fast parse does not support locale-specific parsing, special currency symbols, and date formats other than year-month-date. Also, fast parse can be used only when using flat file source, data conversion transformation or derived column transformation, and flat file destination data flow components because these are the only components that convert data between string and binary data types. You may use fast parse for performance reasons when your data meets these requirements, but for all other occasions, you will be using standard parsing. Before deciding to use fast parsing, refer to Microsoft SQL Server 2005 Books Online to know the data types supported by fast parse.

Standard parsing uses a rich set of parsing routines that are equivalent to OLE DB parsing APIs and supports all the data type conversions provided by the automation data type conversion APIs available in Oleaut32.dll and Ole2dsip.dll. For example, standard parsing provides support for locale-sensitive parsing and international data type conversions.

Returning to the data flow, as the data rows arrive and are parsed, they are validated against the external columns metadata. The data that passes this validation check at run-time is copied to the output columns; the data that doesn't pass is treated slightly differently. You can define the action the component can take when a failure occurs. Generally, the types of errors you expect at the validation stage include data type mismatches or a data length that exceeds the length defined for the column. Integration Services handles these as two different types of errors—data type errors and data length issues—as data truncations. You can specify the action you want the data flow component to take for each type of error from the three options—fail the component, ignore the error, or redirect the failing row to error output fields. You can specify these actions or different actions for each column. If you redirect the failing rows to the error output fields and link the error output to a data flow destination, the failing rows will be written to the data flow destination you specified.

The error output contains all the output columns and two additional columns for the failing rows, ErrorCode and ErrorColumn, which indicate the type of error and the failing column. In Figure 9-1, note that the record holding data for Sarah has a wrong date specified and hence fails during extract process. As the source was configured to redirect rows, the failing row data is sent to the Error Output column. Also, note that the two rightmost columns indicate the type of error and the column number. Every output field is assigned an ID automatically, and the number shown in the ErrorColumn is the ID number of the column failing the extract process.

As the data flow source pulls in data rows, it passes the output rows to the next data flow component—generally a transformation—and the failing rows are passed to another data flow component—which can be a data flow destination, if configured to redirect the failing rows. However, you can also redirect the failing rows to a transformation in which you apply a logic to correct the data in the failing rows and bring them back into the data flow after correcting the data. This is a powerful feature that, if used properly, can reduce wastage and improve data quality. When the output columns of the data flow source are connected to the input columns of a downstream data flow transformation, the data flows from the input columns of the transformation, through the processing logic of transformation, and then to the output columns. Based on the logic of transformation, some rows may fail the process and may be outputted to the error output columns. The main difference to note in comparison to a data flow source is that the transformations do not have external columns and have input columns instead. Figure 9-2 shows the functional layout of a data flow transformation.

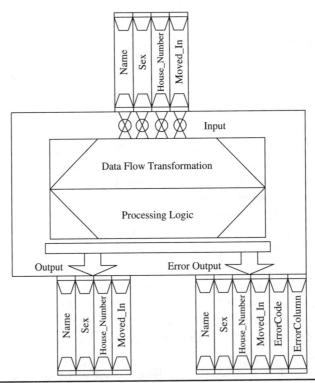

Figure 9-2   *Data Flow transformation showing Input, Output, and Error Output Columns*

Finally, after passing through the data flow source and the data flow transformations, the data will reach a data flow destination so that it can be written to the external data store. Like data flow sources, a data flow destination can also read the schema information from the external data store and copy the metadata to the external columns. When the data flows through the data flow destination, it gets validated against this metadata before being written to the external data store. If configured to redirect the failing rows, the failing rows may be outputted to the error output columns and the rest of the successful data is written to the external data store. Note that a data flow destination does not have output columns. Figure 9-3 shows the data flow through a data flow destination.

Now you know how the data is extracted from a data source, and how it flows through the transformations and destinations before being written to the external data store. Let's study these components to learn more about them and to learn how many types of data sources or destinations are available in Integration Services data flow.

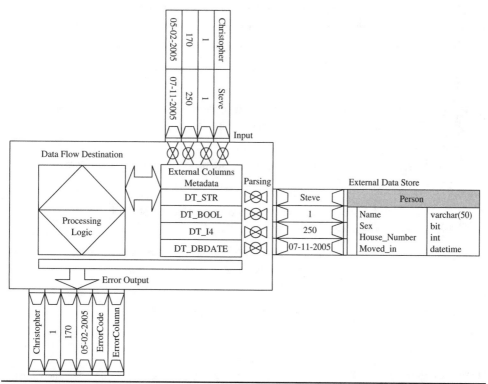

Figure 9-3 *Data flow destination showing the flow of data to the external data store*

Data Flow Sources

While building a data flow for a package using BIDS, your first objective is to bring the data inside the Integration Services data flow so that you can then modify the data using data flow transformations. Data flow sources are designed to bring data from the external sources into the Integration Services data flow. A data flow source reads the external data source, such as a flat file or a table in relational database, and brings in the data to the SSIS data flow by passing this data through the output columns on to the downstream component, usually a data flow transformation. During design time, the data flow source may keep a snapshot of the metadata of external columns and can refer to it at run-time. If the data in certain rows doesn't match with this schema at run-time, the data sources can be configured to redirect those rows to the error output columns that can be dealt with separately. Integration Services provides six preconfigured data flow sources to read data from a variety of data sources, plus a script component that can also be used as a data flow source. However, if some requirement is not met by existing data flow source you can always build a custom data flow source using the Integration Services object model.

The following two tables show the preconfigured source adapters and the interfaces they have in SQL Server 2005 Integration Services data flow.

Source	Description
Data Reader Source	Access data from .NET Framework data providers, such as SQL Server 2005 using ADO.NET Connection Managers.
Excel Source	Extract data from an Excel worksheet using Excel Connection Manager.
Flat File Source	Read data from a text file using Flat File Connection Manager.
OLE DB Source	Extract data from OLE DB–compliant relational databases using OLE DB Connection Manager.
Raw File Source	Extract data from a raw file using a direct connection.
Script Component	Host and run a script that can be used to extract, transform, or load data. Though not shown under data flow sources in the Toolbox, the Script Component can also be used as a data flow source. This component is covered in detail in the next chapter.
XML Source	Read data from an XML data source by specifying the location of the XML file or a variable.

Data Flow Source	Input	Output	Error Output	Custom UI	Connection Manager
Data Reader Source	No	1	1	No	ADO.NET Connection Manager
Excel Source	No	1	1	Yes	Excel Connection Manager
Flat File Source	No	1	1	Yes	Flat File Connection Manager
OLE DB Source	No	1	1	Yes	OLE DB Connection Manager
Raw File Source	No	1	No	No	Not required
XML Source	No	1	1	Yes	Not required

From the preceding table, you can make out that not all data flow sources have a custom user interface—some of them have to use the Advanced Editor to expose their properties, and not all data flow sources require a connection manager to connect to the external data source; rather, some can directly connect to the data source such as XML Source. But the most important thing to understand is that data flow sources don't have an input. They use the external columns interface to get the data and use output columns to pass the data to downstream components. We will study more about each of the data flow source available in BIDS in the following topics.

DataReader Source

When you need to access data from sources such as SQL Server 2005 and you use an ADO.NET Connection Manager to connect to the data source, you can then use the DataReader source to bring the data inside the data flow pipeline. You specify the .NET provider in the ADO.NET Connection Manager to connect to the particular type of data source and then deploy the DataReader source to extract the data from the source and place it into the data flow. The DataReader source has one regular output and one error output.

This component doesn't have a custom user interface; the Advanced Editor is used. The Advanced Editor enumerates all the common and custom properties of the component and exposes them in different tabs on the GUI—Connection Managers, Component Properties, Column Mappings, Input Columns, or Input and Output Properties:

▶ **Connection Managers** Specify the connection manager that the DataReader source uses to connect to the data source. Select one of the ADO.NET connection managers already configured in the package from the drop-down list provided under the Connection Manager column.

▶ **Component Properties** The properties associated with DataReader Source Adapter can be configured in this tab. Most of the fields are not available for editing and are grayed out. You can assign a name and a description to the task and specify a locale in the LocaleID field so that this adapter can interpret the locale sensitive information (such as date, time, and so on) correctly. The other two important fields are ValidateExternalMetadata and SqlCommand. You use the SqlCommand field to specify an SQL statement to select the data. The ValidateExternalMetadata field is used to indicate that the component should be validated during design time or at run-time. This property field has two possible values: True, which implies validation to happen at design time, and False, which implies that the validation should be delayed till run-time. In some situations, you will choose to delay validation until run-time, such as when your data source is created during run-time—i.e., the data source is not available at design time.

▶ **Column Mappings**   Map the available external columns to the available output columns of the component. To create a mapping line, drag a column from the Available External Columns on to the relevant column in the Available Output Columns in the upper section of the tab. Alternatively, you can also create a mapping line between two unmapped columns by clicking in the column listed under the Output Columns in the lower half of the screen and choosing the relevant column from the drop-down list.

▶ **Input and Output Properties**   This tab lists the DataReader Output columns and the DataReader Error output columns. You can click any of the listed columns to see and edit the attributes. Note that an ID is assigned to each column, which is not available for editing. Whenever a column fails, an error output is generated using the output columns and two additional columns, ErrorCode and ErrorColumn, to identify the error-causing column and possibly the error. The ErrorCode contains the error code generated by the DataReader source and the ErrorColumn contains the ID of the column that caused the row to fail.

Finally, a Refresh button is provided to refresh the configurations of the component whenever you change properties.

Excel Source

When you need to work with data in Excel files, you will be using an Excel source to get the data into the pipeline. You will configure the Excel Connection Manager to connect to an Excel workbook and then deploy Excel source to extract the data from a worksheet and bring it to the pipeline. You can treat an Excel workbook as a database and its worksheets as tables while configuring the Excel source. Also, a range in the Excel workbook can be treated as a table or a view on database. The Excel source adapter has one regular output and one error output.

This component has its own user interface, though you can also use Advanced Editor to configure its properties. When you drop the Excel source adapter on the Data Flow Designer surface, double-click it, and then choose Edit from the context menu, the Excel source Editor opens. The Connection Manager page opens by default, where you can select the connection manager from the drop-down list in the OLE DB Connection Manager field. The Data Access Mode drop-down list provides four options. Depending upon your choice in the Data Access Mode field, the interface changes the fields to provide relevant information.

▶ **Table or View**   This option treats the Excel sheet as a table or a view and extracts data from the worksheet specified in the Field Name of the Excel Sheet field.

▶ **Table Name or View Name Variable**   When you select this option, the Name Of The Excel Sheet field changes to Variable Name field. This option works similar to the Table or View option, except instead of reading the name of the worksheet or Excel range from the Name Of The Excel Sheet field, it reads the name of the worksheet or Excel range from the variable specified in the Variable Name field.

SQL Command   Selecting this option in the Data Access Mode field changes the interface to let you provide a SQL statement in the SQL Command Text field to access data from an Excel workbook. A Build Query button lets you build a SQL query. (I recommend you to use this query builder to access data from the Excel sheet, even if you know how to write complex SQL queries for SQL Server, because you might not be aware of some lesser known issues on accessing data from Excel workbooks using SQL.)

You can also use a parameterized SQL query, for which you can specify mapping parameters using the Parameters button. When you click the Parameters button, you get an interface that lets you map a parameter to a variable.

▶ **SQL Command From Variable**   This option works as a SQL command, except it reads the SQL statement from the variable specified in the Variable Name field.

▶ **Columns**   You can map external columns to output columns in this page.

▶ **Error Output**   When outputting the columns read from the Excel sheet, some rows may fail due to wrong data coming through. These failures can be categorized as errors or truncations. Errors can be data conversion errors or expression evaluation errors. The data may be of wrong type—i.e., alphabetical characters arriving in an integer field—causing errors to be generated. Truncation failures are not as critical as errors—in fact, they are sometimes desirable. Truncation lets the data through but truncates the length as specified—for example, if you define the city column as VARCHAR(10), then all the data will be truncated if it exceeds the 10 character length.

You can choose one of the following three options in the Error Output page for each of the column to specify how they should handle errors and truncations:

▶   **Fail Component**   This is the default option for both errors and truncations and will fail the data flow component, Excel source in this case, when an error or a truncation occurs.

▶   **Ignore Failure**   You can ignore the error or the truncation and carry on outputting the data from the Excel source adapter.

▶   **Redirect Row**   You can configure the Excel source to redirect the failing row to the error output of the Excel source adapter, which will be handled by the components capturing the error output rows.

While the Excel Source Editor allows you to configure the properties for Excel source, you may need to use the Advanced Editor to configure the properties not exposed by the Excel Source Editor. These properties include assigning a name and description to the component, specifying a timeout value for the SQL query, or changing the data type for a column. While working with Advanced Editor, get acquainted with the various options available in its interface.

Flat File Source

The Flat File source lets your package read data from a text file and bring that data into the pipeline. You configure a Flat File Connection Manager to connect to the text file and specify how the file is formatted. Also, you will specify the data type and length of each column in the Flat File Connection Manager that will set guidelines for the Flat File source to handle it appropriately. The Flat File source can read a delimited, fixed width, or ragged right formatted flat file. To know more about these file types, refer to Chapter 3.

The Flat File source has a custom user interface that you can use to configure its properties. Also, like the Excel source adapter, its properties can be configured using an Advanced Editor. To open the custom user interface, drag and drop this task on the Data Flow Designer surface, right-click it, and then choose Edit from the context menu. The Flat File Source Editor opens to the Connection Manager page by default.

You can select the Connection Manager from the drop-down list provided in the Flat File Connection Manager field. You can check the box for Retain Null Values From The Source As Null Values In The Data Flow Option to keep the null values. By default, this check box is unchecked, which means the Flat File source will not keep null values in the data and will replace null values with the appropriate default values for each column type—for example, empty strings for string columns and zero for numeric columns. Note that the file you are trying to access must be in a delimited format. This is because the fixed width and/or ragged right format files do not keep blank spaces; you need to pad the fields with a padding character to the maximum width so that the data cannot be treated as null values by the Flat File source adapter. You configure the format of flat file in the Flat File Connection Manager.

The Columns and Error Output pages can be configured as described in the Excel source adapter. You can use Columns page on the Flat File source to map external columns to the output columns and the Error Output page to configure the error and truncation behavior when the mismatched data comes along, using the three options of Fail Component, Redirect Row, or Ignore Failure.

When you open the Advanced Editor For The Flat File Source, you can configure the data parsing option by going to the Input and Output Properties tab. Depending on the data you are dealing with, you can set the FastParse option for each of the columns by selecting the column in the Output Columns section and then going to the Custom Properties category of the column properties. By default, the FastParse option is set to False (see Figure 9-4), which means the standard parsing technique will be used. (Remember that standard parsing is a rich set of algorithms that can provide extensive data type conversions, where as fast parsing is relatively simplified set of parsing routines that supports only the most commonly used data and time formats without any locale-specific data type conversions.)

OLE DB Source

You will be using an OLE DB source whenever you need to extract data from a relational database that is OLE DB–compliant, such as Microsoft SQL Server, Oracle database server, or IBM's DB2 database server. You specify an OLE DB provider in an OLE DB Connection Manager to connect to the database and deploy an OLE DB source to bring the data into the data flow. You should check the documentation of the OLE DB provider that you want to use in your package, as some limitations are associated with different types of OLE DB providers. The OLE DB source has one regular output and one error output.

This data flow component has a custom user interface that is similar to the Excel source adapter discussed earlier, though its properties can also be configured using the Advanced Editor. When you drop this adapter onto the Data Flow Designer surface

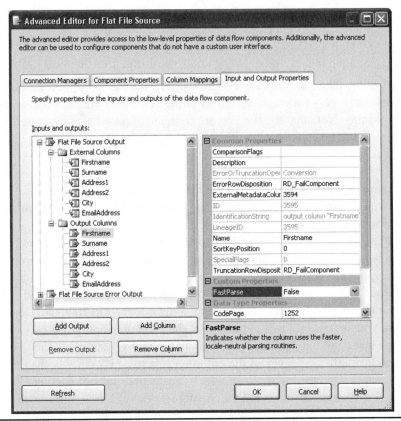

Figure 9-4   *Flat File Advanced Editor showing FastParse data parsing option*

and double-click it, an OLE DB Source Editor dialog box opens, taking you straight into the Connection Manager page. Here you can specify an OLE DB connection manager from the drop-down list provided in the OLE DB Connection Manager field. If you are using Data Sources to create an OLE DB Connection Manager, you can actually make Data Sources or Data Source views available through the OLE DB Connection Manager to all of your projects within an Integration Services project. You get the following four levels of data access mode options:

▶ **Table Or View**   Specify the name of the table or the view from which you want to extract data.

▶ **Table Name Or View Name Variable**   Specify the variable name, which will be the holding name of the table or the view.

▶ **SQL Command** Write an SQL statement to extract data. You have the option of using a parameterized SQL query here.

▶ **SQL Command From Variable** Specify the variable name that will be holding a SQL statement to be passed on to OLE DB source.

For more details on these options, refer to the Excel Source Adapter section where they have been discussed in detail.

In the Columns page, you can map Output Columns to the External Columns using the drop-down list provided for each column under External Column. The matching name will be written for you in the Output Column, which you can change if you wish to do so.

In the Error Output page, you can specify how the OLE DB source should handle an error or a truncation for each column.

Raw File Source

The Integration Services sources that we have studied till now require a connection manager to connect to a data source. The Raw File source doesn't require a connection manager. The Raw File source establishes a direct connection to the file containing the raw data and brings that raw into the data flow. The raw data written in the raw file is native to the source and requires no translation during import, so the Raw File source can extract the data much faster. If you are concerned about the speed of export and import from your system, you can consider saving your data in raw format. In scenarios for which you export data from your system for later transformation and loading back into the similar system, this may be the ideal choice. The Raw File source has only one output and no error output.

The Raw File source has no custom user interface, so the Advanced Editor is used to expose its configurable properties. To open the Advanced Editor, drag and drop the Raw File source from the Toolbox onto the Data Flow Designer surface and choose Show Advanced Editor from the context menu. As this source doesn't require a connection manager, the Advanced Editor uses the following three tabs to expose Raw File source properties:

▶ **Component Properties** This tab has two sections, one for common properties and one for custom properties of the task. In the Common Properties section, you can specify Name, Description, LocaleID, and ValidateExternalMetadata properties. In the Custom Properties section, you can configure AccessMode options. Depending on your choice of access mode, the interface changes the available fields to collect relevant information. Choosing File Name lets you specify the raw file name in the FileName field, and choosing File Name From Variable lets you specify the name of the variable that holds the raw file name in the FileNameVariable field.

▶ **Column Mappings**   Used to map external columns to output columns and input.

▶ **Output Properties**   Lists the column details such as name, data type, or length for external columns and output columns. Note that there are no error output columns as were available for other sources.

Script Component Source

The preconfigured data flow sources in Integration Services have a fixed number of outputs available—for example, Flat File source, Excel source, and OLE DB source have single outputs. If you need to output data to more than one downstream component in the data flow, you can't do that using these preconfigured components. The only option you have in this case is to create your own data flow source using the script component. The script component has not been shown under data flow sources as a data source, but it can be used as a data source as well. When you drop the Script component on to the Data Flow Designer surface, you are asked to select whether you want to configure this component as a source, a transformation, or as a destination in a Select Script Component Type dialog box. Based on your selection, the script component customizes the interface and options appropriate for the purpose. To use the Script component as a data source, select the source option in the dialog box and click OK. The script component will be added to the data flow configured for data flow source options.

As a source, the script component doesn't have any input and only one output to start with. You can add additional outputs using the Add Output button in the Inputs and Outputs page. We won't cover other details for this component here but will cover the script component in detail in the next chapter.

XML Source

XML Source reads the XML data from the XML file or from a variable containing XML data and brings that data into the data flow. This source has a custom user interface to edit properties but also uses the Advanced Editor for configurations of some of the properties.

When you open the XML Source Editor, the Connection Manager page appears, where you specify how you want to connect to and access data from the XML data file. Depending upon the option you choose, the interface changes to collect the relevant information:

▶ **XML File Location** Lets you specify the location and the file name for the XML data file in the XML Location field.

▶ **XML File From Variable** Allows you to use a variable to specify the XML data file name and location. You then provide name of the variable containing XML data file details in the Variable Name field.

▶ **XML Data From Variable** Access XML data directly from a variable by specifying the name of the variable in the Variable Name field.

Next you can choose schema options: inline schema or provide an XML schema definition file in the XSD format. When the XML data file contains the XSD schema itself to validate its structure and data, you will be using inline schema option; otherwise you will have to supply an external schema definition file (XSD). If you don't have an XSD file with you, you can generate this file by clicking the Generate XSD button and providing a location and name for the XSD file. This file is required to interpret the relationships among the elements in the XML data file.

In the Columns page, you can map output columns to external columns and in the Error Output page, you can specify how the XML Source should handle errors and truncations of data for each column. This source can have multiple regular outputs and multiple error outputs.

Data Flow Transformations

Once the data has been captured by source adapters and passed on to data flow path, you can modify this data using a vide range of data flow transformations provided in SSIS. You can use data flow transformations to aggregate column values, update column values, add columns to the data flow, merge data, and many perform more to apply data modifications. The Output columns of the data flow source provide data to the Input columns of the data flow transformation. Data flow transformations can have single or multiple inputs or outputs depending upon the type of transformation you choose. After applying transformations on to the data, the data flow transformation provides the output through its output columns to the input columns of the downstream component that can be another data flow transformation or a data flow destination. Some of the data flow transformations can have error outputs. The data flow transformations output the data rows that fail to transform to the error output columns that can be dealt with separately. Data flow transformations do not have external columns, but you can create one with external columns programmatically.

The following tables list the 28 data flow transformations grouped together in categories on the basis of the function they perform in Integration Services of the final release of SQL Server 2005. Future service packs or add-ons may bring in more transformations. These transformations provide a rich set of functionalities in many areas such as data cleansing, data standardization, BI functionalities, loading slowly changing data warehouse dimension tables, pivoting and unpivoting, and facility to write script using Script Component transformation. However, if you still need a functionality that can't be met by preconfigured components, you can write custom transformations with synchronous outputs or asynchronous outputs. Transformations with synchronous outputs make modifications to data inline—i.e., as the data rows flow through the component—whereas transformations with asynchronous outputs need all the rows before it could output any row—for example, an aggregate transformation needs all the rows before it can perform an operation across rows. For more details on how to create such transformations, refer to Microsoft SQL Server 2005 Books Online.

Business Intelligence Transformations

This category groups together the transformations that allows you to perform business intelligence operations such as data cleansing, data standardizing, text mining, and running DMX prediction queries.

Transformation	Description
Fuzzy Grouping Transformation	Standardize values in column data.
Fuzzy Lookup Transformation	Use fuzzy matching to cleanse or standardize data.
Term Extraction Transformation	Extract term from text in the input columns and write the extracted term to an output column.
Term Lookup Transformation	Count for the terms in a table that are defined in a lookup table.
Data Mining Query Transformation	Create DMX queries for performing prediction queries against data mining models.

Row Transformations

The transformations in this category allow you to update column values or create new columns on a row-by-row basis.

Transformation	Description
Character Map Transformation	Apply string functions to string data type columns.
Copy Column Transformation	Create new columns in the transformation output by copying input columns.
Data Conversion Transformation	Convert data type of the input column and copy the converted data to a new output column.
Derived Column Transformation	Create new derivations of data by applying expressions to a combination of input columns, variables, functions, and operators and the results of this derivation can be copied to either an existing column or in a new column in the output.
Script Component Transformation	Host and run a script that can be used to transform data.
OLE DB Command Transformation	Update, insert, or delete rows using SQL commands in a data flow.

Rowset Transformations

The transformations in this category work on collections of rows and allow you to perform operations such as aggregate, sort, sample rowset, pivot, and unpivot row sets.

Transformation	Description
Aggregate Transformation	Perform aggregate functions such as average, sum, and count and copy the results to an output column.
Sort Transformation	Sort input columns in ascending or descending order and copy the sorted data to the output columns.
Percentage Sampling Transformation	Create a sample data set by specifying a percentage to randomly select from input rows.
Row Sampling Transformation	Create a sample data set by specifying the exact number of output rows to randomly select from input rows.
Pivot Transformation	Pivot the input data on a column value to get a less normalized but compact view of data.
UnPivot Transformation	Create a more normalized version of an denormalized table.

Split and Join Transformations

This category groups the transformations that allow you to distribute rows to different outputs, multicast input rows, join multiple inputs into one output, and perform lookup operations.

Transformation	Description
Conditional Split Transformation	Route data rows to different outputs depending on the content of the data.
Multicast Transformation	Distribute the input dataset to multiple outputs.
Union All Transformation	Merge multiple input datasets into one output.
Merge Join Transformation	Merge two sorted datasets into a single output dataset.
Merge Transformation	Join two sorted input data sets using a FULL, LEFT, or INNER join into a single output.
Lookup Transformation	Perform lookups by joining data in the input columns with reference dataset columns.

Other Transformations

These transformations are used to export and import data, add audit information, count rows, and work with slowly changing dimensions.

Transformation	Description
Export Column Transformation	Export DT_TEXT, DT_NTEXT, or DT_IMAGE data type data from the data flow into a file.
Import Column Transformation	Read data from a file and add it to the columns in the data flow.
Audit Transformation	Include the system environment information in the data flow.
RowCount Transformation	Count the rows flowing through the data flow and write the final count in a variable.
Slowly Changing Dimension Transformation	Configure the updating of slowly changing dimension in data warehouse dimension tables.

Data Flow Destinations

A data flow destination is the last component in the Integration Services data flow, as this component has no output columns, though it may have error output columns for redirecting error rows. The data flow destination writes the data that flows to it after undergoing various transformations to an external data store or to an in-memory dataset. You can configure the data flow destination for how to handle errors in data. You can choose to fail the component, ignore the error, or redirect the error rows to the error output columns. If the data flow destination can't write some of the data rows to the external data store due to errors in data or data not matching with the external columns, it will redirect those rows to the error output columns depending how it is configured to redirect error rows.

Integration Services provides 11 preconfigured destinations plus a script component that can be used as a destination. The following tables list the available destinations and the function they perform.

Destination	Description
Data Mining Model Training Destination	Pass the data to train data mining models through the data mining model algorithms.
DataReader Destination	Read the data in a data flow using ADO.NET DataReader Interface.
Dimension Processing Destination	Load and process an SQL Server 2005 Analysis Services Dimension.
Excel Destination	Output data from a data flow to an Excel workbook.
Flat File Destination	Output data from a data flow to a text file.
OLE DB Destination	Output data from a data flow to the OLE DB–compliant data stores.
Partition Processing Destination	Load and process an SQL Server 2005 Analysis Services partition.
Raw File Destination	Output data to a raw file.
Recordset Destination	Create and populate an in-memory ADO record set.

Destination	Description
Script Component Destination	Host and run a script that can be used to load data. Though not shown under Data Flow Destinations in the Toolbox, Script Component can be used as a data flow destination. This component is covered in detail in the next chapter.
SQL Server Mobile Destination	Insert rows into an SQL Server Mobile database.
SQL Server Destination	Bulk load data into an SQL Server table or view.

All these destinations have an input, and some of them have an error output to meet most of your requirements to write data to external stores. However, if you find that existing data flow destinations do not do what you want, you can custom build a destination to suit your requirements in the Integration Services object model. The following table lists input and outputs available in each data flow destination.

Data Flow Destination	Input	Output	Error Output	Custom UI	Connection Manager
Data Mining Model Training Destination	1	No	No	Yes	Analysis Services Connection Manager
DataReader Destination	1	No	No	No	Not required
Dimension Processing Destination	1	No	No	Yes	Analysis Services Connection Manager
Excel Destination	1	No	1	Yes	Excel Connection Manager
Flat File Destination	1	No	No	Yes	Flat File Connection Manager
OLE DB Destination	1	No	1	Yes	OLE DB Connection Manager
Partition Processing Destination	1	No	No	No	Analysis Services Connection Manager
Raw File Destination	1	No	No	No	Not required
Recordset Destination	1	No	No	No	Not required
SQL Server Mobile Destination	1	No	Yes	No	OLE DB Connection Manager
SQL Server Destination	1	No	No	Yes	OLE DB Connection Manager

Data Mining Model Training Destination

Data changes with time, and the type of information that can be gathered from the data changes along with it. Mining data for useful and relevant information requires data mining model training that can keep up with the challenges of ever-changing data. The data mining model training destination passes data to train data mining models through the data mining model algorithms.

You need a connection to Microsoft SQL Server 2005 Analysis Services, where the mining structure and the mining models reside. You can use Analysis Services Connection Manager to connect to the computer running Analysis Services or to the Analysis Services project. Double-clicking this destination adapter will open the Data Mining Model Training Editor with two tabs, Connection and Columns, which you can use to configure the properties exposed by the editor. In the Connection tab, you specify the connection manager for Analysis Services in the Connection Manager field and then specify the mining structure that contains the mining models you want this data to train. The list of mining models is provided in the Mining Models area, and this destination adapter will train all the models contained within the specified mining structure. In the Columns tab, you can map available input columns to the Mining structure columns.

This destination adapter has one input and no output. The processing of the mining model requires data to be sorted. It is worth considering adding a sort transformation before the data mining model training destination.

DataReader Destination

When your application needs to access data and you are using ADO.NET, Integration Services can provide data straight to your application. ADO.NET can access data using the ADO.NET DataReader interface from the DataReader destination used in an Integration Services project.

Like the DataReader Source, the DataReader destination doesn't have a custom user interface. The Advanced Editor is used to expose the properties of the DataReader destination and represent them using three tabs in the Advanced Editor. You can specify Name, Description, LocaleID, and ValidateExternalMetadata properties in the Common Properties section of the Component Properties tab. In the Custom Properties section, you can specify a ReadTimeout value in milliseconds, and if this value is exceeded, you can choose to fail the component in the FailOnTimeout field.

In the Input Columns tab, you can select the columns you want to output, assign each of them an output alias, and specify a usage type of READONLY or READWRITE from the drop-down list box. As DataReader destination has one input and no error output, the Input and Output Properties tab lists only the input column details.

Dimension Processing Destination

One of the frequent uses of Integration Services might be loading your data warehouse dimensions, and this is where the dimension processing destination comes in play. This destination can be used to load and process an SQL Server 2005 Analysis Services dimension. Being a destination, it has no output and one input, and it does not support an error output.

The dimension processing destination has a custom user interface but you can also use the Advanced Editor to modify properties that are not available in the custom editor. In the Dimension Processing Destination Editor dialog box, the properties are grouped logically in three different pages. In the Connection Manager page, you specify the connection manager for Analysis Services to connect to the Analysis Services server or an Analysis Services project. Using this connection manager, the Dimension Processing Destination Editor accesses a list of dimensions from the source and lists for you to select. Next you can choose the processing method from add (incremental), full, or update options. In the Mappings page, you can map Available Input Columns to the Available Destination Columns using drag and drop operation.

The Advanced page in the editor dialog box allows you to configure error handling in the dimension processing destination. You can choose from among several options to configure the way you want the errors to be handled:

▶   By default, this destination will use default Analysis Services error handling that you can change by setting the Use Default Error Configuration option to False.

▶   When the dimension processing destination processes a dimension to populate values from the underlying columns, an unacceptable value may be encountered; you can specify that the record be discarded by selecting the DiscardRecord option, or you can convert the unacceptable key value to the UnknownMember value. UnknownMember is a property of the analysis services dimension indicating that the supporting column doesn't have a value.

▶   You can select to ignore errors or stop on error threshold using the Ignore Errors and Stop On Errors options. You can specify the error threshold using the Number Of Errors option. Also, you can specify the On Error Action option when the error threshold is reached by setting the StopProcessing or StopLogging options.

▶   When the destination raises an error of Key Not Found, you can configure it to IgnoreError or ReportAndStop. By default, it will ReportAndContinue.

▶   Similarly, you can configure for Duplicate Key error for which default action is to IgnoreError. You can configure it to ReportAndStop or ReportAndContinue.

▶ When a null key is converted to the UnknownMember value, you can choose to ReportAndStop or ReportAndContinue. By default, the destination will IgnoreError.

▶ When a null key value is not allowed and an error null key not allowed is raised when a null key is found in data, this destination will ReportAndContinue by default. However, you can configure it to IgnoreError or ReportAndStop.

▶ You can specify a path for the error log using the Browse button.

Excel Destination

Using the Excel destination, you can output data straight to an Excel workbook, worksheets, or ranges. While configuring this destination adapter, you use an Excel Connection Manager to connect to an Excel workbook and then deploy the adapter. Like an Excel Source, the Excel destination treats the worksheets and ranges in an Excel workbook as tables or views. The Excel destination has one regular input and one error output.

This destination has its own custom user interface that you can use to configure its properties; the Advanced Editor can also be used to modify some properties. Double-clicking the Excel destination opens the Excel Destination Editor dialog box that lists properties in three different pages.

In the Connection Manager page, you can select the name of the connection manager from the drop-down list in the OLE DB Connection Manager field. Then you can choose one of the three following data access mode options:

▶ **Table Or View** Lets the Excel destination load data in the Excel worksheet or named range; specify the name of the worksheet or the range in the Name Of The Excel Sheet field.

▶ **Table Name Or View Name Variable** Works like Table Or View option except the name of the table or view is contained within a variable that you specify in the Variable Name field.

▶ **SQL Command** Allows you to load the results of an SQL statement to an Excel file.

In the Mappings page, you can map Available Input Columns to the Available Destination Columns using a drag-and-drop operation. In the Error Output page you can configure the behavior of the Excel destination for errors and truncations. You can ignore the failure, redirect the data, or fail the component for each of the columns in case of an error or a truncation.

Flat File Destination

Every now and then you may require outputting some data from disparate sources to a text file, as this is the most convenient method to share data with external systems. You can build an Integration Services package to connect to those disparate sources, extract data using customised extraction rules, and output the required data set to a text file using the flat file destination adapter. This destination requires the Flat File Connection Manager to connect to a text file. When you configure a Flat File Connection Manager, you also configure various properties to specify the type of the file and how the data will reside in the file. For example, you can choose the format of the file to be delimited, fixed width, or ragged right (also called mixed format). You also specify how the columns and rows will be delimited and the data type of each column. In this way, the Flat File Connection Manager provides a basic structure to the file, which the destination adapter uses as is. This destination has one output and no error output.

The flat file destination has a simple customized user interface. You can also use Advanced Editor to configure some properties. When you double-click the flat file destination after having it dropped on to the Data Flow Designer surface, the Flat File Destination Editor dialog box opens up with Connection Manager page displayed by default. You can specify the connection manager you want to use for this destination in the Flat File Connection Manager field and select the check box for Overwrite Data In The File if you want to overwrite the existing data in the flat file. Next you are given an opportunity to provide a block of text in the Header field, which can be added before the data as a header to the file. In the Mappings page, you can map Available Input Columns to the Available Destination Columns using a drag-and-drop operation.

OLE DB Destination

You can use the OLE DB destination when you want to load your transformed data to OLE DB–compliant databases, such as Microsoft SQL Server, Oracle, or Sybase database servers. This destination adapter requires an OLE DB Connection Manager with an appropriate OLE DB provider to connect to the data source and write the data to the destination. The OLE DB destination has one regular input and one error output.

This destination adapter has a custom user interface that can be used to configure most of the properties, or you can use the Advanced Editor. When you double-click it on the Data Flow Design surface and choose Edit from the context menu, the OLE DB Destination Editor opens. In the Connections Manager page, choose an OLE DB connection manager from the drop-down list. If you haven't configured an OLE DB Connection Manager in the package, you can create a new connection by clicking the New button. Once you've specified the OLE DB Connection Manager, you can select the Data access mode from the drop-down list. Depending on the option you choose, the editor interface changes to collect the relevant information. You get the following five options:

▶ **Table Or View**   You can load data into a table or view in the database specified by OLE DB Connection Manager. Select the table or the view from the drop-down list in the Name Of The Table Or The View field. If you don't already have a table in the database where you want to load data, you can create a new table by clicking the New button. You'll see an SQL statement for creating a table has been created for you. All the specified columns use the data type and the length from the input columns, which you can change if you want. However, if you provide the wrong data type or a shorter column length, you will not be warned and may get errors at run-time. If you are happy with the CREATE TABLE statement, all you need to do is provide a table name instead of the [OLE DB Destination] string after CREATE TABLE in the SQL statement.

▶ **Table Or View—Fast Load**   You can load data into a table or view as in the previous option. However, you can configure additional options of data loading when you select fast load data access mode. The additional fast load options are:

  ▶ **Keep Identity**   During loading, the server needs to know whether it has to keep the identity values coming in the data or it has to assign unique values itself to the columns configured to have identity key.

  ▶ **Keep Nulls**   Tells the server to keep the null values in the data.

  ▶ **Table Lock**   Acquires a table lock during bulk load operation to speed up the loading process.

  ▶ **Check Constraints**   Checks the constraints at the destination table during data loading operation.

  ▶ **Rows Per Batch**   Specifies the number of rows in a batch in this box. The loading operation handles the incoming rows in batches.

  ▶ **Maximum Insert Commit Size**   You can specify a number in this dialog box to indicate the maximum size that the OLE DB destination handles to commit during loading. The default value of 0 indicates that all the rows are considered in a single batch and they will be handled together—i.e., they will commit or fail as a single batch.

Make sure you use fast load data access mode when loading with double-byte character set (DBCS) data; otherwise, you may get corrupted data loaded in your table or view. The DBCS is a set of characters in which each character is represented by 2 bytes. The environments using ideographic writing systems such as Japanese, Korean, and Chinese use DBCS as they contain more characters than can be represented by 256 code points. These double byte characters are commonly called Unicode characters. Examples of data types that support Unicode data in SQL Server are nchar, nvarchar, and ntext, whereas Integration Services has DT_WSTR and DT_NTEXT data types to support Unicode character strings.

▶ **Table Name Or View Name Variable**   This data access mode works like table or view access mode except that in this access mode you supply the name of a variable in the Variable Name field that contains the name of the table or the view.

▶ **Table Name Or View Name Variable—Fast Load**   This data access mode works like table or view—fast load access mode except here you supply the name of a variable in the Variable Name field that contains the name of the table or the view. You still specify the fast load options in this data access mode.

▶ **SQL Command**   Load the result set of an SQL statement using this option. You can provide the SQL query in the SQL Command Text dialog box or build a query by clicking the Build Query button.

In the Mappings page, you can map Available Input Columns to the Available Destination Columns using a drag-and-drop operation, and in the Error Output page, you can specify the behavior when an error occurs.

Partition Processing Destination

The partition processing destination works like dimension processing destination and is used to load and process an SQL Server 2005 Analysis Services partition. This destination has a custom user interface that is exactly like dimension processing destination. This destination adapter requires Analysis Services Connection Manager to connect to the cubes and its partitions that reside on Analysis Services server or the Analysis Services project.

Open the custom user interface by choosing Edit from the context menu. You can choose from the three processing methods—add (incremental) for incremental processing; full, which is a default option performs full processing of the partition; and data only to perform update processing of the partition. In the Mappings page, you can map Available Input Columns to the Available Destination Columns using a drag-and-drop operation. In the Advanced page you can configure error-handling options when various types of errors occur. Error-handling options are similar to those available on the Advanced page of dimension processing destination.

Raw File Destination

If you want to extract data at the fastest possible speed from your system, you may consider using the raw file destination. This destination writes raw data that is native to the destination and doesn't require translation. This raw data can be imported back to the system using the raw file source discussed earlier. Using the raw file destination to export and raw file source to import data back into the system results in high performance for the export/import operation. If you have multiple packages that work on a data set one after another—i.e., a package needs to export the data at the end of its operation for next package to continue its work on the data, raw file destination and raw file source combination can be excellent choices. However, if you have binary large object (BLOB) data that needs to be handled in such a fashion, Raw File Destination cannot help you, as it doesn't support BLOB objects.

Raw File Destination doesn't have a custom user interface and uses the Advanced Editor to expose its properties. When you double-click the raw file destination on the Designer surface, the Advanced Editor for Raw File Destination dialog box opens, showing three tabs to expose the properties of this destination adapter. No Connection Managers tab appears, as the Raw File Destination doesn't use a connection manager to connect to the raw file; it connects to the raw file directly using the specified file name or by reading the file name from a variable.

In the Component Properties tab, you can specify common properties such as Name, Description, LocaleID, and ValidateExternalMetadata. In the Custom Properties section, you can choose the AccessMode from two options—File Name and File Name From Variable. The File Name option allows you to specify the file name and path in the FileName field, and the File Name From Variable option lets you use a variable to specify the file name and path. You specify the variable name in the FileNameVariable field that becomes available after you choose the File Name From Variable option. Next, you can choose from the following four options to write data to a file in the WriteOption field:

▶ **Append**   Lets you use an existing file and append data to the already existing data. This option requires the metadata of the appended data must match the metadata of the exiting data in the file.

▶ **Create Always**   Always creates a new file using the file name details provided either directly in the FileName field or indirectly in a variable specified in the FileNameVariable field.

▶ **Create Once**   In the situations where you are using the data flow inside a repeating logic—i.e., inside a loop container—you may want to create a new file in the first iteration of the loop and then append the data to the file in the second and higher iterations. You can achieve this requirement by using this option.

▶ **Truncate And Append**   If you've an existing raw file that you want to use to write the data into but want to delete the existing data before the new data is written into it, you can use this option to truncate the existing file first and then append the data to this file.

In all these options, wherever you use an exiting file, the metadata of the data being loaded to the destination must match with the metadata of the file specified.

In the Input Columns tab, you can select the columns you want to write into the raw file and assign them an output alias as well. As this source has only one regular input and no error output, so the Input and Output Properties tab of the Advanced Editor shows only the input columns.

Recordset Destination

Sometimes you may need to extract a record set from the data flow to pass it over to other elements in the package. You can achieve this by using a variable and the recordset destination that populates an in-memory ADO record set to the variable at run-time.

This destination adapter doesn't have its own custom user interface and uses the Advanced Editor to expose its properties. When you double-click this destination in the Data Flow Designer surface, the Advanced Editor for Recordset Destination dialog box opens to show three tabs. In the Component Properties tab, you can specify the name of the variable to hold the record set in the VariableName field along with specifying common properties. In the Input Columns tab you can select the columns you want to extract out to the variable and assign an alias to each of the selected column along with specifying whether this is a read-only or a read-write column. As this source has only one input and no error output, the Input and Output Properties tab lists only the input columns.

Script Component Destination

You can use script component as a data flow destination when you choose Destination in the Select Script Component Type dialog box. On being deployed as a destination this component supports only one input and no output, as you know data flow destinations don't have an output. We will not be covering the script component here because is covered in detail in Chapter 10.

SQL Server Mobile Destination

SQL Server 2005 Integration Services stretches out to give you SQL Server Mobile destination, enabling your packages to write data straight to a SQL Server mobile database table. This destination uses SQL Server Mobile Connection Manager to connect to a SQL Server Mobile database. The SQL Server Mobile Connection Manager lets your package connect to a mobile database file and the SQL Server Mobile destination specifies the table it wants to update.

You need to create a SQL Server Mobile Connection Manager before you can configure SQL Server Mobile destination. This destination does not have a custom user interface, so it uses the Advanced Editor to expose its properties. When you double-click this destination in the Data Flow Designer surface, the Advanced Editor for SQL Server Mobile Destination dialog box opens with four tabs. Choose the connection manager for mobile database in the Connection Manager tab. Specify the table name you want to update in the Table Name field under the Custom Properties section of the Component Properties tab. You can configure Common Properties for this destination in this tab also.

In the Column Mappings tab, you can map Available Input Columns to the Available Destination Columns using a drag-and-drop operation. The Input and Output Properties tab shows you the External Columns and Input Columns in the Input Collection and the Output Columns in the Error Output Collection. SQL Server Mobile destination has one input and supports an error output.

SQL Server Destination

We have looked at two different ways to import data into SQL Server—using the Bulk Insert Task in Chapter 5 and the OLE DB destination earlier in this chapter. Though both are capable of importing data into SQL Server, they suffer from limitations. The Bulk Insert task is a faster way to import data but is a part of control flow not the data flow and doesn't let you transform data before import, whereas the OLE DB destination is part of the data flow and lets you transform the data before import; however, it isn't the fastest method to import data into SQL Server. The SQL Server destination combines benefits of both the components—it lets you transform the data before import and use the speed of the Bulk Insert task to import data into SQL Server tables and views. So, if you want to import data to an SQL Server table or a view, use an SQL Server destination rather than an OLE DB destination. Being a destination adapter, this has one input only and does not support an error output.

SQL Server destination has a custom user interface, though you can also use Advanced Editor to configure its properties. Double-clicking this destination on the Data Flow Design Surface opens the SQL Destination Editor dialog box. Specify a connection manager, data source, or data view in the OLE DB Connection Manager field to connect to an SQL Server database in the Connection Manager page, and select a table or view from the drop-down list in the Use A Table Of View field. You can also create a connection manager and a table or view by clicking the New button if you don't find them in the drop-down lists provided. In the Mappings page, you can map

Available Input Columns to the Available Destination Columns using a drag-and-drop operation.

You specify the Bulk Insert options in the Advanced page of SQL Destination Editor dialog box. You can configure the following ten options in this page:

► **Keep Identity**   This check box option is not checked by default. Check this box to keep the identity values coming in the data rather than using the unique values assigned by SQL Server.

► **Keep Nulls**   This check box option is not checked by default. Check this box to retain the null values.

► **Table Lock**   This check box option is checked by default. Uncheck this option if you don't want to lock the table during loading time. This option may impact the availability of tables being loaded to users. If you want to allow concurrent use of SQL Server tables that are being loaded by this destination, uncheck this box; however, if you are running this package at the quite times i.e. when no other users are accessing the tables being loaded, or you do not want to allow concurrent use of those tables, it is better to leave the default setting.

► **Check Constraints**   This check box option is checked by default. This means any constraint on the table being loaded will be checked during loading time. For faster import of data, you may uncheck this box to save processing overhead of checking constraints.

► **Fire Triggers**   This check box option is not checked by default. Check this box to let the bulk insert operation execute insert triggers on target tables during loading. Selecting to execute insert triggers on the destination table may affect the performance of loading operation.

► **First Row**   Specify a value for the first row from which the bulk insert will start.

► **Last Row**   Specify a value in this field for the last row to insert.

► **Maximum Number Of Errors**   Provide a value for the maximum number of rows that cannot be imported due to errors in data before the bulk insert operation stops. A value of −1 indicates unlimited errors.

► **Timeout**   Specify the number of seconds in this field before the bulk insert operation times out.

► **Order Columns**   Specify a comma-delimited list of columns in this field to sort data on in ascending or descending order.

Data Flow Paths

First, let me remind you how you connect tasks in the control flow. You click the first task in the control flow to highlight the task and add a green arrow, representing output from the task. Then you drag the green arrow to the input of the next task in the downstream to create a connection between the tasks, represented by the green line by default. The green line, called a *precedence constraint*, enables you to define some conditions when the following tasks can be executed. In the data flow, you connect the components in the same way you did in the control flow—drag the output of a data flow component and drop it on to the input of the next component, and the line formed connecting the data flow components on the Data Flow Designer surface is called the *data flow path*. They may look similar on the Designer, but there are major differences between a precedence constraint and a data flow path, as both represent different functionalities in their own right.

You will notice that the data flow path line is thinner than the precedence constraint line and can be either green or red, depending on whether it is representing Output Path or Error Output Path. When you connect a task to another using a precedence constraint and click the task again, you will see another green arrow, indicating that you can configure multiple precedence constraints for the tasks; in the data flow, the data flow paths are limited to the number of outputs and error outputs available to the source component. There's another important difference, too: the data flow path actually simulates a pipe connecting the pipeline components in the data flow path (remember that *data flow* is also known as *pipeline*) through which data flows, whereas a precedence constraint specifies a condition when the next task can be executed in the workflow.

When you click a component, for example OLE DB Source, in the Data Flow Designer surface, depending upon the outputs available from the component, you may see a combination of green and red arrows. Some components have both outputs and error output paths; some have only one and some have no output, such as destinations. Our example component, OLE DB Source, has both output and error output available and hence shows both green and red arrows. After you connect a component to another component using a data flow path on the Data Flow Designer, you can configure the properties of the data flow path using Data Flow Path Editor dialog box. This editor can be opened by choosing the Edit command from the context menu or simply by double-clicking the path. Once in the Data Flow Path Editor, you will be able to configure properties such as name, description, and annotation of the path on the General page; you can see the metadata of the data columns flowing through the path on the Metadata page; and you can add data viewers on the Data Viewers page. We will configure the properties of the data flow path in the following Hands-On exercise.

Hands-On: An Introduction to Data Flow Task

The purpose of this Hands-On exercise is to introduce you to the data flow task and how you can monitor the data flowing through the package by exporting data from [Person].[Contact] table of AdventureWorks database to a flat file.

Method

We will not do much research in this package but will keep it simple as this is just an introduction to data flow. You will drop a Data Flow task on the control flow and then go on to configure this Data Flow task. The Data Flow task has its own development and designer environment. In BIDS, data flow is designed and developed in Data Flow tab, which opens when you double click the Data Flow task or by clicking the tab. Following are the steps used in this exercise:

1. Configure a connection manager for connecting to the AdventureWorks database and add a Data Flow task to the package.

2. Add an OLE DB Source and a Flat File Destination in the data flow and connect them together using a data flow path.

3. Configure the data flow path to view the flow of data at run-time and execute the package.

Exercise (Configure an OLE DB Connection Manager and Add a Data Flow Task)

We will configure a connection manager for connecting to the Adventure Works database and add a Data Flow task to our newly created package.

1. Start BIDS. Choose File | New | Project. In the New Project dialog box, click the OK button after specifying the following:

Template	Integration Services Project
Name	Introduction to Data Flow
Location	C:\SSIS\Projects

2. When the blank solution is created, go to Solution Explorer and right-click Package.dtsx under the SSIS Packages folder and choose Rename from the context menu. Rename the package My First Data Flow.dtsx and click the OK button in the confirmation dialog box.

3. As we will be exporting data from Adventure Works database, we need to have a connection manager to establish a connection to the database. Right-click anywhere in the Connection Managers area and choose New OLE DB Connection

from the context menu. In the Configure OLE DB Connection Manager dialog box, click the New button to specify settings for the Connection Manager dialog box. Specify your computer name in the Server Name field, which is SARTH in my case, and leave the Use Windows Authentication radio button selected. Choose AdventureWorks database from the drop-down list in the Select Or Enter A Database Name field. Test the connection to the database using Test Connection button before closing the open windows by clicking the OK button twice.

4. Go to Toolbox, drag and drop the Data Flow task onto the Control Flow Designer surface. Right-click the Data Flow task and choose Rename Command from the context menu. Rename the Data Flow Task as Export PersonContact.

5. Double-click the Export PersonContact and you will be taken to the Data Flow tab. The Data Flow Task field on the top of the Data Flow tab shows you the currently selected Export PersonContact Data Flow task. This field shows in a drop-down list the configured data flows for the package as an Integration Services can have multiple Data Flow tasks.

6. Go to the Toolbox, and you will notice that the available list of tasks in the Toolbox has changed. The Data Flow tab has a different set of Integration Services components that are designed to handle data flow operations and are divided into three sections: Data Flow Sources, Data Flow Transformations, and Data Flow Destinations, with fourth section General being empty by default. See the list of components available under each section.

Exercise (Add an OLE DB Source and a Flat File Data Flow Destination)

Now you can build your first data flow using an OLE DB Source and a Flat File Destination.

7. From the Data Flow Sources section in the Toolbox, drag and drop the OLE DB Source on to the Data Flow Designer surface. Double-click the OLE DB Source to open the OLE DB Source Editor dialog box. You will see that the OLE DB Connection Manager field has automatically picked up the already configured connection manager. Expand the list of Data Access Mode to see the available options. Leave the Table Or View option selected.

8. When you click in the Name Of The Table Or The View field, the Data Flow Source goes out using the connection manager settings to fetch a list of tables and views. Click in this field to see the list of available tables and views in the AdventureWorks database and select [Person].[Contact] table from the list. Click the Preview button to see the first 200 rows from the selected table. Once done, close the preview window.

9. Click the Columns page from the left pane of the editor window. Note that all the external columns have been automatically selected. Uncheck the last five columns—PasswordHash, PasswordSalt, AdditionalContactInfo, rowguid, and ModifiedDate—as we do not want to output these columns. The Output Column shows the names given to the output columns of OLE DB source, though you can change these names if you wish to do so (see Figure 9-5).

10. Go to the Error Output page and note that the default setting for any error or truncation in data for each column is to fail the component. This is fine for the time being. Click the OK button to close the OLE DB Source Editor.

11. Right-click the OLE DB Source and choose the Show Advanced Editor context menu command. This will open the Advanced Editor dialog box for OLE DB

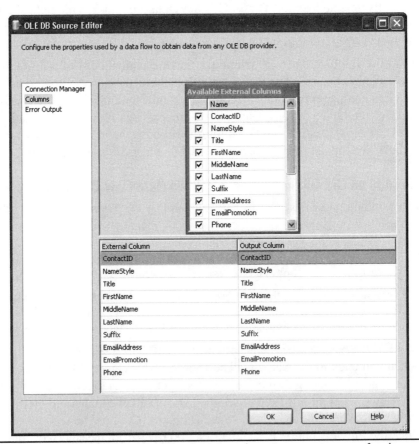

Figure 9-5   *You can select the external columns and assign output names for them*

Source in which you can see its properties exposed in four different tabs. The Connection Managers tab shows the connection manager you configured in earlier steps. Click the Component Properties tab and specify the following properties:

Name	Person_Contact of AdventureWorks
Description	OLE DB source fetching data from [Person].[Contact] table of AdventureWorks database.

Go to the Column Mappings tab to see the mappings of the columns from Available External Columns to Available Output columns. Go to the Input and Output Properties tab and expand the list of columns there. You will see the External Columns, Output Columns, and the Error Output Columns. If you click a column, you will see the properties of the column in the right side. Depending upon the category of the column you're viewing, you will see different levels and types of properties that you may be able to change as well. Click the OK button to close the advanced editor and you will see the OLE DB Source has been renamed as defined above. If you hover your mouse over the OLE DB Source, you will see the description appear as a screen tip. Make a habit to clearly define the name and description properties of the Integration Services components as this helps in self documenting the package and goes a long way in reminding you what this component does, especially when you open a package after several months to modify some details.

12. Go to the Toolbox and scroll down to the Data Flow Destinations section. Drag and drop the Flat File destination from the Toolbox on to the Designer surface just below the Person_Contact of AdventureWorks OLE DB Source. Click the Person_Contact of AdventureWorks and you will see a green arrow and a red arrow emerging from the source. Drag the green arrow over to the Flat File Destination to connect the components together.

13. Double-click the Flat File destination to invoke the Flat File Destination Editor. In the Connection Manager page of this editor, click the New button shown opposite to the Flat File Connection Manager field. You will be asked to choose a format for the flat file to which you want to output data. Click the Delimited radio button and click OK. This will open a Flat File Connection Manager Editor dialog box. Specify **C:\SSIS\Extracts\PersonContact.txt** in the File Name field and check the box for Column Names In The First Data Row. All other fields will be filled in automatically for you. Click the Columns page from the left pane of the dialog box and see that all the columns you've selected in the OLE DB Source have been added. This list of columns is actually taken by the Flat File Destination's input from the output columns of OLE DB Source. If you go to the Advanced page, you will see the available columns and their properties.

Click OK to add this newly configured connection manager to the Flat File Connection Manager field of the Flat File Destination Editor dialog box. Leave the Overwrite Data In The File option checked.

14. Go to the Mappings page to review the mappings between Available Input Columns and Available Destination Columns. Click the OK button to close the Flat File destination. Right-click the Flat File destination and choose Rename to rename it to PersonContact Flat File.

Exercise (Configure the Data Flow Path and Execute the Package)

You will configure the Data Flow path that you've used to connect the two components you added in the last exercise to view the flow of data at run-time and execute the package to see this.

15. Double-click the green line connecting Person_Contact of AdventureWorks and PersonContact Flat File components to open the Data Flow Path Editor. In the General page of the editor, you can specify a unique Name for the path, type in a Description, and annotate the path. The PathAnnotation provides four options for annotation: Never for disabling path annotation, AsNeeded for enabling annotation, SourceName to annotate using the value of SourceName field, and PathName to annotate using the value specified in Name field.

16. The Metadata page of the Data Flow Path Editor shows you the metadata of the data flowing through it. You can see the name, data type, precision, scale, length, code page, and source component of each column. The source component is the name of component that generated the column. You also get a facility to copy this metadata to the Clipboard.

17. In the Data Viewers page you can add data viewers to see the actual data that is flowing through the data flow path. This is an excellent debugging tool, especially when you're trying to find out what happened to the data. Let's add a data viewer. Click the Add button to configure a data viewer. In the General tab of the Configure Data Viewer dialog box, choose how you want to view the data by selecting from Grid, Histogram, Scatter Plot (x,y), and Column Chart types of the data viewers. Depending upon your choice of data viewer type, the second tab is changed appropriately.

    ▶ **Grid**   Shows the data columns and rows in a grid. You can select the data columns to be included in the grid in the Grid tab.

    ▶ **Histogram**   Select the numerical column in the Histogram tab to model the histogram when you choose this data viewer type.

    ▶ **Scatter Plot (x,y)**   Select this option and the second tab changes to Scatter Plot(x,y), in which you can select a numerical column each for x-axis and y-axis. The two columns that you select here will be plotted against each other to draw a one point for each record on the Scatter Plot.

▶ **Column Chart** Visualize the data as column charts of counts of distinct data values. For example, if you are dealing with persons and use City as a column in the data, then the Column Chart will show the number of persons for each city drawn as columns on the chart.

For our exercise, choose Grid as a data viewer type and leave all the columns selected in the Grid tab. Click the OK button to return to the Data Flow Path Editor dialog box, where you will see a grid type data viewer has been added in the Data Viewers list. Click the OK button to close this editor and you will see a Data Viewer icon alongside the Data Flow path on the Designer.

18. The package configuration is complete now, but before we execute the package, it is worth exploring two of the properties of the data flow engine that affect the flow of data buffer by buffer through it. Right-click anywhere on the Data Flow Designer surface and choose Properties. Scroll down to the Misc section in the Properties window and note the following two listed properties:

DefaultBufferMaxRows	10000
DefaultBufferSize	10485760

These properties define the default size of the buffer as 10 MB and maximum rows that a buffer can contain by default as 10,000. These settings give you control to optimize the flow of data through the pipeline.

19. Press the F5 key on the keyboard to execute the package. As the package starts executing you will see a Grid Data Viewer window. As the package executes and starts sending data down the pipeline, the data viewer gets attached to the data flow and shows the data in the buffer flowing between the two components. If you look on the status bar at the bottom of the data viewer window, you can see the counts of the total number of rows that have passed through the data viewer, the buffer number, and the rows displayed in this buffer. On the top of the data viewer window, you can see three buttons: Copy Data allows you to copy the data currently shown in the data viewer to the Clipboard, Detach toggles to Attach when clicked and allows you to detach the data viewer from the data flow and lets the data continue to flow through the path without being paused, and the green arrow button allows you to move data through the data flow buffer by buffer. When the package is executed, the data is moved in the chunk sizes (buffer by buffer) limited by the default buffer size and the default buffer maximum rows, 10 MB and 10,000 by default. Clicking this green arrow button will allow the data in the first buffer to pass through and the data in the second buffer will be held up for you to view (see Figure 9-6). Click the green arrow to see the data in the next buffer.

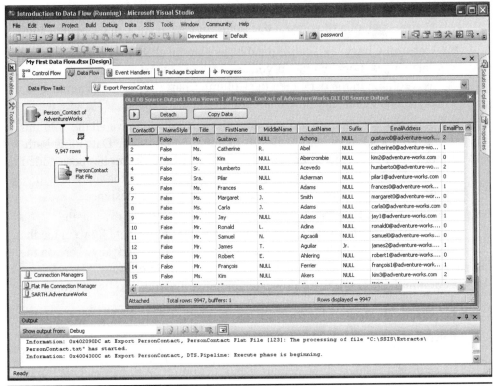

Figure 9-6 *Data Viewer showing the data flow in the grid*

20. After a couple of seconds, you will see the data in the next buffer. This time the total rows will be shown at a little less than 20,000; the buffer number will be shown as 2; and the rows displayed will be a little less than 10,000. The total number of rows is also shown next to the Data Flow path on the Designer surface. This number of rows may vary for a different data flow depending upon the width of the rows. Click the Detach button to complete the execution of the package.

21. Press SHIFT-F5 to stop debugging the package. Press CTRL-SHIFT-S to save all the items in this project.

Review

In this exercise, you built a basic data flow for a package to extract data from a database table to a flat file. You've also used the Data Viewer to see the data flowing past and learned how to optimize the data buffer settings to fine tune the data flow buffer by buffer through the data flow.

Summary

You are now familiar with the components of data flow and know how the data is being accessed from the external source by the data flow source, passes through the data flow transformations, and then gets loaded into the data flow destinations. You studied the data flow sources, data flow destinations, and data flow path in detail in this chapter and briefly learned about the data flow transformations. In the next chapter, you will learn more about data flow transformations by studying them in detail one by one and doing Hands-On exercises using many of the transformations.

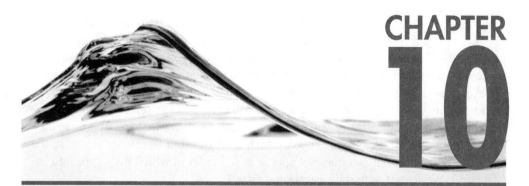

Data Flow Transformations

M ost of your packages will require that you work with and modify data. The data and schema are modified in Integration Services using Data Flow transformations. In this chapter, you will explore these preconfigured transformations in detail. You will also be working with five Hands-On exercises that will cover most of the transformations from the perspective of their usability. As you progress in the chapter, the Hands-On exercises will include more and more complex transformations and business scenarios, and of course they will be more interesting as well. To keep such a progression and your interest in the chapter, the transformations may not appear in the order in which they appeared in Chapter 9. We'll start with the easiest ones first.

Row Transformations

Row transformations are simple compared to other types of transformations. As we did with the control flow, the order of the transformations will be changed to suit your learning requirements. Starting with the simplest transformation—i.e., Copy Column transformation—to copy an input column to output columns, we will study the Character Map transformation, Data Conversion transformation, and then the Data Derivation transformation. The ability to perform more complex functions will increase as we go till we reach the last two transformations, Script Component and OLE DB Command, in this category, which can be programmed to perform precisely the functions you want. Let's start our journey with Copy Column transformation.

Copy Column Transformation

The Copy Column transformation is probably the simplest of the transformations available in SQL Server Integration Services. It does precisely what it says—it copies a column in the data flow to add a new column whose name you can specify in the transformation. To perform the desired function, this transformation has been designed to support one input and one output. The Copy Column transformation has a custom user interface, hence when you double-click this transformation, the Copy Column Transformation Editor window opens.

In the Copy Column Transformation Editor window, you can select the columns you want to copy either from the upper half by checking the boxes in front of columns in the list under Available Input Columns or select from the drop-down list provided in the Input column. You can select multiple columns to be copied or choose to create multiple copies of a column in the same transformation. The selected columns will be copied and added as new columns to the data flow as output columns of this transformation. When you select a column in the Input column, the Output Alias shows an alias for the column, which defaults to the Input column name prefixed with *Copy of.* You can change this alias and specify a more appropriate name for the column. As this transformation does not cause any changes to the data schema or data quality, this transformation doesn't introduce any errors in the data flow and hence doesn't have error output.

Character Map Transformation

You use this transformation to apply string functions to the string data type columns. Configuring this transformation and applying any of the following string functions to one of the columns are simple operations. The converted data can then be populated either in a new column or it can perform an in-place data conversion. An *in-place conversion* means that the data will be modified in the existing column and no new column will be added to the data flow. To perform a function, this transformation supports one input, one output, and one error output. This transformation is categorized as a row transformation; hence the string operation you specify is applied row by row as the data flows through this transformation.

Operation	Description
Lowercase	Convert characters of a column to lowercase.
Uppercase	Convert characters of a column to uppercase.
Byte reversal	Reverses the byte order of a column data.
Hiragana	Convert katakana characters of a column data to hiragana characters.
Katakana	Convert hiragana characters of a column data to katakana characters.
Half width	Convert full-width characters of a column data to half-width characters.
Full width	Convert half-width characters of a column data to full-width characters.
Linguistic casing	Apply linguistic casing instead of the system rules.
Simplified Chinese	Convert traditional Chinese characters of a column data to simplified Chinese characters.
Traditional Chinese	Convert simplified Chinese characters of column data to traditional Chinese characters.

To add Character Map transformation to the data flow part of a package, you need to open the package using BI Development Studio (BIDS) and go to the Data Flow tab. Drag this transformation from the Toolbox onto the Data Flow Designer surface. To understand a data flow component, open the editor for the data flow component and work through its available options. To open the editor, right-click the transformation and choose Edit from the context menu.

The user interface in the Character Map Transformation Editor is simple and intuitive. In the upper part, a list provides the Available Input Columns with a check box in front of each column. Select a column by clicking the check box, and a line is added in the lower half of the window with the selected column shown in the Input column. Alternatively, you can select a column for applying string operations by clicking in the Input column, then clicking the arrow button that appears to select a column from the drop-down list. Note that the Character Map transformation can be used only for string columns and not for columns with different data types. If you configure this transformation with a column that has a data type other than string, validation errors will occur and a red *X* will appear on the transformation with the error message stating that the input column has an unsupported data type.

The Destination column allows you to specify whether you want the modified data to be copied into a New Column(the default) or treated for an In-place Change. You select either option by clicking in the column and choosing it from the drop-down list. When you select the New Column value, the Output Alias field shows Copy Of Column Name for the new column, and when you choose In-place Change, the Output Alias shows Column Name as is. The Operation column allows you to select from any of the string operations listed in the preceding table. You can select multiple operations by clicking the multiple check boxes in the list; the Operation column will show the selected operations in a comma-delimited list. However, there are some restrictions on the selection of multiple operations on the same column— for example, you cannot select Uppercase and Lowercase operations to be applied on the same column in one transformation. Refer to Microsoft SQL Server 2005 Books Online for more details on these restrictions.

You can specify the error handling behavior of this transformation by clicking the Configure Error Output button. As this component applies string transformations to the text columns, truncations can occur in the transformed data. For example, when you convert Half Width data to Full Width data, the column length may not support that and can cause the data to be truncated. In such cases, you can use the Configure Error Output button to specify the action that this component should take. When you click this button, the Configure Error Output dialog box opens, where you can specify whether errors should fail the component, be ignored, or redirect the failing rows to the error output for each of the input or the output column that you've selected or created in the transformation.

Data Conversion Transformation

When data is coming from disparate sources in to a data warehouse or a data mart, data type mismatches can occur during the data upload process. One of the functions performed during data loading to a data warehouse or a data mart is to convert the data type to one that matches the data type of the Destination column. This transformation supports one input, one output, and one error output to perform its functions.

When the data is read from the data source, depending on the data and the data source, a data type is assigned to the Input column, which may not be exactly what you want. For example, a date column read from a text file is generally assigned a string data type that needs to be converted into a datetime data type before loading into a destination expecting a date time data type. This problem was handled in DTS 2000 using CAST or CONVERT functions of T-SQL within the Execute SQL task. SSIS provides Data Conversion transformation as a preconfigured task to perform this operation, though you still can write T-SQL code using OLE DB command transformation within SSIS.

The Data Conversion transformation allows you to convert the data type of an input column to a different data type and add the converted data to a new output column. During data conversion, the data of the input column is parsed and then converted into a new Integration Services data type before being written to a new output column. By now you know that Integration Services provides two types of parsing routines—locale-insensitive fast parsing and the locale-sensitive standard parsing routine. You can specify the parsing routines for each of the output columns in the Advanced Editor for Data Conversion. To specify the parsing method, open the Advanced Editor for Data Conversion, go to the Input and Output Properties tab, click the appropriate output column by expanding the Output Columns folder under Data Conversion Output. Go to the Custom Properties section of the selected output column and choose between the False and the True value for the FastParse option.

You can open the Data Conversion Transformation Editor by double clicking on this transformation. You can select the input columns that you want to convert to a different data type in the input column or select check boxes in the list of Available Input Columns. You can select multiple columns for conversion or apply multiple conversions to the same column. As the converted data is copied into a new output column, you can define an output alias for the newly created column in the data flow. In the Data Type column, you can specify the data type to which you want to convert the selected input column. Click the Data Type column and you'll see a drop-down list of data types available in Integration Services. Depending on the data type you select, you can set other attributes of the new data type such as length, precision, scale, and code page. While specifying the code page for the new string data type output column, you must keep the code page for the new output column the same as the input column code page when you are converting data between string data type columns.

As Data Conversion transformation creates new data types and modifies the data flow, error and truncation occurrences in data are possible. To handle these, this transformation provides an error-handling mechanism via the Configure Error Output button. In the Configure Error Output dialog box, you will find a list of all the output columns that you have created in this transformation. You can specify whether to fail the component, ignore the error, or redirect the failing row against error and truncation for each of the column.

Derived Column Transformation

The Derived Column transformation enables you to perform more complex derivations on an input column data. Till now you've been performing simple operations on the data, such as copying a column, applying string transformations using Character Map transformation, or even changing data types. With this transformation in your toolkit, you can derive your columns using complex derivation rules. Using this transformation, you will be able to perform operations such as deriving sensible information from the Notes or Comments column, concatenating two text strings using two columns or a column and a variable to populate in a single column, performing mathematical operations on a numerical column, using conditional derivations, and much more. This transformation is designed to have one input, one regular output, and one error output.

This transformation's user interface resembles the expression builder dialog box. In the lower half of the window, you can specify in the Derived Column whether you want to add the derived data as a new column or replace the data in one of the existing columns and specify the name of the derived column in the Derived Column Name field. Depending on your choice, different default names are shown in the Derived Column Name field, which can be changed in either case.

The Expression field is the most important field in the Derived Column Transformation Editor. Here you specify the expression to derive the data. You can use any combination of variables, input columns, mathematical functions, string functions, date/time functions, null functions, type casts, and operators to build this expression. After specifying expression to derive data, you can specify the data type, length, precision, scale, and code page for the data. Once you have successfully configured one row in the expression builder, you can add more rows below the first row in the lower half of the window. This enables you to perform multiple derivations using the same transformation. The left upper half of the window lists variables and input columns that you can drag and drop in the Expression field. Similarly, the right upper half of the window lists functions and operators that can be embedded in the expression simply by dragging and dropping.

As this transformation will be making changes to the data and the data schema, an error or a truncation can occur in the data. To handle such an instance, this transformation provides a Configure Error Output button to invoke the Configure Error Output dialog box, where you can specify either to fail the transformation, ignore the error, or redirect the failing rows to an error output for each of the derived column for errors and for truncations.

Script Component

You have learned about this Data Flow component in the Data Flow Sources and Destinations. By now you also understand that this component can be used as a transformation. The basic functionality of this component remains the same—i.e., it enables you to write custom code and include that custom code as a component inside the package. This custom code will be executed for every row of data, as the Script component is part of the row transformations. Using the Script component as a transformation, you can write custom code to call functions that are not available in SSIS—i.e., you can call the .NET assembly to use working code that is available outside SSIS; build transformations that are not available in SSIS; or apply multiple transformations with custom code to enhance the performance of your package. You can in fact write custom code to do all the transformations within the Script component. When the Script component is configured to work as a transformation, it provides an input and multiple outputs but no error output.

Drag and drop this component onto the Data Flow Designer surface, the Select Script Component Type dialog box will pop up on the screen (see Figure 10-1), asking how you want to use this component in the data flow. Select a radio button to configure the component as a Source, a Destination, or a Transformation. Selecting any of the options configures the component suitable for that type as the component behaves differently for different types—acting as source, the component won't have any input, whereas acting as a transformation, the component supports both input and outputs. Selecting the Transformation radio button and clicking the OK button will place this task as a transformation on the Data Flow Designer surface.

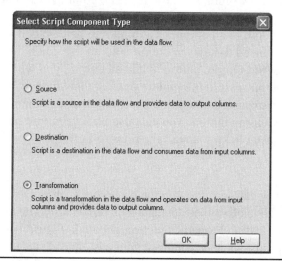

Figure 10-1 *Selecting the Script component type in the Data Flow Designer*

After connecting the Script component to the upstream Data Flow component, you can double-click the Script component to open Script Transformation Editor. You will see four pages available on the left pane of the Script Transformation Editor window that can be used to set the properties of the component.

Input Columns

In this page, you specify the input columns you want to work with in your script. When you select an input column, you can specify the Usage Type as ReadOnly or ReadWrite. This is quite a handy feature from the data security perspective, as it won't let the columns marked for the ReadOnly usage type get accidentally updated. For example, you may want to derive data using your custom code and want to output that derived data in the new output column; it is advisable to mark the input column's usage type as ReadOnly. You can assign an alias to the output column in the Output Alias column. Also, note that Input 0 shown in the Input Name field represents the first and only input available to this transformation.

Inputs and Outputs

In this page, you can configure the properties of available input columns and configure outputs for the Script Component transformation. As the component can support multiple outputs, you can add outputs and output columns in this page, which is not the case with inputs, as the Script component supports only one input. You will see Input 0 and Output 0 in the Inputs and Outputs pane in the middle. When you expand Input 0 and then Input Columns below it, you will see the input columns you have selected in the Inputs page earlier. However, if you expand Output 0 and then expand Output Columns, you will see no column available there. Starting with this component doesn't provide any output column. In real life, you will be adding an output column to an output as a minimum here. When you want to output the derived data, you need to have an output column that can hold the derived data. When you click the Add Output button to add an output, you will see *Output 1* added in the Inputs and Outputs list in the middle pane of the window. To add an output column, you have to expand an output, click the Output Columns folder under it, and then click the Add Column button. You can also remove output or an output column by selecting it and then clicking any of the remove buttons.

Script

In the Script page, you can specify common properties such as Description, LocaleID, and Name and set ValidateExternalMetadata to True or False. The more important properties are in the Custom Properties section, shown in Figure 10-2. The PreCompile property lets you specify whether you want your custom code to be compiled in

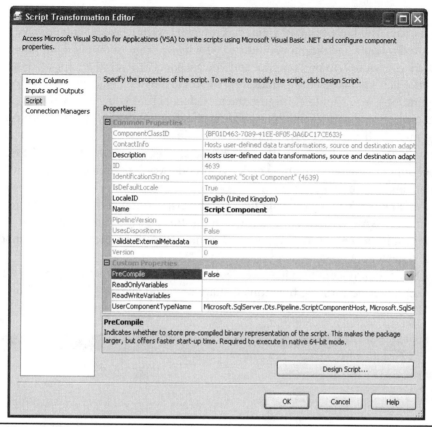

Figure 10-2 *Custom properties of the Script page*

advance—before the run-time—or just in time. When you set PreCompile to True, the script is compiled and stored as a binary within the package. This increases the performance—i.e., the script component execution time reduces—though this also means a slightly larger package size, as the compiled binary code requires more space. Setting PreCompile to False saves the script as Visual Basic code and compiles it just in time during run-time. You might think that this will require more time to complete, as it has to compile the code before executing it. If you are running on a 64-bit version of SQL Server 2005 Integration Services, you must set the PreCompile property to True, as the 64-bit version cannot do the just in time compilation. The ReadOnlyVariables property lets you specify the variables you want to work with in the script but do not want to update their values, and the ReadWriteVariables allow you to provide a list of variables that you do want to update. For both the properties, you can specify multiple variables in a comma-delimited list.

By now you've done everything that is required before you start writing the custom code. You have selected input columns you want to work with; you've configured outputs and output columns to which you want to output data; you've specified your option to precompile; and you've specified variables for read only or read/write access. These configurations are categorized as metadata-design mode configurations. You should configure the metadata before you start writing code, because when you start Visual Studio for Applications (VSA), you enter into code-design mode and the VSA environment automatically generates the base code using the metadata you've already configured. If you change the metadata after the Script component has generated the base code, your code won't remain compatible with the metadata and hence will cause errors.

You can invoke VSA by clicking the Design Script button, as shown in Figure 10-2. The default VSA environment is shown in the Figure 10-3 when the Script Component is used as a transformation. (For more details on the VSA environment, refer to Chapter 5.)

The Script component provides the VSA environment, making it simple to write custom code for performing functions that are not available in SSIS. Sometimes you

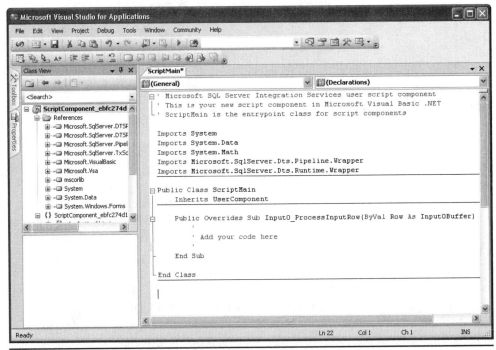

Figure 10-3 *VSA environment for the Script component*

may want to reuse functionality you developed using the Script component, and this gives you the flexibility to reuse the code. Depending on the quantum of reuse, you may be better off creating a custom component for Integration Services that can be included in your packages along with other components. For more information on creating custom components for Integration Services, refer to Microsoft SQL Server 2005 Books Online.

Let's have a quick look at the default script provided by the Script component. The first three lines are comments, which you can change to match more appropriately the code functionality. Following the comments, you can see Imports statements that extend SSIS functionality to .NET Framework system libraries and Imports Pipeline and Runtime wrappers to access resources outside the script task, such as variables.

```
' Microsoft SQL Server Integration Services user script component
' This is your new script component in Microsoft Visual Basic .NET
' ScriptMain is the entrypoint class for script components

Imports System
Imports System.Data
Imports System.Math
Imports Microsoft.SqlServer.Dts.Pipeline.Wrapper
Imports Microsoft.SqlServer.Dts.Runtime.Wrapper
```

After the Imports statements, the Script component provides the `ScriptMain` class as the entry point class where you will write your custom code. The next two lines in the `ScriptMain` make sure that the custom code is called for each row. Finally, you start writing your custom code after `Add your code here` comment and before the `End Sub` statement. When you are done with your code, you can simply close the VSA and the code will be saved for you.

Connection Managers

You can add connection managers in this page that are required by the Script component to access external data sources or destinations.

OLE DB Command Transformation

The Execute SQL task of DTS 2000 is used commonly for variety of functions, including truncating tables and log files, creating or dropping tables and views, and updating, deleting, or inserting data in the database objects. As the control flow and the data flow engines have been separated in SQL Server 2005 Integration Services, so the Execute SQL task has been made available in both the engines of Integration Services to perform the appropriate functions within that engine.

The Execute SQL task provided in control flow of Integration Services is designed to perform the workflow functions such as truncating tables, creating and dropping tables, updating variable values using results of an SQL statement, and in the data flow engine, Integration Services provides OLE DB command transformation for performing data related operations. This transformation allows you to run an SQL statement that can insert, update, or delete rows in a database table. As this transformation is designed to be a part of the Row transformations category, the SQL statement is actually run for each row of the data flowing through this transformation. The real power of the OLE DB transformation lies in the ability to run a parameterized query to perform insert, update, or delete operations against each row. This also means that you can use a stored procedure with parameters to run against each row of the data. To meet its functionality, this transformation has one input and one output and also supports one error output.

The OLE DB transformation doesn't have a custom user interface and hence uses the Advanced Editor to expose its properties. When you add this transformation in the data flow of your package and double-click it, the Advanced Editor for OLE DB Command dialog box opens. You will see four tabs.

In the Connection Managers tab, you specify the connection to the database that you want to update, delete, or insert into. For example, if you want to update [Person].[Contact] table in AdventureWorks database, you will specify a connection manager for AdventureWorks database.

In the Component Properties tab, you specify common and custom properties for this component. Here, you can specify the number of seconds before the command times out in the CommandTimeout field. By default, this field has a value of 0, which indicates an infinite timeout value. You can specify the code page value in the DefaultCodePage field when the data source is unable to provide the code page information. And in the SQLCommand field, you can type in the SQL statement that this transformation runs for each row of the input data. You can use parameters in your SQL statement and map these parameters to the input columns so that the SQL statement is modifying the data, made available by OLE DB Connection Manager, on the basis of values in the input columns. These parameters are named as Param_0, Param_1, and so forth—and you cannot change these names.

The mappings between parameters used in SQL statement and input columns are defined in the Column Mappings tab. In this tab, after typing the SQL statement in the SQLCommand field, you will see the Available Destination Columns populated with parameters for you (You may have to click the Refresh button to see the parameters). The automatic population of parameters is dependant on the ability of the OLE DB provider you've specified earlier. For some third-party OLE DB providers that do not support deriving parameter information from the SQL statement, you will manually create parameter columns in the External Columns node in OLE DB Command Input by going to Input and Output Properties tab; assigning them names such as Param_0, Param_1, and so on; and specify a value of 1 to the DBParamInfoFlags custom property of the column. You can then manually create mappings between Available Input Columns and Available Output Columns by using the drag-and-drop technique.

Split and Join Transformations

These transformations can create multiple copies of input data, split input data into one or more outputs, merge multiple inputs, or add columns to the pipeline by looking up exact matches in the reference table. After reading through the descriptions for these split and join transformations, you will complete your first Hands-On exercise for this chapter that will cover some of the Row transformations also.

Conditional Split Transformation

When you want to apply transformation operations based on a particular type of data set, you need to split data to match the specific criteria. To split data into multiple data sets using conditions, you will use Conditional Split transformation. This transformation allows you to create more than one output and assign a condition (filter) to the output for the type of data that can pass through it. Among the outputs has to be a default output for the rows that meet no criteria. When an input data row hits the Conditional Split transformation, it passes the data row through a set of conditions one by one and will route the data row to the output to which it matches the criteria first. Each row can be diverted only to one output, and this output has to be the one for which the condition evaluates to True. This transformation has one input, one error output, and as you can make out, multiple outputs.

When you drop this transformation on the Data Flow panel and double-click it to open the editor to configure it, you will see that the interface is similar to that of a property expression. You can select variables and columns from the top left section and functions and operators from the top right section of the editor window. You can build an expression using variables, columns, functions, and operators in the Condition field for an output. As you add a condition, an output is created and a name is assigned to it in the Output Name field along with an order number. The order number plays a vital role in routing the rows to outputs, as the row is matched to these conditions in ascending order and the row is diverted to the output for which the condition becomes true first. Once the row has been diverted, the rest of the conditions are ignored, as a row is always sent only to one output. If a row doesn't meet any condition, it will be sent to the default output of the transformation. This transformation has a default output built-in, as it is a mandatory requirement.

You can guess that the syntax you use to build an expression for a condition uses the expression grammar. For example, if you want to split Contacts data on the basis of countries—i.e., you want to separate out rows for UK, USA, and rest of the world—your Conditional Split transformation will have three outputs with the following configurations:

Order	Output Name	Condition
1	Case 1	[Country] == "UK"
2	Case 2	[Country] == "USA"

The default output will collect all the rows for which Country is neither UK nor USA.

Multicast Transformation

The Conditional Split transformation enables you to divert a row to an output and split a data set. It doesn't allow you to divert a row to more than one output and hence does not create a copy of the data set. However, sometimes you may need to create copies of a dataset during run-time so that you can apply multiple sets of transformations to the same data. For example, you may want to load data to your relational database as well as the Analysis Services database, with both having different data models and obviously different loading requirements. In this case, you will create two sets of data, apply different transformations to the data to bring them in line with the data model requirements, and then load the data to the destination database. This transformation has one input and supports multiple outputs to perform multicast operation.

The Multicast transformation creates copies of a dataset by sending every row to every output. It does not apply any other transformation to the data other than diverting a dataset to more than one output. The transformation is simple to use and doesn't require much to configure. When you connect an input to this transformation and double-click to open the editor, you will be surprised to see only two blank panes in the Multicast Transformation Editor dialog box. This is because you configure this transformation by connecting its outputs to inputs of multiple components and not by setting properties on the attributes. On the Data Flow surface, when you click the Multicast transformation after connecting its first output to a downstream component, you will see that it provides another output (a green arrow emerging from the transformation) for you to connect to another downstream component. If you double-click the Multicast transformation after connecting the second output to another downstream component, you will see two outputs listed in the left pane of the editor window, and the right pane shows the properties of the output selected in the left pane. You can modify the name of the output and write a description for it. That's it.

Union All Transformation

This component works similar to the Union All command of T-SQL and combines two or more inputs into a single output. To support this functionality, this transformation has multiple inputs and one output and does not support an error output. During run-time, the transformation picks up all the rows from one input, sends them to output, picks up all the rows from second input, and then combines them after all the rows of the first input in the output of the transformation till all the inputs have been combined. Note that this transformation can select inputs in any random order based on when the data is available at the inputs. Also, it does not sort the records in any way. All the rows from a particular input will be output together.

When you drop this transformation into the data flow of your package and connect an input to it, this transformation copies the metadata from this first input to its output so that the columns of this first input are mapped to the output created by the transformation. The columns having matching metadata of any input you connect after the first input are also mapped to the corresponding output columns. Any column that does not exist in the first input but is a part of subsequent input will not be copied in the output columns by the transformation. You must create and map this column manually in the Output Column Name field of the output with the corresponding input column. If you don't create and map a column that exists in subsequent input but not in the first input, that column will be ignored in the output. You can also change mappings in the editor by clicking in the Input field and choosing an option from the drop-down list.

Merge Transformation

As its name suggests, the Merge transformation combines two inputs into a single output but not without the preconditions that the inputs must be sorted and the columns must have matching metadata. To perform merge functionality, this transformation has two inputs and one output. It does not have an error output. The Merge transformation can even provide you sorted output by inserting rows from inputs based on their key values. This transformation is similar to the Union All transformation with some key differences:

▶ Merge transformation requires sorted inputs whereas Union All transformation does not.

▶ Merge transformation can combine only two inputs whereas Union All can combine more than two inputs.

▶ Merge transformation can provide sorted output whereas Union All transformation cannot.

When you add Merge transformation in to a package's data flow, you won't be able to open its editor until you have attached two sorted inputs that have properly defined sort-key positions for the columns on which they are sorted. The input datasets must be sorted physically—for example, using sort transformation—which must be indicated by setting the sort options on the outputs and the output columns of the upstream components.

Once the sorted inputs are connected to the inputs of this transformation and you are able to open the editor, you will see the output columns mapped to the input columns of both the inputs. This transformation creates the output by copying the metadata of the first input you connect to it. You can make changes to the mappings. However, the metadata of the mapped columns must match. If the input that you connect second has a column that is not in the output columns list, you can add and map this column manually.

Merge Join Transformation

The Merge Join transformation joins two sorted inputs into one but using an inner, left, or full join. For merging two inputs, this transformation supports two inputs and one output and does not support error output. The joins work exactly as it does in T-SQL. For the benefit of those who haven't worked with joins, following are brief descriptions of these joins.

Inner Join

An inner join returns the rows that have a join key present in both the datasets. For example, suppose you have a table for all the customers and a table for products that the customers have purchased during 2005. An inner join will return the list of products and the customers who purchased in 2005.

Left Outer Join

A left outer join returns all the rows from the first (left side of the join) table and the rows from second table for the matching key. For the rows that don't have a matching key in the second table, the corresponding output columns are filled with nulls. For the customer 2005 example, a left outer join will list all the customers without regard to whether they purchased products in 2005, with the products listed against the customers who have made purchases in 2005 and nulls against the customers who didn't make a purchase in 2005.

Full Outer Join

A full outer join returns all the rows from both tables joined by the key—simply put, it is a list of all the data. If the rows from first table don't have a matching key in the second table, the corresponding second table columns are filled with nulls. Similarly, if the rows from the second table don't have a matching key in the first table, the corresponding first table columns are filled with nulls.

When you add merge join transformation into a package's data flow, you won't be able to open the editor until you have attached two sorted inputs to the merge join left input and to the merge join right input. The input datasets must be sorted physically—for example, using sort transformation—which must be indicated by setting the sort options on the outputs and the output columns of the upstream components.

Once the sorted inputs have been connected to the left and right inputs of this transformation and you are able to open the editor, you can choose a join among inner join, left outer join, or full outer join types in the Join Type field. If you select Left Outer Join, you can also swap your inputs for the left outer join by clicking the Swap Inputs button. After selecting the join type, you can specify the join keys if they have not already been picked up by the transformation. The joined columns must have the matching metadata and the join key must be in the same order as specified by the sort key. Next, you can select the output columns by selecting the check boxes or using the drop-down lists in the Input columns in the lower section of the Transformation Editor. You will also be able to assign an alias to the output. Lastly, you can specify to treat null values equal by using the TreatNullsAsEqual property of the transformation; the default is True for this property. If you decide not to treat nulls as equal, the transformation treats nulls similar to the database engine.

Lookup Transformation

With the ever-increasing use of the Web to capture data, lookup operations have become quite important. Web page designers tend to ask users to fill in the most critical data in a web form, and the form fills in rest of the information for them. For example, you may ask a visitor on your site to fill in a street address and postal code during registration, and based on these two pieces of information, you can fill the city and state address fields. This is done by looking up a database table that contains all the postal information keyed in with postal codes. So, you simply look for the row that contains the particular postcode and you will be able to complete the address fields. You can perform such lookup operations in Integration Services using the Lookup transformation.

This transformation lets you perform lookups by joining the input columns in the data flow with columns in a reference dataset. The resulting values can be included in the data flow in the new columns, or you can replace the existing column values. For example, when a value of a record in the postal code column in the data flow is equal to a record in the postal code column in the reference dataset, the lookup transformation will be able to get data for all the other address columns. This equality operation makes this join as an *equi-join*, requiring that all the values in the data flow match at least one value in the reference dataset. In a complex lookup operation, you may be joining more than one column in the input to multiple columns in the reference dataset. Other than connecting to this external source to get reference data, this transformation supports one input, one output, and one error output.

To configure this transformation, you connect an input to it and double-click the input to open the Transformation Editor. You will see that the Lookup Transformation Editor provides three tabs.

You can specify the connection settings for the reference dataset in the Reference Table tab. The reference dataset can be a table or view in a database or in data source view or can be a result of an SQL statement. This transformation uses the OLE DB Connection Manager to connect to the lookup reference dataset, which you can provide in the OLE DB Connection Manager field. Next you can choose between Use A Table Or A View option or Use Results Of An SQL Query option by clicking the corresponding radio button. If you select Use A Table Or A View, you will have an opportunity either to create a new table or view or select it from the drop-down list of existing tables or views. If you select Use Results Of An SQL Query, you can either type in your SQL statement directly in the Option field or you can build the query with the Query Builder, which you can invoke by clicking the Build Query button. You can also read the query from a file by clicking the Browse button.

You specify the join columns in the Columns tab and can also select reference columns that you want to include in the data flow. To make a join drag a column from Available Input Columns and drop it on the column you want to join with in the Available Lookup Columns list. You won't be able to map or join two columns that don't have matching data types. To select a column, check the box provided for the Available Lookup Columns. As you select a column, it will be listed in the lower half of the editor window, where you can select the lookup operation and assign an output alias as well to the selected column. You can add the selected column as a new column or replace the values of this column in the Data Flow column.

At run-time, this transformation has to make connection to the reference dataset for every row, and this takes a big performance hit. To improve performance, the data in the reference set can be cached in the memory used by this transformation. For this reason, the default behavior of the Lookup transformation has been configured to cache the entire reference table in the memory. This is called *full precaching*, which means that the Lookup transformation caches the entire reference dataset in memory before processing input. However, in some situations—for example, memory limitations on the computer—this behavior may not be desirable. When you open the Advanced tab, you will be able to apply restrictions to the default caching by selecting the check box for Enable Memory Restriction. If you do not select any other check box here, no caching will be used, which means that the transformation will make a connection to the reference dataset for each row in the input dataset. After enabling restrictions, you will be able to select Enable Caching check box to specify the Cache Size in megabytes. Using this check box, you can control the size of the cache manually and specify partial caching to improve performance. You can also limit the size of the cache by selecting the Modify The SQL Statement check box. Using this option, you can use an SQL statement to select a subset of the reference dataset. For example, if your reference dataset contains address details for the whole country and your package contains records for a state only, you don't need to load all the reference dataset in the memory; rather, you need to load only the particular state's address details. To limit the reference dataset dynamically, you can also use values or parameters in the WHERE clause of the SQL statement and use provided Parameters button to map parameters to input columns. When you use parameters in the WHERE clause mapped to input columns, these parameters are first evaluated from the input dataset at run-time to load the partial reference dataset in the memory before it starts processing input rows. You can also use the SQL statement in combination with specifying the cache size to fine-tune the balance between performance and memory requirements.

Finally, note a few cautions when you add this transformation in the data flow. The Lookup transformation's lookup operation is case-sensitive. So you need to be careful with the input dataset case, *vis-à-vis* with case of reference dataset. One solution may be to convert both the datasets to either lowercase or uppercase for this transformation. You may also consider using a case-insensitive database to avoid lookup failures. Another reason for lookup failures could be the null values in data. If the lookup operation matches columns that contain null values, it will fail when you are using partial or no caching. A possible solution for this can be either using the full caching or remove null values by modifying the SQL statement.

Hands-On: Updating PersonContact Data

You receive contact details for persons interested in your products from different sources. As a policy, you standardize data as you insert it into a PersonContact table by performing lookups for address details on the basis of postal code, which is a mandatory requirement for you to accept data. You also need to derive a Salutation before loading data and do not want data to be duplicated in the table.

Method

In this exercise, you receive data in two different file formats, Microsoft Excel file format and flat file format, and you will load this data into a PersonContact table in the Campaign database after applying the required transformations. In the data flow of this package, you'll combine the data from these two files, format it to the required data types, generate a salutation in the data flow, perform a lookup on the postal code to get the correct city, and delete duplicate records before loading it into the table. Here is the step by step process:

- Add data flow sources to get the data in the data flow.

- Convert the data to match the data types outputted by both the data flow sources and then combine the data from both data streams.

- Derive a salutation.

- Enhance address details.

- Delete duplicates and insert data into the PersonContact table.

- Execute the package to see the results.

Exercise (Add Data Flow Sources)

You will create a new Integration Services project that will subsequently be used for all the packages developed in this chapter. You will add a data flow in a package in this project and then will add data flow sources in the data flow of this package.

1. Run BIDS and create a new Integration Services project with the following details:

Name	Data Flow transformations
Location	C:\SSIS\Projects

Do not select the check box to Create Directory For Solution. Click OK to create this project.

2. When the blank project is created, go to the Solution Explorer and right-click the Package.dtsx under the SSIS Packages node; choose Rename from the context menu and rename the package Updating PersonContact.dtsx; then click the Yes button on the confirmation dialog box.

3. Drop the Data Flow task from the Toolbox onto the Control Flow Designer surface and double-click it to open the Data Flow tab.

4. In the Data Flow tab, drag and drop a Flat File source and an Excel source from the Toolbox onto the Designer surface.

5. Double-click the Flat File source to open the Flat File Source Editor. Click the New button opposite the Flat file Connection Manager field to create a connection manager.

6. In the Flat File Connection Manager Editor, type **PersonDetails01** in the Connection Manager Name field. Type **C:\SSIS\RawFiles\PersonDetails01 .txt** in the File Name field, or you can click the Browse button to select this file. Select the check box for Column Names in the first data row option. The rest of the options should be automatically selected for you by default, as shown in Figure 10-4.

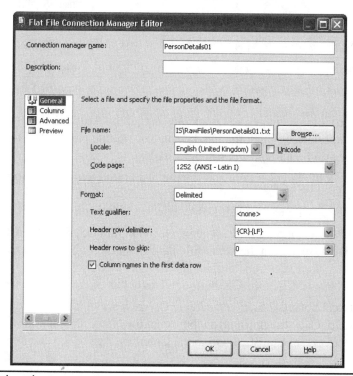

Figure 10-4 *Flat File Connection Manager settings*

7. Go to the Columns page and the columns will be listed for you as the Flat File Connection Manager selects {CR}{LF} as the row delimiter and comma {,} as column delimiter values automatically.

8. Go to the Advanced page to specify the column data type details. In the real world, you would know these details, as you know the destination where your data will finally rest. In this exercise, our final destination is the PersonContact table, so you can check the schema of this table and update column data types accordingly. The following table shows these details, which you need to apply to the column properties in this page. For example, to specify settings for the Postcode column, click this column and then in the right side pane, go to the OutputColumnWidth field and change it to 12. Make sure DataType is set to String [DT_STR]. Similarly apply the following settings to all the columns. After having applied all the settings, click the OK button to close the page and return to the Flat File Source Editor.

Name	OutputColumnWidth	DataType
FirstName	50	string [DT_STR]
LastName	50	string [DT_STR]
Gender	1	string [DT_STR]
Married	1	string [DT_STR]
AddressLine1	255	string [DT_STR]
AddressLine2	255	string [DT_STR]
Postcode	12	string [DT_STR]

9. Go to the Columns page and check out that all the Available External Columns have been selected. Click the OK button to close the editor. Right-click the flat file source and rename it **PersonDetails01**.

10. Right-click the Excel source and rename it **PersonDetails02**. Double-click PersonDetails02 to open the Excel Source Editor. Click the New button provided opposite to the OLE DB Connection Manager field.

11. In the Excel Connection Manager dialog box, specify **C:\SSIS\RawFiles\ PersonDetails02.xls** in the Excel File Path field. Leave Microsoft Excel 97-2005 specified in the Excel Version field and the check box selected for First Row Has Column Names. Click the OK button to create this connection manager.

12. In the Excel Source Editor, leave Table Or View selected in the Data Access Mode field. Click the down arrow button in the Name Of The Excel Sheet field and select PersonDetails02$. Go to the Columns page to see that all the Available External Columns have been selected. Click the OK button to close this editor.

13. Right-click the Excel Connection Manager in the Connection Managers area and select Rename from the context menu. Rename it **PersonDetails02**.

14. Press CTRL-SHIFT-S to save all the files in this project.

Exercise (Combine Two Data Streams)

In this part of the exercise, you will add a Data Conversion transformation to convert the data type of columns coming from the Excel source to match with the data types of columns coming through Flat File source and then use Union All transformation to combine these two data streams.

15. Right-click the Excel source and choose Show Advanced Editor from the context menu. Go to the Input and Output Properties tab and check out the properties of columns listed in External Columns and Output Columns under Excel Source Output. Note that these columns are of Unicode string [DT_WSTR] data type with column width (Length) equals 255. These columns need to be converted to the data type so that you can combine them with the columns from the Flat File source.

16. Drop a Data Conversion transformation from the Toolbox onto the Data Flow surface just below the Excel source. Join the Excel source with this transformation using the green arrow.

17. Double-click the Data Conversion transformation to open its editor. As you want to convert the data type of all the columns, select the check boxes provided in front of all the columns in the Available Input Columns. As you select the columns, a row for each column will be added in the lower grid section where you can configure the changes.

18. For the FirstName Input Column, note its Output Alias, which means the converted column will be added to the transformation output as Copy of FirstName. Click in the Data Type field and change it to string [DT_STR] from the drop-down list and change the Length to 50. The Code Page will be selected as the default code page of the computer; however, you can change it if you need to by selecting a different code page from the drop-down list. Similarly, change settings for all the columns as shown in the Figure 10-5.

19. Click OK to close the transformation. Rename the Data Conversion transformation **Converting PersonDetails02**.

20. Drop the Union All transformation from the Toolbox on the Data Flow surface between PersonDetails01 and Converting PersonDetails02. Join both of these components to the Union All transformations using green arrows.

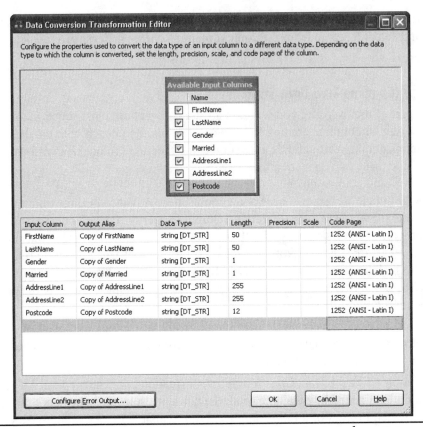

Figure 10-5 *Converting Excel source data using Data Conversion transformation*

21. Double-click the Union All transformation to open the editor. You will see that output columns are mapped to Input 1 and Input 2 columns. In this exercise, you will see Output Column Name columns automatically mapped to Union All Input 1 columns, whereas you have to map Union All Input 2 columns yourself. Click in the FirstName column under Union All Input 2 and select the converted Copy of FirstName column. If you select FirstName in this column, you will get an exception error for incompatible data type. Map all the output columns to the converted columns as you did for FirstName column (Figure 10-6).

22. Click the OK button to close the editor. Rename Union All transformation **Merging PersonDetails01** and **PersonDetails02**.

Exercise (Derive Salutation)

You will use a Derived Column transformation in this part to derive a salutation. You need to derive a salutation as Mr., Mrs., and Miss.

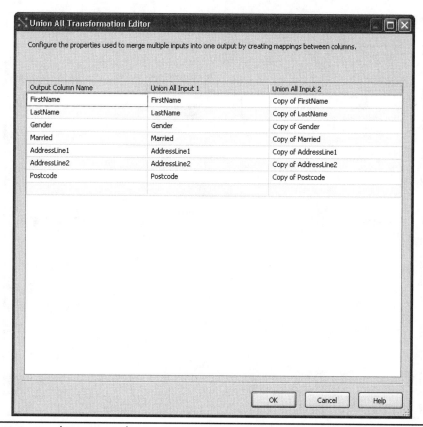

Figure 10-6 *Combining two data streams using the Union All transformation*

23. Drop a Derived Column transformation from the Toolbox below the Merging PersonDetails01 and PersonDetails02 and join both of them by dragging the green arrow on to the Derived Column transformation.

24. Double-click the Derived Column transformation to open the editor. This transformation has an Expression Builder interface. Click in the Derived Column Name field and type **Salutation**. By default, <add as new column> will be displayed in the Derived Column field as shown in Figure 10-7. You can change this by clicking in the field and choosing from the drop-down list.

25. Type the following expression in the Expression field:

```
Gender == "m" ? "Mr." : (Gender == "f" && Married == "y" ? "Mrs." : "Miss")
```

In this expression, you are using a conditional operator that returns one of the two expressions based on the evaluation of the Boolean expression.

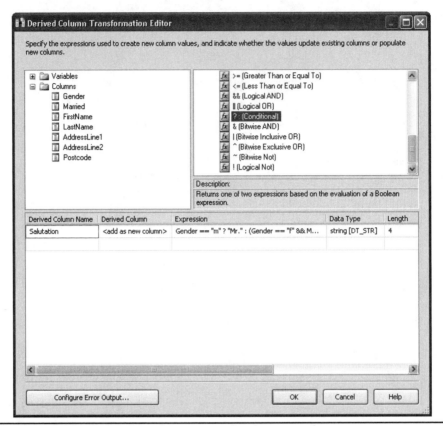

Figure 10-7 *Deriving a salutation using Derived Column transformation*

26. Select string [DT_STR] from the drop-down list in the Data Type field and specify 4 in the Length column if not automatically specified. Click the OK button to close the editor. Rename this transformation **Deriving Salutation**.

Exercise (Enrich Address Details)

One of the requirements you will address in this exercise is to standardize the address detail by including City on the basis of Postcode available in the data. You've a table called PostalCity in the Campaign database that contains a list of cities against postal codes and you will perform a lookup operation to get the correct city against a postal code. As lookup operation is a case-sensitive operation in SSIS, so you will convert the Postcode column in the data to UPPERCASE using a Character Map transformation.

27. Drop a Character Map transformation from the Toolbox on the Data Flow Designer. Join the Character Map transformation with Deriving Salutation by dragging and dropping the green arrow from the latter.

28. Double-click the Character Map transformation to open the editor. Click in the check box next to the Postcode column to select it. A row will be added in the lower grid area with Input Column selected as Postcode. Alternatively, you can select any column by clicking in the Input Column cell and invoking the drop-down list containing input columns.

29. The Destination column has two possible values, New Column and In-place Change, which can be seen by invoking the drop-down list by clicking in the field. Change the default New Column value to In-place Change in the Destination column.

30. Click in the Operation field and click the down arrow to see the list of available operations that can be performed using this transformation. Select Uppercase by clicking the check box in front of it. The list will stay open so you can select multiple operations, but for this exercise, you will be using only one operation. Click the OK button to complete your selection. Make sure Output Alias shows Postcode as a specified value (see Figure 10-8).

31. Click the OK button to close the editor. Rename Character Map transformation **Uppercasing Postcode**.

32. Now drop a Lookup transformation on the Data Flow surface after the Uppercasing Postcode transformation. Join both of these transformations using a green data flow path.

33. Double-click the Lookup transformation and open the editor. In the Reference Table tab, click the New button next to the OLE DB Connection Manager field and choose (local).Campaign from the Data Connections list; then click the OK button to add this connection manager. Click in the Use A Table Or A View field to open the drop-down list of tables and views in the Campaign database. Select [dbo].[PostalCity] from the list.

34. Go to the Columns tab. You will see that the Postcode column is automatically mapped from Available Input Columns to Available Lookup columns.

35. Click in the City Column check box to add this column as a new column in the output, as shown in Figure 10-9.

36. In our data stream, some of the postal codes will not find matches for cities, so they will fail the Lookup transformation. You will configure this transformation to divert these mismatching records to a flat file so that you can review them

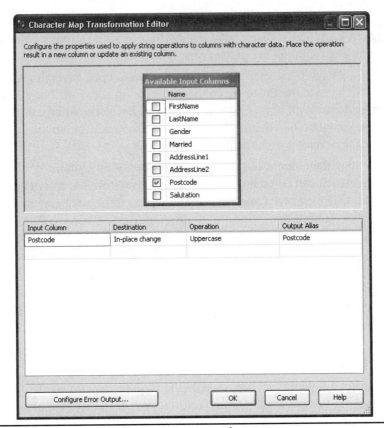

Figure 10-8 *Configurations of Character Map transformation*

later on. Click the Configure Error Output button. For the Lookup Output, click under the Error column and change the Fail Component Value to Redirect Row Value and click the OK button.

37. Click OK again to close the Lookup transformation. You will see a validation error on the Lookup transformation suggesting that rows sent to error output will be lost. This is because you have not yet connected any destination for collecting error rows to the error output of this component. Don't worry about this, as you will be adding a destination in the next step. Rename this transformation **Adding City Column**.

38. From the Data Flow Destinations section of the Toolbox, drag and drop the Flat File destination below the Adding City Column transformation. Drag the red arrow from the Adding City Column and drop it on the new destination. This will open the Configure Error Output dialog box for you to configure and confirm the settings. Click the OK button to accept the settings.

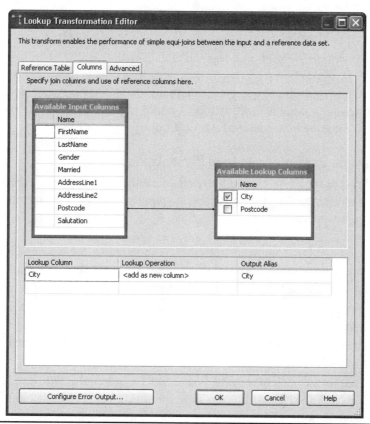

Figure 10-9 *Adding a new column in the output using Lookup transformation*

39. Double-click the Flat File destination to open its editor and click the New button next to Flat File Connection Manager. Select the Delimited Option radio button in the pop up dialog box asking you to select a Flat File Format, and then click OK. This will open the Flat File Connection Manager Editor.

40. Type **Lookup Errors** in the Connection Manager Name field and **C:\SSIS\ RawFiles\Lookup Errors.txt** in the File Name field. Most of the options will be filled in for you automatically. Click to check Column Names in the first data row option.

41. Go to the Columns page and check out that {CR}{LF} is selected as Row delimiter and Comma {,} is selected as Column delimiter. Go to the Advanced page and check out the properties of the columns. Note that the connection manager has correctly picked up the data types and the length of the columns. Click the OK button to close it and return to the Flat File Destination Editor,

where you will see that Lookup Errors has been specified in the Flat File Connection Manager field. Leave the Overwrite Data In The File option selected. You may consider it otherwise in the production environment based on your requirements.

42. Go to the Mappings page to create mappings between the Available Input Columns and Available Destination Columns and then click the OK button to close it. Rename Flat File Destination **Lookup Errors File**.

Exercise (Delete Duplicates and Load PersonContact)

In this final part of the exercise, you will first delete the records from the PersonContact table that are in the data flow to be updated and will then insert all the records in the data flow into the PersonContact table.

43. Drop the OLE DB command from the Toolbox below the Adding City Column transformation. Connect both of these using the green data flow path from the Adding City Column to the OLE DB command.

44. Double-click the OLE DB command to open the Advanced Editor for OLE DB Command. Choose (local).Campaign in the Connection Manager field from the drop-down list in the Connection Managers tab. Go to the Component Properties tab.

45. Type **Deleting Duplicates** in the Name field. Click in the **Sql**Command field and then click the ellipsis button. Type the following SQL statement in the editor and click the OK button.

```
Delete PersonContact Where FirstName = ? and LastName = ?
```

46. Go to Column Mappings page where you will see Param_0 and Param_1 columns in the Available Destination Columns. These represent parameters that you've used in the above SQL statement. Map Param_0 to FirstName and Param_1 to LastName columns in the Available Input columns (see Figure 10-10) and click the Refresh button. This should remove any validation error appearing at the bottom of the Advanced Editor. Click the OK button to close.

47. Drop an OLE DB destination on the Designer surface and join it with the green data flow path from the Deleting Duplicates transformation.

48. Double-click the OLE DB destination to open the editor. You will see (local). Campaign selected in the OLE DB Connection Manager field as this is the only OLE DB Connection Manager configured in the package. Leave Table or View—Fast Load selected in the Data Access Mode field. Select [dbo].[PersonContact] table from the drop-down list in the Name Of The Table Or The View field.

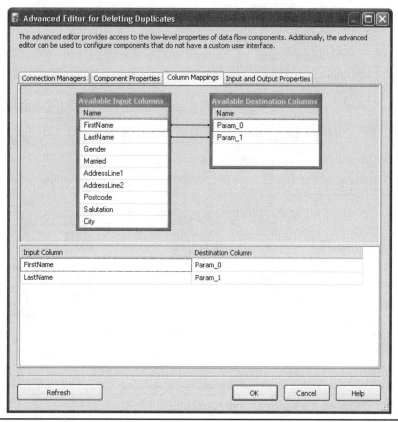

Figure 10-10   *Mapping parameters in the OLE DB Command transformation*

49. Go to the Mappings page to create the required mappings. Click the OK button to close this. Rename this destination **PersonContact**. After some adjustments, your package should look like one shown in Figure 10-11. Press CTRL-SHIFT-S to save all the items in the project.

Exercise (Execute the Package)

50. You can add as many data viewers to the package as you like before executing the package, but as a minimum, add a data viewer before the Deriving Salutation component and before the Deleting Duplicates component. To add a data viewer, double-click the green line joining the two components to open the Data Flow Path Editor. Go to Data Viewers page, click the Add button, and then click OK in the Configure Data Viewer dialog box to return; then click OK again to add a grid type data viewer.

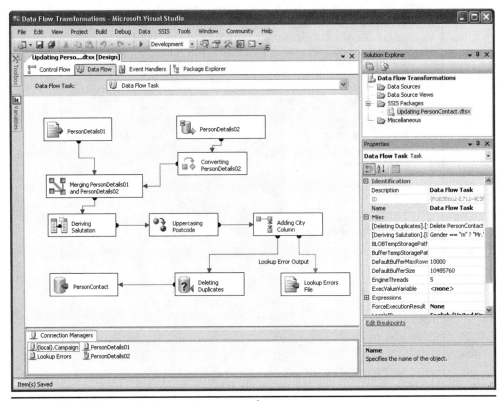

Figure 10-11   *Updating the PersonContact package*

51. Press F5 to execute this package. As the package is executed, you will see two data viewer output windows appear. If you adjust them on the screen (without dropping them on each other) so that you can see the background package as well, you can notice that the package execution is halted till the place where the data viewer is added in the data flow. To continue processing of data further, click the Detach button on the data viewer to detach it from the package and let the data flow.

52. In the beginning of the package execution, note that 20 rows from flat file and 30 rows from Excel file are combined by the Union All transformation. In the first data viewer, you can see that 50 records have been combined and are flowing as a single data collection. Detach this data viewer and see the data in the second data viewer, where the Salutation has been derived and the City column has been populated with city names. This data viewer shows

only 46 records, as 4 records did not find an exact match in the lookup table so were sent out to error output—i.e., Lookup Errors File by the Lookup transformation. Click the Detach button to complete the package execution.

53. Press SHIFT-F5 to stop debugging. Close project and exit BIDS.

Review

In this first data flow Hands-On exercise, you used several components that are the basic building blocks in a data flow. You also saw how you can use these components one after another to convert data to match the succeeding components requirements, while keeping in line with the final destination's requirements. You also captured records from the Lookup transformation for which there were no exact matches in the Lookup table. The concept of a Lookup table is extensively used to standardize data critical to any good customer relationship management (CRM) database.

Rowset Transformations

The Rowset transformations work on record sets. These transformations first receive all the rows and then do the processing bit as the operations they perform need all the rows upfront. Among these are Aggregate transformation, Sort transformation, Percentage and Row Sampling transformations, and Pivot and Unpivot transformations. You will work through two Hands-On exercises built around these transformations—one built around the Aggregate transformation and the other one built around the Pivot transformation, in which you will also use Sort transformation along with other data flow components.

Sort Transformation

The Sort transformation allows you to sort input rows in ascending or descending order by selecting one or more input columns for sort order criteria, similar to the ORDER BY clause of T-SQL. The user interface of this transformation is simple and has list of Available Input Columns in the upper half of the dialog box, along with check boxes before and after the column names. The selection of the check boxes after the column names—i.e., the Pass Through check boxes—allow the columns to be included in the sorted output; the selection of check boxes before the column names allow you to sort the input records on those columns. The lower half of the dialog has five fields to specify the columns you want to work with and the criteria to apply for sort order. To sort the records, this transformation requires that all the rows first be made available. While sifting through the records, this transformation can look for duplicate records with the same sort key values to "de-dupe" them. The Sort transformation supports one input and one output to perform its operation.

To configure this transformation, you select the input columns by clicking the check boxes for the Available Input Columns. Alternatively, you can select a column from the drop-down list invoked by clicking in the Input Column field. As you select an input column, notice that Output Alias, Sort Type, and Sort Order are automatically assigned to this column, though you can modify these values. The default value for Sort Type is Ascending, that can be changed to Descending. The Sort Order is a numerical value assigned to a column on the basis of its position in the sort order. This value starts with 1 for the first column and is increased by 1 for subsequent columns selected. The Sort Order value determines which column is sorted first. The column with the smaller value is always sorted before a column with bigger Sort Order value—i.e., the column with a Sort Order value of 1 will be sorted before the column with a Sort Order value of 2, and so on. This works similar to the ORDER BY clause of T-SQL.

The Sort Type and Sort Order are represented by a single property of the input column in the Advanced Editor. If you open the Advanced Editor for Sort Transformation, go to the Input and Output Properties tab, expand Sort Input under Inputs and Outputs, and then expand Input columns, you will see a list of input columns that are available to the transformation. If you click any of the input columns and scroll to the bottom of its properties, you will see the property NewSortKeyPosition that holds a positive or negative value. The positive value indicates that the sort type is ascending and a negative value indicates that the sort type is descending. The numerical value—i.e., 1, 2 or 3 and so on—represents the sort order property of customer user interface. A value of 0 indicates that the column is not included in the sort criteria; in fact, these are the columns that have only Pass Through check boxes selected against them. The input columns that are not included in the sort criteria are copied along with the sorted columns to the output columns.

Once the Sort transformation collects all the rows, it can apply the sorting criteria to the data rows. A sort operation can be an expensive process and can cause performance issues. You need to decide what you want to achieve before using this transformation; for example, do you want to provide all the server power to the sort process or want to limit usage of resources for sort operation? In the Advanced Editor for Sort Transformation, you can specify the maximum number of threads that can be used by Sort transformation in the MaximumThreads property of the Component Properties tab. The default value for this property is –1, which indicates an infinite number of threads available to the transformation.

Returning to the Sort Transformation Editor, where you've selected input columns and specified sort criteria, notice the Comparison Flags field. If you click in this field, you will see a list of options. The purpose of this field is to specify how the sorting should handle comparing the data. As you sort columns, the Sort transformation compares the data to allocate a proper sort order for the data rows.

You can specify the options in this field that can affect the sensitivity of the comparison of the data. For example, you can choose the Ignore Case option to specify that uppercase and lowercase data is to be treated equally. Six options are available, and you can choose more than one option provided in the drop-down list:

▶ **Ignore Case**   You choose this option to specify that while comparing data, the Sort transformation will not distinguish between uppercase and lowercase letters.

▶ **Ignore Kana Type**   If you are using the Japanese language, selecting this option requires the Sort transformation to ignore the distinction between hiragana and katakana, the two types of Japanese kana characters. For the benefit of those who are less acquainted with Japanese, kana is a general term used to express the two types of Japanese syllabic scripts. Hiragana is a cursive and flowing variety of kana used in most modern Japanese texts, and katakana is a relatively angular kana used for writing foreign words or official documents such as telegrams.

▶ **Ignore Nonspacing Characters**   The data you deal with may contain diacritics, especially in the age of Internet when the data entry is left in the hands of end users across the globe. A diacritic is a mark added to a letter to indicate a special phonetic value—such as the acute accent of *resumé*. Selecting the check box for this option treats the spacing characters and diacritics alike.

▶ **Ignore Character Width**   Using this option allows you to treat the single-byte characters (non-Unicode) and double-byte characters (Unicode characters) alike. Integration Services may automatically convert the data to Unicode data before comparing text data.

▶ **Ignore Symbols**   Sometimes it is useful to compare the string data by eliminating the symbols and white-space characters. This may be due to poor data quality or standardization, again due to free style data entered by users. The Sort transformation ignores the symbols when you select this option and treats *HNO#* and *HNO* as identical.

▶ **Sort Punctuation As Symbols**   You can configure the Sort transformation to remove all punctuation symbols except hyphens and apostrophes appended before the string data before comparison. Using this option treats *.NET* and *NET* as identical.

After configuring these options for sort criteria, you can add more sort criteria. The sort criteria you specify for the input generates a sort key value used to compare string data and sort it appropriately. If duplicate rows are included and you want to remove these, you can do so by selecting the Remove Rows With Duplicate Sort Values option provided on the lower left side of the Sort Transformation Editor dialog box.

Percentage Sampling Transformation

When you need to give out data to call centers for telesales activities, you are generally asked to create a sample set from a data segmentation. Sometimes the requirement is defined in percentage—for example, you may be asked to create a sample set of a randomly selected 15 percent of the total records in the segment. In such a case, you can use the Percentage Sampling transformation to create a sample data set from the input rows using the specified percentage. This transformation helps you create a representative data set much smaller in size that you can use for variety of purposes such as testing your packages in a development environment or using the sample data set for surveys and marketing purposes.

The Percentage Sampling transformation has a simple and intuitive user interface with just four fields. The first field, Percentage Of Rows, allows you to specify a percentage of sampling. The Percentage Sampling transformation uses an algorithm to select at random the number of rows according to the specified percentage. However, the number of rows that this transformation selects does not precisely match with the percentage calculations—i.e., the output rows may be a little bit too much or a little bit too little. The next two fields allow you to specify the names for selected sample output rows and the remaining unselected output rows. As this transformation selects rows for sampling, it outputs those rows onto its first output and the remaining unselected rows are outputted on to its second output. This transformation supports one input and two outputs to support both the selected and unselected data sets and supports no error output.

The last field is a check box and a value pair that lets you select that you want to specify a sampling seed and if yes, a value can be specified in the field provided. If you choose to specify a sampling seed and use the same sampling seed, it will produce the same sample output no matter how many times you run the packages with the same data set. This is helpful in testing of packages. Alternatively, if you don't specify a sampling seed, this component will generate a random number using the tick count of the operating system. Hence, each time you run a package, a different random number is generated and a different data set is sampled.

Row Sampling Transformation

The Row Sampling transformation works quite similar to the Percentage Sampling transformation in sampling a data set. However, the Row Sampling transformation outputs an exact number of rows as specified in the transformation. This random selection of a precise number of rows is useful, for example, if you're running a campaign to introduce your new product to different segments of your customers and prospects by sending them an e-mail every week. To promote Readers interest, you decide to award gifts to a random selection of 50 persons who show interest in your product by evaluating it every week. You can easily build this package by bringing into the data flow the records for the persons who evaluated the product in the current week and then apply a Row Sampling transformation to select 50 persons out of these records.

After you add this transformation to your package data flow, you can double-click it to open the custom editor interface to specify the number of rows you want to output (Figure 10-12). This transformation supports two outputs—one for extracting the selected records and the other for unselected records. You can type in the names for both the outputs in the user interface. It is not necessary for you to configure a downstream data flow to capture the unselected records. You can simply ignore this output, and the records appearing on this output will not be included in the data flow.

You can choose to specify a random seed for selection of records by clicking in the Use The Following Random Seed check box. This transformation selects random records on the basis of an algorithm that uses the random seed. If you specify the same random seed, the algorithm will select the same random records for the same input data. When you check this option, a message will pop up to tell you that using the same random seed on the same input data always generates the same sample, and specifying a random seed is recommended only during the development and

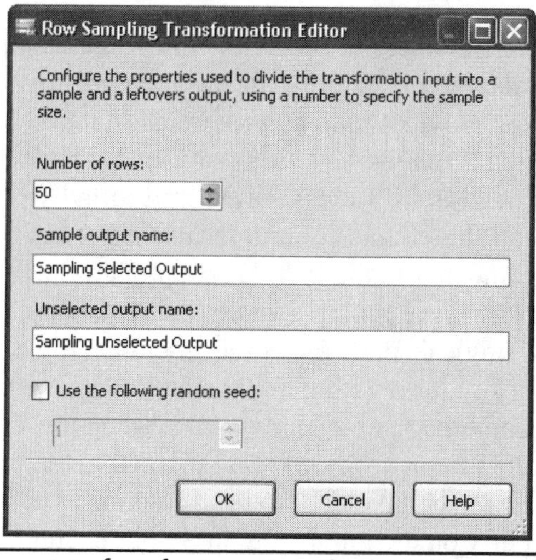

Figure 10-12 *Custom user interface for Row Sampling transformation*

testing of a package. Specifying a random seed affects the selection of records, and considering the example above, it would be quite naughty on your part to do that for selecting persons for awarding gifts. When you don't specify a random seed, the transformation uses the tick count of the operating system to create the random number that is obviously different each time you run the package, and hence the selected random records will be different even for the same input data.

Pivot Transformation

Relational databases are modeled to store normalized data. This normalization of data changes the data view that sometimes may not be as intuitive as businesses desire. The process that is used to convert data from a normalized form to a denormalized form is called *pivoting*. To understand how you can use this transformation, you will be working through a Hands-On exercise later; for now, let's discuss what a normalized data is by looking at the data we are going to use.

The data you will use in the following exercise is in an Excel spreadsheet that keeps sales order details in three columns: SalesOrderID, ProductName, and OrderQuantity. To keep the data in a normalized form, the table contains multiple entries or rows for the same SalesOrderID. For example, if three products have been purchased under a single SalesOrderID, the normalized data is represented by listing three rows for the same SalesOrderID with a different ProductName in each row to show the purchase quantity for that product. The sales manager may want to see the sales order details with the products and the quantity for each of them listed against the SalesOrderID on the same row. This is when you need to use pivot function to denormalize the data.

Before SSIS made it available, the pivot function was available in Microsoft Excel or third-party tools, or you had to write custom code to accomplish the task. Integration Services now provides both a Pivot transformation and an UnPivot transformation to provide different data views or forms. The Pivot transformation converts a normalized data set into a less normalized form by pivoting the input data on a column value. The value of this column forms the set key for pivoting, and this column is assigned a value of 1 to the PivotUsage property, which defines the role each input column performs. Assigning a value of 1 to a column indicates that it is part of the set key of a single or multi-rows set. In our example, the SalesOrderID column will act as a set key for pivoting and the multiple rows with the same SalesOrderID will be combined into one row. Also, when the data is pivoted, the values in a column, called *Pivot key values*, are pivoted to the columns in the output. For specifying the values to be pivoted to output columns, you assign a value of 2 to the PivotUsage property on the input column. In our example, the ProductName column has 10 different values for the products. When this data is pivoted,

10 columns are created on the basis of 10 different values in the ProductName column—i.e., value Mountain–100 of the ProductName column becomes the Mountain–100 column in the pivoted output. These newly created columns in the pivoted output get the values from the third column, which is used to provide values for newly created columns in the pivoted output by specifying a value of 3 to the PivotUsage property. All other input columns that don't participate in the pivoting process are assigned PivotUsage value of 0, and the first input value for the column is copied to the output column from the set of input rows with the same set key.

The Pivot transformation pivots the data on the basis of set key column value. For the same value of set key, the Pivot transformation merges multiple rows into a single row and pivots the input rows into columns. This implies that if the data is not sorted to list the same set key values in one collection of rows, this transformation will output the same key values multiple times. In our example, to get only one record for a SalesOrderID, the data must be sorted on SalesOrderID. However, if the data is not sorted on SalesOrderID, this transformation will generate multiple records for same SalesOrderID, as it will pivot the rows to columns each time the value of SalesOrderID changes.

All this may appear quite complex, but it is not that complicated when it comes to configuring the Pivot transformation. Let's see how to use this transformation to pivot data from an Excel worksheet.

Hands-On: Pivoting Sales Order Records in an Excel Worksheet

The records exported from the Sales order database to an Excel worksheet are in the normalized form—i.e., one sales order number appears in multiple rows to store details for the products ordered against it. The sales manager wants to see details of all the products ordered against each sales order in a single row.

Before starting this exercise, open the C:\SSIS\RawFiles\SalesOrders.xls file to determine whether the file has only one worksheet labeled *Normalized*. This exercise adds another worksheet to this file and it is likely that the file may have two worksheets. If it does have two, delete the second worksheet and then start this exercise. Also, if you are using the package code provided with the book, you may see a validation error as some of the worksheets are created at package run-time. To remove the errors, open the component, go to mappings page, and close it without making any changes; this will clear any validation error.

Method

To achieve the objective, you will be using a Pivot transformation to transform this data to the required format and put the data in a new worksheet. As Pivot transformation pivots the data every time the set key column value changes, you will sort the data before sending it down to Pivot transformation. The step by step method follows:

▶ Add a connection manager and Data Flow task to the package.

▶ Configure the Data Flow task.

▶ Add data viewers to monitor the data flow at run-time and execute the package.

Exercise (Add Connection Manager and Data Flow Task)

1. Open the Data Flow transformations project in BIDS. Right-click the SSIS Packages in the Solution Explorer and choose New SSIS Package. This will add a new SSIS package called Package1.dtsx.

2. Right-click Package1.dtsx and choose Rename from the context menu. Rename the package **Pivoting SalesOrders.dtsx**.

3. Right-click in the Connection Managers area and choose New Connection from the context menu. Select Excel Connection Manager Type from the list in the Add SSIS Connection Manager dialog box and click the Add button. Type **C:\SSIS\RawFiles\SalesOrders.xls** in the Excel File Path field in the Excel Connection Manager dialog box. Leave the Excel Version selected as Microsoft Excel 97-2005 and the checkbox for First Row Has Column Names checked. Click the OK button to add this connection manager. You will see *Excel Connection Manager* added under Connection Managers area. Double-click this and rename it SalesOrders Connection Manager by choosing Rename from the context menu.

4. Drag the Data Flow Task from the Toolbox and drop it on to the Control Flow Designer surface. Rename this task **Transforming SalesOrders**. Double-click it to open the Data Flow tab and configure this task.

Exercise (Configure the Data Flow Task)

To configure data flow for pivoting SalesOrders data, you will first add an Excel source to extract data from a normalized worksheet of SalesOrders.xls file and then sort this data on SalesOrderID as a Pivot transformation requires all the rows having same set key to get together in a single set for merging them to a single row. After sorting the data, you will configure the Pivot transformation to pump the pivoted data through to an Excel destination that will write the pivoted output to an Excel worksheet.

5. From the Toolbox, drag and drop Excel source onto the Data Flow Designer surface. Rename this adapter **Normalized Data Source**. Double-click the Normalized Data Source to open the Excel Source Editor. You will see SalesOrders Connection Manager listed in OLE DB Connection Manager

field and the Table Or View option selected in Data Access Mode field. Leave them as is and click the down arrow in the Name Of The Excel Sheet field. Choose Normalized$ from the drop-down list to extract data from Normalized worksheet of the SalesOrders workbook.

6. Go to the Columns page, and note that all the three fields selected from the Available External Columns and the Output Column shows the names that have been assigned to them automatically. By default, it is same as the external column name.

7. Go to the Error Output page and note that this page displays error handling properties for the output columns of Excel Source Output. By default, all the columns are configured to fail the Excel source component for any error or truncation of data. A handy option—Set This Value To Selected Cells, below the error handling configuration box—allows you to configure multiple error or truncation fields for error handling quickly and easily. Select multiple error and truncation fields in the error handling box using the SHIFT or CTRL key while clicking the fields; then select one of the three options listed in the Set This Value To Selected Cells field and click the Apply button. The selected option will be applied to all the fields you selected. For this exercise, leave the fields selected to Fail Component Setting. Click the OK button to close this editor.

8. Drop the Sort transformation from the Toolbox onto the Data Flow Designer surface just below the Normalized Data Source. Rename this **Sort on SalesOrderID**. Click the Normalized Data Source and drag the green arrow on to the Sort on SalesOrderID. Double-click it to open Sort Transformation Editor. You will see the three columns listed under Available Input Columns. Note that these columns have check boxes before and after the column names. Click to select the check box before the SalesOrderID column. This column will appear in the lower half of the dialog box with Sort Type as Ascending and Sort Order equals 1. Leave these setting as is and click the OK button to close this editor.

9. Drop the Pivot from the Toolbox onto the Designer surface just below the Sort on SalesOrderID. Connect the two transformations using the green arrow. Double-click the Pivot to open the Advanced Editor for Pivot. In the Component Properties tab, change the Name field to **Pivot on ProductName**.

10. Go to the Input Columns tab and select all the three columns.

11. Move on to the Input and Output Properties tab. Expand the Input Columns under Pivot Default Input on the left side of the dialog box to reveal the three columns you selected in the Input Columns tab. Click the SalesOrderID to list the properties of this column on the right pane of the dialog box. Scroll down in the properties of the SalesOrderID column and locate PivotUsage property. Assign a value of 1 to PivotUsage, indicating that this field will be treated as a set key. Move on to the ProductName field and assign a value of

2 to its PivotUsage property to indicate that this field is a pivot key field and the distinct values in this field will create corresponding columns in the output. Next, click the OrderQuantity field and assign a value of 3 to its PivotUsage property to indicate that the values from this field will be populated in the columns generated by the pivot key column.

12. Expand Pivot Default Output and then click Output Columns. You will notice that no output column appears in this transformation yet. Click the Add Column button and rename the newly added column **SalesOrderID**. This output column needs to be linked to an input column. In the properties of this column, locate the SourceColumn property. This property tells the Pivot transformation to populate this output column using values from the input column specified. To specify the source of data for this column, click the SalesOrderID column under Input Columns and note the LineageID. Specify this value of LineageID in the SourceColumn property of SalesOrderID output field. The value *282* shown in the SourceColumn property in Figure 10-13 is the LineageID of SalesOrderID column.

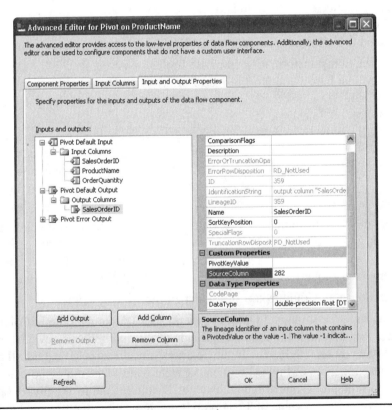

Figure 10-13   *Setting LineageID on the SourceColumn property*

13. As you did in step 12, add 10 more columns in the Output Columns and rename them as per the following table. Also, assign values to the PivotKeyValue and SourceColumn properties of the new output columns. Remember that PivotKeyValue is one of the distinct values of pivot key column and the SourceColumn indicates from which input column the data will populate the concerned output column. The new columns added here will be populated by OrderQuantity input column, so the LineageID of OrderQuantity will be used to populate all of them.

Output Column	Renamed to	PivotKeyValue	SourceColumn
Column	Mountain-100	Mountain-100	LineageID Value of OrderQuantity column
Column1	Mountain-200	Mountain-200	LineageID Value of OrderQuantity column
Column2	Mountain-300	Mountain-300	LineageID Value of OrderQuantity column
Column3	Road-150	Road-150	LineageID Value of OrderQuantity column
Column4	Road-250	Road-250	LineageID Value of OrderQuantity column
Column5	Road-350	Road-350	LineageID Value of OrderQuantity column
Column6	Touring-1000	Touring-1000	LineageID Value of OrderQuantity column
Column7	Touring-2000	Touring-2000	LineageID Value of OrderQuantity column
Column8	Touring-3000	Touring-3000	LineageID Value of OrderQuantity column
Column9	Sport-100	Sport-100	LineageID Value of OrderQuantity column

Refer to Figure 10-14 to see how this will look. In the figure, the value *292* appears in the SourceColumn of the LineageID of OrderQuantity input column. Click the OK button to close this transformation

14. Drop the Excel destination from the Toolbox just below the Pivot on ProductName and connect the two transformations using the green arrow. Rename Excel Destination **Pivoted Data Destination**. Double-click the Pivoted Data destination to open the Excel Destination Editor dialog box. You will use the same connection manager and the same Excel workbook. But you will add a new worksheet called Pivoted to the Excel workbook to store pivoted data. Click the New button opposite the Name Of The Excel Sheet field and you will see a script to create a new table (worksheet in Excel). Change the Pivoted Data Destination appearing just after CREATE TABLE statement to *Pivoted* only. This will create a new worksheet named Pivoted in the SalesOrders.xls file. Click the OK button and you will see Pivoted listed in the Name Of The Excel Sheet field.

15. Go to the Mappings page. As you click Mappings, you should see all the mappings created for you automatically. Click the OK button to close the editor for this component.

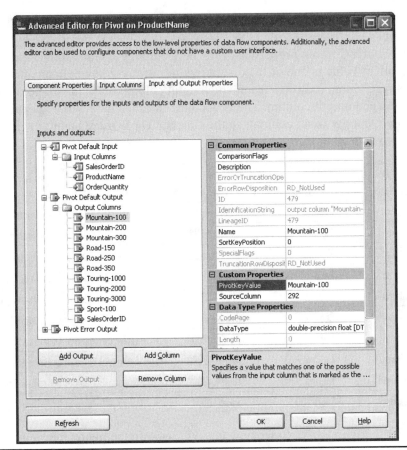

Figure 10-14 *Configuring output columns for Pivot transformation*

Exercise (Add Data Viewers and Execute the Package)

After having configured all the data flow components, you are ready to execute the package. However, in this exercise, you will also add couple of data viewers that will show the flow of data from a component to the other component at run-time.

16. Double-click the data flow path connecting Sort on SalesOrderID and Pivot on ProductName. In the Data Flow Path Editor, click the Data Viewers page, and then click the Add button and add a grid type data viewer. Click the OK button twice to close the editor window.

17. Similarly, add another grid type data viewer on the data flow path between Pivot on ProductName and Pivoted Data Destination.

18. Press F5 to execute the package. As the Normalized Data Source extracts data and passes to the Sort on SalesOrderID, you can see Normalized Data Source turns green, indicating a successful extraction of data and a total of 2187 records extracted. The next two components will appear in yellow, as the data viewer is holding the execution process for you to check the data and give your permission to go further. The second data viewer will be blank, as no data has reached it yet. Click the Detach button on the first data viewer to let the execution process proceed. As you detach the first data viewer, you will see the second data viewer populated with data and the Pivot on ProductName outputting 1302 rows. As the data passes the Sort on SalesOrderID, it will turn green to indicate a successful sort operation (see Figure 10-15). When you are done checking the data, click the Detach button on the second data viewer and let the package complete successfully.

19. Stop debugging by pressing SHIFT-F5. Save and close the project. Open the SalesOrders.xls file and check out the Pivoted worksheet to see how the data has been pivoted.

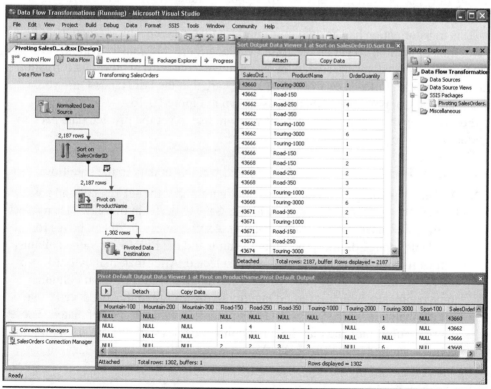

Figure 10-15 *Data viewers showing data before and after Pivot transformation*

Review

You've used a Pivot transformation to convert normalized data to a less normalized form. During this exercise, you sorted the data before sending it to the Pivot transformation and created output columns for the pivoted data. Finally, you created a new Excel worksheet using an Excel destination. Note that you've used only one connection manager to connect to Excel file for both extraction of data using source adapter and loading of data using destination adapter.

Unpivot Transformation

This transformation works in an opposite way to the Pivot transformation and converts a denormalized dataset into a more normalized version—i.e., one row may be broken down into multiple atomic rows so that they can be stored in a relational database. We will use the data you derived in the last exercise, in which each row lists multiple products against a single SalesOrderID. When you run this transformation, the records will be broken up into multiple rows containing the same value for SalesOrderID but having only one product in each row. To support its functions, this transformation uses one input, one output, and an error output.

This transformation has its own user interface that is much simpler than that of the Pivot transformation. To get an idea of how to configure this transformation, consider the pivoted data that you created in the preceding exercise. To get the data formatted in the normalized form—i.e., from where you started in the last Hands-On—you will configure the Unpivot transformation, as shown in Figure 10-16.

Following is the step by step method you will use to get the pivoted data back to normalized form:

1. Use the Excel source to bring the Pivoted worksheet data in the data flow.

2. Add an Unpivot transformation and configure it. Let the set key column pass through the transformation as is, which is SalesOrderID in this case. Then select all the columns that you want to unpivot. As you select the check boxes for Available Input Columns, the Input Column and the Pivot Key Value columns will be filled in using the column name selected. After that, manually fill in the Destination Column value where you want the values of input columns to be populated, which is OrderQuantity in this example. Lastly, specify the column name in which you would like pivot key values to be populated. These configurations indicate that the input column names will be converted into the values specified in the Pivot Key Value, which will then be populated in the

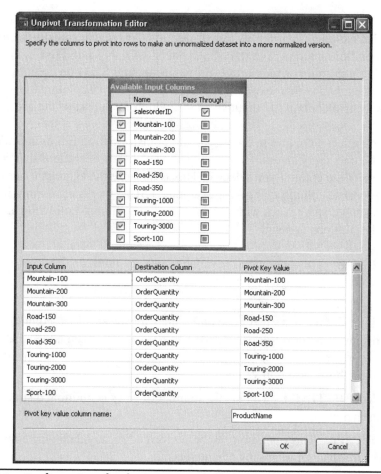

Figure 10-16 *Configurations for the Unpivot transformation*

pivot key value column (ProductName in this case), and input column values will be populated in a new column specified in the Destination Column, which is OrderQuantity column in this example.

3. Finally, add an Excel destination to collect the normalized data in an Excel worksheet.

Aggregate Transformation

To perform operations such as SUM, AVERAGE, and so on, you need to have a complete data set. Aggregate transformation consumes all the rows before applying any transformation and extracting the transformed data. Because of this, it is also called *asynchronous* transformation. Aggregate transformation can perform operations such as AVERAGE, COUNT, COUNT DISTINCT, GROUP BY, selecting minimum or maximum from a group, and SUM on column values. The aggregated data is then extracted out in the new output columns. The output columns may also contain the input columns, which form part of the groupings or aggregations.

When you select a column in the Aggregate Transformation Editor and click in the Operation field to apply an operation, you will see a list of operations that coincide with the type of the column you selected. This is because the aggregate operations require appropriate column types—for example, a SUM works on a numeric data type column and doesn't work with a string data type column. Following are the operation descriptions in detail:

▶ **AVERAGE**   This operation is available only for numeric data type columns and returns the average of the column values.

▶ **COUNT**   Counts the number of rows for the selected column. This operation will not count the rows that have null values for the specified column. In the Aggregate Transform Editor, a special column (*) has been added that allows you to perform the COUNT ALL operation to count all the rows in a data set, including those with null values.

▶ **COUNT DISTINCT**   Counts the number of rows containing distinct non-null values in a group.

▶ **GROUP BY**   This operation can be performed on any data type column and returns the data set in groups of row sets.

▶ **MAXIMUM**   This operation can be performed on numeric, date, and time data type columns and returns the maximum value in a group.

▶ **MINIMUM**   This operation can be performed on numeric, date, and time data type columns and returns the minimum value in a group.

▶ **SUM**   This operation is available only for numeric data type columns and returns the sum of values in a column.

The Aggregate transformation's user interface provides features and options to configure to apply aggregations. We will cover configurations in the following

Hands-On exercise, as they will be easier to understand as you work with them. Before we dive in, consider the following:

▶ You can perform multiple aggregate operations on the same set of data. For example, you can perform SUM and AVERAGE operations on a column in the same transformation. As the result from these two different aggregate operations will be different, you must direct the results to different outputs. This is fully supported by the transformation as you can add multiple outputs to this transformation.

▶ The null values are handled as specified in SQL-92 standard that is in the same way they are handled by T-SQL. The COUNT ALL operation will count all the rows including those containing null values, whereas COUNT or COUNT DISTINCT operations for a specific column will count only rows with non-null values in the specified columns. In addition, GROUP BY operation put null values in a separate group.

▶ When an output column requires special handling because it contains an oversized data value greater than 4 billion, or the data requires precision that is beyond a float data type, you can set the IsBig property of the output column to 1 so that the transformation uses the correct data type for storing the column value. However, columns that are involved in a GROUP BY, MINIMUM, or MAXIMUM operation cannot take advantage of this.

Hands-On: Aggregating SalesOrders

The SalesOrders.xls file has been extended with the pricing information by adding unit price and total price columns. The extracted data has been saved as SalesOrdersExtended.xls. From this extended sales orders data that has a price listed for each product against the SalesOrderID, you are required to aggregate a total price for each order and calculate the average price per product and the number of each product sold.

Before starting this exercise, open the SalesOrdersExtended.xls Excel file to determine whether the file has only one worksheet named SalesOrders. This exercise adds two more worksheets to this file, and the file may already include three worksheets. If so, delete the other two worksheets before you start this exercise. Also, if you are using the provided package code, you may get a validation error, as the Excel Destination used in the package looks for the worksheets created at run-time. In this case, leave the worksheets as is.

Method

As with the Pivot transformation Hands-On exercise, you will use an Excel file to access the data from a worksheet and create two new worksheets in the same Excel file to extract the processed data. The step by step method is as follows:

▶ Create a new package and add a connection manager and Data Flow task.

▶ Configure the Aggregate transformation and the Data Flow task.

▶ Execute the package and check the results.

As most of these steps have been explained in detail in earlier exercises, only a brief reference will be mentioned here. For more details on how to configure components in detail, refer to earlier exercises. The new components will, however, be explained in detail.

Exercise (Add Connection Manager and Data Flow Task to a New Package)

1. Open the Data Flow transformations project in BIDS. Right-click the SSIS Packages in Solution Explorer and choose New SSIS Package. This will add a new SSIS package named Package1.dtsx.

2. Right-click Package1.dtsx and choose Rename from the context menu. Rename the package **Aggregating SalesOrders.dtsx** and click the Yes button on the pop-up dialog box to confirm the new name.

3. Add an Excel Connection Manager to connect to an Excel file C:\SSIS\ RawFiles\SalesOrdersExtended.xls.

4. Add a Data Flow task from Toolbox and rename it **Aggregating SalesOrders**. Double-click it to open the Data Flow tab. Press CTRL-SHIFT-S to save all the files.

Exercise (Configure Aggregating SalesOrders)

The main focus of this exercise is to learn how to configure an Aggregate transformation. You will configure the Excel source and Excel destination as well to complete the data flow configurations.

5. Add an Excel source to extract data from the SalesOrders worksheet in the SalesOrdersExtended.xls file. Rename this Excel Source **Sales Orders Data Source**.

6. Drag and drop an Aggregate transformation from the Toolbox onto the Data Flow surface just below the Excel source. Connect both the components with a data flow path.

7. Double-click the Aggregate transformation to open the Aggregate Transformation Editor with two tabs—Aggregations and Advanced. In the Aggregations tab, you select columns for aggregations and specify aggregation properties for them. This tab has two display types: basic and advanced. An Advanced button on the Aggregations tab converts the basic display of the Aggregations tab into an advanced display. This advanced display allows you to perform multiple GROUP BY operations. Click the Advanced button to see the advanced display. Selecting multiple GROUP BY operations—i.e., adding rows using multiple Aggregation Names in advanced display—means you will be generating different types of output data sets that will be sent to multiple outputs. Adding an Aggregation Name adds an additional output to the transformation outputs.

8. Click the Advanced tab to see the properties you can apply at the component level. Notice that the same properties are available for configurations in more than one place. You can configure this transformation at three levels—the component level, output level, and column level. The properties you define on the Advanced tab apply at a component level, the properties configured in the advanced display of the Aggregations tab apply at the output level, and the properties configured in the column list at the bottom of the Aggregations tab apply at the column level. Specifying properties at different levels provides performance benefits to the transformation. Following are descriptions for properties in the Advanced tab:

Key Scale   This property helps the transformation decide the initial cache size. By default, this property is not used and is optional for you to specify low, medium, and high options. Using the low value, the aggregation can write approximately 500,000 keys, medium enables it to write about 5 million keys, and high enables it to write approximately 25 million keys.

Number Of Keys   This optional setting is used to override the value of a key scale by specifying the exact number of keys that you expect this transformation to handle. Specifying the keys upfront allows the transformation to manage cache properly and avoids reorganizing the cache at run-time and will enhance performance.

Count Distinct Scale   You can specify an approximate number of distinct values that the transformation is expected to handle. This is an optional setting and is unspecified by default—that means this property is not used. You can specify low, medium, or high. Using the low value, the aggregation can write approximately 500 thousand distinct values, medium enables it to write about 5 million distinct values and high enables it to write approximately 25 million distinct values.

Count Distinct Keys   Using this property, you can override the count distinct scale value by specifying the exact number of distinct values that the transformation can write. This will avoid reorganizing cached totals at run-time and will enhance performance.

Auto Extend Factor   Using this property, you can specify by how much percentage of memory this transformation can extend its memory during run-time. You can use a value between 1 to 100 percent—the default is 25 percent.

9. In the Aggregations tab, select SalesOrderID and TotalPrice from the Available Input Columns. As you select them, they will be added to the columns list below as SalesOrderID with GROUP BY operation and TotalPrice with SUM operation being applied. You can select one of the comparison flags for the GROUP BY operation to specify how to compare data. The available options are Ignore Case, Ignore Kana Type, Ignore Non-spacing Characters, and Ignore Character Width. These comparison flags were explained earlier in this chapter. You can also specify the Count Distinct Scale and the Count Distinct Keys properties to specify the number of keys and distinct count keys that each column contains, at column level to boost the performance. For our example, the data is too small, so ignore these settings.

10. Click the Advanced button to display the options for configuring aggregations for multiple outputs; the button will change to Basic, and clicking it will hide these options. You will see Aggregate Output 1 already configured using SalesOrderID as a GROUP BY operation. Rename Aggregate Output 1 **Total Per Order** and click in the second row in the Aggregation Name field. Type **Products Sold and Average Price** in the cell. Then select ProductName, OrderQuantity, and UnitPrice columns from the Available Input Columns list. These columns will appear in the columns list with default operations applied to them. Change these operations as follows: GROUP BY operation to the ProductName column, SUM operation to the OrderQuantity column, and AVERAGE operation to the UnitPrice column, as shown in the Figure 10-17.

Note that you can specify key scale and keys in the advanced display for each output, thus enhancing performance by specifying the number of keys the output is expected to contain. Similarly, you can specify Count Distinct Scale and Count Distinct Keys for each column in the list to specify the number of distinct values the column is expected to contain to enhance the performance.

11. You're done with the configuration of Aggregation transformation. Click the OK button to close the editor. Before you start executing the package, check out one more thing. Open the Advanced Editor for Aggregate Transformation and go to the Input and Output Properties tab. You'll see the two outputs you

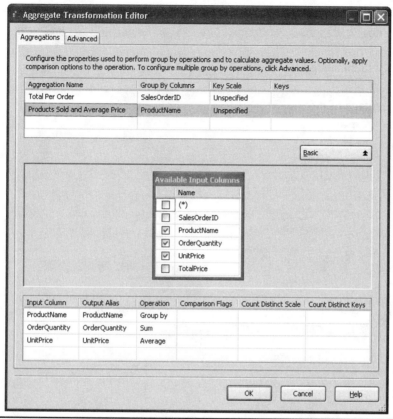

Figure 10-17 *Configuring Aggregate transformation for multiple outputs*

created earlier in the advanced display of Aggregations tab of the custom editor. Expand and view the different output columns to see how easy it can be to manage multiple outputs and output columns. Also, note that you can specify the IsBig property in the output column of Aggregate transformation in the Advanced Editor, as shown in Figure 10-18. Click the OK button to return to the Designer.

12. Let's direct the outputs to different worksheets in the same Excel file. Add an Excel destination on the left, just below the Aggregate transformation, and drag the green arrow from Aggregate transformation to Excel destination. As you drop it on the Excel destination, an Input Output Selection dialog box will pop-up, asking you to specify the output you want to send to this destination. Select Total Per Order in the Output field and click OK to add the connector.

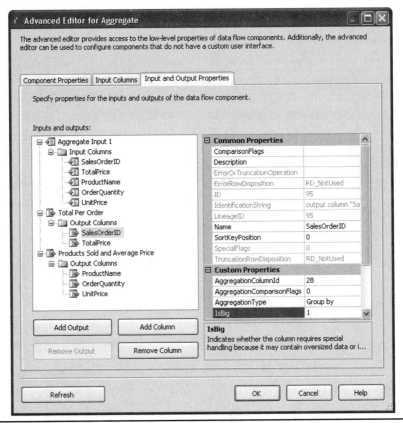

Figure 10-18   *Multiple outputs of Aggregate transformation*

13. Double-click the Excel Destination and click the New button opposite to the Name Of The Excel Sheet field to add a new worksheet in the Excel file to which you are connecting. In the Create Table dialog box, change the name of the table from Excel Destination to **Total Per Order** and click OK to return to the Excel Destination Editor dialog box. Go to the Mappings page and the mappings between the Available Input Columns with the Available Destination Columns will be done for you by default. Click the OK button to close the Destination Editor. Rename this destination **Total Per Order**.

14. Similar to steps 12 and 13, add another Excel destination below the Aggregate transformation on the right side (see Figure 10-19) and rename it **Products Sold and Average Price**. Connect the Aggregate transformation to the Products Sold and Average Price destination using the second green arrow. Add a new worksheet by clicking the New button next to the Name Of The Excel Sheet

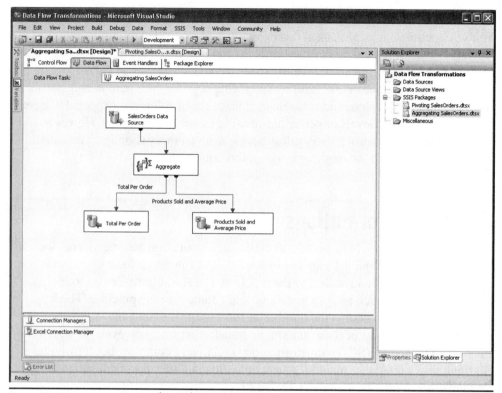

Figure 10-19   *Aggregating the SalesOrders package*

field and click the OK button to add a worksheet by the name of Products Sold and Average Price. Go to the Mappings page to create the mappings. Click the OK button to close the editor.

Exercise (Run the Aggregations)

In the final part of this Hands-On, you will be executing the package and seeing the results. If you wish, you can add data viewers at a couple of the data flow paths.

15. Press F5 to run the package. The package will complete execution almost immediately. Stop the debugging by pressing SHIFT-F5. Save all files and close the project.

16. Explore to the C:\SSIS\RawFiles folder and open the SalesOrdersExtended.xls file. You will see two new worksheets created in the file. Check out the data to appreciate the Aggregate transformation a bit more.

Review

You've done some aggregations in this exercise and have added multiple outputs to the Aggregate transformation. You've also learned that the Aggregate transformation can be configured at the component level by specifying the properties in the Advanced tab, can be configured at the output level by specifying keys for each output, and can also be configured at the column level for distinct values each column is expected to have. You can achieve high levels of performance using these configurations. However, if you find that the transformation is still suffering from memory shortage, you can use Auto Extend to extend the memory usage of this component.

Other Transformations

Other transformations are important as well. The Export Column transformation exports partial data from the pipeline into a file. The Import Column transformation reads data from a file and adds into the pipeline. The Audit transformation includes environmental data such as system data or login name into the pipeline. The Row Count transformation counts the number of rows in the pipeline and stores the data to a variable. Most of these are simple transformations; however, the Slowly Changing Dimension (SCD) transformation is relatively complex, but it provides a configuration wizard that makes the task of loading a dimension table much easier. You will be working through a Hands-On exercise to use a SCD transformation.

Export Column Transformation

The Export Column transformation has one input, one output, and one error output. Using this transformation, you can export data from the data flow to an external file. For example, you can export images from the data flow and save them to individual files. To use this transformation, two columns must exist in the data flow: one that contains data—i.e., images—and the second that contains the paths for the files to which you want to save those images. By properly configuring the Export Column transformation, you can save each image in every row to a separate file specified by the column that contains the file path information. When you open the transformation editor after connecting an input, you can select columns that you want to extract in the Extract Column field and select the columns in the File Path Column that specify file paths for the extracted data. The Extract Column and the File Path Column fields provide drop-down lists of the columns in the data flow; however, the Extract Column displays only the columns that have DT_TEXT, DT_NTEXT, or DT_IMAGE data type.

You will be able to select Allow Append and Force Truncate check boxes as well. The Allow Append check box allows the transformation to append data to an existing file, and the Force Truncate check box allows transformation to delete and re-create the file before writing data into it. The editor's user-interface doesn't allow you to select both the check boxes simultaneously; however, if you set these properties programmatically, the component fails. At run-time, the transformation exports data row by row and writes the exported data to the files. Depending on your selections of Allow Append and Force Truncate options and the existence of files to which you want to save data, the transformation decides the appropriate action. For example, if the file to which data is to be inserted does not exist, the transformation creates a new file and writes the data to it irrespective of your settings of these check boxes. However, if the file to which data is to be inserted already exists, the transformation uses information from the check boxes. In this case, if the Allow Append check box is selected, the transformation opens the file and writes the data at the end of the file, and if the Force Truncate option is checked, the transformation deletes and re-creates the file and writes the data to the file. If you do not select any of the check boxes and the file exists, a run-time error occurs because you are effectively not letting the transformation append or truncate the file and prohibiting it from writing data to the file.

The last option you may find on the user-interface is a check box to Write Byte-Order Mark. A Byte-Order Mark (BOM) is a ZERO-WIDTH NO-BREAK SPACE character used to denote Endianness of a string. This is particularly useful for images saved in the TIFF format that store pixel values as words, and BOM makes a difference in performance. Images stored in JPEG or GIF format are not word-oriented and Byte-Order does not matter. Note that BOM is written only when the data type is DT_NTEXT and data is written to a new file.

Import Column Transformation

The Import Column transformation has one input, one output, and one error output and is the reverse of the Export Column transformation. Using this transformation, you can read data from files and add the data to the columns in the data flow. For example, you can add images using this transformation in the data flow along with the text fields. An input column in the transformation input contains the file paths for the files that contain data that you want to add to the data flow. At run-time, this transformation processes each row, gets the file path information from the input column, and then opens the file to load the data from it to an output column in the data flow.

This transformation doesn't have its own user interface and uses the Advanced Editor to expose its properties for configurations. When you double-click this transformation after connecting an input to it in the data flow of your package, the Advanced Editor for Import Column dialog box opens. To configure this transformation, select the input column that contains the file path information in the Input Columns tab. In the Input and Output Properties tab, you add an output column under Output Columns collection in the Import Column Output node. When this new column is added, select the desired data type for the column. The data type of the output column must be DT_TEXT, DT_NTEXT, or DT_IMAGE. Note the ID of this column and expand Input Columns collection in the Import Column Input node. You will see here the column that you've selected in the Input Columns tab earlier. Scroll down to the Custom Properties section in this column's properties and specify the ID of the new output column in the FileDataColumnID field. By specifying the ID of the output column in the FileDataColumnID property of the input column, you indicate the transformation ID of the column in which you want imported data to receive. If the data type of the new output column is DT_NTEXT, you can also specify True in the ExpectBOM field if the file is expected to begin with a BOM.

Audit Transformation

One of the common requirements of data maintenance and data warehousing is to timestamp the record whenever it is either added or updated. Generally in data marts, you get a nightly feed for new as well as updated records and you want to timestamp the records that are inserted or updated to maintain a history, which is also quite helpful in data analysis. By providing Audit transformation, Integration Services has extended this ability and allows an environment variable values to be included in the data flow. With Audit transformation, not only can you include the package execution start time but you can include much more information—for example, name of the operator, computer, or package to indicate who has made changes to data and the source of data. To perform the assigned functions, this transformation supports one input and one output.

Audit transformation provides nine system variables. Following is a brief description of each of these variables:

▶ **Execution Instance GUID**   Each execution instance of the package is allocated a GUID that is available in this variable.

▶ **Package ID**   Represents the unique identifier of the package.

▶ **Package Name**   A package name can be added in the data flow.

▶ **Version ID**   Holds the version identifier of the package.

▶ **Execution Start Time**   Include the time when the package started to run.

▶ **Machine Name**   Provides a computer name.

▶ **User Name**   Add the login name of the person who runs the package.

▶ **Task Name**   Holds the name of the Data Flow task to which this transformation belongs.

▶ **Task ID**   Holds the unique identifier of the Data Flow task to which this transformation belongs.

When you open the editor for this transformation after connecting an input, you will be able to select the system variable from a drop-down list by clicking in the Audit Type column, as shown in Figure 10-20. When you select a system variable, the Output Column Name shows the default name of the variable, which you can change. This Output Column will be added to the data flow as a new output column in the transformation output.

Row Count Transformation

Using the Row Count transformation, you can count the rows that are passing through the transformation and store the final count in a variable that can be used by other components, such as a script component and property expressions. This transformation uses the Advanced Editor to expose its properties. To store the count of rows into a variable, you need to define a variable before you can use this task. The variable must

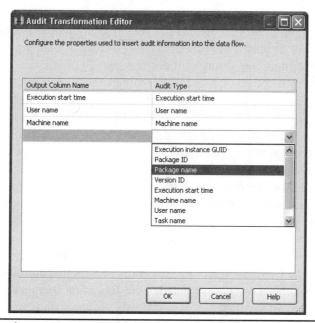

Figure 10-20   *Configuring Audit transformation*

be in the scope of the Data Flow task to which the transformation belongs. To count the rows in the data flow and update the variable value, you simply specify the variable in the VariableName field in the Component Properties tab.

Slowly Changing Dimension Transformation

SCD helps you manage slowly changing data attributes in a data warehouse. To describe this transformation clearly and for the benefit of those who are new in data warehousing, I will explain it starting with some conceptual details. When a database for a data warehouse is built using the dimensional modeling design, the data is sliced across many dimensions, such as time, location, and product, and is stored in two types of tables called the *fact table* and the *dimension table*. A dimension table stores records for that particular dimension and a fact table contains measures for the dimensions. For example, a product dimension table contains information about products such as product category, model details, and product features. A sales fact table contains measures of sales across different dimensions, such as total sales of a product, total sales in a month, and total sales at a location. The advantage of dimensional data modeling is that you can aggregate data across multiple dimensions—for example, total sales of a product at a location in a year.

One of the issues you will face while maintaining a data warehouse is how to handle changes to the dimensional data across time. For example, contacts may change their addresses, products can change over time, new products may be introduced, some old products may be removed, or your company may decide to reorganize its sales regions. These changes may pose some challenges when you're tasked with maintaining the history of these changes. To provide complex reports, maintaining history in a data warehouse, or online analytical processing (OLAP) system, is much more important compared to online transaction processing (OLTP) systems, which are generally designed to represent the current state. For example, if a sales representative is allocated a new sales region, the commission for the sales she has made in the previous region should still go to her; this makes it necessary to keep a history of changes to her sales region.

To maintain a history for changing data while dealing with restrictions imposed by data complexity and storage limitations, information engineers have been adopting different approaches to different types of data. When maintaining a history for a particular data type is not important, an existing record simply gets overwritten by a new record. This is the simplest form of handling a slowly changing dimension and is classified as Type 1. When preserving the history of changing attributes of data is critical to business, the new record is added to the dimension along with the existing original record. This is classified as a Type 2 slowly changing dimension. This is a more commonly used form that allows you to maintain accurate historical data; however, if the dimension sizes become too big and the number of rows is too high, you may have to work on storage and performance issues. In Type 3 slowly changing dimension, the issue of additional rows with each change is addressed by adding new columns for the current value and when the current value became effective. Hence the dimension contains the original value and the current value, irrespective of how many changes have occurred in between, thus limiting the ability to register changes accurately; this does overcome the limitations of Type 2, however. In Integration Services, the slowly changing dimension transformation doesn't support Type 3 changes.

You can use the Slowly Changing Dimension transformation to update and insert records in data warehouse dimension tables for different types of changes. This transformation contains a wizard that helps you configure various selections. You set various change types on the columns and select attribute options to configure SCD transformation in this wizard. When you click the wizard's Finish button, the wizard creates the logic for updating or inserting the records in the dimension table and outputs records for different types of operations to different outputs. But the wizard does not stop at simply outputting the records, but also creates a downstream data flow by adding the required components to load incoming data to the SCD table. The great thing about this is that you have complete flexibility to modify the data flow created by SCD wizard.

The SCD transformation supports up to six different outputs to output records for different types of processing before loading them into the dimension table. These outputs have different names assigned on the basis of different Change Type records they carry. For example, the Changing Attribute Updates Output carries all the records specified for Changing Attribute Change Type, and New Output outputs all the records that are to be inserted to dimension table. The outputs are discussed in more detail later in this chapter.

When you connect an input to this transformation in the data flow and double-click it, you invoke Slowly Changing Dimension Wizard. The SCD wizard allows you to select a dimension table and specify business keys to map transformation input columns to the dimension table columns. Then you can manage the changes to column data in SCD by specifying a change type for various dimension columns. You can configure this transformation for the following change types using the SCD wizard:

▶ **Fixed Attribute** Configure the transformation not to change the column value by selecting Fixed attribute Change Type for a column. At run-time, the SCD transformation performs a lookup of the incoming row against the dimension table to check for a match. If SCD doesn't find any match for a particular row, it diverts that row to the New Output; however, if a match is found and the matching key contains the columns with Fixed Attribute changes, the SCD transformation diverts the row to the Fixed Attribute Output. As these changes are not to be applied to the dimension table, the SCD wizard creates no data flow for this output. However, if you want to capture such rows, you can create a data flow and connect to this output by dragging the green arrow from the transformation to the downstream component and selecting Fixed Attribute Output from the Input Output Selection pop-up dialog box. If you do not expect any changes in the columns specified for Fixed Attribute Change Type, you can also specify to fail the transformation if changes are detected in a fixed attribute in the next screen of the wizard.

▶ **Changing Attribute**   The columns that you select for Changing attribute Change Type are treated as Type 1 changes, and the changed rows will overwrite the existing rows. At run-time, the SCD transformation performs a lookup for the incoming row against the dimension table and checks for the match. If a match is found and the matching key is found to have the specified columns with changed values, the transformation directs the row to the Changing Attributes Updates Output, which is further connected to an OLE DB Command transformation to perform the UPDATE operation on the dimension table. If the SCD transformation finds a matching row during the lookup operation but the row doesn't contain any change, such rows are diverted to the Unchanged Output and the SCD wizard doesn't create any data flow for this output by default. However, if you want to capture such rows, you can create a downstream data flow and attach it to this output. Your data warehouse will contain multiple records for a business key as it keeps the history depending on what kind of changes it has been through. So when an SCD transformation gets a Changing Attribute type record, it may match against multiple records. To update all the records in that case, you can specify your option in the next screen of the wizard, where you can select an option to indicate whether the task should change all matching records, including outdated records, when a change is detected in a Changing attribute.

▶ **Historical Attribute**   Create a new record and mark existing records as expired by changing the date fields or setting a flag in an indicator column by setting Historical Attribute Change Type. These changes are treated as Type 2 changes. At run-time, when the SCD transformation finds a matching row that has Historical Attribute changes, it diverts the row to a Historical Attribute Inserts Output. SCD Wizard creates a data flow, which updates the existing record and then inserts the incoming record as a new record with the same business key in the dimension table. The data flow first adds a new column to the incoming record as an expiry indicator using the Derived Column transformation and then uses an OLE DB Command transformation to update the existing record in the dimension table with the newly added column to mark it expired. After updating the existing record, it adds all the columns, but the newly added indicator column of the incoming record to the New Output Data Flow path uses Union All transformation so that a new record is added to the dimension table. Refer to Figure 10-26, later in the chapter, for clarity on the data flow it creates. (If you find this difficult to understand, try rereading this description. After you've completed the Hands-On exercise, it will make much more sense!) The New Output also gets all the new records for which SCD did not find any match within the dimension table. The New Output combines new records and the records coming from the OLE DB Command component of the Historical Attribute Inserts Output Data Flow path using the Union All transformation. These records are then added with a new column and the value to indicate that the record is current (for example, StartDate if using dates to indicate the current state of the record) before being added to the dimension table.

In addition to the outputs specified in these Change Type descriptions, SCD includes one more, called *Inferred Member Updates Output*. This output gets all the inferred members' records. An inferred member record is created in the dimension table with the minimal data, anticipating that more details of the record will arrive when a later loading process runs. An inferred member is created because the fact table contains foreign keys for the dimension tables, and sometimes the loading of the fact table fails because facts data arrives when a key doesn't yet exist in the dimension table. To avoid the failure of a fact table loading process, you should create a record in the dimension table with minimal data so that when the fact arrives earlier than its attributes, it can still be loaded. This inferred member record is updated later when the attribute data arrives. Support for uploading inferred members details when they arrive is inbuilt in the SCD transformation and the SCD wizard allows you to choose one of the following methods (see Figure 10-25) to identify an inferred member while uploading:

▶ All columns with a change type are null.

▶ Use a Boolean column to indicate whether the current record is an inferred member.

You will use the first option if you have created a minimal record in the dimension table while loading the fact table, when all the columns with a change type have null values. Alternatively, you can use a Boolean column to indicate that the incoming record is an inferred member record. After you specify the inferred member identification and finish the SCD wizard, you will see that the wizard has created a data flow with lot of data flow components connected to different outputs to load the dimension table.

Now you'll work through another Hands-On exercise to see for yourself how easily you can load a dimension using the SCD Wizard.

Hands-On: Loading a Slowly Changing Dimension

You are tasked with loading the DimCustomer dimension using a SCD transformation from the Customer table. The challenge is that the customers were registered using a variety of methods, and not all customers were allocated a customer number, so the Customer table contains some records that do not have a Customer ID assigned to them. You need to identify those customers as well. The other business requirements are that changes to phone numbers are allowed and you don't need to keep a history for these changes; however, a complete history is to be retained for change of address. As an Email attribute is required for logging on to the customers portal, this attribute is not allowed to be changed.

Email → fixed

phone → Type 1

Address → Type 2

Method

The Campaign database contains a Customer table that you will use to load the DimCustomer dimension table. In real life, DimCustomer would be in a different database, but to keep things simple for this exercise, the DimCustomer table has been created in the Campaign database. The exercise is divided in four parts:

▶   In the first part you will create a new package and add starting components to the package.

▶   In the second part you will filter out records that do not have a CustomerID allocated to them.

▶   In the third part you will configure SCD transformation using the SCD Wizard.

▶   In the final part you will execute the package to see how SCD deals with different types of updates.

Exercise (Add Data Flow Task and OLE DB Source to a New Package)

1. Open the Data Flow transformations project in BIDS. Right-click the SSIS Packages in Solution Explorer and choose New SSIS Package. This will add a new SSIS package named Package1.dtsx.

2. Right-click Package1.dtsx and choose Rename from the context menu. Rename the package **Loading Slowly Changing Dimension.dtsx** and click the Yes button on the pop-up dialog box to confirm the rename.

3. Drop the Data Flow task from the Toolbox onto the Control Flow surface and rename it **Loading SCD**. Press CTRL-SHIFT-S to save all the files.

4. Double-click the Loading SCD to go to the Data Flow panel. Drop the OLE DB source from the Toolbox on to the Data Flow surface. Rename the OLE DB Source **Customer**.

5. Double-click Customer to open the OLE DB Source Editor. Click the New button next to the OLE DB Connection Manager field. Choose (local). Campaign in the Configure OLE DB Connection Manager window and click OK. Leave Table Or View selected in the Data Access Mode field. Click the down arrow button in the Name Of The Table Or The View field and choose [dbo].[Customer] table from the drop-down list. Go to the Columns page and all the External Columns will be mapped to the Output Columns. Click the OK button to close the OLE DB Source Editor. You've added a connection manager to connect to the Customer table in the Campaign database and an OLE DB source to extract data from this table.

Exercise (Identify Customers that Do Not Have a Customer ID)

An SCD transformation needs to have a business key so that it can do a lookup with the dimension table using this key. As a requirement, the SCD transformation doesn't allow this key to contain null values. In this part, you will filter out all the records coming in the pipeline that have Customer ID equal to Null.

6. From the Toolbox, drag and drop the Conditional Split transformation below the Customer source. Connect both the components by dragging the green arrow from the Customer and dropping it on the Conditional Split component. Rename the Conditional Split component **Customers Filter**.

7. Double-click the Customers Filter component to open the Conditional Split Transformation Editor. The interface of this component is basically an Expression Builder UI. Expand the NULL Functions node in the top right section of the dialog box and drag and drop ISNULL(<<expression>>) in the Condition column in the grid. The expression will be displayed in red, indicating that there is an error with the expression syntax. This will add an output with the name *Case 1* to this component.

8. Expand the Columns node in the top left box and drag the CustomerID on the <<expression>> part of the ISNULL function so that the Condition field contains ISNULL([CustomerID]). When you click outside the Condition field, the expression turns black, indicating that the expression syntax is correct. The ISNULL function will be true for the null values of CustomerID column.

9. Click in the Output Name column and change Case 1 to **Customers without CustomerID**. Click in the Default Output Name field and rename it **Customers with CustomerID**, as shown in Figure 10-21. This component has been configured to output records to two outputs on the basis of whether the CustomerID is a null or a non-null value. Click the OK button to close the editor.

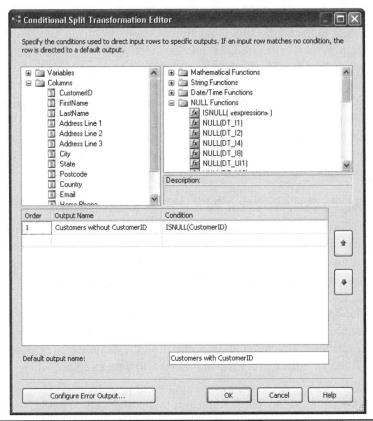

Figure 10-21   *Conditionally splitting customers on the basis of the CustomerID column*

10. Drag an Excel destination onto the Data Flow surface below the Customers Filter. Click the Customers Filter and drag the green arrow onto the Excel Destination. Select Customers without CustomerID in the Output field of the Input Output Selection dialog box. Click OK to return to the Designer.

11. Double-click the Excel destination to open the editor. Click the New button next to OLE DB Connection Manager field. Type **C:\SSIS\RawFiles\ Customers without CustomerID.xls** in the Excel File Path field in the Excel Connection Manager dialog box and click OK to return. The specified file will be created at run-time.

12. Click the New button next to Name Of The Excel Sheet field and replace Excel Destination written after CREATE TABLE with Customers without CustomerID in the Create Table dialog box; then click OK. Go to the Mappings page to create mappings between the input and destination columns. Click the OK button to close the editor.

Exercise (Configure the Slowly Changing Dimension Transformation)

13. Drag the Slowly Changing Dimension transformation from the Toolbox on to the Data Flow surface just below the Customers Filter component. Connect Customers Filter by dragging the green arrow connector to the Slowly Changing Dimension transformation. Rename Slowly Changing Dimension to **Loading DimCustomer**.

14. Double-click the Loading DimCustomer transformation. This will start the SCD Wizard. Click the Next button to go to Select a Dimension Table and Keys screen.

15. Make sure that (local).Campaign is selected in the Connection Manager field. Click the down arrow button next to the Table Or View field and choose [dbo].[DimCustomer] from the drop-down list of Campaign database. As you select the dimension table, you will see that the Input Columns are mapped to Dimension Columns in the grid. Click in the Key Type column of the CustomerID field and select Business Key from the drop-down list, as shown in Figure 10-22. Click the Next button to move on.

16. Specify the change types for various columns. As per the requirements set out in the initial statement of this exercise, you are to select all the address fields as the historical attribute, e-mail as the fixed attribute, and phone numbers as the changing attribute. Click in the first row of the Dimension Columns and select Address Line 1 from the drop-down list; then click in the Change Type field to set it as a historical attribute from the drop-down list. Set the different columns to different change types as per the following table.

Dimension Columns	Change Type
Address Line 1	Historical attribute
Address Line 2	Historical attribute
Address Line 3	Historical attribute
City	Historical attribute
State	Historical attribute
Country	Historical attribute
Email	Fixed attribute
Home Phone	Changing attribute
Work Phone	Changing attribute
Mobile Phone	Changing attribute

When you've configured all the columns, the wizard screen should look as shown in Figure 10-23. Click the Next button to move on.

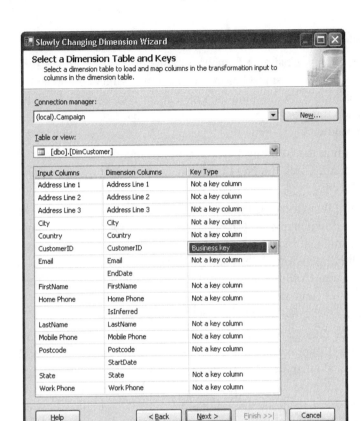

Figure 10-22 *Selecting Business Key in the SCD Wizard*

17. In the Fixed And Changing Attribute Options screen, uncheck the Fail The Transformation If Changes Are Detected In A Fixed Attribute option, because we will make changes to the Email field to test how it goes. In a production environment, you need to consider both of these options in light of your requirements. Click the Next button to open the Historical Attribute Options screen.

18. You have two options to record a Historical attribute. If you select a single column option, you can then select a column and the value pair to indicate the Current/ Expired or True/False values. Alternatively, you can select start and end dates to identify current and expired records. Select the radio button next to Use Start And End Dates To Identify Current And Expired Records. Select StartDate in the Start Date Column and EndDate in the End Date Column fields. Then select System:: StartTime in the Variable To Set Date Values field, as shown in Figure 10-24. This will update the values of StartDate and EndDate fields using the start time of the package provided by the specified system variable. Click the Next button.

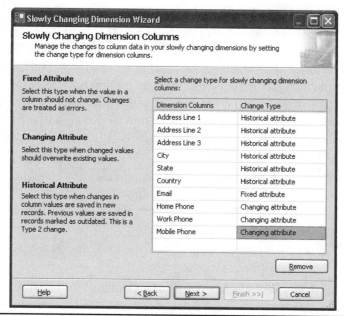

Figure 10-23   *Setting change types on the dimension columns*

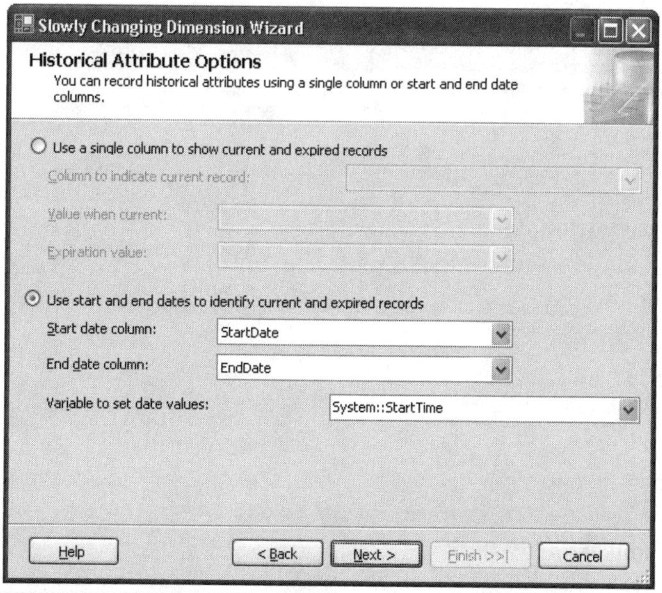

Figure 10-24   *Setting historical attribute options in the SCD Wizard*

19. By default, the inferred member support is enabled in the SCD transformation, and you can select from either of the two options to identify the inferred member record. In the first option, you can specify the column values for inferred members with change type equal to null and in the second option you specify an indicator column. Select the radio button for Use a Boolean Column To Indicate Whether The Current Record Is An Inferred Member. Select IsInferred Column from the drop-down list in the Inferred Member Indicator field as shown in Figure 10-25. Click the Next button to review the outputs summary of the SCD Wizard.

20. Click the Finish button after reviewing the summary information. The SCD Wizard will take a while to build the data flow for you, but when it's done, you will have a lot to review. After moving some of the components around, your data flow should look like the one shown in Figure 10-26.

The SCD Wizard has added a data flow to the four outputs out of six outputs available. Let's do a quick review.

▶ **Inferred Member Updates Output**   Double-click the OLE DB Command transformation attached to this output and go to the Component Properties tab. Check the SQL Statement in the SqlCommand field to find that this statement will update the DimCustomer table, where IsInferred = 1 for the matching CustomerID, and also sets IsInferred = 0 during update. Click Cancel.

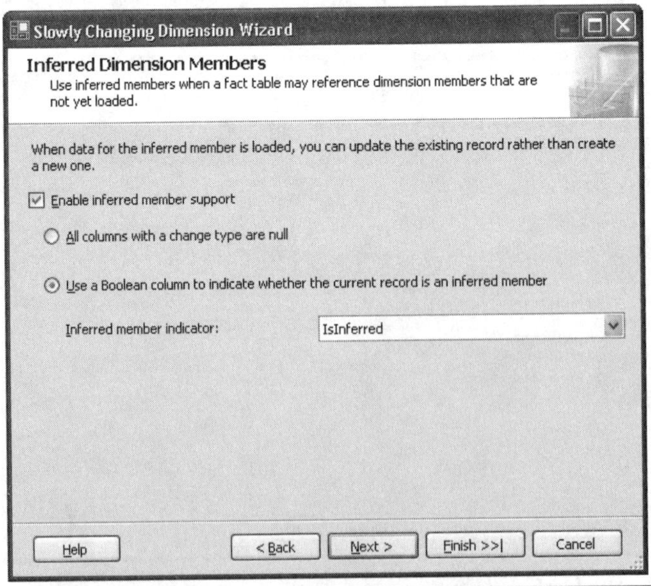

Figure 10-25   *Inferred member support in the SCD Wizard*

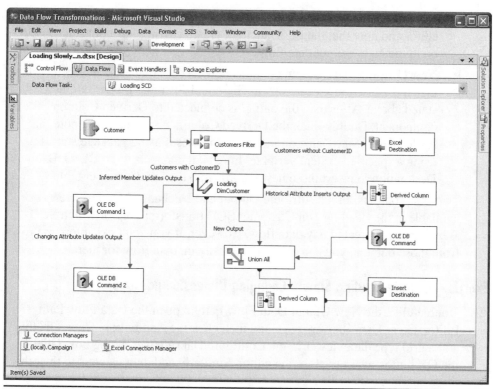

Figure 10-26   *Data flow created by the SCD Wizard*

▶ **Changing Attribute Updates Output**   Double-click the OLE DB
Command attached to this output and go to the Component Properties tab.
Check the SQL Statement in the SqlCommand field to find that this statement
will update the current records of the DimCustomer table for changes to
phone numbers for the matching CustomerID. Click Cancel to exit.

▶ **Historical Attribute Inserts Output**   Double-click the Derived Column
component attached to this output and note that this transformation creates
a new column EndDate and populates the package start time in this new
column. Click Cancel. Double-click the OLE DB Command attached to
the output of the Derived Column transformation and go to the Component
Properties tab. Check the SQL Statement in the SqlCommand field to find
that this statement will update the current records of the DimCustomer
table with the EndDate populated in the previous component for the
matching CustomerID. Click the Cancel button. The output from the OLE
DB Command is combined with the data flow of New Output using the

Union All component. Double-click the Union All component to open the editor and note that the EndDate field created earlier has not been passed on to the New Output data flow.

▶ **New Output** This output contains new records that are combined with the "to be inserted" records from Historical Attribute Inserts output as stated above. After that, the output is connected to Derived Column component. Double-click the Derived Column component and note that it adds a new StartDate column and populates it using package start time using a specified system variable. Finally, it connects to an OLE DB Destination to insert these new records into the DimCustomer table.

Two other outputs, Fixed Attribute Output and Unchanged Output, are available at the Loading DimCustomer SCD transformation for which SCD Wizard has not created any data flow. However, if you want to capture the rows from those outputs, you can create a downstream data flow for them.

Exercise (Execute Loading Slowly Changing Dimension package)

21. Double-click the New Output Data Flow Path to open the Data Flow Path Editor. Go to Data Viewers page and then click the Add button. Click OK to add a grid type data viewer in the Configure Data Viewer dialog box. Click the OK button again to close the editor. Similarly add data viewers to the other three outputs.

22. You are now ready to run this package. First, though, let's see the data that is going to be played and replayed to see the responses of SCD transformation to different changes. Open SQL Server Management Studio and connect to the database engine. Open a new query pane and run the following query to see records in the Customer table:

```
Select * from [Campaign].[dbo].[Customer]
```

Note that the Customer table contains 14 records and the CustomerID of the last four records is NULL. As per our package design, the Conditional Split transformation should filter out these records. Switch to BIDS, right-click the Loading Slowly Changing Dimension.dtsx package in the Solution Explorer, and choose Execute Package from the context menu.

As the package executes, four data viewers will pop up. If you move around on the screen, as shown in the Figure 10-27, you will note that the Customers Filter component diverts four rows to the Excel destination and sends the other 10 rows to Loading DimCustomer SCD transformation. Further, the SCD transformation identifies that all these records are in fact new records and diverts them to New Output. No records flows through any other output.

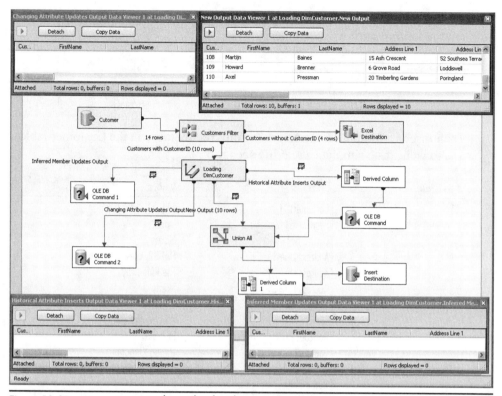

Figure 10-27 *Executing Loading Slowly Changing Dimension Package*

Click the Detach button on the New Output Data Viewer to let the data flow to the destination and be inserted into DimCustomer table. Click the Detach button on other data viewers and close them. Press SHIFT-F5 to return to design mode.

23. Let's make changes to Customer's data and see how this transformation works with them. Run the CustomerChanges.sql from the C:\SSIS\RawFiles folder in the query pane of SQL Server Management Studio. This script makes changes to the first three records in Customer table as follows:

CustomerID	Column Changed	New Value
101	[Home Phone]	020885711000
102	[Email]	peter.gormlay@AffordingIT.co.uk
103	[Address Line 1] [Address Line 2]	15 Abercrombie Avenue Wooburn Green

Then it adds an Inferred member record first in DimCustomer table with minimal information as shown here:

CustomerID	Columns	Value
111	[IsInferred]	1
	[StartDate]	getdate()

Then inserts additional information for inferred member in the Customer table, as shown next, to simulate a real life scenario:

CustomerID	Columns	Value
111	[CustomerID]	111
	[FirstName]	Mark
	[LastName]	Morris
	[Address Line 1]	Flat 22, Crescent Flats
	[Address Line 2]	The Ridgeway
	[Address Line 3]	Sketty
	[City]	Chertsey
	[State]	West Midlands
	[Postcode]	PE7 3RQ
	[Country]	United Kingdom
	[Email]	mmark@AffordingIT.co.uk
	[Home Phone]	
	[Work Phone]	
	[Mobile Phone]	079576516756

24. After running the CustomerChanges.sql script successfully, switch to BIDS and run the package again by pressing the F5 key. As the package executes, four data viewers will pop up on screen. First, you will see a record in the data viewer attached to Changing Attribute Updates output. Note that this is the record for which you changed the home phone number, which is allowed, and no history is to be kept. Click the Detach button to let it process. Then the data viewer attached to the Historical Attribute Inserts Output will display a record with CustomerID = 103. Note that this is the record that changed the address for which a history is to be kept. This record will first update the existing record with EndDate and then will be combined with the New Output using Union All transformations so as to be inserted as a new record. Click the Detach button to let it process. Next you will see that the data viewer attached to Inferred Member Updates Output shows up as a record with CustomerID = 111. This record will be updated in the DimCustomer table. Click the Detach button to let it process. The New Output path will also be processed and the package will complete.

25. Press SHIFT-F5 to switch back to design mode. Press CTRL-SHIFT-S to save all the files and close the project.

26. Switch to SQL Server Management Studio and check the DimCustomer table to see that it has been loaded with the expected values.

Review

This exercise has been explained in as much detail as possible; loading a dimension is a daily chore of a DBA's life. Loading a data warehouse dimension has been made easy with the Slowly Changing Dimension transformation, and configuring this transformation has been made easier still by the SCD Wizard. The SCD Wizard does so much work for you that you will probably use it every time you need to configure a SCD transformation.

Business Intelligence Transformations

The Business intelligence transformations enable you to perform data cleaning, data standardization, text mining operations, and run data mining prediction queries against data mining models. You will be performing a data cleaning Hands-On exercise to remove duplicates from data using Lookup, Fuzzy Lookup, and Fuzzy Grouping transformations.

Data Mining Query Transformation

You can use a Data Mining Query transformation whenever you want to perform prediction queries against data mining models. This transformation has one input and one output and no error output. The user interface for this transformation's editor has Mining Model and Query tabs. In the Connection Manager field of the Mining Model tab, you specify the Analysis Services Connection Manager to connect to an Analysis Services project or server. You select the mining structure from the drop-down list in the Mining Structure field. Once you've selected a mining structure, the Mining Models field lists the mining models associated with that mining structure.

In the Query tab, you can either type in your query or use the graphical query designer by clicking the Build New Query button. The graphical query designer helps you build Data Mining Extensions (DMX) queries. If you type directly in the query mode and later on switch to design mode, you will get a prompt alerting you that your changes may get lost. The designer in the query builder allows you to select mining models and data flow input columns from two list boxes. You can drag and drop fields from these boxes on to the designer cells and build custom DMX queries for evaluating data flow input data against an existing mining model.

You can create more than one prediction query using multiple mining models. However, the mining models you select must belong to the same mining structure.

Term Lookup Transformation

Using the Term Lookup transformation, you can count the number of times a text term occurs in the input data row and create custom word list along with word frequency statistics. This transformation reads the terms from a lookup table that can be in SQL Server 2000, SQL Server 2005, or in an Access database to look for matches in an input column and then adds two columns named Term and Frequency by default to the output containing the term and the count for the term. The transformation supports one input and one output and can do a lookup only on a column that is either the DT_WSTR or the DT_NTEXT data type.

After adding this transformation in the data flow, you can double-click it and open the editor. You will see the following three tabs.

▶ **Reference Table**   Specify an OLE DB Connection Manager and a reference table name from where the transformation can read lookup terms.

▶ **Term Lookup**   Map an input column to a reference column to specify the input column in which the terms are to be counted. You also select the columns that you want to pass through the data flow. Based on your selections, the InputColumnType property of the input column is set. Selecting a column only for pass-through sets the InputColumnType property to 0, mapping a column for lookup only sets the InputColumnType property to 1, and selecting a column for both pass-through and lookup operations sets the InputColumnType property to 2. This can be viewed by going to the Input Columns in Input and Output Properties tab of the Advanced Editor and looking at the properties of an input column.

▶ **Advanced**   Select to use a case-sensitive term lookup in which uppercase words are treated separate from lowercase words. However, if a word is a first word in a sentence and its first letter is capitalized, this can still match with a lowercase equivalent—so, for example, the word *travel* will match with the word *Travel* in the sentence "Travel in style and comfort."

From these configuration details, you can see that it is relatively straightforward to configure this transformation. The mechanics are also simple. This transformation loads the terms it is to lookup from the reference table in its private memory. It works in a fully pre-cached mode only, so it loads all the values before processing lookups against the input column. However, to get accurate results you need to understand how this transformation behaves for different types of matches. The Term Lookup transformation extracts the required term from the input column by breaking the text into sentences, breaking sentences into words, and then normalizing the words. To extract the matching term, this transformation observes the following rules:

- If you specify the singular form of the word or phrase in the reference table, this transformation will match both singular and plural forms of the word or phrase.

- If you use a plural form of the noun or noun phrase in the reference table, the transformation matches it only with a plural form of the noun or noun phrase in the input data.

- If you want to do a match for nouns and noun phrases that contain special characters such as %, @, &, $, #, *, :, ;, ., , , !, ?, <, >, +, =, ^, ~, |, \, /, (,), [,], {, }, ", and ', you can do so by including these special characters in the nouns and noun phrases in the reference table.

- The Term Lookup transformation returns only one result for any lookup input column in which multiple overlapping terms are involved.

- While normalizing the input column words, the Term Lookup transformation will affect the last word in the lemmatized noun phrase for normalization.

Term Extraction Transformation

Using a Term Extraction transformation, you can extract terms from the text of an input column and can thus build a list of terms used repeatedly in the input column for text mining and data analysis. This transformation, however, is limited in that it can extract only nouns or noun phrases or a combination of both, in English text only. It is aware of linguistic information about English and comes with its own English dictionary. At run-time, the Term Extraction transformation reads the specified input column and uses its internal algorithms and statistical models in line with the options you've selected to generate the output results. The output of this transformation contains only two columns, Term and Score by default. The Term column contains the extracted term while the Score column contains the number of times that term is found in the input column. To meet its objective of reading from an input column and writing to an output, this transformation supports one input and one output along with one error output. This transformation can extract terms from the input column that of either the DT_WSTR or DT_NTEXT data type.

Generally, you will use this transformation as the last transformation in that branch of the data flow as it doesn't let the input columns pass through. However, it does provide an output that contains only the two resulting output columns. When you open Term Extraction Transformation Editor, you will see the following three tabs:

▶ **Term Extraction**   In this tab, you can select an input column from the list of Available Input Columns from which you want this transformation to extract a term. You also can specify the names for the two output columns in this tab, which by default are Term and Score.

▶ **Exclusion**   You can choose to use exclusion terms by clicking the check box, which tell the transformation to exclude some of the terms from extraction. While you are trying to build a meaningful list of terms that you can use for data mining purposes, you may want to exclude certain terms because they are appearing everywhere and causing you to lose focus from key terms. You can specify the exclusion terms in a lookup table that must be in SQL Server 2000, SQL Server 2005, or Access. This lookup operation works in a fully pre-cached mode, which means that the transformation loads the exclusion terms from the lookup table into its private memory before it starts extracting terms from input column.

You specify an OLE DB Connection Manager to let it connect to the data source. Then you choose a table or view from the drop-down list, which this transformation can access using the OLE DB Connection Manager specified previously; finally you select the column from the drop-down list of columns that contains exclusion terms in the specified table or view.

▶ **Advanced**   This tab has four sections. In the Term Type section, select one of the radio buttons to specify that the term is a Noun, Noun phrase, or a combination of Noun and noun phrase. For this transformation, a noun is a single noun; a noun phrase is at least two words, of which one is a noun and the other one is a noun or an adjective. For example, *car* is a noun and *red car* is a noun phrase.

In the Score Type section, you choose either Frequency or TFIDF by selecting either of the radio buttons. While the Frequency represents the number of times the normalized term appears in the input, the TFIDF (Term Frequency Inverse Document Frequency) is a statistical technique used to evaluate the importance of a term in a document. This importance weight increases with the number of times the term or the word appears in the document but is also offset by the commonality of the word in all the documents. This is an important measure used in text mining and is often used by search engines.

In the Parameters section, you specify values for the frequency Threshold and the Maximum Length Of Term. Frequency Threshold is the minimum number of times a term must occur for it to be extracted and the Maximum Length Of Term is applicable for noun phrases only and specifies the maximum number of words in a noun phrase. For example, the noun phrase "top-of-the-line competition mountain bike" contains seven words.

You can select to use a case-sensitive match for extracting a term from the input column in the Options section. When you select this option, you tell the transformation to treat uppercase words different from lowercase words. In that case, *bicycle* and *Bicycle* will be treated as two separate terms. However, if *Bicycle* is the first letter in the sentence, it will still be treated as the same as *bicycle*.

As you can see, configuring this transformation for use in your package is not difficult; however, you need to work with it a few times to get the results you want to see, because this transformation behaves quite different with different types of terms in the data, so you need to work out exactly what you are going to get for a given set of data. The term extraction process is based on its internal English language dictionary and statistical model that may not be 100 percent accurate; however, understanding the process that this transformation uses to extract terms from the input column will help you get going. Following are the steps used by this transformation in the process of term extraction process:

▶ **Tokenizing** The Term Extraction transformation identifies words by first breaking down the text into sentences and then separating the words from the sentences. To break the text into sentences, this transformation reads ASCII line break characters such as a carriage return (0x0d) or a line feed (0x0a). It is clever enough to recognize other characters as a sentence boundary, such as a hyphen (-) or an underscore (_), when neither the character to the left nor to the right of a hyphen or an underscore is a letter. It can recognize an acronym separated by one or more periods (.) and does not break it into multiple sentences. For example, it does not convert G.T.I. into multiple sentences. After separating the sentences, it breaks down the sentences further into separate words using spaces, tab characters, line breaks, and other word terminators but preserves the words that are connected by hyphens or underscores. This transformation takes care of other special characters and is intelligent to extract the words properly, sometimes by separating the special characters and sometimes not. For example, (bicycle) is extracted as *bicycle*, whereas the term *you're* will generate only *you*. For more details on how this transformation handles tokenization, refer to Microsoft SQL Server 2005 Books Online.

▶ **Tagging** Depending upon your choice of Term type in the Advanced tab, the Term Extraction transformation will keep and tag only the words that match with your selection—i.e., if you've selected Noun Only, it will tag only the singular and plural nouns and reject all others; if you've selected Noun Phrase

Only, it will tag only the terms that have two or more words containing at least one noun. After the words have been separated out by the Tokenizing process, they are tagged as either a singular noun, plural noun, singular or plural proper noun, adjective, comparative or superlative adjective, or number. All other words are discarded.

▶ **Stemming**   After tagging the words, especially plural nouns that are not lemmatized, this transformation stems those words to their dictionary form by using its internal dictionary. For example, it converts cars to *car* and *lorries* to *lorry*.

▶ **Normalizing**   Once the words have been separated and tagged, they are normalized so that the capitalized words and non-capitalized are treated alike. This process converts the capitalized letters in a word (for example, first letter of a word may be capital because it is the first word in the sentence) to lowercase—so, for example, *Cars* becomes *car*. However, note that the capitalized words that are not the first word in a sentence are not normalized and are marked as proper nouns, which are not included in its internal dictionary and hence not normalized.

Fuzzy Grouping Transformation

This transformation is part of the Enterprise Edition of SQL Server 2005 and is designed to help in the data cleaning process by grouping duplicate records that appear in data in the data flow. At run-time, this transformation first groups together all the likely duplicate rows and then identifies a canonical row of data for each group. This identified canonical row and other likely duplicate rows are outputted after marking them with proper tokens in additional output columns. The duplicate rows are not deleted from the data; instead, they are outputted but marked so that you can identify and remove them from the data flow using the downstream components (such as Conditional split) if you want. This transformation uses a comparison algorithm to compare rows in the transformation input. You can customize this algorithm to be exhaustive if you want to compare every row in the input to the every other row in the input. Though this is quite an expensive method from the performance point of view it can yield more accurate results. To compare rows against each other in the input, this transformation creates temporary tables in an SQL Server 2005 database. To perform groupings of likely duplicate rows on the input data, this transformation supports one input and one output only.

When you add the Fuzzy Grouping transformation into the data flow of your package and open its editor, you will see the following three tabs.

Connection Manager Tab

You can create a new connection manager in this tab by clicking the New button, or you can select already configured OLE DB Connection Manager. While specifying the connection manager here, you need to think seriously about the operations that this transformation will be performing in the database using this connection. First of all, this transformation will create temporary tables and their indexes in the database, which requires that the user account you use in the connection manager setup must have necessary permissions to create tables in the database. Secondly, to compare rows against each other in the input dataset, the algorithm that this transformation uses will create temporary tables much larger than the input dataset. The size of the tables and indexes are proportional to the number of rows flowing through the transformation and the number of tokens you select to tokenize the data elements. This gets further aggravated if you select to perform an exhaustive comparison. This may put quite stringent requirements of space on the database to which this transformation is connecting. You must ensure that the referenced database has enough free space to perform a fuzzy comparison given the dataset and your selections while configuring this transformation.

Some performance controls are provided in this transformation. If you go to Component Properties tab of the Advanced Editor, you will see four properties under the Custom Properties section that help you fine-tune the balance between accuracy and performance. The Delimiters field lets you specify additional characters that you can use to separate strings into multiple words. Use only the required ones that generate the acceptable level of results. The Exhaustive property, discussed earlier, lets you specify whether you want to compare each input row with every other row in the input. If your dataset is a few thousand rows long, you can use this option without any major impact. However, if you are dealing with dataset that has millions of rows, consider using it only during the design and debugging phase or on a subset of data to fine-tune the similarity threshold requirements. You can also control memory requirements by using the MaxMemoryUsage property, for which you can specify a value in megabytes to limit its usage or specify 0 to enable dynamic memory usage based on requirements and available system memory. Finally, using MinSimilarity, you can specify the minimum similarity threshold value between 0 and 1. The closer the value to 1, the less rows will be selected as likely duplicates, which means less processing required by the transformation. Some of these properties are also available in the custom UI editor, which we will discuss as the properties are discussed.

Columns Tab

In the Columns tab, you select the columns that you want to pass through as is, the columns you want to compare with other rows in the input. When you select the check box in front of a column that column will be selected for comparison and a row will be added in the lower grid section of the editor window. In the grid, you can further specify the criteria you want this column to be compared against other columns. Using the Match Type field, you can either specify the column to be exactly matched or fuzzy matched. For the columns for which you select Match Type as Exact, the Minimum Similarity is set to 1, indicating that the column has to be matched 100 percent; however, for other columns that you set Match Type as Fuzzy, you can specify a Minimum Similarity value between 0 and 1. The column value closer to 1 indicates the closer it is matched. Using this, you can specify the values that match the rows that are approximately same. The transformation identifies duplicates with more efforts for the Minimum Similarity values closer to 1. Here you specify this value for each column. It is also possible to specify minimum similarity thresholds at the component level in the Advanced tab. At run-time, the Fuzzy Grouping transformation measures the similarity and groups together the rows on the basis of similarity score. The rows that fall below the specified minimum similarity score are not grouped together. In real life, you may not know the minimum similarity score that works for your data. You can determine it by running the Fuzzy Grouping transformation several times using different minimum similarity threshold values against the subset or sample data, which you can obtain using the Row Sampling or Percentage Sampling transformations. Once you find out the minimum similarity value, you can use it to group similar rows together.

So, in the output of the transformation, you will get all the input columns that you've selected to pass through or compare, the columns with standardized data (taken from canonical row), and a column containing the similarity score for each column that you select to participate in the Fuzzy grouping. The aliases of these columns are specified in the Similarity Output Alias fields in this tab. Finally, you can also use Comparison Flags, such as Ignore Case or Ignore Character Width, to specify how this transformation should handle the string data in the column while doing comparison.

Advanced Tab

At run-time, the transformation tokenizes each of the columns selected for comparison and then compares them against the columns of other rows. Based on the algorithm and the settings, it then produces output, which is basically one output row for each input row with additional columns that are specified in the Advanced tab. The Input key Column Name field contains the _key_in value by default, which is the name of a new column it adds in the output. You can change this name if you want. This new column, _key_in, contains a string value that uniquely identifies each row. The Output Key Column Name field also specifies the name assigned to a new column added in the output. By default, this name is _key_out and it can be changed. This new column, _key_out, contains a string value that is same for all the rows that have been identified as likely duplicates and grouped together. After having identified and grouped together the likely duplicates at run-time, it carries on to select a canonical row and copies its _key_in value in the _key_out column of all the rows in the group, making both values the same for the canonical row. This makes it possible for you to identify the rows in the group because they all have the same _key_out value, and the row that has _key_in value equal to _key_out value is the canonical row.

The third column added in the output is shown by the Similarity Score Column Name field, for which the default name is _score. This column holds values between 0 and 1, indicating the similarity of the input row to the canonical row. When the input row is selected as the canonical row, the value of _score is 1. For other rows in the group, the value of _score will vary depending on how closely they match with the canonical row. The more the similarity, the closer the value of _score will be to 1. The exact duplicates to the canonical row will also be included in the output and will have a _score of 1.

You can specify a value for the Similarity threshold attribute using the slider. You've used a similar attribute in the Columns tab called Minimum Similarity. That value is applied against each column, whereas the Similarity threshold is applied at the component level. The rows that have values smaller than the value you set for the Similarity threshold will not be considered as duplicates and hence will not be grouped together. As explained earlier, you may have to run the package containing a Fuzzy Grouping transformation several times to find the value that works with your data. Finally, you can select the Token Delimiters from space, tab, carriage return, and line feed by clicking the appropriate check boxes to tokenize data. You can also specify additional tokens in the Additional Delimiters field. This is the Delimiters property in the Advanced Editor discussed earlier in this transformation.

Fuzzy Lookup Transformation

Earlier you studied The Lookup transformation and also used it in a Hands-On exercise. You used the Lookup transformation to look for exact matches of Postcodes in the database table and to add a City column in the output; if there was no match for Postcode, the transformation extracted those rows into a flat file for your review. The Fuzzy Lookup transformation does more than the Lookup transformation because it can do a fuzzy match and return one or more similar matches from the lookup table. The Lookup transformation's strength is that it can enhance and standardize data by looking up matches from the reference table; however, this strength is limited by the fact that the lookup has to be an exact lookup—so, for example, Postcode has to match exactly. If you need to match First Name for *Stephen* who may write his name as *Steve* also, you can't use an exact match. Your matching criterion has to pick up similarity in the text in a matching column to locate matching data, and this is precisely why the Fuzzy Lookup transformation was designed. This transformation enables you to correct, standardize, and enrich data by providing missing information using fuzzy matching technique. As you would expect, the Fuzzy Lookup transformation has one input and one output to support its operation. This transformation is available in the Enterprise Edition of SQL Server 2005 and requires a connection to a SQL Server 2005 database to create temporary tables.

The Fuzzy Lookup transformation creates tokens of the data to be fuzzy matched and uses a lookup technique to fuzzy match these tokens. To create tokenized data, this transformation needs a SQL Server 2005 connection where it can create a temporary table and index to store the tokenized information. As it will be matching tokenized data, there is a possibility that this transformation may return more than one match for a row. These matches carry different confidence levels for determining how close the match is. This transformation also takes into consideration the minimum similarity value before outputting that a row as a possible match.

At design time, you specify the connection to the SQL Server 2005 database, select how you would like to create or use an existing match index, and then specify the columns you want to match for, pass through, and add in the output. You also specify the number of rows that should be outputted per lookup, similarity threshold before considering the row a match, and the token delimiters for tokenizing data. At run-time, the transformation creates or uses an existing match index to perform the fuzzy lookup and outputs the pass-through columns, plus the columns added from the lookup table, plus the additional columns carrying component level similarity score and confidence level information and the column level similarity score column for the each column that participates in performing a fuzzy lookup.

The custom UI for Fuzzy Lookup transformation is similar to that of the Lookup transformation. It provides three tabs.

Reference Table Tab

In the Reference Table tab, you specify the connection manager that this transformation uses to connect to the reference table and the match index options that this table will use to create, use, and maintain the index for fuzzy lookup matches. You specify the connection manager in the OLE DB Connection Manager field. Next, you choose whether to use and existing index or create a new index. At run-time, the Fuzzy Lookup transformation connects to the reference table using the specified OLE DB Connection Manager and creates a copy of the reference table, adds an integer data type key to the copied reference table, and builds an index on the key column. Then, this transformation tokenizes the data in the columns that you want to reference and stores them in an index table called *match index*.

You can select the Generate New Index radio button to specify the creation of the new match index each time the Fuzzy Lookup transformation runs. When you select this option, you can then select the reference table from the drop-down list in the Reference Table Name field. You will also see that the Store New Index option becomes available, which allows you to save the match index for use in the subsequent processing of this transformation. If you select the Store New Index check box, you can assign a name to the newly created index, which by default is FuzzyLookupMatchIndex. If you prefer to save the match index so that you can reuse it and avoid high processing costs at package run-time, you may want to keep this index fresh and up to date all the times—i.e., you may want to update the match index whenever the reference table is updated with new records. Select the Maintain Stored Index check box. The transformation then creates triggers on the reference table to keep the match index table synchronized with the reference table.

The process of creating a match index can be an expensive process depending upon the size of data you're dealing with. So this transformation provides a facility with which you can reuse an existing match index if the reference data is fairly static. When you select the Use Existing Index radio button, you can then choose a match index table from the drop-down list, which this transformation can use for repeated operations.

If you are dealing with millions of rows in the reference table, the recommended way to implement Fuzzy Lookup transformation will be to generate and save the match index the first time by running the package containing this transformation and then reusing it using the Use Existing Index option in subsequent executions of the package. You may also prefer to use Maintain Stored Index option to keep the match index updated. However, if you are thinking of using this option, you need to understand the effect of triggers on database performance and maintainability of reference table. Refer to Microsoft SQL Server 2005 Books Online for more details on how to manage triggers when using this option with the Fuzzy Lookup transformation.

Columns Tab

In the Available Input Columns you can select the Pass Through check boxes for the columns that you want to be passed through to the output as is. And in the Available Lookup Columns ,you can select the check boxes for the columns that you want to add in the output for the fuzzy lookup matching rows. You can create mappings in this tab between Available Input Columns and the Available Lookup Columns for which you want to perform lookup operations. The mappings you create here are visually different than those you create in the Lookup transformation because they are displayed as dotted lines in this transformation. You can perform exact matches for some of the columns in the Fuzzy Lookup transformation as long as you keep at least one column using Fuzzy match. You can specify the match type as Exact or Fuzzy using the JoinType property of the input columns in the Input and Output Properties tab of the Advanced Editor.

Advanced Tab

You set the Maximum number of matches to output per lookup by specifying an integer value in this field. At run-time, the transformation identifies matches considering similarity threshold and can return the matches up to the number you have specified in this option. These matches may contain duplicates if you're looking for more than one output per lookup. Next, you can specify the Similarity Threshold value using the slider. This value can be a floating-point value from 0 to 1. When you specify a similarity threshold here, you apply it at the component level. You can also apply a similarity threshold at the column level—also known as join-level—using the MinSimilarity property of the input columns, which is accessible in the Input and Output Properties tab of the Advanced Editor. The closer its value is to 1 for a row or a column, the closer the row or column will be to match against the reference table and qualify as a duplicate. As mentioned, the output also contains a column for confidence score. The combination of similarity score and confidence determines how close the input row or a column is to the reference table column or row. Similarity score describes the closeness or the textual similarity between the input columns and the reference table columns, whereas the confidence describes the quality of this fuzzy match. Columns having a high similarity score and high confidence score are the most likely candidates for duplicates; however, not all columns having high similarity score will always have high confidence score as well. You should understand a subtle difference between the two terms: for example, if you are looking for match on a series of cars, then the 3 series, 5 series, or 7 series returns a high similarity score but the confidence score will be poor. Similarly, if you are looking for a PC and the only term used in reference table is *Personal Computer*, then the confidence for this will be high whereas similarity, as you can see, is low.

Finally, you can select the token delimiters by clicking the check boxes provided for space, tab, carriage return, and line feed default delimiters. You can also specify Additional Delimiters in the provided field. Delimiters are the characters used to tokenize and separate fuzzy match fields into the words used for matching and scoring.

Other Considerations

Having configured all the options, you are ready to run the transformation. However, consider the following performance issues before you begin:

▶   As this transformation needs an SQL Server 2005 connection to create and maintain a match index table, connecting to a database server that has lots of free space is advisable. At index creation time, the reference table is locked by this transformation, so consider using another machine for the reference table if multiple users access this table. Also, it is a good idea to copy the reference table to a non-production server if the data changes regularly, especially during package execution, in which case results may be inconsistent.

▶ The Exhaustive property in the Custom Properties section of Component Properties in the Advanced Editor can be set to True or False. This property yields more accurate results if set to True. However, setting the Exhaustive property to True should be done with care, because it will mean that each row in the input will be matched against every row in the reference table. Also, to perform this match, the entire reference table will be loaded in to the main memory, which will put high pressure on memory requirements. If your reference table is extremely large and you have little free memory available, avoid using this option. However, for smaller reference table with lots of free memory on the system, setting this option to True will yield better results.

▶ You can specify the maximum amount of memory in megabytes that this transformation is allowed using the MaxMemoryUsage option. Specifying a maximum amount of memory to match its requirements will greatly improve its performance. However, if not enough free memory is available on the system or you do not know how much memory will be required by this transformation, you can specify a value of 0, which indicates that the transformation will manage memory dynamically based on the requirements and available free memory.

▶ You can manage memory on the basis of input rows. If you have many input rows to process, you can set WarmCaches to True to indicate that the match index and the reference table are to be loaded into memory. This can greatly enhance the performance by caching reference data and index in the main memory before the transformation starts processing input rows.

Hands-On: Removing Duplicates from Owners Data

The Fuzzy Lookup and Fuzzy Grouping transformations provided in Integration Services are the main components that provide data cleaning facility. One of the main issues with data quality is to remove duplication in data whether it occurs at loading time or it already exists in the data that you want to cleanse. Till now, you've worked on a couple of instances to remove duplicates in the earlier Hands-On exercises, but those instances were dealing with exact duplicates. In this exercise, you will deal with fuzzy duplication of data. You will work with these components to remove exact as well as fuzzy duplicates from the input data.

You are maintaining an Owner table that contains contact details for the owners of your products. You regularly receive Owners data feed that sometimes contains duplicate data. This duplicate data is not consistent, as users tend to provide their details differently at different occasions. You need to make sure no duplicate record is added to the Owner table.

Method

You have the Owner table in the Campaign database and receive OwnersFeed.xls files regularly that contain owner records. This Excel file can contain duplicate records for the same person. The complication, however, is that these records may not be exact duplicates, as persons provide their contact details differently at different occasions. Our sample OwnersFeed.xls file contains 13 records, of which 3 are unique records and the other 2 records have five variants each, with different name spellings and address details; one of these 2 records already exists in the Owner table. Open the OwnersFeed.xls file to have a look at the incoming data (see Figure10-28).

The owner with first name Johnathon already exists in the table and has five different variants of contact details. The other owner with first name Katherine is a new owner but has five different variants of contact details in the feed. You want to load four records into the Owner table consisting of three unique records plus the owner record for Katherine. All the duplicate variants and the owner record for

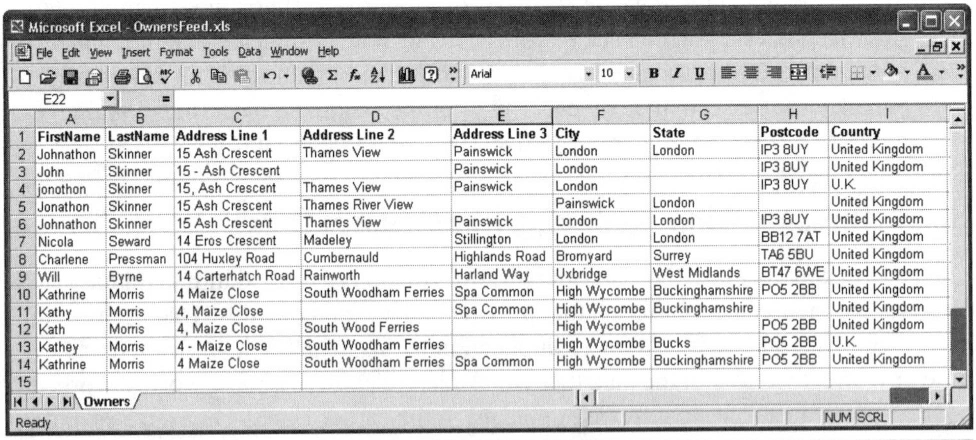

	A	B	C	D	E	F	G	H	I
1	FirstName	LastName	Address Line 1	Address Line 2	Address Line 3	City	State	Postcode	Country
2	Johnathon	Skinner	15 Ash Crescent	Thames View	Painswick	London	London	IP3 8UY	United Kingdom
3	John	Skinner	15 - Ash Crescent		Painswick	London		IP3 8UY	United Kingdom
4	jonothon	Skinner	15, Ash Crescent	Thames View	Painswick	London		IP3 8UY	U.K.
5	Jonathon	Skinner	15 Ash Crescent	Thames River View		Painswick	London		United Kingdom
6	Johnathon	Skinner	15 Ash Crescent	Thames View	Painswick	London	London	IP3 8UY	United Kingdom
7	Nicola	Seward	14 Eros Crescent	Madeley	Stillington	London	London	BB12 7AT	United Kingdom
8	Charlene	Pressman	104 Huxley Road	Cumbernauld	Highlands Road	Bromyard	Surrey	TA6 5BU	United Kingdom
9	Will	Byrne	14 Carterhatch Road	Rainworth	Harland Way	Uxbridge	West Midlands	BT47 6WE	United Kingdom
10	Kathrine	Morris	4 Maize Close	South Woodham Ferries	Spa Common	High Wycombe	Buckinghamshire	PO5 2BB	United Kingdom
11	Kathy	Morris	4, Maize Close		Spa Common	High Wycombe	Buckinghamshire		United Kingdom
12	Kath	Morris	4, Maize Close	South Wood Ferries		High Wycombe		PO5 2BB	United Kingdom
13	Kathey	Morris	4 - Maize Close	South Woodham Ferries		High Wycombe	Bucks	PO5 2BB	U.K.
14	Kathrine	Morris	4 Maize Close	South Woodham Ferries	Spa Common	High Wycombe	Buckinghamshire	PO5 2BB	United Kingdom
15									

Figure 10-28 *Incoming data contains variants of duplicate records*

Johnathon should be removed by the Integration Services package. The following steps are involved in the development of this package:

▶ Create a new package, add the Data Flow task, and add the Excel Source to get the data in the data flow.

▶ Remove exact duplicates from the OwnersFeed file using the Sort and Lookup transformation.

▶ After removing exact and matched duplicates, you will use the Fuzzy Lookup transformation to remove fuzzy matched duplicates.

▶ At this stage the data will be left with only the duplicates that exist in variant forms in the input file only and not in Owner table. You will remove the duplicates using the Fuzzy Grouping transformation.

▶ Finally, you'll execute the package to see how the various transformations remove the duplicate data.

Exercise (Create Removing Duplicate Owners Package)

1. Open the Data Flow transformations project in BIDS. Right-click the SSIS Packages in Solution Explorer and choose the New SSIS Package option to add a new SSIS package named Package1.dtsx. Rename the package **Removing Duplicates.dtsx** and click the Yes button on the pop-up dialog box to confirm the new name.

2. Drop the Data Flow task from the Toolbox onto the Control Flow surface and rename it **Removing Duplicates from OwnersFeed**.

3. Double-click Removing Duplicates from OwnersFeed to go to Data Flow panel. Drop the Excel Source from the Toolbox onto the Data Flow surface. Rename the Excel Source **OwnersFeed**.

4. Double-click OwnersFeed to open Excel Source Editor. Click the New button next to the OLE DB Connection Manager field. Type **C:\SSIS\RawFiles\ OwnersFeed.xls** in the Excel File Path field. Leave the First Row Has Column Names option checked. Click the OK button to add an Excel Connection Manager and return to the Excel Source Editor. Leave Table Or View selected in the Data Access Mode field. Click in the Name Of The Excel Sheet field and select Owners$ from the drop-down list.

5. Go to the Columns page and verify that all the columns have been selected. Click the OK button to close the Excel Source Editor.

6. Right-click the Excel Connection Manager in the Connection Managers area and choose Rename from the context menu. Rename it **OwnersFeed Connection**.

7. Right-click anywhere on a blank surface in the Connection Managers area and choose New Connection from the context menu. Select Excel from the Connection Manager Type list and click the Add button. This will open the Excel Connection Manager dialog box. Type **C:\SSIS\RawFiles\DuplicateOwners.xls** in the Excel File Path field. Leave the First Row Has Column Names check box selected and click the OK button to add this connection manager. Once added, rename this connection manager **DuplicateOwners Connection**. Press CTRL-SHIFT-S to save all the files.

Exercise (Remove Exact Duplicates)

If you look at the data in the Figure 10-28, you will see that Johnathon Skinner and Katherine Morris have duplicate records in the OwnersFeed. You will use a Sort transformation to remove these duplicates. Then you will check the OwnersFeed to see whether any of the record exists in the Owner table. Johnathon Skinner also exists in the Owner table and will be removed from the input data flow using a Lookup transformation. The other variants of these owners will remain unaffected and will have to be dealt with separately.

8. Drop the Sort transformation onto the Data Flow surface and join OwnersFeed with it using the green path.

9. Double-click the Sort transformation to open the editor. Select all the Available Input Columns starting with FirstName, as shown in Figure 10-29. Select the check box for Remove Rows With Duplicate Sort Values and click OK to close the editor. Rename Sort transformation **Removing Exact Duplicates by Sort Key**.

10. Add a Lookup transformation to the data flow and join the Sort transformation by dragging the green arrow on to it.

11. Double-click the Lookup transformation to open the Lookup transformation Editor. Click the New button next to the OLE DB Connection Manager field and choose (local).Campaign connection manager. Then click OK. Choose [dbo].[owner] table from the drop-down list in the Use A Table Or A View field.

12. Go to the Columns tab, and note that all the mappings will be created for you between Available Input Columns and the Available Lookup Columns. Click to select the OwnerID column in the Available Lookup Columns to add it as a new column in the output (see Figure 10-30). In this transformation, you are matching input records with the records in the Owner table and for the matching record, you are adding OwnerID in the output to indicate the record with which a match has been found. Click the OK button to close this editor. Rename the Lookup transformation **Removing Exact Duplicates by Lookup**.

13. Drop an Excel destination just below Removing Exact Duplicates by Lookup and join both of these components. Rename this Excel Destination **Exact Duplicates**.

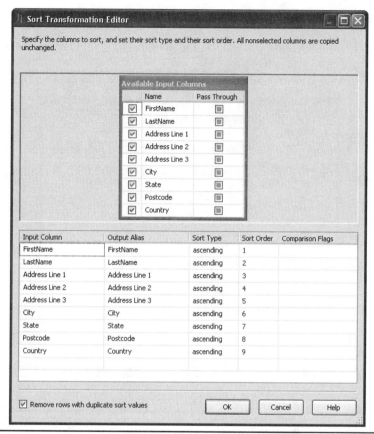

Figure 10-29   *Removing exact duplicates using a Sort transformation*

14. Double-click the Excel Destination to configure it. Choose DuplicateOwners Connection in the OLE DB Connection Manager field if it's not already selected.

15. Click the New button next to the Name Of The Excel Sheet field and verify the CREATE TABLE statement that it is creating an Exact Duplicates table (i.e., a worksheet in Excel). Click OK to accept. Go to the Mappings page to create the necessary column mappings automatically. Click the OK button to close this editor.

Exercise (Remove Fuzzy Duplicates)

You've extracted exact duplicates from the Lookup transformation to an Excel destination. Now you will redirect the remaining rows to a Fuzzy Lookup and

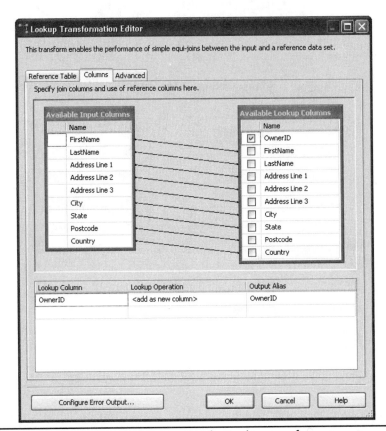

Figure 10-30   *Removing exact duplicates using the Lookup transformation*

extract the duplicates using fuzzy match logic. You will be removing all the variants of Johnathon Skinner.

16. Drop a Fuzzy Lookup transformation onto the Data Flow surface to the right of Removing Exact Duplicates by Lookup component. Click Removing Exact Duplicates by Lookup and drag and drop the red arrow onto the Fuzzy Lookup transformation. Configure the Error Output dialog box to change Error and Truncation column values from Fail Component to Redirect Row by choosing options in the drop-down menus. Click the OK button to close the dialog box. You have redirected all the remaining rows that did not match in the exact lookup operation to the Fuzzy Lookup transformation.

17. Double-click the Fuzzy Lookup transformation and make sure Generate New Index Radio Button is selected. Select the [dbo].[Owner] table from the drop-down list in the Reference Table Name field. Go to the Columns tab.

18. As the data is flowing through the error output of Lookup transformation, two error columns are added in the Available Input Columns. Uncheck the Pass Through check boxes for ErrorCode and ErrorColumn columns in the Available Input Columns and check the OwnerID column in the Available Lookup Columns to add it in the fuzzy matched records, as shown in Figure 10-31.

19. Go to the Advanced page and set the Maximum Number Of Matches To Output Per Lookup equal to 3. Slide the Similarity Threshold slider to 0.30. Click the OK button to close the Transformation Editor. Rename this transformation as **Identifying Duplicates by Fuzzy Lookup**.

20. Drop the Conditional Split transformation just below the Identifying Duplicates by Fuzzy Lookup transformation and connect both the components using a green data flow path. Double-click the Conditional Split to edit it. You need to identify the duplicates using _Similarity and _Confidence columns added by the Fuzzy

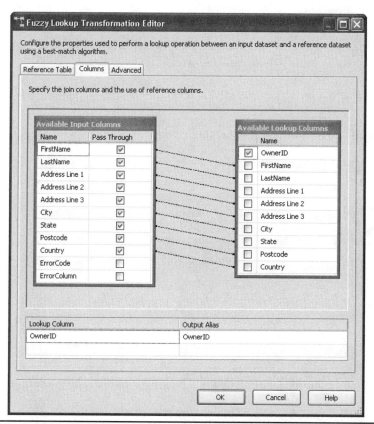

Figure 10-31 *Identifying fuzzy matched records with Fuzzy Lookup*

Lookup transformation in the pipeline. You may have to run your package several times before you can get workable values for this identification. Here, I've done the work for the exercise data we have; add the following in the Condition field:

```
_Similarity >= 0.60 && _Confidence >= 0.85
```

Type **Fuzzy Lookup Matches** in the Output Name field and **Remaining Owners** in the Default Output Name field, as shown in Figure 10-32. Click the OK button to close the editor. Rename this transformation **Splitting Fuzzy Matched Duplicates**.

21. Drop an Excel Destination below the Conditional Split transformation and join both of these components using a green arrow. Select Fuzzy Lookup Matches in the Output field of Input Output Selection dialog box. Rename this Excel Destination **Fuzzy Matched Duplicates**.

22. Double-click the Excel Destination to configure it. Select DuplicateOwners Connection in the OLE DB Connection Manager field if it is not already selected.

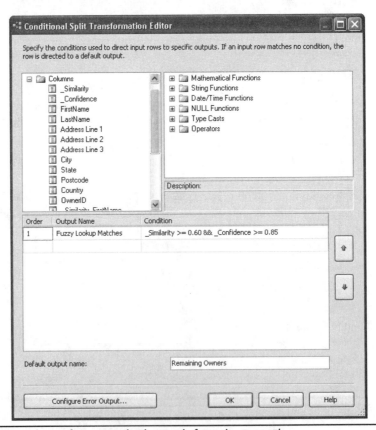

Figure 10-32   *Splitting fuzzy matched records from the Data Flow.*

23. Click the New button next to Name Of The Excel Sheet field, verify in the CREATE TABLE statement that is creating the Fuzzy Matched Duplicates table (i.e., the worksheet in Excel), and click OK to accept. Go to the Mappings page to create necessary column mappings automatically. Note that apart from adding _Similarity and _Confidence columns, the Fuzzy Lookup transformation has added one _Similarity_ColumnName column for each column that participated in the fuzzy match. Click the OK button to close this editor.

Exercise (Remove Duplicates by Fuzzy Grouping)

Here you will remove duplicate variants of the Katherine Morris entries. These records do not exist in the reference table but appear multiple times in the input file in variant forms. You will capture the Remaining Owners from Split transformation and use Fuzzy Grouping to identify canonical row and the likely duplicates.

24. Drop Fuzzy Grouping in the pipeline to the right of the Splitting Fuzzy Duplicates component. Click Splitting Fuzzy Duplicates and then drag the available green arrow from the Splitting Fuzzy Duplicates and drop it on the Fuzzy Grouping transformation.

25. Double-click the Fuzzy Grouping transformation and verify that (local). Campaign is selected in the OLE DB Connection Manager field. Go to the Columns tab. Note that all the Available Input Columns have Pass Through check boxes selected. Uncheck all of them. Select only the columns that are coming from OwnersFeed—i.e., from FirstName to Country, as shown in Figure 10-33. As you select these columns, a line corresponding to each selected column will be added in the grid. Type **0.25** in the Minimum Similarity column for the FirstName and LastName cells.

26. Go to the Advanced tab and set the Similarity threshold to 0.50 using the slider. Click the OK button to close this editor. Rename the Fuzzy Grouping transformation **Identifying Duplicates by Fuzzy Grouping**.

27. Drop the Conditional Split transformation just below the Identifying Duplicates by Fuzzy Grouping transformation and connect both the components using a green data flow path. Double-click the Conditional Split to edit it. You need to split the duplicates using _key_in and _key_out columns added by the Fuzzy Grouping transformation in the pipeline. Add the two rows in the grid by adding the following in the Condition field:

```
_key_in == _key_out
_key_in != _key_out
```

Type **Canonical Row** in the first row and **Fuzzy Grouped Matches** in the second row of Output Name field, as shown in Figure 10-34. Click the OK button to close the editor. Rename this transformation **Splitting Fuzzy Grouped Duplicates**.

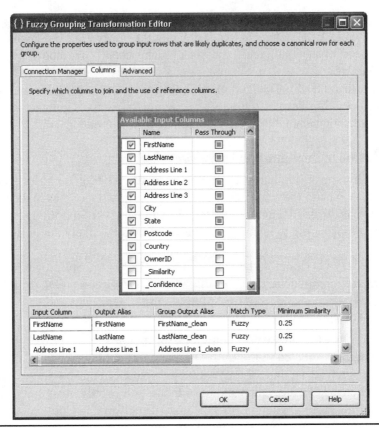

Figure 10-33   *Identifying and grouping duplicates using the Fuzzy Grouping transformation*

28. Drop an Excel Destination just below the Splitting Fuzzy Grouped Duplicates component and join both of these components using the green arrow. Select Fuzzy Grouped Matches in the Output field of Input Output Selection dialog box and click the OK button. Rename this Excel destination **Fuzzy Grouped Duplicates**.

29. Double-click the Excel destination to configure it. Select DuplicateOwners Connection in the OLE DB Connection Manager field if it's not already selected.

30. Click the New button next to Name Of The Excel Sheet field and verify in the CREATE TABLE statement that it is creating the Fuzzy Grouped Duplicates table (i.e., worksheet in Excel); then click OK to accept. Go to the Mappings page to create the necessary column mappings automatically. Note that apart from adding

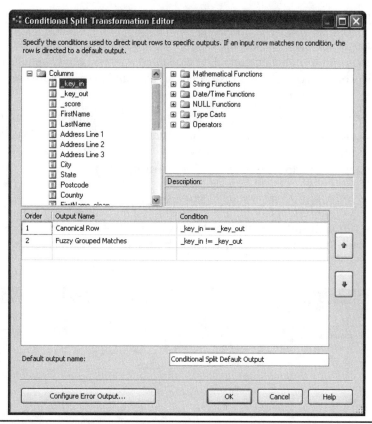

Figure 10-34 *Splitting fuzzy grouped and unique records in the data flow*

_key_in, _key_out and _score columns, the Fuzzy Lookup transformation has added one _Similarity_ColumnName column for each column that participated in the fuzzy grouping. Click the OK button to close this editor.

31. Drop an OLE DB destination on the Data Flow surface below the Splitting Fuzzy Grouped Duplicates component and join the component to the OLE DB destination using the available green arrow. Select Canonical Row in the Output field of Input Output Selection dialog box and click the OK button.

32. Double-click the OLE DB destination and select [dbo].[Owner] table in the Name Of The Table Or The View field. Go to the Mappings page and verify that the necessary mappings have been automatically created. Click the OK button to close this editor. Rename the OLE DB Destination **Owner**. Press CTRL-SHIFT-S to save all the files in the project.

Exercise (Execute Removing Duplicates Package)

33. You can add the data viewers after each transformation to see the records that have been removed from the pipeline. I've explained how you can re-run the package to see the workings of various transformations over and over. As a first go, just run it without any data viewer.

34. Press F5 to execute the package. When the package completes execution, note the number of records after each transformation (see Figure 10-35).

Following is an explanation of the execution results:

► The Excel source brings 13 rows into the data flow.

► The Sort transformation removes two exact duplicate records—one for Johnathon Skinner and one for Katherine Morris.

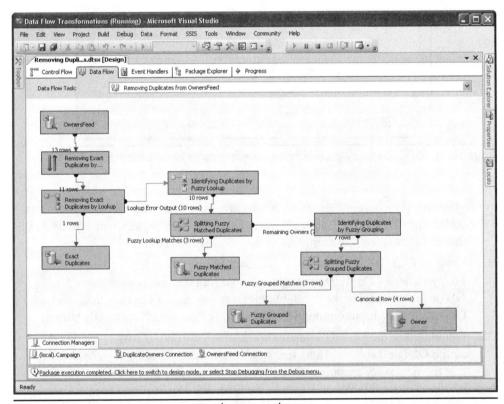

Figure 10-35 *Executing Removing Duplicates package*

▶ The Lookup transformation then matches Johnathon Skinner in the reference table and diverts it to the Excel destination; the remaining 10 rows are then passed on to the Fuzzy Lookup transformation.

▶ The Fuzzy Lookup transformation fuzzy matches John, Jonothon, and Jonathon with the Johnathon in the reference table and marks all three records with a high similarity and confidence score. This high similarity and confidence score is then used by the Conditional Split transformation to filter out these three records to the Excel destination.

▶ The remaining seven records are then passed on to Fuzzy Grouping transformation, which looks for records that are likely duplicates in the data flow and groups them together using _key_in, _key_out, and _score column values. These values are then used by the conditional Split transformation to filter out records for Kathy, Kath, and Kathey that are fuzzy grouped together. The remaining four unique records are then sent to the OLE DB destination for loading into the Owner table.

Review

You've seen various types of duplicates and the methods for removing them in this package. This package will give you a kick start into real life de-duplication problems. However, bear in mind that whenever you use Fuzzy Lookup and Fuzzy Group transformations, you need to find the similarity threshold values by running the package on a sample data that correctly represents the main data. The more effort you put into find the value of the similarity threshold that works with your data, the more accurate your results.

If you want to re-run the package, you need to execute the following SQL statement against the Campaign database in the SQL Server Management Studio. This will refresh the Owner table for you to run the package with the same results.

```
USE Campaign;
DROP TABLE [dbo].[Owner];
SELECT * INTO [dbo].[Owner] FROM Owner_original;
```

Summary

Having used lots of Data Flow transformations, you must by now feel a lot more confident and ready for real life challenges. You have used various transformations to perform functions such as pivoting, sorting, performing an exact lookup for de-duplication of data, and standardizing data, fuzzy lookup, and fuzzy group to eliminate duplicates in a pipeline, aggregate data, and load a slowly changing dimension table. You've also studied several other pre-configured transformations that are straightforward to use in your packages. Having come so far, you can now create control flow and data flow in your packages to perform workflow and transformation functions, store and manage your SSIS packages, and secure them as well. This chapter ends the development related stuff about Integration Services packages. In the next chapter, you will study how to deploy your packages in an enterprise environment.

Deploying Integration Services Packages

Till now you have learned how to build SSIS packages on a server and run them from within BI Development Studio (BIDS) or using the dtexec command prompt utility, but you have not deployed the packages to other servers. In real life, you may be required to develop packages on development environments and then deploy them in the production environment. The predecessor of SSIS i.e., DTS 2000 struggled with the limitation of moving packages between development, test, and production environments. Typically, you had to edit your packages manually to point the connection objects to the server to which you were deploying your packages. DTS 2000 used an object called the Dynamic Properties task to update package properties with the values retrieved from sources outside a DTS package during run-time to overcome the deployment issues, but this wasn't sufficient to address the problems associated with complex deployments. This object has been removed from the SSIS object model and has been replaced with SSIS package configurations.

SQL Server 2005 Integration Services addresses this issue, as you will learn in this chapter. You will use different tools and utilities to deploy a package in a step by step process. Using package configurations, you can update properties of package elements at run-time, create a deployment utility to deploy the package, and finally run the Installation Wizard to install the package either to the file system or to an instance of SQL Server 2005.

The following table lists the deployment journey of a package:

Action	Tool Used	Result
Create package	SSIS Import and Export Wizard or BIDS	An SSIS package created in XML format—e.g., package.dtsx.
Create package configurations	BIDS Package Creation Wizard	Package configurations created in XML/SQL.
Create deployment utility	Build project from within Solution Explorer	Package deployment utility with manifestation file.
Install package	Package Installation Wizard	Package deployed in SQL or file system.

The first step in the deployment journey is to create a package, which you have already learned in other chapters; you will be using those packages here to learn about the various aspects of deployment.

Package Configurations

The next step in the deployment journey after having created a package is to create package configurations. By now, you should understand the versatility of variables and their preferable use in packages over hard-coding the values. Also in Integration Services, you can update the variable values using other components at run-time to add some dynamics to your package. This concept has been extended to properties of SSIS control flow components by package configurations. As mentioned, package configurations allow properties of a package, its control flow container, or any of the tasks, variables, or connection managers to be changed at run-time. Package configurations are in fact property/value pairs that you use to update the values of properties of a package or its control flow components at run-time. The package configurations make deploying a package to the other servers easier by allowing you to update properties exposed by the package and its tasks at run-time without actually editing them. You can use the same configurations to deploy a package to several servers.

To use package configurations, you must first enable them for your package using the Package Configurations Organizer utility provided in BIDS. Once enabled, you can add package configurations. You can define more than one configuration for a package or apply the same configuration to more than one package defined in your solution. You can enable package configurations for one of your packages without affecting the way the configurations are used in other packages. Various storage options are available for storing your configurations, including reading them directly from the environmental variables. The storage options for package configurations, discussed in detail in the following section, include an XML configuration file, an SQL Server table, a registry entry, or a variable.

Types of Package Configurations

You can open the Package Configurations Organizer dialog box by choosing the Package Configurations option under the SSIS menu and enable the package configurations. After you add package configurations, you will choose the configuration types (see Figure 11-1) in the Package Configuration Wizard before you can proceed to building package configurations.

Depending on the configuration type you choose here, the package configurations will be stored to different storage locations. The following list shows five different types of stores supported by Integration Services package configurations. You can

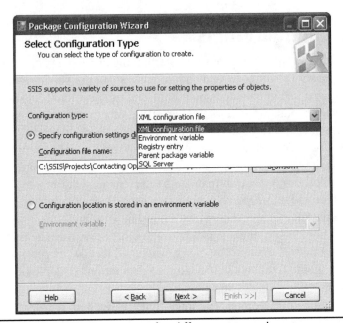

Figure 11-1   *Choosing configuration type for different storage locations*

choose any of these configuration types while adding a package configuration using the Package Configuration Wizard:

► XML configuration file

► Environment variable

► Registry entry

► Parent package variable

► SQL Server table

XML Configuration File

When you select XML Configuration File in the Package Configuration Wizard, you must then provide an XML file name, including the path. Here you can create a new configuration file or open an existing file. Then you will be able to select any of the properties or variable to add to the configuration file. You can include multiple property/value pairs of configurations within the same configuration object using an XML configuration file type. Selecting an executable (container) or a task adds all the configurable properties in the scope of that container or task.

If you open the configuration file after it has been created, using any XML editor or Notepad, you will notice that the root element, <DTSConfiguration>, has two child elements, <DTSConfigurationHeading> and <Configuration>. The <DTSConfigurationHeading> element contains details about the file, such as the name of the login that generated the file, the package name, the ID from where this file was generated, and the generated date; the <Configuration> element contains information about the configurations, such as the property path and the configured value.

Environment Variable

Selecting this option in the Package Configuration Wizard allows you to choose an environment variable from the list provided. Using this type of configuration allows you to update a property directly based on an environment variable.

Registry Entry

Integration Services allows you to store the configuration in a registry key by using the Registry Entry configuration type. When you select this configuration type, you must then specify a registry key and choose a target property that will have its value updated by the registry key.

Parent Package Variable

When the Package Execute task in the parent package is using your package as a child package, you may want to use a variable defined in the parent package to set a property in the child package. To do this, you use the Parent Package Variable configuration type in the Package Configuration Wizard. You can then specify a variable name defined in the parent package to store the configuration value used to set a property in the child package.

The package configurations are applied at package loading time and not at execution, which occurs after the package is loaded and the configurations have been applied. So, when you run the package, first the package is loaded, then package configurations are applied, and then the package is executed, though there is one exception to this: when you use the Parent Package Variable configuration option, the configuration is applied at the execution time. This makes perfect logical sense, as the parent package variable needs to be already populated by the time the child package is executed.

SQL Server

By choosing SQL Server as the configuration type in the Package Configuration Wizard, you can specify a table or create a new table to store the configurations.

The connection to the database that you have selected to host the table can be created as a new OLE DB Connection Manager or you can specify an already existing connection manager. This configuration creates ConfigurationFilter, ConfiguredValue, PackagePath, and ConfiguredValueType columns in the new table you create.

Using the SQL Server configuration type, you can store multiple property/value pairs of configurations within the same configuration object. You can use the SQL Server configuration type to store all the configurations for your project in the same table and use it as a central store to keep configurations.

Hands-On: Applying Configurations to Contacting Opportunities

In this Hands-On exercise, you will use package configurations to change e-mail addresses and demonstrate how package configurations can affect the working of a package. For demonstration purposes, you will use Mailing Opportunities.dtsx package you built in Chapter 4.

Method

As you will be modifying an existing package, to avoid any confusion with package names, you will create a new project in which you will add the Mailing Opportunities.dtsx package with a new name: Mailing Opportunities With Configurations.dtsx. You will then open the newly added package Mailing Opportunities With Configurations.dtsx and enable package configurations. The ToLine property of the Mailing Opportunities task determines who will receive the e-mail message. You will change this property in the package configuration file to demonstrate how the properties of a package can be modified at run-time.

Exercise (Enable and Add Package Configurations)

You will enable configurations using the Package Configurations Organizer utility provided in BIDS. Then you will add a ToLine configuration in the package.

1. Choose Start | All Programs | Microsoft SQL Server 2005, and run SQL Server BIDS. Create a new Integration Services package with the following details:

Name	Contacting Opportunities With Configurations
Location	C:\SSIS\Projects

2. Go to the Solution Explorer and right-click the SSIS Packages node. Choose Add Existing Package to open the Add Copy of Existing Package dialog box. Select File System in the Package Location field and specify **C:\SSIS\Projects\ Contacting Opportunities\Mailing Opportunities.dtsx** in the Package Path field. Click the OK button to add this package. When the package is added, right-click the Mailing Opportunities.dtsx package and choose Rename from the context menu. Rename this package **Mailing Opportunities With Configurations.dtsx** and click OK in the confirmation dialog box. Then click Package.dtsx and press the del et e key on the keyboard to delete this blank package. Click the OK button on the confirmation dialog box.

3. Double-click the Mailing Opportunities With Configurations.dtsx package to load it. When the package is loaded completely, right-click anywhere on the blank surface of the Designer and choose Package Configurations from the context menu. This will open the Package Configurations Organizer dialog box. You can also open it by choosing SSIS | Package Configurations.

4. Select the Enable Package Configurations check box. Any configurations you define in other packages in your multi-package project will remain unaffected whether you enable or disable configurations for your current package.

5. Now you can add configurations in this package. Click the Add button to start the Package Configuration Wizard. Click the Next button on the Welcome screen.

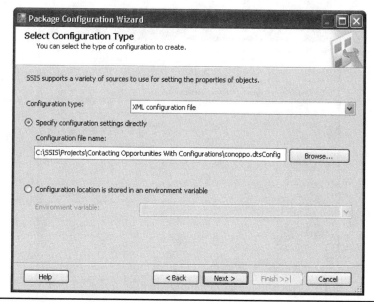

Figure 11-2 *Specifying configurations directly*

6. Leave the XML Configuration File option selected in the Configuration Type field.

7. Next, choose to specify a configuration directly or indirectly by using an environmental variable to pass the value. In this exercise, you will use the direct package configuration. In the Specify Configuration Settings Directly field, type the file name and path for XML configuration file as shown in Figure 11-2— **C:\SSIS\Projects\Contacting Opportunities With Configurations\conoppo .dtsConfig**. Note that the package configuration file has a .dtsConfig extension when saved as an XML file. Click the Next button.

8. In the Select Properties to Export page, you can select to export the Variables, properties of the package, properties of the connection managers, or properties of any of the executables or tasks used in the package. Under the Objects pane, expand the Executables folder in Mailing Opportunities package. Under the Executables folder, expand Iterating May Opportunities followed by the Executables subfolder used in this package. Again under Executables, expand the Mailing Opportunities subfolder, followed by Properties, and then check in the Subject and ToLine properties to select them, as shown in Figure 11-3. After selecting these properties, click the Next button to move on to the Completing the Wizard window.

9. Type **Config_emails** in the Configuration Name field and review the options before clicking the Finish button.

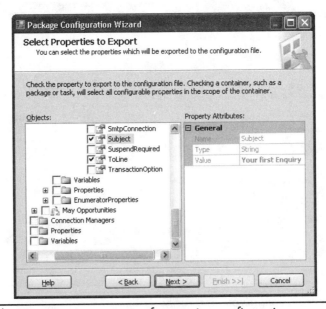

Figure 11-3 *Selecting properties to export for creating configurations*

10. When you return to the Package Configurations Organizer dialog box, you will see the configuration you just added listed there. You can return to this dialog box later to add configurations, edit already defined configurations, or remove configurations from the package. The configuration we added updates multiple properties. You can add multiple configurations in the way you've added Config_emails configuration into your packages. The configurations are applied in the order they appear in this list. The configurations are applied at loading time, so when multiple configurations update the same property, the value updated last is used at run-time. You can control this order by using the direction arrow buttons provided on the right side of the dialog box (shown in Figure 11-4) to move configurations up or down.

11. Pay some attention to the columns that appear under the Configurations area. The configuration name you defined is shown under Configuration Name; Configuration Type shows the type of configuration you have chosen; Configuration String shows the path where the configuration is located. You can create multiple configurations and group them logically for a package or set of packages in the Configuration Name column. In this exercise, we have created two configurations under one configuration name Config_emails. Two more columns, Target Object and Target Property, refer to the name of an object and that of a property, respectively. The use of an XML configuration file renders the Target Object and Target Property columns blank, as it can update multiple objects. Click the Close button to close the dialog box.

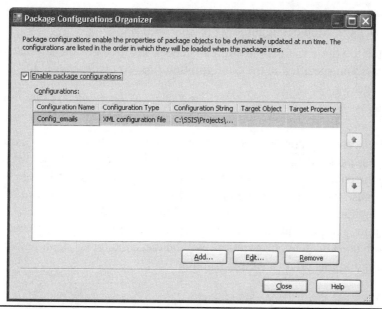

Figure 11-4 *Package Configurations Organizer dialog box showing a configuration*

Exercise (Assign a Value to the Package Configurations and Debug)

In this part of the Hands-On exercise, you will assign an e-mail address to the Subject and ToLine configurations and see how they are being used by the package during run-time to update the values specified (hard-coded) in the package.

12. So far, you have defined a package configuration for the ToLine property. The next step is to assign a value to this configuration. Choose File | Open | File, or press CTRL-O, to open a file. In the Open File dialog box, open the conoppo .dtsconfig file by exploring to the C:\SSIS\Project\Contacting Opportunities With Configurations folder and clicking the Open button.

13. When the conoppo.dtsconfig file opens in a new tab, locate the <ConfiguredValue> element after the following configuration:

```
<Configuration ConfiguredType="Property" Path="\Package\Iterating May
Opportunities\Mailing Opportunities.Properties[ToLine]" ValueType="String">
```

Type your alternative e-mail address between <ConfiguredValue> and </ConfiguredValue>. Alternatively, choose View | Data Grid and you will see a new tab with the configuration file shown in a data grid format. Click the Configuration on the left side of the screen (see Figure 11-5) and type **Your first Enquiry** in the first line (referring to Subject). Type an alternative e-mail address in the second line (referring to the ToLine property shown in the Path column).

14. Now you'll test your configurations. Save your package by pressing ctrl-shift-s, and then press the f5 function key to start debugging the package.

15. You will see the tasks turning green from yellow and successfully completing the package. Stop debugging by pressing shift-f5.

16. Switch to your e-mail application and check the inbox of the alternative e-mail address you specified in the configuration file. You will see e-mails from your package.

Review

You have successfully created a configuration for two of the properties exposed by a task in your package and have assigned values to the exposed properties. Upon executing the package, you saw that the values configured in the package were modified to use the values specified for the configuration. The value can be assigned to the configuration either directly, as you did in this Hands-On exercise, or by directing it to read from an environment variable. In situations when you are sure that the path used by the configurations will be the same for all deployments, use of direct configurations offers a simple solution.

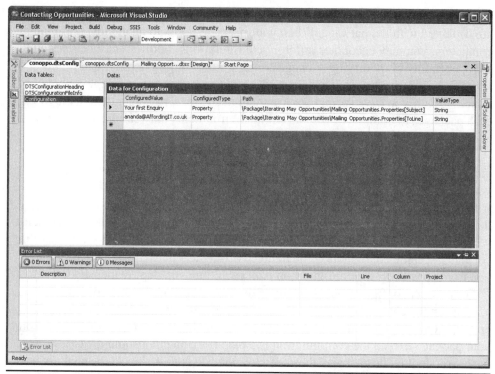

Figure 11-5 *Assigning values to exported properties in package configurations*

Direct and Indirect Configurations

You can specify the package configurations in two ways—direct and indirect. In direct configuration, you specify the configuration using any of the five configuration types mentioned earlier. For example, you specify a configuration for a property in an XML configuration file and then assign a value to that configuration. As you deploy the package, this configuration gets deployed with the package. You get an opportunity to specify the configuration file path and modify the configuration value during deployment.

If you decide to deploy the configuration file in such a way that you can keep the same configuration file path and the value of the variable, you can hard-code the configuration values. In this type of deployment, Integration Services reads the configuration file from the path specified during deployment and links directly the configured property in the package and the value assigned to it in the configuration. For simple environments—i.e., those in which you can specify the deployment path and the configuration values during deployment—direct configurations are a better choice because they offer flexibility of making changes during deployment.

However, bear in mind that the configurations become part of the package and are deployed with the package. When your package needs to be deployed to many computers, you may encounter different configurations for different machines and the opportunity of modifying package configurations during deployment in this situation becomes a hassle. This can cause some management and deployment issues—i.e., if you have special environment needs for a package, then deploying such packages to computers with different environments may call for lot more work at deployment time and cause some deployment grief.

The solution to this problem lies in using indirect configurations, in which you create a configuration file for each computer once and then use an environment variable to access the computer-specific file. This computer-specific file doesn't flow with the package during deployment; instead, it lies at the deployment computer all the time and becomes responsible for creating an environment into which the package will be deployed. Unlike direct configuration, in this case the package will access this computer-specific configuration file indirectly using an environment variable to free you from specifying the configuration path each time you deploy the package.

For indirect configurations, you create the configuration file and copy it to a folder on the computer where you want to deploy the package, and create an environment variable that points to this file; on the development computer you point your package to read the configuration file path from an environment variable. So when you deploy the package, the configuration file is available to the package via the environment variable.

When you create an indirect configuration for an XML configuration file, instead of specifying the file path directly, you point your package to read the file path for the XML configuration file from an environment variable. The computer-specific XML configuration file defines the environment on the deployment computer. Once you have created such XML configuration files for each computer, the package deployment gets reduced to copying your package to these computers.

For still more complex environments, you can update the variable values in the package during run-time using configurations, and the variables in turn modify properties of the package through the use of property expressions. In this way, you can have a totally disjointed configuration for your package with different bits playing their roles independently of each other, yet in a coordinated way.

The concept of indirect configurations may seem complex but in reality is simple to adapt and use; quite interestingly, we already use this concept in real life. Think of your car as a package that has properties such as steering wheel position, pressure on brake pedal, and so on. These properties change the behavior of the package, the car in our analogy. You, the driver, are modifying these properties that are analogous to property expressions. To modify the properties of car, you are guided by the road conditions (variable values in package analogy), such as traffic lights or traffic signs.

And, above all, these road conditions are regulated and applied by a traffic regulating agency, which is the configuration file in our package. So the package configuration sets the environment (traffic lights), the environment changes the variable values (traffic light turning green), and using those modified values, property expressions modify the behavior of the package (applying the brake to stop the car).

Hands-On: Using Indirect Configurations

You will be creating an indirect package configuration for downloading zipped files package that you created in chapter 5.

Method

For Indirect configurations, you create a configuration file on the computer to which you want to deploy the package. This configuration defines the environment for the computer, which is used by the package to modify its properties. The following steps will be used for this exercise:

▶ Create a computer-specific package configuration.

▶ Create an environment variable.

▶ Use property expressions to update the ConnectionString property.

▶ Create indirect package configuration.

▶ Deploy and execute the package.

Couple of points to note: If you want to use the Downloading zipped files package provided with this book, you will receive an error when opening the package. When you Click OK for the error dialog, the package will load properly sans the connection string in the FTP task. This is because, by default, the sensitive information (passwords, connection strings, and so on) in the packages get encrypted using the user key, and when some other user tries to open the package, an error will occur and sensitive information will be removed from the package. However, if you open the Downloading zipped files package that you developed yourself in Chapter 5, you will not get this error.

This package requires a connection to an FTP server. If you skipped building this package in Chapter 5, I would recommend that you find an FTP server (Many FTP sites allow you to download files that you can use to build this package—e.g., FTP sites for anti-virus updates) and build the package to work through this Hands-On exercise. The provided package may not be of much help, as it is pointing to my second computer, which is obviously not accessible to you.

Exercise (Create a Computer-Specific Package Configuration)

To deploy the package to multiple computers, you need to develop a configuration for each computer. You may do this at the development computer or at the deployment computer, depending upon the available resources. Once the configuration has been created, you then deploy the configuration file on the deployment computer. In this exercise, you will be using a development computer to create this configuration file.

1. Start SQL Server BIDS. Create a new Integration Services project with the following details:

Name	Downloading zipped files with Indirect Configurations
Location	C:\SSIS\Projects

2. After a blank project is created in BIDS, go to Solution Explorer and right-click the SSIS Packages node. Choose Add Existing Package. This will open Add Copy of Existing Package dialog box. Select File System in the Package Location field and specify **C:\SSIS\Projects\Control Flow Tasks\ Downloading zipped files.dtsx** in the Package Path field. Click the OK button to add this package. Right-click the Package.dtsx package and choose Delete from the context menu to delete this blank package. Click the OK button on the confirmation dialog box. Open the Downloading zipped files.dtsx package by double-clicking it.

3. Verify that fpath variable is added to the package with the details shown. Otherwise add this variable by right-clicking anywhere on the blank surface of the Designer and choose Variables from the context menu. Add a variable with the following details:

Name	fpath
Data Type	String

   While specifying the name, keep in mind that variables are case-sensitive.

4. Again, right-click anywhere on the blank surface of the Designer and choose Package Configurations from the context menu. Select the Enable Package Configurations check box.

5. Click the Add button to start the Package Configuration Wizard. Click Next on the first screen, and on the Select Configuration Type screen, choose the Configuration Type as XML Configuration file.

6. Select the Specify Configuration Settings Directly radio button. This will highlight the Configuration File Name field in which you can type **C:\SSIS\Projects\Downloading zipped files with Indirect Configuratiuons\ Configurations for DZF.dtsConfig** as the file name (see Figure 11-6). Click the Next button to move to the Select Properties to Export screen.

   This file path is not of much relevance, as we will finally move this file to the computers where the package will be deployed.

7. In the Objects pane, under the Downloading zipped files, expand the Variables\ fpath\Properties. Check the Value property, as shown in Figure 11-7. Click the Next button to go to the next screen.

8. Type **Downloaded files path** in the Configuration Name field on Completing the Wizard screen. Note that the Preview section shows the Type as Configuration File and tells you that a new configuration file will be created. Also note that the property \Package.Variables[User::fpath].Properties[Value] has been structured in a particular way. The basic rule here is that executables (containers or tasks) will start with a backslash (\); variables, properties, and connection managers will start with a dot (.); and an item in the collection will be enclosed within square brackets ([ ]). Starting with \Package, variables collection has been started with a dot, which is then followed by the [User::fpath] variable enclosed in square brackets because it is one in the collection of variables. This is then followed by

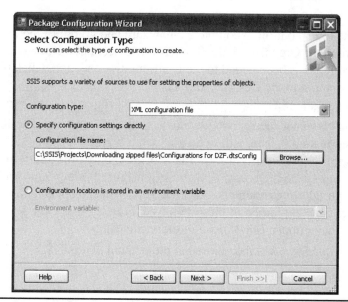

Figure 11-6 *Creating configurations for deployment computer*

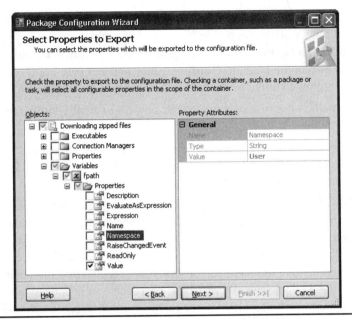

Figure 11-7 *Selecting properties to export*

Properties, starting with a dot and the [Value] item in the properties collection enclosed within square brackets.

Click the Finish button to complete the wizard and go return the Package Configurations Organizer dialog box. You will see that the newly created configuration has been added to the Configurations section. Click the Close button to return to the Designer surface.

9. Open the newly created configuration file Configurations for DZF.dtsConfig from the Designer menu: choose File I Open I File and provide the path specified in step 6. This will open a new tab on the Designer surface showing the XML configuration file. Locate the <ConfiguredValue> element and specify C:\SSISDeploy after the <ConfiguredValue> and before </ConfiguredValue> element. Alternatively, you can specify this value using a data grid, as explained in the previous exercise. Press ctrl-s to save this file and then choose File I Close to close this file.

10. Choose File I Save All; then close the project and exit BIDS.

Exercise (Create an Environment Variable)

Let's now move the configuration file to the deployment computer and set up an environment variable on the deployment computer to point to the configuration file. In real life, you will be setting up an environment variable on a development computer as well as all the deployment computers, but the path value defined for the environment variable on the deployment computer will differ from computer to computer, depending on your requirements.

11. Create a folder on the deployment computer named C:\SSISDeploy, and move the newly created configuration file Configurations for DZF.dtsConfig from your development computer to this folder on the deployment computer.

12. Right-click My Computer on the computer where you will be deploying the package, and choose Properties from the context menu. Go to the Advanced tab and click the Environment Variables button.

13. In the Environment Variables window, click the New button in the System Variables section and click the OK button in the pop-up window after typing in the following details:

Variable Name	DZFConfig
Variable Value	C:\SSISDeploy\Configurations for DZF.dtsconfig

14. You can scroll through the list of system variables to see this variable added to the list (Figure 11-8).

    Repeat steps 11 to 13 on the development computer so that you have access to the run-time environment on the development computer as well as for designing and testing purposes.

Exercise (Use Property Expressions to Update Exported Properties)

Now you'll use property expressions to update the ConnectionString property of the Downloads Connection Manager so that the downloaded zipped files can be saved to a folder specified by the `fpath` variable. BIDS requires a restart to load new environment settings. So if BIDS is already open, exit from it and then start it again to load the newly created the environment variable.

15. Return to the development computer and open the Downloading zipped files with Indirect Configurations project using BIDS.

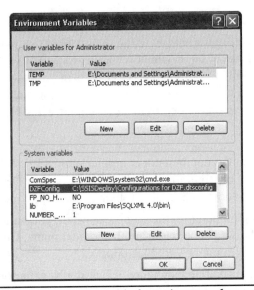

Figure 11-8 *Creating an environment variable for indirect configuration*

16. Right-click Downloads Connection Manager in the Connection Managers area and choose Properties from the context menu. In the Properties window, click in the Expressions field and then click the ellipsis button to open Property Expressions Editor. Click in the field under the Property column and select ConnectionString from the drop-down list. Click the ellipsis button next to the Expressions field to build an expression.

In the Expression Builder dialog box, expand Variables and then drag the User::fpath variable to drop in the Expression box. Click the OK button twice to return to the Properties window, shown in Figure 11-9.

Exercise (Create Indirect package Configuration)

Till now you have created a configuration file to update the value of the fpath variable and the property expression to use fpath to update the ConnectionString property of the Downloads Connection Manager. Also, you have moved the configuration file to a different computer, which is now not accessible to your package. You have created an environment variable that points to the already created configuration file. In this part you will point your package to read the configuration file from the location specified by the environment variable you created earlier. To do this, you will use an indirect configuration.

17. In BIDS, right-click anywhere on the blank surface of the Designer and choose Package Configurations from the context menu. In the Configurations list box,

Figure 11-9   *Creating a property expression for ConnectionString property*

you will see the previously configured Downloaded files path configuration listed there. Click the Remove button to delete this configuration.

18. Click the Add button to create a new configuration. Click Next on the Welcome screen of the Package Configuration Wizard.

19. In the Select Configuration Type screen, in the Configuration Type field, choose XML Configuration File, and instead of specifying XML file name, click the radio button for Configuration Location Is Stored In An Environment Variable. Select DZFConfig from the drop-down list in the Environment Variable field (see Figure 11-10). You are telling your package that you are using an XML configuration file to define your configurations whose location information is located in the environment variable DZFConfig. Click the Next button.

20. Type **DZFConfig file connection** in the Configuration Name field on the Completing the Wizard screen. Note that the Preview section shows the Type as Indirect Configuration File and Environment Variable Name as DZFConfig. Click the Finish button to complete the wizard and return to the Package Configurations Organizer. You will see that the newly created configuration has been added to the Configurations list.

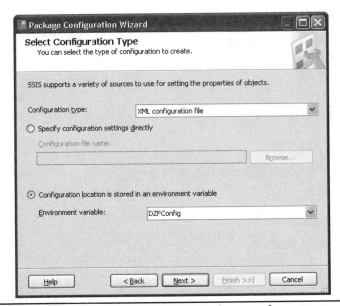

Figure 11-10   *Using environment variable to create indirect configurations*

21. Click the Close button to return to the Designer surface. With the creation of this configuration, you have completed the entire configuration steps required for indirect package configurations. Pointing the package to read information from an environment variable doesn't result in creation of any file; rather this information is embedded in the package itself. This enables you to copy your package to any computer and the package will look to the environment on the computer to get the location information for the configuration file from environment variable. Press ctrl-shift-s to save the package and then exit from BIDS.

Exercise (Deploy and Execute the Package)

In the final exercise, you will deploy your package to the computer where you want to run it and execute to see how the package behaves with the indirect package configurations.

22. Copy the Downloading zipped files.dtsx file from C:\SSIS\Projects\Downloading zipped files with Indirect Configurations folder on the development computer to the root folder of the C: drive on the deployment computer. (Actually, you can choose any folder on the deployment computer to host your package file.)

23. Open the command prompt window by choosing Start | Run and type **cmd** before clicking the OK button.

24. At the command prompt, execute the following command:

```
dtexec /file "Downloading zipped files.dtsx"
```

You will see the package executed successfully with a DTSER_SUCCESS message, as shown in Figure 11-11.

25. Go to C:\SSISDeploy folder and notice that the two zipped files have been downloaded in that folder.

Review

You have learned how to use indirect package configurations to simplify the deployment or redeployment process to a mere copy operation in situations for which you must deploy many machines or you must deal with complex requirements of applying configurations. During package loading time, as the configurations have been enabled, the package knows that it has to load configurations from an XML configuration file, which can be accessed from the path specified by the environment variable. So, the package goes to the environment variable DZFConfig, which directs it to the C:\SSISDeploy\Configurations for DZF.dtsConfig file. On reading this file, the package sets the fpath variable value to C:\SSISDeploy. And during the package execution time, the property expressions read the value of User::fpath variable and update the ConnectionString property of the Downloads Connection Manager and hence copies the zipped files to C:\SSISDeploy folder. Last point on running package on the deployment computers, you can actually run SSIS packages on a computer that doesn't necessarily have SQL Server 2005 installed. All you need is to run SSIS packages on a computer is the .NET framework and SSIS run-time environment installed.

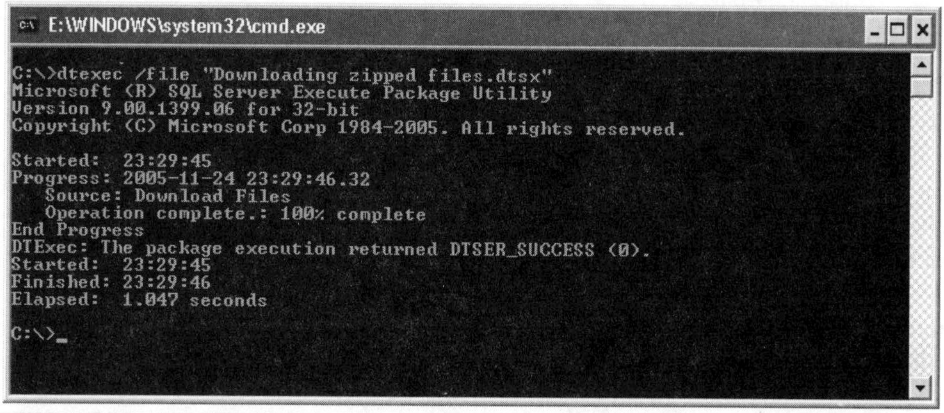

Figure 11-11   *Using the dtexec utility to execute the package on the deployment computer*

Deployment Utility

When you have created the package and the package configurations, you are ready to deploy your package to the various computers that are going to do the work. You might not understand the difference between copying a package and deploying a package. Truth is, there's no difference if your package is simple enough that it has no configuration file or miscellaneous files that have to be taken care of. Deploying a package takes into consideration the package configuration file and any other miscellaneous files when pushing the package to the deployment computer. The following scenarios can be used to deploy a package to a computer:

► Using import and export facility of Integration Services within SQL Server Management Studio.

► Saving a package to the file system or to the SQL Server store.

► Copying or moving packages using the dtutil utility.

► Using a package deployment utility.

You have used the first three methods in Chapter 6 when you were learning about administration of Integration Services. This approach is suitable for simple single package projects or when you develop a package on the machine where you want to use it. This approach is not much help when you are dealing with some or all of the following situations:

► The project contains several small packages as modules of a parent package.

► You need to deploy Integration Services project to several computers.

► You will use package configurations to set the properties.

► You will store miscellaneous files within the package.

Under these conditions, you will be using a package deployment utility, which can deploy multiple-package projects along with package configurations and miscellaneous files. A package deployment utility is used after you've created a package and package configurations.

You configure the Deployment Utility section of the project properties, accessed from Solution Explorer, before building the project to create a package deployment utility. Three properties here can be configured to control deployment of your project.

AllowConfigurationChanges

You can assign True or False value to this property. The True value lets you update configurations during deployment of the package; False lets you omit the update option during deployment. You can use this feature when you have to distribute a deployment utility to remote administrators for deploying the project but do not want them to be able to make changes to configurations. This is also useful when you are redeploying packages after making a few changes but do not want configurations to be changed.

CreateDeploymentUtility

This property also has True or False value options. A True value lets the build process create a deployment utility for the Integration Services project; a False value prohibits the creation of deployment utility. You need to specify a True value if you want to create a deployment utility, as the default value of this property is False.

DeploymentOutputPath

Whenever you create a new project using BIDS, a bin subfolder is also created along with other files within the project folder. The default path shown in this property— i.e., bin\Deployment—refers to the same bin folder under the project. When you build the project, and then packages, the package configurations, miscellaneous files, and the deployment utility file are added in this folder. You can change this path to create your deployment utility at a central location within the organization.

Once you configure these properties, you can create a package deployment utility by building a project on the computer where the Integration Services project is stored. The build process automatically includes the packages in a project, the package configurations, and the files saved to the miscellaneous folder in the project and adds a manifestation file that is gracefully called the Deployment Utility.

Deploying Integration Services Projects

The last step in the Integration Services project deployment journey is the deployment of the project. After having created packages for the project, package configurations, and the deployment utility, there isn't much left other than actually running the deployment utility to deploy the Integration Services project.

As you create the deployment utility, a manifestation file with the extension SSISDeploymentManifest is created along with packages, configurations, and miscellaneous files in the folder specified in the DeploymentOutputPath property of Integration Services project. You need to copy this deployment folder to the deployment computer and execute the SSISDeploymentManifest file to install the Integration Services project. Executing the SSISDeploymentManifest file starts the Package Installation Wizard, which then guides you through the process of package installation.

You decide where you want to install the package. If you choose to install your package in the file system, the package and other files such as configurations and miscellaneous files will be saved to the specified folder on the file system. However, if you choose to install the Integration Services package in the SQL Server, the package will be saved in the sysdtspackages90 table in the msdb system database and the other files will still be saved to the file system in the folder specified.

After you have deployed a project and start using the packages to do the work for you, you may find that you need to make changes to these packages, either to add functionality or to accommodate changes happening somewhere else in the environment. In such cases, you may be making changes to your project in the development environment and then testing in the staging environment. Once those changes have been tested successfully, you are again facing the task of deploying your project. This redeployment differs slightly from the first deployment of the project. You may want to change the deployment process during redeployment— i.e., you may not want to make any change during deployment and set the AllowConfigurationChanges property to False. Secondly, if you've made changes only to some of the packages and do not want to redeploy all the packages within a project, you can create a new Integration Services project and add only the packages to the project you want to redeploy. When you add a package to an Integration Services project, the configurations associated with the package are automatically added to the new project and you don't have to worry about them.

The following Hands-On exercise lets you create a deployment utility and then install the Integration Services package to the deployment computer.

Hands-On: Deploying an Integration Services Project

Create a package deployment utility for Contacting Opportunities with configurations project.

Method

Deploying a project involves going through three simple steps:

- ▶ Configure the Integration Services project properties.
- ▶ Build an Integration Services project.
- ▶ Install the Integration Service project.

Exercise (Configure Project Properties)

Before you can create a deployment utility, you must configure the project properties. These properties provide you with additional control and security over deployment process.

1. Open Contacting Opportunities With Configurations project using BIDS.
2. In the Solution Explorer, right-click the Contacting Opportunities With Configurations project and choose Properties from the context menu.
3. In the Contacting Opportunities With Configurations Property Pages window, click the Deployment Utility under Configuration Properties on the left pane. Specify True in the AllowConfigurationChanges and CreateDeploymentUtility properties (see Figure 11-12). Leave the default bin\Deployment path in the DeploymentOuputPath property. Click the OK button to close the property pages.

Exercise (Build the Project)

Building an Integration Services project is quite easy using the Solution Explorer in BIDS.

4. In the Solution Explorer, right-click the Contacting Opportunities With Configurations project again and choose Build from the context menu.
   Alternatively, you can also do this from the Build menu.

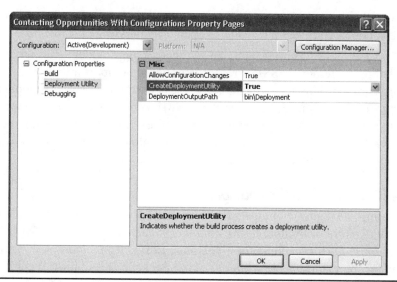

Figure 11-12 *Configuring Project properties*

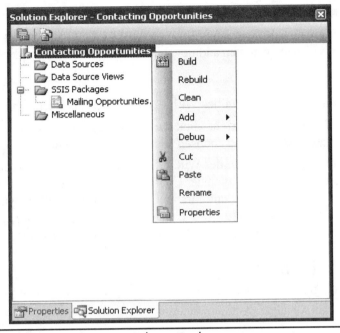

Figure 11-13   *Building a project using Solution Explorer*

5. You will see a success message in the Output window in BIDS. If this window doesn't open up by default, you can open it by pressing ctrl-alt-o.

6. Using Windows Explorer, you can see that the deployment files have been added in the folder C:\SSIS\Projects\Contacting Opportunities With Configurations\bin\Deployment. These files constitute of Mailing Opportunities With Configurations.dtsx, the package XML file and Contacting Opportunities With Configurations.SSISDeploymentManifest, the package deployment utility. Copy the Deployment folder to the deployment computer in C:\SSISDeploy folder.

Exercise (Install and Run the Package)

After creating the deployment utility, you can install your package using the DTSInstall.exe tool or by double-clicking the SSISDeploymentManifest file. If you want to use DTSInstall.exe tool, you have to specify the complete path and file name for the manifest file while invoking Package Installation Wizard.

7. On the deployment computer, go to the C:\SSISDeploy\Deployment folder using Windows Explorer and double-click the Contacting Opportunities With Configurations.SSISDeploymentManifest file. This will start the Package Installation Wizard after a few seconds. Click Next on the Welcome screen.

8. On the Deploy SSIS Packages screen, you can choose between File System Deployment and SQL Server Deployment of the package. Select the File System Deployment radio button. Click the Next button.

9. Click the Browse button and browse to C:\SSISDeploy folder, and then click the Make New Folder button to create a Contacting Opportunities With Configurations folder. Select this folder and click the OK button to return and see C:\SSISDeploy\Contacting Opportunities With Configurations listed in the Folder field. Click the Next button to go to the next screen. Click Next again in the Confirm Installation screen.

10. In the Configure Packages screen, expand Property under the Configurations section. You can see the two properties Subject and ToLine listed there. You can modify the value of any configuration here by clicking in the Value field of the configuration. Click Next when you're done.

11. In the Finish the Package Installation Wizard screen, review the summary that tells you about the package to be deployed, the configuration file to be used, the folder where it will be installed, and the log file name. Click Finish to deploy the package.

12. Browse to C:\SSISDeploy\Contacting Opportunities With Configurations folder using Windows Explorer. You will see Mailing Opportunities With Configurations.dtsx file in the folder.

13. Open the command window, go to C:\SSISDeploy\Contacting Opportunities With Configurations directory, and type the following at the command prompt:

```
dtexec /file "Mailing Opportunities With Configurations.dtsx"
```

You will see the various steps being completed and scroll through the window, finally returning a DTSER_SUCCESS message.

Review

To deploy a project, you need to configure its deployment properties and make sure that the CreateDeploymentUtility property is set to True. Once the deployment utility is created, you can install the package by running the deployment manifest file. You can also invoke the Package Installation Wizard using the DTSInstall.exe tool. You have also seen that if the AllowConfigurationChanges property is set to True during deployment utility creation, you get an opportunity to modify package configurations during deployment of the package. Make sure you use this aspect when you are deploying to several computers with different environments, if you are not using indirect package configurations.

Summary

You have completed an interesting journey to deploy Integration Services packages. You have created package configurations, used direct and indirect methods to specify configurations for a package, created a deployment utility, and deployed a package using the Package Installation Wizard. You now understand the difference between copying a package and deploying a package and you're now able to create indirect configurations to make the deployment process as easy as a copy operation.

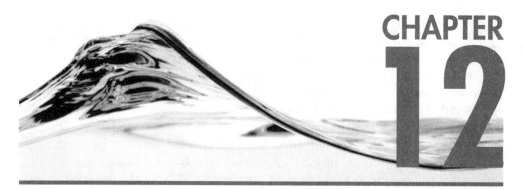

CHAPTER

12

Migrating to Integration Services

After having worked with various components of Integration Services such as Control Flow tasks, Data Flow transformations, connection managers, variables, property expressions, and package configurations, you should be confident in knowing that Integration Services is totally different from Data Transformation Services of SQL Server 2000. Integration Services is not an upgrade of DTS rather it is altogether a new tool.

For one thing, Data Transformation services have been deprecated from SQL Server 2005 and are no longer supported. With that in mind, you may be wondering what will happen to your existing DTS 2000 packages. Integration Services provides options that you can use to migrate DTS packages into SSIS. In Hands-on exercises in this chapter, you will use a DTS 2000 package provided in the RawFiles folder. Before you start checking out the options, you'll need to analyze your packages to determine whether they can be migrated; if they can be, you need to be aware of issues that might come up during migration. You can analyze your DTS 2000 packages using the Upgrade Advisor. Let's start the chapter with a discussion of the Upgrade Advisor, and then we will look at the migration options.

Upgrade Advisor

As a DBA of SQL Server 2000, you will sooner or later find yourself face to face with having to upgrade to SQL Server 2005. This may be due to an end of support for legacy software, or you may want to use the enhanced performance and new features provided in SQL Server 2005. Microsoft provides the Microsoft SQL Server 2005 Upgrade Advisor and recommends that you run it to analyze how your upgrade project will go before you get started on any project upgrades.

Upgrade Advisor is used to analyze the configurations of installed SQL Server 7.0 or SQL Server 2000 components and generate a report about the issues that you must address to ensure a successful upgrade. The reports generated by this tool let you plan how to deal with issues during an upgrade and the migration process. You can install Upgrade Advisor in the following ways:

▶ If you have SQL Server 2005 product media, you can go to the redist\Upgrade Advisor folder on the CD and run the installation by double-clicking the SQLUASetup.msi file.

▶ If you don't have SQL Server 2005 product media, you can download SQLUASetup.msi file by going to http://www.microsoft.com/downloads and searching for Microsoft SQL Server 2005 Upgrade Advisor.

Before you can successfully install Upgrade Advisor, you must comply with following prerequisites:

▶ **Supported OS**   Windows 2000 SP4 or later, Windows XP SP2 or later, or Windows Server 2003 SP1 or later.

▶ **Microsoft Windows Installer 3.1 or later**   This is available in the redist folder on the SQL Server 2005 product media, or you can download it from Microsoft's download site.

▶ **The Microsoft .NET Framework version 2.0 or later**   The .NET Framework version 2.0 is also available on the SQL Server 2005 product media or can be downloaded from the Microsoft download site.

▶ **SQL Server 2000 Client components**   These are required to scan DTS packages. These components should already be available on the computer you want to upgrade; however, if you want to run Upgrade Advisor from a remote computer, you need to install the SQL Server 2000 client components on the remote computer where you will install Upgrade Advisor.

In the following Hands-On exercise, you will install Upgrade Advisor and then run it to analyze your DTS 2000 packages.

Hands-On: Analyzing DTS 2000 Packages Before Upgrading to SSIS

You need to analyze your existing DTS 2000 packages before upgrading them to SQL Server 2005 Integration Services format to learn about any issues that may come up during migration.

Method

In this Hands-On exercise, you will be using Upgrade Advisor to analyze an existing package, Importing Contacts.dts, provided in C:\SSIS\RawFiles. This exercise is divided into two main parts:

▶ Installing Upgrade Advisor.

▶ Running Upgrade Advisor and viewing an analysis report.

Exercise (Install Upgrade Advisor)

You will use SQL Server 2005 product media to install the required software in the following steps. However, if you don't have the product media, these software add-ons are freely downloadable from Microsoft downloads site.

1. Using Windows Explorer, go to the redist folder on the SQL Server product media where you will see the following three folders:

   Windows Installer   Contains Windows Installer 3.1 installable files

   2.0   Contains Microsoft .NET Framework version 2.0 installable files

   Upgrade Advisor   Contains Microsoft SQL Server 2005 Upgrade Advisor installable files

2. Go to the Windows Installer folder and install the software. If you are using Windows XP SP2 or Windows 2003, this might be already present on your system.

3. When installation completes, go to the folder named 2.0 and install the .NET Framework by double-clicking the dotnetfx.exe file if your server is on 32-bit technology. The dotnetfx64.exe file installs a 64-bit version of .NET Framework.

4. When the .NET Framework installation completes, go to the Upgrade Advisor folder and double-click the SQLUASetup.msi file and start installing Upgrade Advisor. You will see a Welcome screen, as shown in Figure 12-1. Click Next to move on.

5. Accept the terms of the License Agreement screen and Click the Next button.

6. Provide your name and company name in the Registration Information screen and click Next.

7. In the Feature Selection screen, note the installation path where Upgrade Advisor will be installed. You can change this path by clicking the Browse button and locating the preferred path (Figure 12-2). Click Next when you are ready to proceed.

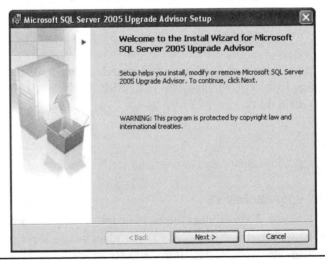

Figure 12-1 *Starting Installation of Upgrade Advisor*

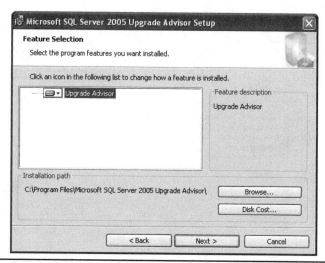

Figure 12-2 *Installation path of Upgrade Advisor*

8. Click the Install button in the Ready to Install the Program screen. The files for Upgrade Advisor will be copied to the selected folder. Click the Finish button when the installation completes.

Exercise (Run the Upgrade Advisor to Analyze DTS 2000 Packages)

You will run the Upgrade Advisor to analyze the Importing Contacts.dts package and will see the report.

9. Choose Start | SQL Server 2005 Programs Group and start the Upgrade Advisor. You'll see the Welcome page, which provides links to documentation, latest updates, and two links for Launch Upgrade Advisor Analysis Wizard and Launch Upgrade Advisor Report Viewer. These two components are the main components of the Upgrade Advisor.

10. Click the Launch Upgrade Advisor Analysis Wizard to analyze DTS 2000 package. Click Next on the Welcome screen of the Analysis Wizard.

11. Select the components you want to analyze in the SQL Server Components screen. For this exercise, make sure you select the Data Transformation Services check box as shown in Figure 12-3. You can also use the Detect button to let Upgrade Advisor detect and select the services installed on the specified computer. Click Next to move on.

Figure 12-3 *Selecting Data Transformation Services for analysis*

12. Type or select an Instance name from the drop-down list box in the Connection Parameters screen. Specify the authentication details for the selected instance and Click the Next button when ready. Don't get confused between versions of SQL Server. The Upgrade Advisor connects to SQL Server 2000 to analyze and report, so specify an instance of SQL Server 2000 here and not of SQL Server 2005.

13. On the DTS Parameters screen, you can select whether you want to analyze DTS 2000 packages that are saved in the SQL Server or the packages saved on the file system. Select the Analyze DTS Package Files radio button and then type **C:\SSIS\RawFiles** in the field provided next to this option (see Figure 12-4). Click the Next button to move on.

14. Review the settings in the Confirm Upgrade Advisor Settings screen. Click the Run button to analyze the selected package.

15. In the next screen, the Upgrade Advisor will analyze the package; when it completes analysis, you can see the report by clicking the Launch Report button. The analysis report will be displayed in the Upgrade Advisor Report Viewer. The key messages that you can spot in the report among other messages are

   ▶ That you need to install SQL Server 2000 DTS Designer Components to edit the packages in Integration Services.

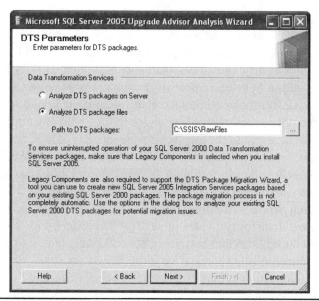

Figure 12-4 *Selecting DTS packages on the basis of storage location*

▶   Packages stored in Meta Data Services are not supported.

▶   SQL Server 2000 Data Transformation Services has been deprecated.

Review

Depending on the complexity and the components used in the package, you will see different messages for your packages. But you will find that the above mentioned three key messages are common to all types of packages, as these are generic messages representing major differences between DTS and SSIS. In the following section, you will read about these differences in detail and see how you can best manage your upgrade project and use your existing packages.

Migration Options

After having run Upgrade Advisor, you can view the report that will tell you whether your package can or cannot be upgraded based on the complexity and the components used in the package. At that time, you need to consider the options available for the DTS 2000 packages you've already developed and are still running. Some preconditions will affect your choice of options.

While considering crossing the migration bridge, one thing you need always to bear in mind is that Integration Services is a new software that has been developed from the ground up. Though it has adopted most of the DTS 2000 concepts, it is totally different in usability, operation, and, above all, not all DTS 2000 tasks are available in Integration Services. Some of them have been deprecated and some have been removed. But the good news is that Integration Services can coexist with DTS and provides necessary tools to migrate along with other options.

You also need to be aware of the fact that not all versions of SQL Server 2005 include Integration Services. SQL Server 2005 Express Edition and Workgroup Edition do not include Integration Services, though the Workgroup Edition has an Import/ Export Wizard that doesn't use Integration Services. SQL Server 2005 Standard Edition has basic Integration Services transformations, whereas Developer and Enterprise Edition has advanced transformations built into it. While discussing your options, we will focus only on the editions that have Integration Services built into them.

Another consideration is the storage location of your package. You were able to store your DTS 2000 packages in SQL Server, Structured Storage File, or in Meta Data services, also known as the repository. Integration Services fully supports DTS 2000 packages that were saved in SQL Server 2000 or Structured Storage File for executing or migrating, but Integration Services does not support Meta Data services. You can export the packages from Meta Data services to SQL Server or Structured Storage File for easily migrating them to Integration Services. However, if you cannot do this, you will have to install SQL Server 2000, SQL Server 2000 tools, or repository redistributable files on your local computer to enable Integration Services to scan and migrate the packages saved in Meta Data services.

At the time of upgrading your database server, you may suppose that you have to migrate all your packages and test them on the SSIS environment before you can commission an SQL Server 2005 migration project. This alone can be a deterrent to upgrading a project and can cause long delays. The following options are available while moving to SQL Server 2005 Integration Services:

▶ Running DTS 2000 packages with run-time support.

▶ Including DTS 2000 packages in Integration Services packages using a wrapper task.

▶ Migrating DTS 2000 packages to Integration Services using Package Migration Wizard.

Let's discuss these options in detail and see how well they fit with your scenario.

Running DTS 2000 Packages with Run-time Support

If you are busy dealing with other stuff while migrating to SQL Server 2005, you may want to leave your DTS packages running as is and focus on migration later. You can run the DTS 2000 run-time environment and Integration Services on the same computer. However, some of the databases to which DTS 2000 package connects may be upgraded to SQL Server 2005 leaving DTS 2000 unable to access them. To deal with this issue, Integration Services installs an updated version of the DTS 2000 run-time environment that is capable of accessing SQL Server 2005 databases.

To install Integration Services backward-compatibility features, you need to select the check box for Integration Services during installation in the Components to Install screen. This was explained in Chapter 1—Figure 12-5 shows this screen for your quick reminder.

Selecting Integration Services installs Microsoft SQL Server 2005 backward-compatibility software, visible in the Add or Remove Programs applet of the Control Panel. The installation of backward-compatibility components enhances the DTS 2000 run-time engine to enable DTS 2000 packages to access SQL Server 2005 data sources, adds a legacy support to enumerate DTS 2000 packages in SQL Server Management Studio, and provides Package Migration Wizard for migrating DTS 2000 packages. For example, the DTS run-time environment of SQL Server 2000 has dtsrun.exe file

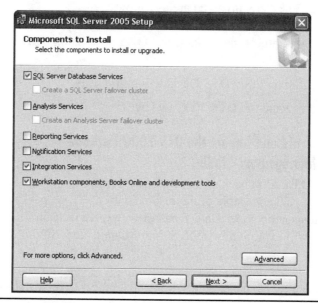

Figure 12-5 *Selecting Integration Services during installation*

dated 17/12/2002 that has version 2000.80.534.0, and when you upgrade to SQL Server 2005 and install Integration Services, this file is replaced with a newer file called DTSRun.exe dated 29/09/2005, with a version of 2000.85.1054.0. This new file enables DTS packages to access SQL Server 2005 data sources.

In the following Hands-On exercise, you will discover what happens to the packages after upgrade.

Hands-On: Executing a DTS 2000 Package

You have upgraded SQL Server 2000 to SQL Server 2005 and installed Integration Services. Here you will learn how you can manage and run DTS 2000 packages.

Method

A DTS 2000 package, Importing Contacts, is available in a C:\SSIS\RawFiles folder saved in a structured storage file. This package imports records from the C:\SSIS\RawFiles\Contacts.txt flat file to the Contacts table of the Campaign database. Contacts.txt is a fixed-width file and the Importing Contacts package uses a flat file source, an OLE DB provider for SQL Server, and a Transform Data task to import data into SQL Server.

Starting with structured storage file, you will investigate how the package can be managed and modified in SQL Server Management Studio based on the various storage locations. The steps involved are as follows:

▶ Enumerate and import the package to SQL Server using SQL Server Management Studio.

▶ Install SQL Server 2000 DTS Designer components.

▶ Export and execute the DTS 2000 package.

Exercise (Enumerate and Import the DTS 2000 Package in SQL Server Management Studio)

When you save DTS 2000 packages to SQL Server, you know that SQL Server saves them to the sysdtspackages table of the msdb database. These packages are visible in the Local Packages node under Data Transformation Services in Enterprise Manager. In this part, you will explore how SQL Server Management Studio enumerates legacy packages.

1. Start SQL Server Management Studio and connect to the database engine.

2. In the Object Explorer window, expand Management/Legacy/Data Transformation Services. Your legacy packages—i.e., DTS 2000 packages—will show up under this node.

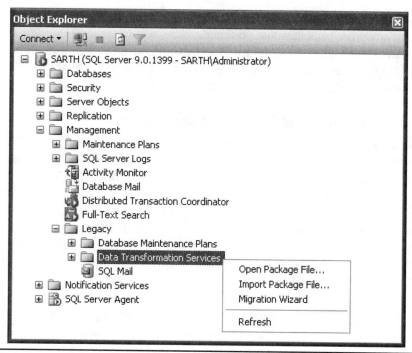

Figure 12-6 *Importing a DTS 2000 package in SQL Server Management Studio*

3. Right-click the Data Transformation Services and choose Import Package File from the context menu, as shown in Figure 12-6.

   In the Import DTS 2000 Package dialog box, choose Importing Contacts.dts Package from C:\SSIS\RawFiles and click the Open button.

4. Because a structured storage file can have more than one package and package versions, you are asked to choose the package you want to import in the Select Package dialog box. Expand the Importing Contacts package and choose any of the versions; then click OK to select your package. These packages are the same, just saved a few seconds apart.

5. Go back to Data Transformation Services node to see that the Importing Contacts package has been added there.

6. Click the New Query button and run the following query in the New Query tab.

```
select * from msdb.dbo.sysdtspackages
```

You will see the Importing Contacts package listed in the output results along with any other packages that you might have in sysdtspackages table. This means that all the DTS 2000 packages are still saved in the msdb.dbo .sysdtspackages table and can be added to this table using the import facility provided by SQL Server Management Studio.

Exercise (Install SQL Server 2000 DTS Designer Components)

You can import and export DTS 2000 packages from the sysdtspackages table and enumerate DTS 2000 packages with SQL Server Management Studio. However, if you need to modify the DTS 2000 packages, you must have SQL Server 2000 tools on the computer or take them away to a computer where SQL Server 2000 is installed. This is not a very helpful situation. To overcome such issues, Microsoft has released a Feature Pack for SQL Server 2005 with various add-on components. You will download and install Microsoft SQL Server 2000 DTS Designer Components that allow you to modify DTS 2000 packages from SQL Server Management Studio.

7. In SQL Server Management Studio, expand the Management/Legacy/Data Transformation Services node to see the package you've just added. Right-click the Importing Contacts package and choose Open from the context menu. You will see an alert message that SQL Server 2000 DTS Designer components are required to edit a DTS package (see Figure 12-7). Click OK to close the message.

8. Go to http://www.microsoft.com/downloads using Internet Explorer and search for the Feature Pack for SQL Server 2005 and follow the link.

9. From the Feature Pack for SQL Server 2005 page, locate Microsoft SQL Server 2000 DTS Designer Components section and download SQLServer2005_DTS .msi file. When the download is complete, double-click the downloaded file to start the installation wizard (see Figure 12-8) for DTS Designer Components. Click Next on the Welcome screen.

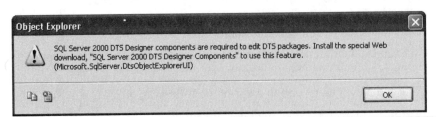

Figure 12-7 *Alerting you to install SQL Server 2000 DTS Designer Components*

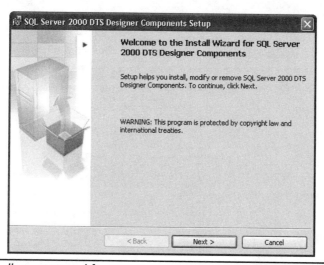

Figure 12-8 *Installation Wizard for SQL Server 2000 DTS Designer components*

10. On the License Agreement screen, accept the license agreement (see Figure 12-9) and click Next.

11. Provide your name and your company's name in the Registration screen and click Next.

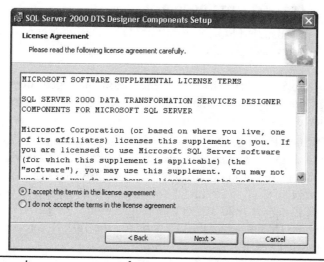

Figure 12-9 *Accept license agreement for SQL Server 2000 DTS Designer components*

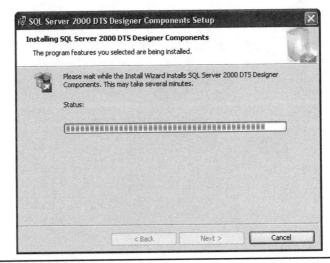

Figure 12-10 *Installing SQL Server 2000 DTS Designer components*

12. As you click Install in the Ready to Install confirmation screen, the SQL Server 2000 DTS Designer Components start to install as shown in Figure 12-10.

13. Finally, click the Finish button to complete the installation. You've now installed SQL Server 2000 DTS Designer Components that allow you edit and maintain DTS 2000 packages until they can be migrated to Integration Services.

Exercise (Edit and Execute a DTS 2000 Package)

You will use the just installed SQL Server 2000 DTS Designer components to edit the Importing Contacts package and then run the package.

14. Switch back to SQL Server Management Studio and repeat step 7 to open the Importing Contacts package. This time the package will open up in the DTS 2000 Package Designer, as shown in Figure 12-11.

15. In the DTS 2000 Package Designer, double-click the Campaign to open the Microsoft OLE DB Provider for SQL Server Connection Properties and provide the name of your server in the Server field. The provided name SARTH is the name of computer used in set-up lab for this book. Change it to your computer name. In the Database field, select Campaign (Figure 12-12). Click OK to close this dialog box. Do not select the check box in the Task References dialog box, and click OK to close it.

16. You can also execute your package in this Designer in the usual way by clicking the Execute button. Save your package and close the Designer.

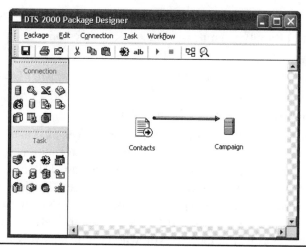

Figure 12-11   *Importing Contacts package in DTS 2000 Package Designer*

17. Using Windows Explorer, browse to the C:\SSIS\RawFiles folder and delete Importing Contacts.dts package.

18. Now, go back to SQL Server Management Studio and right-click the Importing Contacts and choose Export from the context menu.

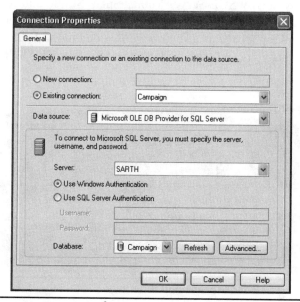

Figure 12-12   *Connection Properties for Campaign database*

19. Specify C:\SSIS\RawFiles path to export Importing Contacts package.

20. Choose Start | Run; type **cmd**; and click OK. At the command prompt, type the following:

```
C:\>dtsrun /F "C:\SSIS\RawFiles\Importing Contacts.dts"
```

You will see that the package executes successfully and 49 rows are added to the Contacts table, as shown in Figure 12-13.

Integration Services lets you run DTS 2000 packages as if using the DTSRun .exe utility. For those who haven't used Data Transformation Services of SQL Server 2000 and are facing migration challenges now, DTSRun.exe is the command line utility used to run DTS 2000 packages. The jobs created in SQL Server Agent to run DTS 2000 packages also use DTSRun to execute the jobs. This also means that all the jobs that were created in SQL Server Agent will keep on running as is. For those of you who have extensively used dtsrun .exe and dtsrunui.exe, Integration Services provides equivalent, rather better utilities called dtexec and dtexecui. The dtexecui utility can be used to create commands for using with dtexec. Refer back to Chapter 6 where these utilities are covered in detail.

Review

In this exercise, you used SQL Server Management Studio to enumerate the packages stored in the sysdtspackages table of the msdb database. You also used the import and export facility provided by SQL Server Management Studio and explored other available options. The important thing you learned is that Microsoft has provided a DTS 2000 Designer package as a separate download in the Feature Pack for SQL Server 2005 that you can install and use to edit existing DTS 2000 packages.

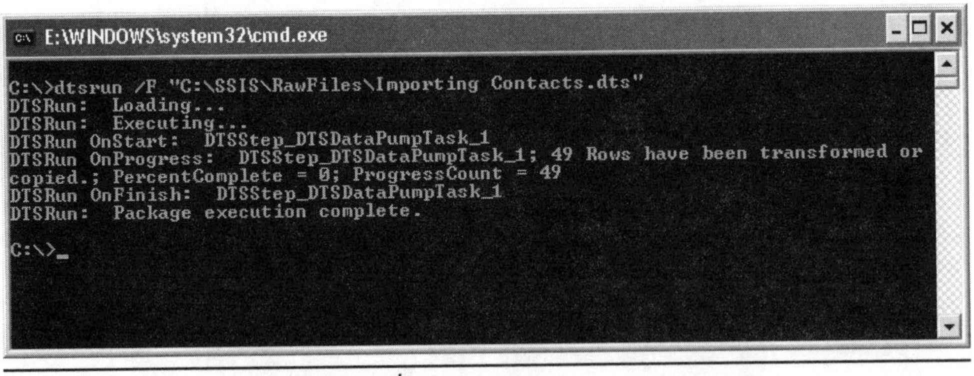

Figure 12-13   *Running DTS 2000 package*

This makes life much easier if you need to manage migration of DTS packages to Integration Services. In the next part of this chapter, you will learn how to include your existing DTS 2000 packages in Integration Services projects.

Embedding DTS 2000 Packages in Integration Services Packages

Integration Services lets you to create business solutions using a modular design so you can build your package as a small unit of work to provide a piece of functionality that can be repeatedly used in various enterprise solutions. You can integrate these smaller units of work to form a complete solution using the Execute Package task. You learned about the Execute Package task in Chapter 5 and used it to build a solution in one of the Hands-On exercises as well. This is relevant if you are developing a new piece of functionality. What about the work that has been developed already using DTS 2000 packages? Do you have to develop that functionality in Integration Services? Various scenarios may guide you to adopt a particular solution, but if you want to use your DTS 2000 package as a module in your Integration Services package, Integration Services provides a wrapper task that lets you do this. And that wrapper task is the Execute DTS 2000 Package task.

Execute DTS 2000 Package Task

Using the Execute DTS 2000 Package task, you can include a DTS 2000 package in your Integration Services project and run it using the enhanced DTS run-time engine. As you are aware, Integration Services installs the enhanced DTS run-time engine (DTSRun.exe), so you must select Integration Services specifically during installation or upgrading to SQL Server 2005. Now you know two ways of running your DTS 2000 packages—one using the enhanced DTS run-time engine and the other using the Execute DTS 2000 Package task. Though this task also uses the DTS run-time engine, it provides additional ability to include your DTS 2000 package in Integration Services as a child package—like including a SSIS package using the Execute Package task. Both the Execute Package task and the Execute DTS 2000 Package task can be used in the same package without worrying about run-time conflicts as Integration Services can coexist with DTS. The other benefits of using this task are similar to those provided by the Execute Package task, such as modularity, reusability, and security.

Let's work through a quick Hands-On exercise to demonstrate usage of the Execute DTS 2000 Package task.

Hands-On: Executing Importing Contacts Using the Execute DTS 2000 Package Task

You will run a DTS 2000 package using the Execute DTS 2000 Package task in this exercise.

Method

You will use the Execute DTS 2000 Package task to run the Importing Contacts package that is saved to the file system in the C:\SSIS\RawFiles folder.

Exercise (Configure the Execute DTS 2000 Package Task)

1. Start BIDS and create a new Integration Services project with the following details:

Name	Executing Importing Contacts
Location	C:\SSIS\Projects

2. When the new project has been created, go to Solution Explorer and rename the Package.dtsx package **Importing Contacts.dtsx** package. Click Yes to accept to rename. Press SHIFT-CTRL-S to save the project.

3. From the Toolbox, drop the Execute DTS 2000 Package task on to the Control Flow Designer surface.

4. Double-click the task to open the Execute DTS 2000 Package Task Editor.

5. In the General page, click in the StorageLocation field under the Location section to enable the drop-down arrow. The drop-down list shows three option: SQL Server, Structured Storage File, and Embedded In Task, as shown in Figure 12-14.

   Depending on the storage location of the DTS 2000 package, choose the relevant option, and based on the option you choose, the editor's interface changes to show only the relevant fields. When you choose the SQL Server option, the task will access packages stored in the sysdtspackages table of the msdb database of the SQL Server you specify in the SQLServer field. If you choose the Structured Storage File option, the package will access the packages from the file stored on the file system. You can specify the path for this file in the File field. The third option, Embedded In Task, means the

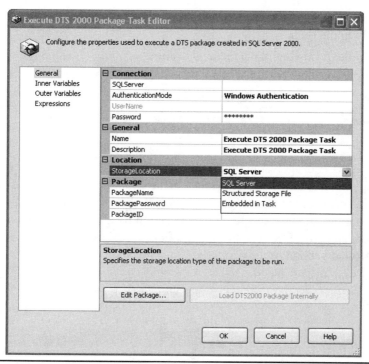

Figure 12-14   *Storage locations supported by Execute DTS 2000 Package Task*

DTS 2000 package has been saved internally in the Execute DTS 2000 Package task and you don't have to specify the connection information of file or SQLS erver for the DTS 2000 package. You can load the DTS 2000 package in this task by clicking the Load DTS2000 Package Internally button. To load the package, you first select either SQL Server or Structured Storage File location in the Location field and specify the relevant connection information in the Connection area. After choosing the PackageName, you can then click the Load DTS2000 Package Internally button and the package will be loaded in the task. When you save this project, the DTS 2000 package is saved within the task. This task will hold all the information required for executing the DTS 2000 package after that and removing the DTS 2000 package from original location wouldn't affect the execution of this task.

6. For this exercise, you will be using Structured Storage File location. Select Structured Storage File in the Location field.

7. Click in the File field to invoke an ellipsis button. Click this button and select Importing Contacts.dtsx package from the C:\SSIS\RawFiles folder.

Alternatively, you can type **C:\SSIS\RawFiles\Importing Contacts.dts** directly in the field.

8. Specify the following in the General section:

Name	Importing Contacts
Description	This task is used to execute the named DTS 2000 package.

9. Click in the PackageName field to invoke the ellipsis button. Click this button and open Select Package dialog box. As the structured storage file can contain multiple packages and package versions, you are asked to choose the package you want this task to execute. Select a version for the Importing Contacts.dts package and click OK. The PackageID field will show the unique identifier for the selected version of the package.

10. As the Importing Contacts package doesn't have a password, leave the PackagePassword field as is. The task should look like Figure 12-15.

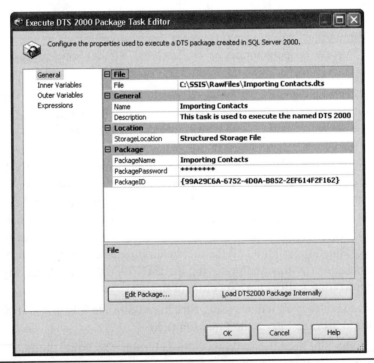

Figure 12-15 *Configurations for the Execute DTS 2000 Package task*

11. You can edit the specified package by clicking the Edit Package button. The DTS 2000 Package Designer will open, where you can edit the package using legacy tools. If you haven't installed the SQL Server 2000 DTS Designer components in the previous Hands-On exercise and you don't have SQL Server 2000 tools installed on your computer, you will get an alert message asking you to install the Designer components. Close the DTS 2000 Package Designer window.

12. Go to Inner Variables page. Here you can specify and configure the inner variables that the DTS 2000 package uses. The variables and their values specified will be passed to the global variables in the DTS 2000 package. You can use the New button to add a new variable for which you can specify a type and can assign a value as well. This value will be used by global variables as the updated value at run-time.

13. Go to Outer Variables page, where you can add an outer variable to the DTS 2000 package. Outer variables are used in the parent package—i.e., in an Integration Services package. When you click the New button, a blank row is added under the Name field, in which you can select a variable from the drop-down list of system and user-defined variables in the parent package.

14. Using the Expressions page, you can write an expression for any of the property for this task to update dynamically at run-time.

15. Click OK to close this task and press SHIFT-CTRL-S to save the project.

16. Press F5 to execute the package. The task will change color to green and you will receive a success message in the Output window.

17. Press SHIFT-F5 to stop debugging and close the project.

Review

In this exercise, you learned another way of executing your DTS 2000 package using Integration Services Execute DTS 2000 Package Task. You can also include your legacy package as a child package in a parent SSIS package using this task. You also learned that you can use inner and outer variables to pass updated variables to the legacy package and can save DTS 2000 package internally in the Execute DTS 2000 Package task. The option of loading and saving DTS 2000 package internally is useful during migration of DTS to SSIS when dealing with custom tasks developed in DTS 2000. As the DTS 2000 custom tasks will not have a directly mapped task in Integration Services, the migration process encapsulates such tasks inside the Execute DTS 2000 Package task using the Embedded in Task feature and adds it in the migrated package.

Migrating DTS 2000 Packages to Integration Services

Once you understand the issues involved in migrating a DTS package to Integration Services, you can begin migrating most of your packages. To make life easier, Integration Services provides the Package Migration Wizard to help you migrate packages to the SSIS format.

Some of the Data Transformation Services tasks didn't fit well in the design and development of Integration Services software. This led to the removal of those tasks from Integration Services. Other tasks were developed into Integration Services. These tasks map directly and are converted to Integration Services tasks during migration, while custom DTS tasks or tasks that have been removed from Integration Services are either encapsulated in the Execute DTS 2000 Package task or replaced with a placeholder task. The following discussion tells you how the various components of SQL Server 2000 Data Transformation Services are mapped to Integration Services components and what happens when they are migrated to Integration Services.

▶ **ActiveX Script Task**   The SSIS version of this task is able to run most of the DTS ActiveX scripts; however, the scripts that reference DTS package objects may not successfully run on migration and you may have to edit the code manually. This task has been marked deprecated in SSIS and is available to support existing DTS scripts.

▶ **Analysis Services Task**   Though Integration Services has two built-in tasks, namely Analysis Services Execute DDL task and Analysis Services Processing task, neither of them directly map to the DTS 2000 Analysis Services task. This is because Integration Services tasks do not work with SQL Server 2000 Analysis Services. The migrated package contains the encapsulated functionality that must be manually migrated to Integration Services.

▶ **Bulk Insert Task**   Directly maps to Bulk Insert task of Integration Services.

▶ **Copy SQL Server Objects Task**   Migrates to Transfer SQL Server Objects task.

▶ **Data Driven Query Task**   This task does not get migrated straight away, as it has no directly mapped task in Integration Services. The migrated package contains the encapsulated functionality of this task, which you have to migrate manually using Data Flow components based on the functionality provided by this task.

▶ **Data Mining Prediction Task**   Directly maps to Data Mining Query task; however, in some cases you may find that the Data Mining Prediction task of SQL Server 2000 gets encapsulated in the Execute DTS 2000 Package task, which you have to convert to a Data Mining Query task.

▶ **Dynamic Properties Task**   There is no direct mapping task to the DTS 2000 Dynamic Properties task that is used to modify the DTS components dynamically at run-time. This functionality has been achieved in Integration Services by the use of package configurations and property expressions. You learned about property expressions in Chapter 3 and package configuration in Chapter 11. On migration, this task is replaced by a placeholder task which you have to convert manually using package configurations, property expressions, and variables in Integration Services.

▶ **Execute Package Task**   This is migrated to the Execute DTS 2000 Package task in Integration Services.

▶ **Execute Process Task**   This is converted to the Execute Process task in Integration Services after migration.

▶ **Execute SQL Task**   Maps directly to the Execute SQL task in Integration Services.

▶ **File Transfer Protocol Task**   Maps directly to the FTP task in Integration Services.

▶ **Message Queue Task**   This task maps directly to the Message Queue task in Integration Services.

▶ **Send Mail Task**   Gets converted to Send Mail task of Integration Services.

▶ **Transform Data Task**   This task has no directly built-in task mapped in Integration Services and gets encapsulated in the Execute DTS 2000 Package task on migration. The functionality provided by this task has been distributed among various data flow components in Integration Services. You must manually convert this functionality to the Integration Services format.

▶ **Various Transfer Tasks**   Gets converted to various transfer tasks in Integration Services. These tasks have direct mapping tasks.

▶ **Passwords**   As the Integration Services packages have totally different security features, the passwords used to protect DTS packages don't get migrated. However, you can configure the package protection level after the package has been migrated to Integration Services. For more details on security features, refer to Chapter 7.

▶ **Variable**   DTS 2000 packages contain only global variables, whereas Integration Services can use system variables, create user-defined variables, assign scope and namespace to variables, attach property expressions to variables to update their values dynamically at run-time, and configure them to raise an event when their values are updated. On migration, the DTS 2000 package variables get migrated to the package scope in the user namespace. You can enhance the use of variables in your package after migration.

▶ **Connections**   The connections in the DTS 2000 package get migrated to connection managers in Integration Services for the tasks that get directly migrated. For the tasks that use connections and cannot be directly migrated, such as the Transform Data task, the connection stays the part of the intermediate package that encapsulates DTS 2000 task.

It should be clear to see that the migration from DTS 2000 to SSIS package may involve some development work due to the tasks that did not find their place in Integration Services. Removing these tasks from Integration Services does not mean that the functionality has been lost; rather, the functionality provided by these tasks has been enhanced. But the enhanced features have been distributed among various other components that must be used together to create the required functionality. Depending on the complexity of your package and the tasks it contain, your package may get migrated without any additional effort or may migrate some of the tasks while encapsulating the others in the Execute DTS 2000 Package task, requiring only a bit of effort on your part to migrate completely; or they may not get migrated at all, and you have to then decide whether to use them with the DTS run-time support or rewrite the packages.

In the following section, you will study the Package Migration tool that you can use to migrate an SQL Server 2000 Data Transformation Services package to an SQL Server 2005 Integration Services package.

Package Migration Wizard

Integration Services provides this tool that guides you step by step to migrate packages stored in SQL Server or a structured storage file. The Package Migration Wizard reads the DTS package and creates a new copy of the migrated package in Integration Services. It does not alter the source package, which stays available as is, if the migration process fails. The Package Migration Wizard can be started using one of the following methods:

▶ From SQL Server Management Studio, right-click the Data Transformation Services node under the Legacy node of Management in Object Explorer (see Figure to 12-6 shown earlier in this chapter) and choose Migration Wizard from the context menu.

▶ From BIDS, by right-click the SSIS Packages node in Solution Explorer and select Migrate DTS 2000 Package from the drop-down list box.

▶ From the command prompt, go to folder C:\Program Files\Microsoft SQL Server\90\DTS\Binn and run the executable DTSMigrationWizard.exe.

Let's do a short Hands-On exercise on using the Package Migration Wizard.

Hands-On: Migrating Importing Contacts to Integration Services

Migrate the DTS 2000 package Importing Contacts into Integration Services format.

Method

You will use the Package Migration Wizard to migrate the package, and after migration is completed you will execute the package to see the results.

Exercise (Use the Package Migration Wizard)

1. Start BIDS and create a new Integration Services project with the following details:

Name	Migrating Importing Contacts
Location	C:\SSIS\Projects

2. When BIDS loads the blank project, go to the Solution Explorer window, right-click the SSIS Packages node, and choose Migrate DTS 2000 Package from the context menu (see Figure 12-16).
3. This will invoke Package Migration Wizard, and you will see the first screen of this wizard. Click Next to move on.
4. The Choose Source Location screen allows you to select the location where your package is stored. Click the down arrow in the Source field to see the list of source locations. Package Migration Wizard can read DTS 2000 packages stored in Microsoft SQL Server or in a structured storage file. As mentioned, SQL Server 2005 does not support Meta Data services (also called the repository). If your DTS 2000 package is stored in Meta Data services, you

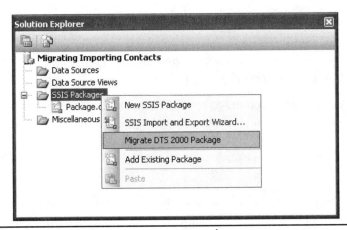

Figure 12-16   *Starting the Package Migration Wizard*

may prefer to save those packages to the locations supported by the Package Migration Wizard. In case you cannot do that, the Package Migration Wizard provides a way to read packages from Meta Data services when SQL Server 2000, SQL Server 2000 tools, or the repository redistributable files are installed on the local computer. For this exercise, select Structured Storage File in the Source field.

5. Specify **C:\SSIS\RawFiles\Importing Contacts.dts** in the File Name field as shown in Figure 12-17. Alternatively, you can choose this file by clicking the Browse button. Click Next to move on.

6. In the Choose Destination Location screen, specify the folder where you want to save the migrated package. The migrated package is created as a new DTSX file, and your DTS 2000 package is left as is without any changes. In the Folder Name field, specify **C:\SSIS\Projects\Migrating Importing Contacts** as the folder where you want to save the migrated package (see Figure 12-18). You can also click the Browse button to choose this folder, which also provides you an opportunity to create a new folder if you need to. Click the Next button.

7. As a structured storage file can have multiple packages and package versions, you can select the packages and their versions you want to migrate in the List Packages screen. You can also modify the name of the migrated package by editing the Destination Package field for the selected package. Select Importing

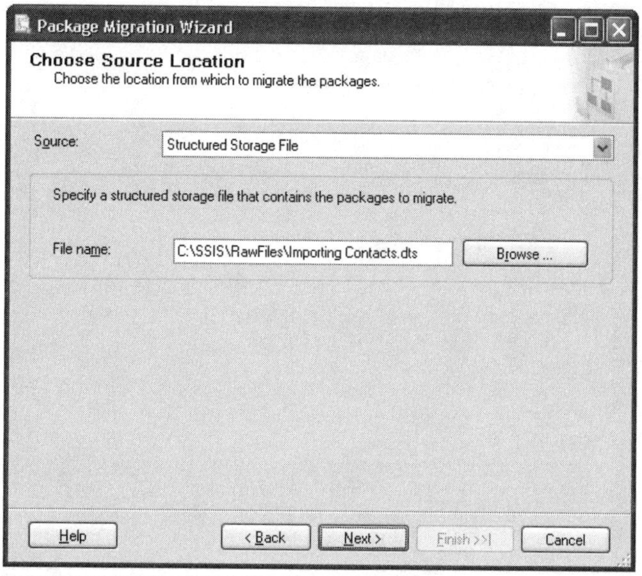

Figure 12-17 *Specifying the DTS 2000 package location*

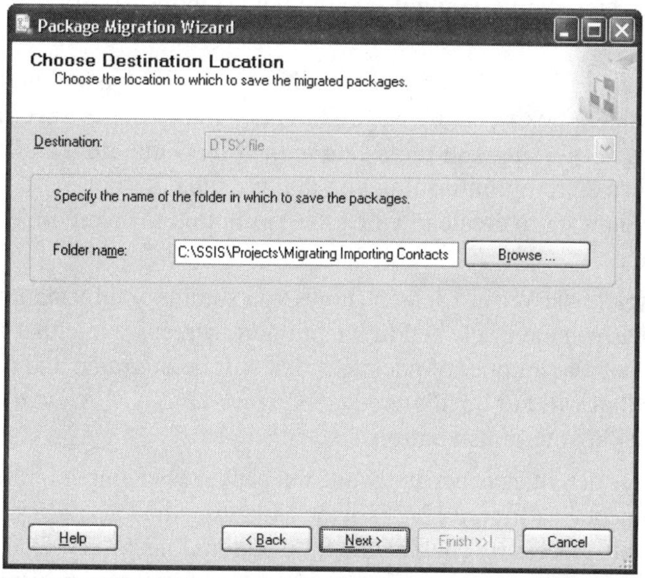

Figure 12-18 *Specifying a destination folder for the migrated package*

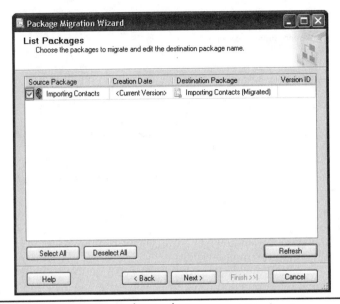

Figure 12-19   *Selecting DTS 2000 packages that you want to migrate*

Contacts package and change the Destination Package to Importing Contacts
(Migrated) by directly typing it into the field (Figure 12-19). Click the Next
button.

8. In the Specify a Log File screen, click the Browse button and in the Choose
   Log File dialog box select C:\SSIS\RawFiles folder in the Save In field. Type
   Migrating Importing Contacts.Log in the File Name field and click Save.
   You will see a prompt informing you that the file does not exist and asking
   whether you want to create it. Click the Yes button to create it. Then click the
   Next button.

9. The Complete the Wizard screen shows you summary information for all the
   options that you have selected in the previous screens. Note that this screen
   also tells you the number of packages that will be migrated and the number of
   packages that will not be migrated (see Figure 12-20). Review the information
   before clicking the Finish button.

10. You will see activities occurring while the package is being migrated, component
    by component (see Figure 12-21) in the Migrating the Packages screen. You can
    interrupt this process by clicking the Stop button if necessary. Once the package
    is migrated completely, you will see a success status for the package. At this
    stage you can see the report by clicking the Report button. Once you're happy,
    click the Close button to close the Package Migration Wizard.

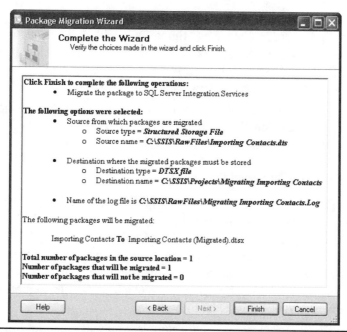

Figure 12-20   *Summary for the options selected in Package Migration Wizard*

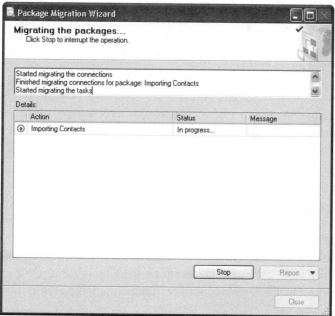

Figure 12-21   *Monitoring progress for migrating DTS 2000 packages*

11. As the Package Migration Wizard is closed, you will notice that a package by the name Importing Contacts (Migrated).dtsx has been added in the SSIS Packages node in the Solution Explorer window. You can delete the blank package Package.dtsx by right-clicking it and choosing Delete from the context menu. Click OK to confirm deletion in the pop-up dialog box.

12. Explore to the C:\SSIS\RawFiles folder and open the Migrating Importing Contacts.Log file using Notepad. This shows you details of how the migration progressed.

Exercise (Execute the Migrated Package)

13. Double-click the Importing Contacts (Migrated).dtsx package to open it. You will see a Data Flow task named DTSTask_DTSDataPumpTask_1 on the Control Flow Designer surface. Notice that this is the DTS 2000 data pump task name. Also, two connection managers were added: the OLE DB Connection Manager for connecting to the Campaign database, and a flat file connection manager for connecting to the Contacts.txt file. Double-click the Data Flow task to open the Data Flow panel.

14. As the DTS 2000 package was quite simple, you will see a flat file source and an OLE DB destination adapters connected by a data flow path only in the Data Flow Designer surface. Press F5 to execute the package and check that it has been migrated successfully. Oops! the package actually fails. The OLE DB Destination component is shown in red, indicating an error with this component.

15. Go to Progress tab and you will see lot of warnings for almost each column, saying that they have not been used in the Data Flow task. If you scroll down to the locate error messages, you will see errors with OLE DB Destination indicating that the number of columns is incorrect, as shown in Figure 12-22. These warnings and errors are pointing to check columns in the OLE DB destination.

16. Press SHIFT-F5 to stop debugging the package. Go to the Data Flow tab and double-click the OLE DB Destination to open the editor. Review the settings in the Connection Manager page. They seem OK, but note an alert message at the bottom of the editor asking you to map the columns on the mappings page. Go to the Mappings page and you'll see that no input column is mapped to the destination column. Map all the input columns to the destination columns by dragging input columns and dropping them on to destination columns, as shown in Figure 12-23. When you're done, click OK to close the editor.

17. Press F5 to execute the package. This time, the package will execute successfully.

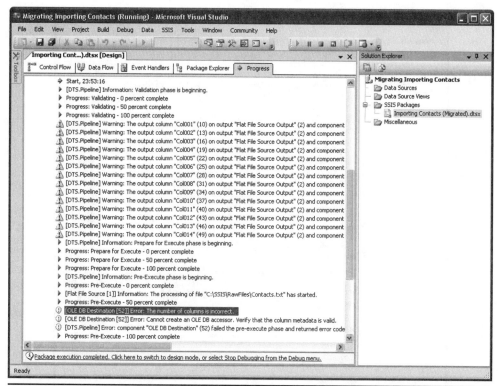

Figure 12-22   *Checking errors for Importing Contacts (migrated) package*

Review

You've used the Package Migration Wizard to migrate a DTS 2000 package to Integration Services. You selected a DTS 2000 package stored on the file system in a structured storage file and saved the destination package in the DTSX format on the file system. The option to select the destination location for migrated package was disabled in the Package Migration Wizard as the wizard was run from BIDS. In the end, you observed that though the package was migrated successfully and no error was reported, the package failed to execute and actually had some errors. The point to be noted is that the Package Migration Wizard migrated all the components, yet it missed mapping the columns in such a simple package. These kinds of errors are simple to fix, but you must be vigilant and expect the Package Migration Wizard to miss some of the validation errors. It is highly recommended that you open the migrated package and test run it to check all the components' behaviors.

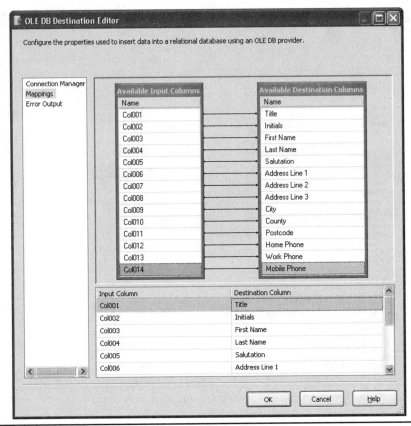

Figure 12-23 *Mapping columns in OLE DB destination*

Summary

Integration Services gives you the option of running your DTS 2000 package without making any changes using the enhanced run-time support. However, you may find yourself at crossroads in deciding when to upgrade your packages, as Data Transformation Services has been marked deprecated and will not be supported in the future. You've also learned about the provision of the SQL Server 2000 DTS

Designer components, the method to include or run your DTS 2000 packages in Integration Services projects using the Execute DTS 2000 Package task, and you have used the Package Migration Wizard to migrate a DTS 2000 package to Integration Services. One important thing you learned about migrating your DTS 2000 packages is that there is no straightforward method, though the Package Migration Wizard makes it easy to do; still, even the wizard misses out on minor errors that you may have to mend yourself.

CHAPTER 13

Troubleshooting and Performance Enhancements

517

Y ou've come a long way with Integration Services and have worked with its various aspects to configure and develop SSIS packages. By now, you can not only develop workflow and data transformations in your packages but you can also deploy them to an enterprise infrastructure securely with complete administration and control over the storage locations. In this chapter, you will learn the skills necessary for debugging your packages, in general and at the component level. You will then learn about the facilities that you can use to determine what happens at package run-time to fix these issues accordingly. You must have come across various alerts and warning messages raised by Integration Services throughout your experience with package development. In this chapter you will explore how Integration Services validates component configurations in your packages and handles errors.

In the second half of the chapter, you will learn to configure your packages to keep them performing at peak levels. You'll explore the performance counters provided by Integration Services, custom events of the Data Flow task, execution trees and execution plans, among other options to help you keep memory usage in control. This chapter also offers a high level discussion on package design techniques to optimize the pipeline and exploit the parallelism features. Let's start the last leg of our journey with Integration Services by learning to troubleshoot SSIS packages.

Troubleshooting Integration Services Packages

As mentioned earlier, during package development, you might have seen various alerts and warnings appear on the screen. For example, when you drop the Execute SQL task on the Control Flow surface, you see a crossed red glyph on the task indicating "No connection manager is specified". These validation alerts are available by default in Business Intelligence Development Studio (BIDS). Some features are available in Integration Services by default, so you don't need to set any configurations; other debugging features, such as breakpoints and logging, must be configured and you must interpret the results. You can broadly lump features into two categories:

▶   Debugging features that are available by default.

▶   Debugging tools that are required to be configured.

The following section covers the features that are available to you by default.

Debugging Features Available by Default

Integration Services provides several features that help you in developing packages by alerting and providing useful information that you might have overlooked while configuring components in your package. Various windows display variable values, expression results, alerts, and other messages. Following are brief descriptions of some of these windows.

Error List Windows

You can launch this window from the View menu in BIDS. It lists errors and warning messages during design time, such as validation errors. The messages are generally descriptive, stating the type of error, source of the error, and description of the error. However, if you find it a bit difficult to link the error message to the source task in a complex package, you can double-click the error message to open the editor for that particular task.

Locals Window

This window is quite helpful in debugging by displaying local variables in the current scope. This window is available only when you've suspended execution in your package using breakpoints. While execution is suspended at breakpoints, you can launch this window by choosing Debug | Windows to see the state or current values of local variables at that time.

Watch Window

This window is a great debugging facility that lets you watch for specific variables during package execution. Like the Locals window, you can launch this window by choosing Debug | Windows when your package has suspended execution after encountering a breakpoint. You can directly type in a variable to see its value or set a watch for that variable. You can also assign a new value to the variable manually and inject this value into the package execution to see the results or modify the execution process. In the first Hands-On exercise, you will use this feature to modify the execution.

Output Window

This window is also available from the View menu. It shows results of execution, like the Progress tab described next, and hence includes errors that occur during run-time.

Progress Tab

The Designer includes a Progress tab during package execution. It displays progress information about the package and its components. You can find start and stop times, validation errors or warnings, and other execution errors or warnings about the components of the package here. When package execution is finished and you switch back to design mode, this tab changes to the Execution Results tab and shows the messages of the last execution of the package.

Debugging Tools Requiring Configuration

The following debugging tools must be configured.

Breakpoints

SSIS Designer is based in the Visual Studio environment, which leverages some of the functionality provided in that programming environment. You can set a breakpoint in your Integration Services package, for example, to help you debug the control flow in your package at run-time. Breakpoints suspend the execution of the package and let you review run-time environment conditions, such as variable values and the state of your package at that particular point in execution. You can set breakpoints at the package level, on containers, and on Control Flow tasks.

You can also use breakpoints in your scripts while working with the Script task and break your code at execution time. The Visual Studio for Applications (VSA) environment is used in Integration Services to develop and debug scripts. This enables you to apply breakpoints to your scripts to pause execution during debugging. You can apply breakpoints in one of the following ways:

▶ Right-click at the left of the row and choose Breakpoint | Insert Breakpoint option from the context menu.

▶ Select the line where you want to insert the breakpoint and choose Debug | Toggle Breakpoint, or press F9 on the keyboard.

When you set a breakpoint on a line, it is highlighted in red and a red circle appears to the left of the line. The run-time handling of breakpoints in VSA is the same as handling them while running the package in the Designer. You use the F10 key to step over the breakpoint and the F5 key or the Continue button on the screen to continue the execution. VSA provides a debugging window that you can use with breakpoints to get information about what's happening with script execution. You can print variable values, execute procedures, or evaluate expressions using this window. This is equivalent to the Locals and Watch windows provided in the SSIS Designer.

Let's work through a Hands-On exercise to see how breakpoints can be set within your packages.

Hands-On: Setting Breakpoints to See Variables Values

You will be setting breakpoints at various levels in an Integration Services package to see how variables change values during execution.

Method

In this exercise, you will be using the Contacting Opportunities with Property Expressions Integration Services project you developed in Chapter 8. This project creates personalized e-mail messages after reading values from a defined data set row by row. The package contains a Foreach Loop container that executes seven times, once for each segmented record; reads the May Prospects contact details such as first name, last name, and e-mail address; and passes this information on to the Send Mail task that creates personalized e-mail using this information. The Foreach Loop container passes this information to the Send Mail task using variables. You've seen the package executing but did not see how the variables change the values. In this exercise, you'll be using breakpoints to see exactly how the variables are getting updated.

Exercise (Set Breakpoints)

1. Open the Contacting Opportunities with Property Expressions project in BIDS and double-click the Mailing Opportunities.dtsx package under the SSIS Packages node in the Solution Explorer window to load it into the Designer.

2. Right-click the Iterating May Opportunities Foreach Loop Container and choose Edit Breakpoints from the context menu. The Set Breakpoints dialog box will open.

3. In this dialog box, you can set breakpoints using various break conditions. Take a moment to read through the conditions that are available here. For this exercise, you will be using the Break At The Beginning Of Every Iteration Of The Loop break condition, the last in the list. Select the check box at the left of this break condition. You will see the Hit Count Type column displaying *Always* for this break condition. Click this and then click the down arrow to see the following four options in the Hit Count Type column:

   Always   Execution will always be suspended.

   Hit Count Equals   Specify a value in the Hit Count column when you want to skip some execution cycles of the component—such as when your container iterates over a record set that contains thousands of records and you want to see the variable values after a few thousand iterations. The breakpoint will suspend execution after the number of breakpoint occurrences has reached the value specified in the Hit Count column.

Hit Count Greater Than Or Equal To   Similar to Hit Count Equals, except the execution is suspended when the number of times the breakpoint has occurred is equal to or greater than the value specified in the Hit Count column. The execution will be suspended each time the breakpoint is hit after the Hit Count value is reached, whereas Hit Count Equals breaks the execution only once when the Hit Count value is equal to the number of times the breakpoint has occurred.

Hit Count Multiple   You may be interested in seeing variable values at intervals to sample test that the package is working as expected. You can use this option and specify a value in the Hit Count column to break the execution only when the breakpoint occurrence is a multiple of this value. For example, you may set a value of 100 in the Hit Count column with this option and the execution will be suspended every 100th time the breakpoint occurs.

For this exercise, leave Always selected, and you don't have to specify any value in the Hit Count column (see Figure 13-1). Click OK to close the Set Breakpoints dialog box.

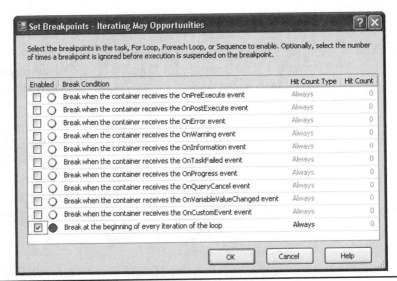

Figure 13-1   *Setting a breakpoint on a Foreach Loop container*

4. You will see a red circle on the Iterating May Opportunities Foreach Loop container, indicating that a breakpoint has been set on this component. Press F5 to execute the package.

5. You will see that the May Opportunities task has been successfully completed and the execution is stopped at Iterating May Opportunities with this container appearing in yellow, and the breakpoint red circle has a yellow arrow inside it. The execution has been suspended at the first hit of the breakpoint. Choose Debug | Windows | Locals to open the Locals window. Expand the Variables node to see the list of system as well as user variables. Note the User::fname and User::lname variable values.

6. Click the Continue button (green triangle) or press F5 to continue execution. This time you will see that the Mailing Opportunities task has been executed successfully and the package execution is stopped again at the Iterating May Opportunities as it hits the breakpoint a second time. Note the User::fname and User::lname variable values, which have been updated with the values of second row in the data set.

7. Go to the Progress tab in the SSIS Designer, and locate the Task Mailing Opportunities section. Note the two rows showing initialization and completion of the task. Continue the package execution by clicking the Continue button or pressing F5.

8. The package executes one more iteration of the Iterating May Opportunities Foreach Loop Container and stops as it hits the breakpoint a third time. Note the User::fname and User::lname variable values, which have been updated with the values of the third row in the data set. Go to the Progress tab and check out the Task Mailing Opportunities section. Note that this time it shows ⇒*Start (2)* at the beginning and ⇐*Stop (2)* at the end of the section, indicating that this task has completed two execution cycles.

9. Go to the Control Flow tab, right-click Iterating May Opportunities, and select Edit Breakpoints from the context menu. For the selected Break Condition, change the Hit Counter Type from Always to Hit Count Equals and specify 4 in the Hit Count column. Click the OK button to close the dialog box and press F5 to continue the execution of the package.

10. This time you will notice that the Mailing Opportunities task has executed a number of cycles—exactly four—and the execution stops again. You can verify this by going to the Progress tab and checking out the Task Mailing Opportunities section, which shows that the task has been executed six times.

11. Choose Debug | Windows | Watch | Watch 1 to add a watch window. In the Watch 1 window, click in the Name column and type **User::email** and then

press ENTER on the keyboard. You will see that this variable is added in the Watch 1 window and displays its current value. Expand the User::email variable and type in an alternative e-mail address in the Value field; then press the ENTER key on the keyboard. You will see the value of User::email is changed to the one you've specified. Figure 13-2 shows the various values in the Progress tab, Watch 1 window, and Locals window.

12. Press F5 to continue execution. This time, the package completes execution successfully and stops. Press SHIFT-F5 to switch to design mode. Check your inbox and the alternate e-mail address inbox. You will receive six e-mails in your inbox and one e-mail at your alternative e-mail address.

13. Remove the breakpoint from Iterating May Opportunities, save all the files, and close the project.

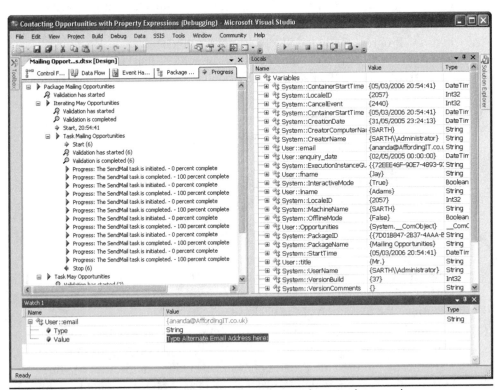

Figure 13-2 *Changing variable value at run-time using the Watch 1 window*

Review

In this Hands-On exercise, you've seen how the Progress tab shows the number of executions of a task along with other information. This tab also displays alert, warning, and error messages while the package executes. These messages are still available after the package completes execution when the Progress tab becomes the Execution Results tab. You've also used the Locals window to see the values of variables that get updated with each iteration of the Foreach Loop container. Then you changed the breakpoint setting and jumped four steps at a time. This powerful feature helps a lot while debugging packages with large data sets, and you need to check the multiple points of failure. The most interesting thing you've learned is how to change the variable value on the fly and inject that value into the package execution. You can easily simulate various values and see how the package responds to these values using this feature.

Logging Feature

The logging feature of Integration Services can be used to debug task failures and monitor performance issues at run-time. A properly configured log schema to log run-time events can be an effective tool in your debugging toolkit. Logging has been discussed in detail in Chapter 8 along with a discussion on various log providers. Refer to that chapter for more details on how to configure logging in your package.

Precedence Constraints and Data Flow Paths

You've used these two connecting elements in package development, so now you understand that precedence constraints are used to connect control flow tasks whereas data flow paths are used to connect data flow components. You can use precedence constraints to control the workflow in a package by configuring the evaluation operation to a constraint or an expression, or a combination of both. Using a constraint as the evaluation operation, you can configure the connected task to run on the basis of success, failure, or completion of the initial task. If you use an expression as an evaluation operation, you can then specify a Boolean expression whose evaluation result of True will let the connected task be executed. You can also choose to use both a constraint and an expression with an AND operator or an OR operator to specify when the next task in the workflow can be executed. You can also set multiple precedence constraints to one task when multiple tasks are connected to this task. You can set it to run when either of the constraint evaluates to True or leave it to default setting of executing the connected task when all the constraints must evaluate to True. By configuring precedence constraints properly, you can control the order of execution of tasks in the workflow to the granular level.

Similar to precedence constraints, you use Data Flow paths in the pipeline to connect components. However, Data Flow paths do not apply any constraints on the data flow as precedence constraints apply to Control Flow tasks. Several of the data flow components support error outputs that are represented by red colored data flow paths. You can configure the error outputs of components to handle the rows that do not pass through the main output successfully and can cause truncation of data or failure of the component. These failing rows can be passed on to error outputs to be treated separately from the main pipeline. You can then log these rows to be dealt with later or you can be more productive by configuring an alternate data flow to fix the errors in the data for such failing rows and put these rows back to the main data flow. This ability to fix errors in the data while processing the bulk of it is extremely powerful and easy to use. You've used error output in Chapter 10 (refer to Figure 10-11) that shows using the Error Output for the rows that don't have a matching city for the postcodes they have. This is a slightly different way of using the error output than was mentioned previously. It is interesting to note that the error output can also be used for obtaining an alternative output. You've used the error output in the same fashion while working through another exercise in Chapter 10 (refer to Figure 10-35). In this exercise, a Lookup Transformation was used to extract to the main output the exact matches from the pipeline and to pass on all the remaining records to an alternate path. So, in the simplistic way, you can use error output to handle errors or the failing rows in the Data Flow component, and in a slightly modified way, you can use them to deploy alternate pipeline paths to create more productive, more resilient, and reliable data manipulation packages.

Data viewers

Data viewers are excellent debugging tools when used in pipeline—just like oscilloscopes that are used in electric circuits. You see traces of the waves and pulses of current flowing in the circuit using an oscilloscope, whereas you use data viewers to see the data flowing from one component to the other in the pipeline. There is a difference between the two though. Oscilloscopes do not tend to affect the flow of current whereas data viewers stop the execution of the data flow engine and require you to click the Continue button to proceed. Data viewers are attached to the path connecting the two data flow components and at run-time, these data viewers pop open windows to show you the data in one of four formats: grid, histogram, scatter plot, or chart format.

You were introduced to data viewers in Chapter 9 and used them extensively in Chapter 10. While working with them, you attached the data viewers to the path and saw the data in the grid format popping on the Designer surface. If you run a package that has data viewers attached in the data flow using any method other than inside BIDS, the data viewers do not show up—i.e., data viewers work only when the package is run inside the BIDS environment.

Performance Enhancements

The next step to improve your package development skills is to consider the proper use of resources. Many scenarios occur in development, staging, and production environments that can affect how packages run. For example, your server may be running other processes in parallel that are affected when an Integration Services package starts execution and puts heavy demands on server resources; or your package may use sorts and aggregations that require lots of memory that may not be available to you because other services such as SQL Server or the tables required by an Integration Services package may be locked by SQL Server to serve queries from other users.

In this section, you will learn skills to design your package and its deployment so that you can manage resources on the server for optimum utilization without affecting other services provided by the server. You will study about optimization techniques to keep your packages running at peak performance levels. Like most database applications, you can enhance the performance of Integration Services by managing memory allocations to various components properly. Integration Services packages can also be configured to work in parallel, which is discussed later in the chapter.

It's All About Memory

One common misconception is to assume that the memory management of Integration Services is either handled by the SQL Server 2005 database engine or can be managed in a similar fashion. However, Integration Services is a totally independent application that is packaged with SQL Server 2005 and runs exactly the way any other application would run. It has nothing to do with memory management of the SQL Server 2005 database engine. It is particularly important for you to understand that Integration Services works like any other application on Windows that is not aware of (Advanced Windowing Extensions) AWE memory. Hence, SSIS can use only virtual address space memory of 2 GB or 3 GB if the /3GB switch is used on 32-bit systems per process. Here a *process* means a package—that is, if you have spare memory installed on the server that you want to use, you have to distribute your work among multiple packages to enable these packages to use more memory at run-time. This goes back to best practices of package design that advocates modular design for developing bigger and more complex packages. You've studied this in Chapter 5. The package modules can be combined using Execute Package Task to form a more complex package.

Also, you will need to run child packages out of process from the parent package to enable them to reserve their own memory pool during execution. You can do this by setting the ExecuteOutOfProcess property to True on the Execute Package task. Refer to Chapter 5 for more details on how this property affects running packages.

If a package cannot be divided into child packages and requires more memory to run, you need to consider moving to 64-bit systems that can allocate large virtual memory to each process. As SSIS has no AWE memory support, so adding more AWE memory on a 32-bit system is irrelevant when executing a large SSIS package.

64-Bit Is Here

With 64-bit chips becoming more affordable and multi-core CPUs appearing on the horizon, performance issues are beginning to disappear—at least for the time being. Utilizing 64-bit computer systems in the online data processing, analytical systems, and reporting systems makes sense. If you are up against a small time window and your data processing needs are still growing, you need to consider moving to 64-bit technology. The benefits of this environment not only outweigh the cost of moving to 64-bit, but it may actually turn out to be the cheaper option when you're dealing with millions of transactions on several 32-bit systems and need to scale up.

Earlier 64-bit versions in SQL Server 2000 provided limited options, whereas SQL Server 2005 64-bit edition provides the same feature set as 32-bit with enhanced performance. SQL Server 2005 and all its components can be run in native 64-bit mode, thus eliminating the earlier requirement to have a separate 32-bit computer to run tools. In addition, the WOW64 mode feature of Microsoft Windows allows 32-bit applications to run on a 64-bit operating system. This is a cool feature of Microsoft Windows, as it lets third-party software without 64-bit support coexist with SQL Server 2005 on the 64-bit server.

While discussing advantages of 64-bit technology, let's quickly go through the following architectural and technical advantages of moving to the 64-bit environment.

Compared to 32-bit systems that are limited to 4 GB of address space, 64-bit systems can support up to 1024 gigabytes of both physical and addressable memory. The 32-bit systems must use Address Windowing Extensions (AWE) for accessing more memory, which has its own limitations. The increase in directly addressable memory for 64-bit architecture enables it to perform more complex and resource-intensive queries easily without swapping out to disk. Also, 64-bit processors have larger on-die caches, enabling them to use processor time more efficiently. The transformations that deal with row sets instead of row-by-row operation, such as Aggregate transformation and the transformations that cache data to memory for lookup operations such as Lookup transformation and Fuzzy Lookup transformations, are benefited with increased availability of memory.

The improved bus architecture and parallel processing abilities provide almost linear scalability with each additional processor, yielding higher returns per processor when compared to 32-bit systems.

The wider bus architecture of 64-bit processors enables them to move data quicker between the cache and the processor, which in-turn provides improved performance.

With more benefits and increased affordability, deployment of 64-bit servers is growing and will eventually replace 32-bit servers. The question is, when is the optimum time to make a switch? As an Integration Services developer, you need to determine when your packages start suffering from performance and start requiring more resources. The following scenarios may help you identifying such situations:

▶ With the increase in data volumes to be processed, especially where Sort and Aggregate transformations are involved, the pressure on memory also increases, causing large data sets that cannot fit in the memory space to be swapped out to hard disks. Whenever this swapping out of data volumes to hard disks starts occurring, you will see massive performance degradation. You can use Windows performance counters to capture this situation so that when it happens, you can add more memory to the system. However, if you've already run out of full capacity and there is no more room to grow, or if you are experiencing other performance issues with the system, your best bet is to replace it with a newer, faster, and beefier system. Think about 64-bit seriously, analyze cost versus performance issues, and go for it.

▶ If you are running SSIS packages on a database system that is in use at the time when these packages run, you may encounter performance issues and your packages may take much longer to finish than you would expect. This may be due to data sets being swapped out of memory and also due to processor resource allocations. Such systems will benefit most due to improved parallelization of processes within 64-bit systems.

The next step is to understand the requirements, limitations, and implications associated with use of 64-bit systems. Review the following list before making a final decision:

▶ Only Developer Edition, Standard Edition, and Enterprise Edition of SQL Server 2005 are available in 32-bit and 64-bit editions. The other editions, Workgroup and Express, are available in 32-bit editions only.

▶ The 64-bit Standard Edition of SQL Server 2005 doesn't include the Slowly Changing Dimension transformation and SCD Wizard, but this transformation is provided in SQL Server 2005 32-bit Standard Edition.

► Not all utilities available in 32-bit editions are available in 64-bit editions. The only utilities available in 64-bit edition are dtutil.exe, dtexec.exe, and DTSWizard.exe (SQL Server Import and Export Wizard).

► When you're populating a database in a 64-bit environment, you must have 64-bit OLE DB providers for all data sources available to you.

► As DTS 2000 components are not available for 64-bit editions of SQL Server 2000, SSIS has no 64-bit design-time or run-time support for DTS packages. Because of this, you also cannot use the Execute DTS 2000 Package task in your packages you intend to run on a 64-bit edition of Integration Services.

► By default, SQL Server 2005 64-bit editions run jobs configured in SQL Server Agent in 64-bit mode. If you want to run an SSIS package in 32-bit mode on a 64-bit edition, you can do so by creating a job with the job step type of Operating system and invoking the 32-bit version of dtexec.exe using the command line or a batch file.

► The Script task provides limited debugging facilities on the 64-bit platform. You will have to debug your scripts on a 32-bit edition of the Script task before deploying them to a 64-bit Script task.

► To run packages successfully in a 64-bit edition of Integration Services, you must use precompiled scripts in the Script task and Script component in the data flow. For this, leave the PreCompile property set to its default value of True.

► Not all .NET Framework data providers and native OLE DB providers are available in 64-bit editions at the time of this writing. You need to check the availability of all the providers you've used in your package before deploying your packages on a 64-bit edition.

► If you need to connect to a 64-bit system from a 32-bit computer where you're building your Integration Services package, you must have a 32-bit provider installed on local computer along with the 64-bit version, because the 32-bit SSIS Designer displays only 32-bit providers. To use 64-bit provider at run-time, you simply make sure that the Run64BitRuntime property of the project is set to True, which is the default.

After you have sorted out the infrastructure requirements of having a 32-bit system or 64-bit system, your next step toward performance improvement is to design and develop packages that are able to use available resources optimally, without causing issues for other applications running in proximity. In the following sections, you will learn some of the design concepts before learning to monitor performance.

Architecture of the Data Flow

The Data Flow task is a special task in your package design that handles data movement, data transformations, and data loading in the destination store. This is the main component of an Integration Services package that determines how your package is going to perform when deployed on production systems. Typically, your package can have one or more Data Flow tasks, and each Data Flow task can have one or more Data Flow sources to extract data; none, one, or more Data Flow transformations to manipulate data; and one or more Data Flow destinations. All your optimization research rotates around these components, where you will discover the values of properties you need to modify to enhance the performance. To be able to decipher the codes and logs, you need to understand how the data flow engine works and what key terms are used in its design.

When a Data Flow source extracts the data from the data source, it places that data in chunks in the memory. The memory allocated to these chunks of data is called a *buffer*. A memory buffer is nothing more than an area in memory that holds rows and columns of data. You've used data viewers earlier in various Hands-On exercises. These data viewers show the data stored in the buffer at one time. If data is spread out over more than one buffer, you click the Continue button on the data viewers to see the data buffer by buffer. In Chapter 9, you saw how data viewers show data in the buffers, and you also explored two other properties on the Data Flow task that are discussed here as well.

The Data Flow task has a property called DefaultBufferSize whose buffer size is set to 10 MB by default (see Figure 13-3). Based on the number of columns (i.e., row size of pipeline data) and keeping some contingency for performance optimizations (if a column is derived, it can be accommodated in the same buffer), Integration Services calculates the number of rows that can fit in a buffer. However, if your row width is small, that doesn't mean that Integration Services will fit as many rows as can be accommodated in the buffer. Another property of the Data Flow task, DefaultBufferMaxRows, restricts a buffer from including more than a specified number of rows, in case the number of columns in the data set are too less or the columns are too narrow. This design is meant to maximize the memory utilization but still keep the memory requirements predictable within a package. You can also see another property EngineThreads in the same figure that is discussed a bit later in this chapter.

While the data flow is executed, you see the data is extracted by Data Flow sources, passed on to downstream transformations, and the data finally lands in the Data Flow destination adapter. By looking at the execution view of a package, you may think that the data buffers move from component to component and data flows from one buffer to another. This is in fact not all correct. Moving data from one buffer to another is quite an expensive process and is avoided by several components of the Integration Services

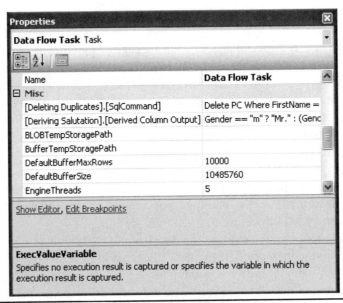

Figure 13-3 *Miscellaneous properties of the Data Flow task*

data flow engine. Data Flow transformations are classified into different categories based on their methods of handling and processing data in buffers. Some components actually traverse over the memory buffers and make changes only in the data columns that are required to be changed, while most other data in the memory buffer remains as is, thus saving the costly data movement operation while other components do require actual movement of data from one buffer to another to perform the required operation. This depends on what type of operation is required and what type of transformation is used to achieve the objective. Based on the functions performed by Data Flow transformations, they may use different types of outputs that may or may not be synchronous with the input. This has quite an impact on the requirement of making changes in place and can force data to be moved to new memory buffers. Let's discuss the synchronous and asynchronous nature of Data Flow transformations before discussing their classifications.

Synchronous and Asynchronous Transformations

Data Flow transformations can have either *synchronous* or *asynchronous* outputs. Components that have outputs synchronous to the inputs are called *synchronous components*. These transformations make changes to the incoming rows by adding or modifying columns but do not add any rows in the data flow—for example, the Derived Column transformation modifies existing rows by adding a new column. If you go to the Input and Output Properties tab in the Advanced Editor for these transformations, you may notice that these transformations do not add all the columns to the Output Columns section, but add only the newly created columns, because all other columns that are available in the input are by default available at the output also. The transformation with synchronous outputs processes and passes the input rows immediately to the downstream components. Such transformations do not block data buffers, and the outputs of these transformations are readily available to the downstream components. These transformations do not move data from one buffer to another; instead, they make changes to the required columns while keeping data in the same buffer. So the operation of these rows is quick and they do not place a heavy load on the server.

In some situations, you need to use transformations that have asynchronous outputs. These transformations add new rows to the data flow—for example, an Aggregate transformation adds new rows containing aggregations of the data columns. The transformations with asynchronous outputs need all the rows before they can start operating on the data rows—for example, a Sort transformation needs all the rows before it can decide which rows could be placed at the top of the data set. These components act as a data source and a data destination at the same time. These transformations provide new rows and columns for the downstream components and hence have to work harder.

If you go to the Input and Output Properties tab in the Advanced Editor for these transformations, you may notice that the transformations define new columns in the Output Columns section. While waiting for the complete data set, these transformations block the data buffers and slow down the processing. These transformations also put a heavy load or huge memory demands on the server to accommodate the complete data set in the memory. If the server doesn't have enough memory, the data will be cached on to the disk, further degrading the performance of the package. For these reasons, you need to make sure that you use only the minimum required number of asynchronous transformations in your package and that the server has sufficient memory to support the data set that will be fed through the asynchronous transformation.

Classifying Data Flow Transformations

You've seen the transformations grouped together differently in Chapter 9. In this chapter, you will study the following three classifications of Data Flow transformations that are based mainly on performance considerations.

Non-Blocking Synchronous Row-Based Transformations

These transformations work on a row-by-row basis and modify the data by changing the data in columns, adding new columns, or removing columns from the data rows, but these components do not add new rows to the data flow. The rows that arrive at the input are those that leave at the output of these transformations. These transformations have synchronous outputs and make data rows available to the downstream components straightaway. In fact, these transformations do not cause data to move from one buffer to another; instead, they traverse over the data buffer and make the changes to the data columns. So these transformations are efficient and lightweight from the process point of view. Their operation is quite visible in BIDS and you can quickly make out the differences by looking at the execution of the components in run-time mode.

When you execute a package in BIDS, look at the data flow execution of the package. You may see certain components processing together with the annotations for row numbers ticking along, though they may be placed one after another in the pipeline; you may also notice that certain transformations do not pass data to the downstream components for some time. The transformations that readily pass the data to the downstream components are classified as row transformations. These transformations do not block data. It's bit difficult to envisage the downstream components working on the data set that is still to be passed by the upstream component. However, in reality, data doesn't flow. Data stays in the same buffer and the transformation works on the relevant column. So as the data is not flowing and is remaining static in the memory buffer, a transformation works on a column while the other transformation performs operations on another column. This is how multiple row transformations can work so fast (almost simultaneously) on a data buffer.

These transformations fall under one execution tree. (You will learn more about execution trees later in the chapter.) The following Row transformations are examples of non-blocking synchronous row-based transformations:

▶ Audit transformation

▶ Character Map transformation

▶ Conditional Split transformation

▶ Copy Column transformation

▶ Data Conversion transformation

▶ Derived Column transformation

▶ Export Column transformation

- ▶ Import Column transformation

- ▶ Lookup transformation

- ▶ Multicast transformation

- ▶ OLE DB Command transformation

- ▶ Percentage Sampling transformation

- ▶ Row Count transformation

- ▶ Script Component transformation

- ▶ Slowly Changing Dimension transformation

Semi-Blocking Asynchronous Row Set-Based Transformations

Integration Services provides some transformations that essentially add new rows in the data flow and hold on to the data buffers before they can perform the transformation. The nature of such transformations is defined as *semi-blocking* because these transformations hold on to data for a while before they start releasing buffers. As these transformations add new rows in the data flow, they are asynchronous in nature. For example, a Merge transformation combines two sorted data sets that may be the same data, but it essentially adds new rows in the data flow. The time taken by this transformation before starting to release the buffers depends on when these components receive matching data from both inputs.

Following is a list of semi-blocking asynchronous row set-based transformations:

- ▶ Data Mining Query transformation

- ▶ Merge Join transformation

- ▶ Merge transformation

- ▶ Pivot transformation

- ▶ Term Lookup transformation

- ▶ UnPivot transformation

- ▶ Union All transformation

Blocking Asynchronous Full Row Set-Based Transformations

These transformations require all the rows be assembled before they can perform their operation. These transformations can also change the number of rows in the data flow and have asynchronous outputs. For example, the Aggregate transformation needs to see each and every row to perform aggregations such as summation or finding an average. Similarly, the Sort transformation needs to see all the rows to sort them in proper order. This requirement of collecting all rows before performing a transformation operation puts a heavy load on both processor and memory of the server. You can understand from the nature of the function they perform that these transformations block data until they have seen all the rows and do not pass the data to the downstream component until they have finished their operation.

If you are working with a large data set and have an Aggregate or Sort transformation in your package, you can see the memory usage ramp up consistently in the Task Manager when the transformation starts execution. If the server doesn't have enough free memory to support this, you may also see disk activity and virtual memory being used, which affects performance drastically. When all the rows are loaded in memory, which you can confirm by looking at the row number shown in the Designer, you may see in the Task Manager that after the processing is done, all the built-up memory is released immediately.

The following are blocking asynchronous full row set-based transformations:

▶ Aggregate transformation

▶ Fuzzy Grouping transformation

▶ Fuzzy Lookup transformation

▶ Row Sampling transformation

▶ Sort transformation

▶ Term Extraction transformation

Optimization Techniques

The techniques used for optimizing your Integration Services packages are quite simple and similar to any other application built around database operations. Here we will discuss the basic principles that help you optimize packages by applying common-sense techniques. For some of us, it is easiest to spend more money to get the fastest 64-bit machines with multi-core CPUs with several gigs of memory and consider optimization done. It definitely helps to throw more hardware and more processing power at performance issues, but if you don't debug the underlying performance bottlenecks, they come back to haunt you a few months after you've upgraded to newer, beefier machines.

From the architecture point of view, you also need to decide whether you'd like to go with Integration Services or with Data Transformation Services of SQL Server 2000 or any other third-party application, or maybe write the scripts directly in SQL to perform the work. A bit of analysis needs to be done before you make a decision.

The choice to use a particular application may be based on its architectural advantages. For example, DTS 2000, which is an ELT (extract, load, and transform) process, can better fit under certain circumstances compared to Integration Services, which is an ETL (extract, transform, and load) tool. Similarly, using custom-built scripts directly on large, properly indexed databases may prove to be more efficient for batch transformations compared to Integration Services, which is more suitable for complex row-by-row transformations. Most of the transformation of Integration Services are row-based and are quite lightweight and efficient for performing transformations compared to row set-based transformations. If you need to use lots of row set-based transformations that move buffers around in the memory, you need to consider whether that can be done using direct SQL. This requires testing and analysis, which you must do to optimize your data transformation operations. Monitoring, measuring, testing, and improving are vital to any optimization plan, and you cannot avoid this process with Integration Services also.

Once you've decided to use Integration Services and are building your package, you can apply the following simple considerations to design your package to perform optimally.

Choose the Right Operation

You need to have a critic's eye when designing an Integration Services package, and whenever you choose a specific operation in your package, keep asking yourself the following:

- ► Why am I using this operation?
- ► Can I avoid using this operation?
- ► Can I share this operation?

It is easy to get carried away when considering what you want to achieve with the various requirements of data flow components. Not all the operations you do in an SSIS package are required from the functionality point of view; some of them are forced on to you because of environmental conditions. For example, you have to convert the text strings coming out of a flat file into the proper data types such as integer and datetime. Though you cannot avoid such a conversion, you can still decide where to perform this conversion—i.e., at a source or a destination, or maybe somewhere in between. Second, you need to consider whether you're using any redundant operations in the package that can be safely removed. For example, you may be converting a text column to a datetime column when you extract data from a flat file and later converting the same column into a date type column because of data store requirements. You can avoid one operation in this case by directly converting the column to the data type required by destination store. Similarly, if you are not using all the columns from the flat file, are you still parsing and converting those columns? When it comes to performance troubleshooting, remember *every little bit helps*! Third, consider whether you can distribute processing on multiple machines. Some other specific and thought-provoking components-based examples are discussed in the following paragraphs.

While designing your package, you should always think of better alternatives for performing a unit of work. This calls for testing different components for performance comparisons within Integration Services or using alternative options provided by SQL Server. For example, if you are loading data to an SQL Server in an Integration Services package, it is better to use a SQL Server destination than OLE DB destination. A SQL Server destination uses memory interfaces to transfer data to SQL Server at a faster rate but requires that the package to be run on the local server. Also, keep in mind that T-SQL can be used to import small sets of data faster than using the Integration Services Bulk Insert task or SQL Server destination because of the extra effort of loading the Integration Services run-time environment.

When you use a Lookup transformation to integrate data from two different sources, think about whether this can be replaced with a Merge Join transformation, which generally performs better than the Lookup transformation for a large data set. Lookup works on a row-by-row basis, whereas Merge Join works on a set basis. From the earlier discussion, you know that a Lookup transformation is a non-blocking synchronous component that wouldn't require data to be moved to new buffers, whereas a Merge Join transformation is a row set-based semi-blocking asynchronous transformation that will move data to new buffers. However, moving to new buffers may call for a new execution tree, which may also get an additional processing thread and increase the number of CPUs used.

Also, a Merge Join transformation requires data inputs to be sorted in the same order by the join columns. You may think that adding a Sort transformation in the pipeline would be expensive, as it is a blocking asynchronous full row set-based transformation that needs to cache all the data before sorting it. However, if your data is coming from an RDBMS where it is indexed on the join column or the source file is already sorted in the required order, you can avoid using a Sort transformation, though you still need to tell the Merge Join transformation that the incoming data is already sorted. You can avoid sorting as long as the data is sorted in the right order in the flat file, or you can use an ORDER BY clause in T-SQL in the Data Flow Source adapter to extract data from an indexed data source. The Data Flow source output has a property called IsSorted that you can use to specify that the data being output by this component is in sorted order. You need to set this property to True, as shown in Figure 13-4.

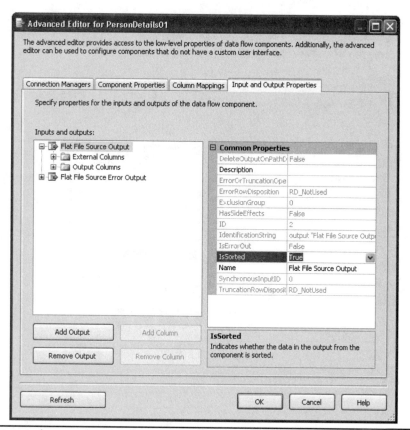

Figure 13-4 *Indicating that the data is sorted using the IsSorted property*

After setting the IsSorted property, you still need to specify the columns that have been sorted and the order in which they have been sorted. This works exactly like the ORDER BY clause in which you specify column names and then the order of the sort by using the ASC or DESC keywords. To set this property, expand the Output Columns node, choose the column, and assign a value of *1* to the SortKeyPosition property for specifying that the column is the first column that is sorted in an ascending order (see Figure 13-5), or use a value of *–1* to specify that the first column is sorted in descending order. For specifying second column in the sort order, set the SortKeyPosition value for that column to either *2* or *–2* to indicate ascending or descending order, respectively. By understanding how you can use a Merge Join transformation with already sorted data, you can determine whether your objectives can be achieved using this transformation instead of using a Lookup transformation.

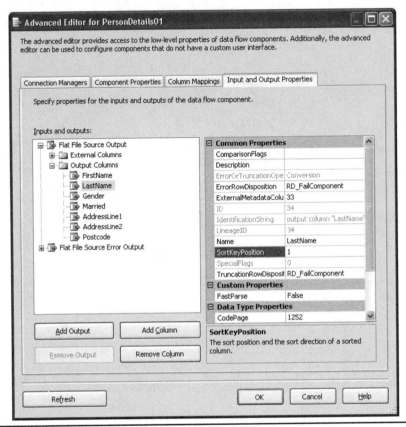

Figure 13-5 *Specifying sort order on the columns.*

I experienced an incident you might find interesting. One of my clients asked me to optimize their DTS package, which was loading about 12 million rows into SQL Server. The package was simple but was taking about one and a half days to complete processing of all the files. I started checking the usual things—that files were copied to a local server before the process, that the database had enough free space, and the disks were configured in RAID 10. The package code was relatively simple. I started believing (against my gut feeling) that this was probably just the time it should take to complete the process. I asked for a baseline. The DBA who implemented the package had done a good job at deployment time by providing the baseline for 100,000 records. The DBA had moved on after implementation of this package and the data grew massively after that. I quickly did the calculations and realized that something was wrong—the package should finish quicker. Further research uncovered the issue:

the commit transaction setting was left blank, which meant that all the rows were being committed together in a single batch. DTS was being required to keep 12 million rows in the memory, so it was no surprise that the server was running out of memory and swapping data out to disks and the processes were taking so much time to complete. I reduced the batch size to 10,000 rows and the package completed in less than 4 hours.

Smaller batches do not put heavy demand on memory and if properly configured, values can be fit in the memory available on the server and the process will complete in much shorter time. Keep the commit size smaller if you do not have to use bigger batches. Figure 13-6 shows two properties of the OLE DB destination Rows Per Batch and Maximum Insert Commit Size that you can use to specify the number of rows in a batch and the maximum size that can be committed together.

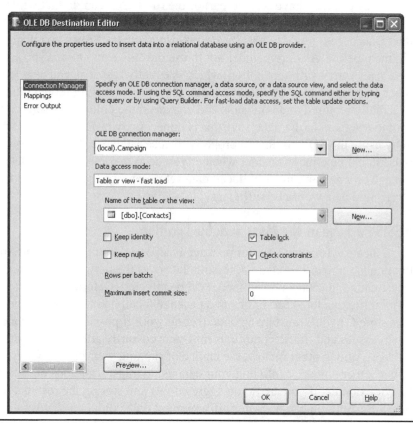

Figure 13-6 *OLE DB destination can control the commit size of a batch.*

Do Only the Work You Need to Do

You should consider this tip seriously as this is generally an overlooked problem that causes performance issues. Always ask yourself these questions:

▶   Am I doing too much?

▶   Can I reduce the amount of work I'm doing?

During design time, developers generally start with a larger data set than required, as they want to build the required functionality quicker to see how the package will work. Once the package is created, the data set is reduced by fine-tuning the data flow sources or other components. For example, you may have imported a complete table in the pipeline using a Data Flow source with a Table or View Data access option, whereas you may have wanted part of the rows. You can do that while trying to build your package as a proof of concept, but preferably you should use SQL Command Data access mode to specify the precise number of rows you want to import in the pipeline. Also, remember not to use the `Select * from [your table name]` query with this option, which is equally bad. You can also reduce the number of data columns from the data set. If you're importing more columns than are actually required and you parse and convert these columns before you decide not to use them in the data flow, this is unnecessary processing that can be avoided by using the SQL command properly to access the precise data that you want to use in the pipeline. Consider whether you need to use a complete data set in your package or whether a much-reduced data set in rows or columns that consist of only incremental data would be sufficient.

Run an SSIS Package at the Most Suitable Location

Choosing a location for running your package is also important when a data source or destination is remote. If you are accessing data over the network or writing to a remote destination, package performance will be affected. Determine whether you can transfer a file to a local server or run a package locally on a machine where the data is stored. Avoid transferring data over network if possible, as network connectivity issues and traffic conditions may unnecessarily affect performance of your package. Among other factors, the choice of running your package may be guided by whether you are exploding your data using transformations or reducing the data. For example, if you are doing aggregations and storing the results on a remote SQL Server, you can be better off running it on a computer that is or near to the data source. Alternatively, if you are expanding a data set by copying columns or using data conversions, you may be better off getting the raw data from the data source and running the package on the computer on or near to destination.

The choice of data type can affect the bytes handled by the package. For example, if you are using an integer data type to specify an integer, it will be represented by a space of 2 bytes in the memory, whereas using a real data type for this number will use 4 bytes. When you are dealing with a large data set that has, say, 10 million rows, you will be adding an extra 20 million bytes to your package that will further degrade the performance when this data is being transferred over the network.

Run an SSIS Package at the Most Suitable Machine

If your SQL Server is being used heavily or scheduled jobs are running on the SQL Server at the same time that you want to run your SSIS package, you can explore the possibility of using a server other than the SQL Server that may have more resources available at that time. This will ease the pressure of a narrow processing window; however, the down side is that you will have to buy an extra license for SQL Server 2005 for the server on which you are running Integration Services.

If you are planning to buy a new machine for SQL Server 2005 or where ever you will be running Integration Services, consider buying the server with the fastest possible drives, as the disk read and write operations are affected by disk performance. Configure RAID on your server with a clear understanding of performance options offered by different types. RAID 10 provides the best read and write performance but uses more disk real estate, whereas RAID 5 offers a balance between the disk read speed and the redundancy cost. Use RAID 10 if you can afford it in your budget.

Avoid Unnecessary Contention for Resources

When deploying your packages, think of the run-time conditions. Ask yourself these questions:

▶ Will other users be accessing the server at the same time?

▶ Will other processes or jobs, such as server maintenance plans or backup jobs, be running at that time?

Integration Services can happily coexist with any other application and run packages with minimal requirements for resources. The amount of data to be processed, the transformations, and the ways you've configured your package to use resources all determine the impact on server performance as a whole. If a server is being used heavily, avoid running your packages on the server, as it may not be able to acquire locks quickly enough and will also affect the users connected to other services on the server. Check out the condition of memory being used on the server at the time when the package will be run. Memory is the most precious resource for any database application, and any contention for memory will negatively affect performance.

Discuss and Optimize

As with database development, you discuss the data modelling with developers and other information analysts to reach properly optimized yet resilient and compliant rules for database design, and adopt a philosophy to discuss designs and techniques used with the development team. You will find this is not only encouraging for the team, but it will provide uniform techniques that can be used throughout the enterprise—and that goes a long way toward developing a culture of adopting best practices.

As mentioned in various Hands-On exercises, make your packages self-explanatory by adding proper descriptions and comments in tasks and annotations. You can annotate your package on the Control Flow surface to explain how the package works, and this helps other developers quickly understand the functionality and will help avoid accidental changes.

Test, Measure, and Record

Performance tuning is a strenuous process. You must clearly define performance requirements and try to keep your packages performing within that matrix. The packages change execution behavior over time as the processing data grows. When you develop an SSIS package, you should first test and document the performance of the package to develop a baseline for comparing future test results. Having a baseline can help you determine how much performance tuning you need to do to optimize the package.

If at some stage you want to break open the pipe and measure the data pressure, as most plumbers do to clear blocked pipes, you can use a trick explained in the following few lines to get a view of how much performance can be achieved with your pipeline. You can replace the downstream components at any stage in your pipeline with a RowCount transformation that is quick to consume the rows coming to it. You can determine maximum speed at any stage of your package and compare this value with the real-time value—i.e., with the real components in place. This is handy for finding out which component is degrading the performance of your package. It is worth recording the values monitored with this technique for future references as well. Various tools and utilities can be used to measure the baseline parameters, and will study these in the following section.

Performance Monitoring Tools

Integration Services provides a number of performance counters that can help you monitor the run-time workings of a package. You can also use tools such as SQL Server Profiler provided with SQL Server 2005 and Windows Performance counters to get a complete picture of run-time activities. These tools can be useful in understanding the internal workings and identifying which components are acting as bottlenecks in the performance of your package. In addition, you can use the Logging tool provided by Integration Services to develop a performance baseline for your package.

Performance Counters

You can use a set of performance counters provided by Integration Services to track pipeline performance. When you open the Windows Performance MMC snap-in to create a log that captures performance counters, you will find performance counters available in the SQLServer:SSIS pipeline object, as shown in Figure 13-7.

These counters provide information about three main types of objects: BLOB data, memory buffers, and the number of rows. Knowing about memory usage is more important, so more counters are provided to track this. The SSIS pipeline uses memory buffers to keep the data and to allocate memory to individual components to meet their processing requirements. The buffers used to hold data are called *flat buffers* and the buffers allocated to components such as Sort, Aggregate, or Lookup

Figure 13-7 *SSIS pipeline counters*

transformations for their internal hashing and calculation purposes are called *private buffers*. Large binary objects can require lot of the memory buffers, so use BLOB counters to check out these values if your data carries BLOB objects. These performance counters are described here:

▶ **BLOB Bytes Read**   Displays total number of BLOB bytes read from all the data sources including Import Column transformation.

▶ **BLOB Bytes Written**   Displays the total number of BLOB bytes written to all data destinations including Export Column transformation.

▶ **BLOB Files In Use**   Displays the number of BLOB spooling files in use throughout the pipeline.

▶ **Buffer Memory**   Displays the amount of memory buffers allocated to the pipeline at different times during the package execution. Compare this value with the memory available (which you can capture using memory object counters) on the computer to track whether the available memory falls short during any time of the package processing.

▶ **Buffers In Use**   Displays the number of buffers used from the allocated buffers for the pipeline.

▶ **Buffers Spooled**   This is the most important counter to observe if your package is taking an exceptionally long time to execute. It will help you determine whether at any time during the package execution, Integration Services starts swapping out buffers to disk. Whenever memory requirements out number the physical memory available on the computer, you will see that the buffers not currently in use are swapped out to disk for later recovery when needed. This counter tells you the number of buffers being swapped out to disk. This is an important event to watch.

▶ **Flat Buffer Memory**   Flat buffers are used to store data when a package runs. This counter displays the total amount of memory allocated to all the flat buffers. If your package has multiple Data Flow tasks, this counter shows consolidated value used by all the Data Flow tasks.

▶ **Flat Buffers In Use**   Displays the number of flat memory buffers used by Data Flow engine.

▶ **Private Buffer Memory**   Some transformations such as Sort transformation and Aggregate transformation need extra memory buffers to perform the operations on the data in flat buffers. These extra memory buffers are locally allocated to the transformation and are called private buffers. This counter shows the total number of buffers allocated as private buffers in the pipeline.

▶ **Private Buffers In Use**   Displays the number of buffers in use throughout the pipeline.

▶ **Rows Read**   Displays the total number of rows read from all data sources. The rows read by the Lookup transformation for lookup operations are not included in the total.

▶ **Rows Written**   Displays the total number of rows that are written to all the Data Flow destinations.

In addition to these performance counters, SQL Server 2005 provides another counter to monitor the number of package instances currently running. The SSIS Package Instances counter is available under SQL Server: SSIS Service Performance object.

SQL Server Profiler

You can use the SQL Server Profiler whenever you're transferring data with SQL Server to determining what's happening inside SQL Server that may be negatively affecting the running of your package. Your package may be simple and straightforward, so it should be running at top speed. But if a SQL Server is also running other processes during that time, your package may find it difficult to transfer data. With SQL Server Profiler, you can monitor the SQL Server not only for data access but also for the performance of the query you may be using in a data source to access the data.

Logging

You've already read about logging of Integration Services, so how to use it is not discussed here; however, it is worth knowing that you can use logging to create a baseline for your package execution. This baseline should be revised from time to time as the data grows or whenever the processing design of the package is changed. It is particularly helpful to watch the time taken by different tasks or components to complete, as you can focus on improving this. For example, if a data source takes most of the processing time to extract data from a source, it is not going to benefit much if you're putting efforts into improving transformations.

The Data Flow task also provides some interesting custom log events that are helpful in debugging issues that affect performance of the pipeline. You can view these events in the Log Events window when the package is being executed by selecting the Log Events command from the SSIS menu or by right-clicking the

Control Flow surface and choosing Log Events from the context menu. Alternatively, you can log these events by configuring logging for the Data Flow task.

Following are descriptions of some of the log events available for the Data Flow task. These can be helpful in monitoring performance-related activities:

- ▶ **BufferSizeTuning**   This event happens whenever the Integration Services pipeline changes the size of a buffer from the default size. This log entry also specifies the reason for changing the buffer size, which is generally about either too many rows to fit in the default buffer size or too few for the given buffer size. It indicates the number of rows that can fit in the new buffer. Refer to the earlier discussion on DefaultBufferSize and DefaultBufferMaxRows for more details on buffer size and rows that can fit in a buffer.

- ▶ **PipelineBufferLeak**   When the pipeline execution stops, some of the components may hold on to the buffers they used even after the buffer manager has stopped. Thus the memory buffers that are not freed will cause a memory leak and will put extra pressure on memory requirements. You can discover such components using this event log, as it will log the name of the component and ID of the buffer.

- ▶ **PipelineExecutionPlan**   SSIS pipeline has an execution plan just as the stored procedures have. This event provides information about how memory buffers are created and allocated to different components. By logging this event and the PipelineExecutionTrees, you can track what is happening within the Data Flow task.

- ▶ **PipelineExecutionTrees**   The pipeline is divided into separate execution trees based on the synchronous relationship among various components of the Data Flow task. (Execution trees are covered in detail later in this chapter.) When Integration Services starts building an execution plan for the package, it requires information about execution trees, and this information can be logged using this event log.

- ▶ **PipelineInitialization**   This log event provides in one or more entries the information about directories to use for temporary storage of BLOB data, the default buffer size, and the number of rows in a buffer at the initialization of the Data Flow task.

You will log these events later in a Hands-On exercise to study them more closely.

Execution Trees

The pipeline of a package is divided into discrete parts for execution purposes by the initialization process. These discrete parts, called *execution trees*, are allocated their own resources to run the package at optimum levels. The number of execution trees in a pipeline depends on the synchronous relationship among the components and their layout in the package. In simplistic terms, if a package consists of only synchronous row-based components, it will have only one execution tree. However, if you introduce a component with asynchronous outputs in the pipeline, it will be executed in two discrete parts and will have two execution trees. The asynchronous output of the component starts a new execution tree, whereas its input is included in the upstream execution tree. So, from this, you can make out that an execution tree starts at a data flow source or a component with asynchronous outputs and ends at a data flow destination or at an input of the component with asynchronous outputs.

Let's review what happens within an execution tree. From earlier discussions, you already know that the components with synchronous outputs—i.e., row-based components—work on the same data buffers and do not require that data be moved to new buffers. This set of buffers constitutes an execution tree. All the components within an execution tree operate on the same set of buffers. As the data is not moved, it allows transformations to perform operations at the maximum attainable speed on the data. However, this is still a queued operation.

When you run a package that has all row-based components in BIDS, you will see that the row counts work almost at the same time for those components. However, if you are working with a massive amount of data and are using process-intensive operations such as lookups in the pipeline, you will see that some downstream transformations have to wait. This is not because some component is blocking, but is due to the limitation of processing power allocated to the pipeline. Though row-based components do not block data from the downstream components, they have an issue with thread allocation. The pipeline engine allocates only one thread to an execution tree irrespective of the number of transformations included in that tree or how much work those transformations have to perform.

Now let's see what happens when we add a component with asynchronous outputs in the data flow. This component causes the data to be moved to new set of buffers because it needs to perform an operation that renders data rows not compatible with the existing buffer set. The movement of data to a new buffer set creates a new execution tree. New execution trees get allocated their own resources, so this new execution tree gets a new thread and a different set of buffers. This is quite an interesting revelation of design criteria that lets you use a blocking transformation, meaning slower performance on the one hand and provides additional processing thread to compensate on the other.

Hands-On: Monitoring Execution Trees in a Pipeline

In this exercise, you will discover the execution trees in the data flow of your package.

Method

You will be using the Updating PersonContact package of the Data Flow transformations project you built in Chapter 10. You will enable logging in the package and add custom log events on the Data Flow task to log what's happening in the package at run-time.

Exercise (Enable Logging on the Data Flow Task)

1. Open the Data Flow transformations project using BIDS.

2. Double-click the Updating PersonContact.dtsx package in Solution Explorer to load this package on the Designer if it doesn't load by itself. Right-click the blank surface of the Control Flow and choose Logging from the context menu.

3. Click in the check box to enable logging for Updating PersonContact in the Containers pane.

4. On the right side, in the Providers and Logs tab, leave SSIS Log Provider For Text Files selected in the Provider Type field and click the Add button to add this provider type. When this provider type has been added, click in the Configuration column, then click the down arrow and select <New connection...> to add the File Connection Manager.

5. In the File Connection Manager Editor, select Create File in the Usage Type field. Type **C:\SSIS\RawFiles\ExecutionLog.txt** in the File field and click OK.

6. On the left side, click the Data Flow task and then click twice in the check box provided next to it to enable logging for this task. The right pane becomes available. Click to select the SSIS Log Provider for the Text files log.

7. Go to the Details tab, scroll down, and select the custom events BufferSizeTuning, PipelineBufferLeak, PipelineExecutionPlan, PipelineExecutionTrees, and PipelineInitialization, as shown in Figure 13-8. Click OK to close this dialog box.

8. Go to the Data Flow tab and double-click the data flow path between Merging PersonDestails01 and PersonDestails02 transformation and Deriving Salutation transformation to open the Data Flow Path Editor. Go to the Data Viewers page, and click the Delete button to delete the data viewer attached to the path. Click OK to close it. Similarly, delete the data viewer attached to the data flow path between Adding City Column transformation and Deleting Duplicates transformation.

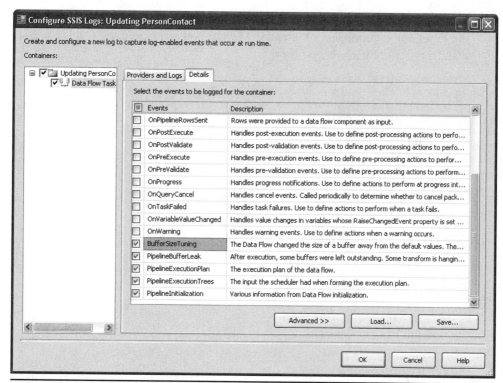

Figure 13-8 *Custom log events provided by the Data Flow task*

9. Right-click the Updating PersonContact.dtsx package in the Solution Explorer window and choose Execute Package from the context menu.

10. When the package has been executed, press SHIFT-F5 to switch back to designer mode.

Exercise (Review the ExecutionLog File)

11. Explore to the C:\SSIS\RawFiles folder and open the ExecutionLog.txt file using Notepad. Read through the messages related to the BufferSizeTuning event at the beginning of the package. Here is one example:

```
"Rows in buffer type 3 would cause a buffer size greater than the
configured maximum. There will be only 2440 rows in buffers of
this type."
```

This event indicates that the buffer size created will be larger than the default size configure and also tells you the number of rows that this buffer will be able to hold.

12. After the BufferSizeTuning event, you will see the list of execution trees under the PipelineExecutionTrees log entry. The log is listed here in case you haven't managed to run the package till now:

```
begin execution tree 0
   output "Flat File Source Output" (2)
   input "Union All Input 1" (241)
end execution tree 0
begin execution tree 1
   output "Flat File Source Error Output" (3)
end execution tree 1
begin execution tree 2
   output "Excel Source Output" (17)
   input "Data Conversion Input" (194)
   output "Data Conversion Output" (195)
   input "Union All Input 2" (265)
   output "Data Conversion Error Output" (196)
end execution tree 2
begin execution tree 3
   output "Excel Source Error Output" (18)
end execution tree 3
begin execution tree 4
   output "Union All Output 1" (242)
   input "Derived Column Input" (439)
   output "Derived Column Output" (440)
   input "Character Map Input" (465)
   output "Character Map Output" (466)
   input "Lookup Input" (494)
   output "Lookup Output" (495)
   input "OLE DB Command Input" (631)
   output "OLE DB Command Output" (632)
   input "OLE DB Destination Input" (692)
   output "OLE DB Destination Error Output" (693)
   output "OLE DB Command Error Output" (633)
   output "Lookup Error Output" (505)
   input "Flat File Destination Input" (590)
   output "Character Map Error Output" (467)
   output "Derived Column Error Output" (441)
end execution tree 4
```

Let's now see how the pipeline engine has created execution trees. The execution trees are numbered beginning with 0, so you have five execution trees in total. Execution trees 1 and 3 have only the error outputs of data sources, which do not have any data flow branch and are ignored for this explanation. Based on the above the execution trees shown in Figure 13-9 have been marked for you.

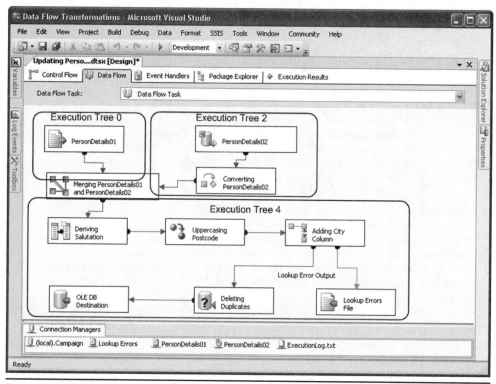

Figure 13-9 *Execution trees in the Updating PersonContact package*

13. The next section of the log shows PipelineExecutionPlan, which is listed here:

```
SourceThread0
   Drives: 1
   Influences: 240 438 464 493 589 626 679
   Output Work List
      CreatePrimeBuffer of type 1 for output ID 2.
      SetBufferListener: "WorkThread0" for input ID 241
      CreatePrimeBuffer of type 3 for output ID 3.
      CallPrimeOutput on component "PersonDetails01" (1)
   End Output Work List
End SourceThread0
SourceThread1
   Drives: 9
   Influences: 193 240 438 464 493 589 626 679
   Output Work List
      CreatePrimeBuffer of type 4 for output ID 17.
      SetBufferListener: "WorkThread1" for input ID 194
      CreatePrimeBuffer of type 7 for output ID 18.
      CallPrimeOutput on component "PersonDetails02" (9)
   End Output Work List
```

```
    End SourceThread1
    WorkThread0
       Drives: 240
       Influences: 240 438 464 493 589 626 679
       Input Work list, input ID 241 (1 EORs Expected)
          CallProcessInput on input ID 241 on component "Merging
    PersonDetails01 and PersonDetails02" (240) for view type 2
          End Input Work list for input 241
       Output Work List
          CreatePrimeBuffer of type 8 for output ID 242.
          SetBufferListener: "WorkThread2" for input ID 439
          CallPrimeOutput on component "Merging PersonDetails01 and
    PersonDetails02" (240)
       End Output Work List
    End WorkThread0
    WorkThread1
       Drives: 193
       Influences: 193 240 438 464 493 589 626 679
       Input Work list, input ID 194 (1 EORs Expected)
          CallProcessInput on input ID 194 on component "Converting
    PersonDetails02" (193) for view type 5
          ActivateVirtualBuffer index 1
          CallProcessInput on input ID 265 on component "Merging
    PersonDetails01 and PersonDetails02" (240) for view type 6
          End Input Work list for input 194
       Output Work List
       End Output Work List
    End WorkThread1
    WorkThread2
       Drives: 438
       Influences: 438 464 493 589 626 679
       Input Work list, input ID 439 (1 EORs Expected)
          CallProcessInput on input ID 439 on component "Deriving
    Salutation" (438) for view type 9
          ActivateVirtualBuffer index 1
          CallProcessInput on input ID 465 on component "Uppercasing
    Postcode" (464) for view type 10
          ActivateVirtualBuffer index 2
          CallProcessInput on input ID 494 on component "Adding City
    Column" (493) for view type 11
          ActivateVirtualBuffer index 3
          CallProcessInput on input ID 631 on component "Deleting
    Duplicates" (626) for view type 13
          ActivateVirtualBuffer index 4
          CallProcessInput on input ID 692 on component "OLE DB
    Destination" (679) for view type 14
          ActivateVirtualBuffer index 7
          CallProcessInput on input ID 590 on component "Lookup Errors
    File" (589) for view type 12
          End Input Work list for input 439
       Output Work List
       End Output Work List
    End WorkThread2
```

The PipelineExecutionPlan shows the number of threads allocated to the pipeline. It also shows that the pipeline uses two different types of threads, SourceThread and WorkThread. Note that two SourceThreads and three WorkThreads have been allocated in our case. The SourceThreads are directly related to the Data Flow sources and their number is determined by the number of Data Flow sources present in the pipeline. On the other hand, WorkThreads are related to the Data Flow task property called EngineThreads. Refer to Figure 13-3, which shows the EngineThreads property set to the default value. Our package also has the default value of 5. As only three execution trees in our pipeline have some logical work to perform, the engine allocated three WorkThreads in this case. You will study more about this later in this chapter.

14. Finally, look through the PipelineInitialization log entries, which tell you important information about your pipeline execution environment.

Review

This exercise showed you that the pipeline engine divides the pipeline work in discrete execution trees on the basis of synchronicity in the package. Whenever it comes across a component with asynchronous outputs, the engine creates a new execution tree by moving the data to the new buffer set. You've also seen that each execution trees gets a WorkThread subject to the EngineThreads setting on the Data Flow task. Finally, the SourceThreads are directly linked to the Data Flow sources present in the pipeline, implying that the total number of threads on a data flow is equal to the number of execution threads plus the Data Flow sources present in the pipeline. Also, note that these threads are applicable to each data flow and multiple data flows on a package allocate threads on their own basis, and hence provide a means of parallel execution.

Using Parallel Processing

By now, you must have sensed that Integration Services packages can be configured to gain from parallel processing. You've learned optimization techniques earlier in this chapter that talked about managing buffers so that you could avoid swapping out buffers to disk and fit maximum rows in a buffer. Now you will learn how to make use of more processors available on your computer so that the packages run faster. Using both techniques—managing buffer utilization and using maximum CPUs on the computer—you can develop highly efficient packages that work with peak performance.

Running Parallel Tasks in the Control Flow

Recall that the tasks in the control flow are connected by precedence constraints and a task in the control flow runs only when the previous task has finished based on the precedence condition specified. However, you can create unrelated parallel workflows (i.e., flows not connected to each other) in the control flow and run them simultaneously. The control flow of a package has a property called MaxConcurrentExecutables, shown in Figure 13-10, that specifies the number of executables—i.e., tasks that can run in parallel.

The value of *–1* shown in the figure is the default value of this property, indicating that the maximum executables that this package can run will be the number of processors on the computer plus 2. It counts the logical processors. On a basic four-CPU server, this value will allow maximum of six executables to run in parallel; however, if you're lucky to work on a server that has four dual core CPUs with hyper threading enabled, the default value will be interpreted as 18. Based on the number of CPUs on the server and whether other applications are also running on the server, you can configure this setting. If you configure this value too low for a package that can run more tasks in parallel than this setting indicates, some of the tasks will have to wait. However, if you configure this value too high and the server

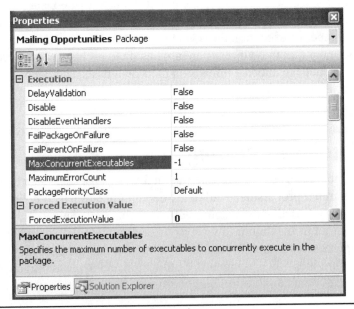

Figure 13-10   *Control flow properties of a package*

also hosts other applications, the performance and usability of those applications will suffer. Before deciding the number of CPUs for the given tasks, consider the types of tasks that are running in parallel. Not all tasks require the same processing power—for example, an FTP task requires much less processing power than Data Flow task.

Creating Multiple Data Flows

If you must deal with massive amounts of data or you've multiple data sources that require independent data conversions and transformations, you can create multiple Data Flow tasks in your package. As mentioned, these tasks can be executed in parallel, so if you've added more than one Data Flow task in your package, all will be executed in parallel and hence perform the work faster depending upon the MaxConcurrentExecutables setting and availability of resources on the server. Remember that the execution trees are created for each Data Flow task, which means multiple Data Flow tasks will create much more execution trees and will help the pipeline to execute faster, though they are subject to availability of sufficient number of CPUs on the computer to support multiple Data Flow tasks.

Enhancing EngineThreads

As discussed earlier and shown in Figure 13-3, the EngineThreads property specifies the maximum number of threads allocated to a data flow. The WorkThreads are related to the EngineThreads property, though they are not hard bound with it. The EngineThreads property hints to the pipeline scheduler about the maximum number of WorkThreads that can be allocated to this data flow. If the value of the EngineThreads property exceeds the maximum number of execution trees, a thread will be allocated to each of the execution trees. However, if the number of execution trees exceeds the EngineThreads value, one WorkThread will be allocated to more than one execution tree and some execution trees have to wait for the upstream components to finish execution. If you have multiple CPUs present on your server that you want to use, increase the value of the EngineThreads property to let more CPUs be used by the data flow execution trees. However, if you don't have enough execution trees on your package, increasing the EngineThreads value will not help much. You need to modify your pipeline first as mentioned next.

Balancing Synchronicity

Components with synchronous outputs operate on the same set of buffers and hence work in the same execution tree. If the pipeline consists of components with synchronous outputs, you may end up having only one execution tree for this pipeline. And if the components are performing process-intensive operations such as lookups, even then the pipeline will use the only thread allocated to this execution tree and the downstream components will have to wait. This wait is not due to blocking of data, but is the result of limited processing power allocated to this execution tree. In this scenario, the pipeline will use only one CPU while other CPUs may be sitting idle. In this case, it wouldn't help even if you increased the EngineThreads value because the pipeline doesn't create any demand for additional threads. You can create this demand for additional thread by modifying your package to have more execution trees by adding a Union All transformation with a single input and single output in the middle of the package. Union All is a semi-blocking transformation with asynchronous outputs. This component moves data buffers to new buffers and creates a new execution tree. With this new execution tree created, the pipeline will use additional threads from the pool. With a sufficient quantum of data and transformations used in the package, the overhead of moving data to new buffers generally results in better overall performance.

Summary

You've learned lots of techniques for debugging and optimizing your packages in this chapter. While learning these techniques, you learned the internal working of Integration Services and saw how it allocates resources at run-time to different components on the basis of execution trees. The chapter discussed troubleshooting your packages using various features such as breakpoints, precedence constraints, and data viewers. You also worked with breakpoints in a Hands-On exercise to see how variable values are changed during execution of a package.

In the performance section, you learned how to manage memory allocation to data buffers and the types of components that work on the data in the same set of buffers while others force the data to move to the new buffers. These components also exhibit blocking, non-blocking, and semi-blocking nature for data. You worked through another Hands-On exercise to learn about execution trees created in a package.

Lastly, you learned how to put all the CPUs in your computer to work. Not only in this chapter, but throughout this book, you learned to use various components by working through Hands-On exercises. I hope this book becomes an oft-consulted source for your use of Integration Services and I hope it sets you free to begin your exciting journey with Integration Services. Best of luck.

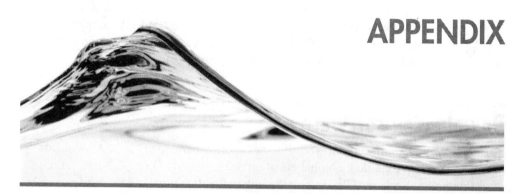

How to Use the Provided Software

IN THIS APPENDIX

Downloaded software

ll the exercises you do in this book have been created for your quick reference along with all the input files. The following steps explain how you can download and use the software provided for this book.

Downloaded software

1. Type www.osborne.com in your internet address bar and click the Downloads tab. Look up the title by alphabetical order i.e., Hands-On SQL Server 2005 Integration Services. Clicking on the link will automatically download a zip file.

2. Expand the zip file to extract all files you need to practice that include input files, developed SSIS packages and SQL Server database files. The zip file contains the folder structure necessary for performing the exercises. All you need to do is copy the root folder SSIS to your C:\. The table below explains the folder structure and its components.

Folder	Description
SSIS	This is the root folder. Copy SSIS folder to C:\.
Database	This folder contains the SQL Server 2005 database files. The following section explains how you can attach database files to your SQL Server 2005 server.
Deployment	Blank folder for exercises in this book.
Downloads	Blank folder for exercises in this book. Contains a sub folder Archive that is also blank.
Freeware	Holds Freezip software used in chapter 5.
Packages	This folder has a backup sub-folder that contains SSIS packages, which you develop in Chapter 2.
Projects	All the SSIS projects, developed for this book, are contained within a backup sub-folder. You will be developing your own projects in this folder.
Rawfiles	Holds all the input files required for various exercises.
Code for individual chapters	This folder contains similar folder structure as contained in SSIS main folder. The code and the input files are relevant for the individual chapter only.

Attaching Campaign database

Once you've copied SSIS folder from the zip file to your C:\, you are ready to attach Campaign database to your SQL Server 2005. As mentioned, C:\SSIS\database folder contains the database files. To attach Campaign database, follow the steps listed below:

1. Run SQL Server Management Studio and connect Database Engine to localhost.

2. Right-Click on the Database node in the Object Explorer window and select Attach.

3. Click Add in the Attach Databases dialog box. Choose Campaign_Data.mdf file from C:\SSIS\Database folder and click OK to attach the selected file as Campaign database.

Index